# New Dynamics in East Asian Politics

# New Dynamics in East Asian Politics

## Security, Political Economy, and Society

Edited by

## Zhiqun Zhu

continuum

2012

**The Continuum International Publishing Group Inc**
80 Maiden Lane, New York, NY 10038
The Tower Building, 11 York Road, London SE1 7NX

www.continuumbooks.com

ISBN:  978-1-4411-6621-0 (PB)
          978-1-4411-8331-6 (HB)

**Library of Congress Cataloging-in-Publication Data**
  New dynamics in East Asian politics : security, political economy,
and society / edited by Zhiqun Zhu.
      p. cm.
  Includes bibliographical references and index.
  ISBN-13: 978-1-4411-8331-6 (hardcover : alk. paper)
  ISBN-10: 1-4411-8331-0 (hardcover : alk. paper)
  ISBN-13: 978-1-4411-6621-0 (pbk. : alk. paper)
  ISBN-10: 1-4411-6621-1 (pbk. : alk. paper)  1. East Asia–Politics
and government–21st century.  2. National security–East Asia.
3. East Asia–Economic conditions–21st century.  4. East Asia–Social
conditions–21st century.  I. Zhu, Zhiqun.
  DS518.1.N387  2012
  327.5–dc23
                                                      2011034352

Typeset by Newgen Imaging Systems Pvt Ltd, Chennai, India
Printed and bound in the United States of America

# Contents

# Notes on the Editor and Contributors

## Editor

**Zhiqun Zhu** is John D. and Catherine T. MacArthur Chair in East Asian Politics and Associate Professor of Political Science and International Relations at Bucknell University in Pennsylvania. He received his PhD in political science from the University of South Carolina in Columbia. His teaching and research interests include Chinese politics and foreign policy, East Asian political economy, East Asian international relations, and US-East Asian relations. His published books include *China's New Diplomacy: Rationale, Strategies and Significance* (Ashgate, 2010); *Understanding East Asia's Economic "Miracles"* (Association for Asian Studies, 2009); *US-China Relations in the 21st Century: Power Transition and Peace* (Routledge, 2006); *Global Studies: China* (ed., 13th and 14th editions, McGraw-Hill, 2009 and 2011); and *The People's Republic of China Today: Internal and External Challenges* (ed., World Scientific Publishing, 2010). His research articles have appeared on *Asian Perspective*, *Global Economic Review*, *Journal of International and Area Studies*, *Journal of Asia-Pacific Affairs*, *Journal of Chinese Political Science*, *Yale Journal of International Affairs*, etc. He has also contributed dozens of book chapters. Dr. Zhu was a POSCO visiting fellow at the East-West Center in Hawaii and a senior visiting fellow at the East Asian Institute of National University of Singapore.

## Contributors

**Il Hyun Cho** is Assistant Professor of Political Science at Cleveland State University. He received his Ph.D. in political science from Cornell University. Dr. Cho's research interests include international relations theory, global governance, nuclear proliferation, East Asian regionalism, and religious politics in East Asia. He has conducted field research in China, Japan, and South Korea. His recent publications include a chapter (with Peter J. Katzenstein) in Jack Snyder, ed., *Religion and International Relations Theory* (Columbia University Press, 2011) and articles in *Foreign Policy Analysis* and *The Chinese Journal of International Politics*. He has been a recipient of fellowships from Harvard University's Belfer Center for Science and International Affairs, the Mellon Foundation, the MacArthur Foundation/Peace Studies Fellowship, and Cornell University's Mario Einaudi Center for International Studies and East Asia Program. He has also held visiting positions at the Center for International Studies at Yonsei University and the Institute of Social Sciences at the University of Tokyo.

**Ken Coates** is Canada Research Chair in Regional Innovation at the Johnson-Shoyama Graduate School of Public Policy, University of Saskatchewan and President of the Japan Studies Association of Canada. He is currently studying the digital content sector in Japan, focusing on the convergence of government policy, academic research and training and the national international business strategies. He and Professor Carin Holroyd have published several books on Japanese innovation, including *Japan and the Internet Revolution* (Palgrave Macmillan, 2003) *Innovation Nation: Science and Technology in 21^st Century Japan* (Palgrave Macmillan, 2007). They are writing a book on the digital revolution in East Asia.

**Mary Alice Haddad** is an Associate Professor of Government at Wesleyan University. Her research has focused on civil society and democracy in Japan, and her current project concerns environmental politics in East Asia. Her publications include *Politics and Volunteering in Japan: A Global Perspective* (Cambridge, 2007), *Building Democracy in Japan* (Cambridge forthcoming), and articles in journals such as *Comparative Political Studies*, *Democratization*, *Journal of Asian Studies*, and *Nonprofit and Voluntary Sector Quarterly*. She is working on a book about environmental politics in East Asia.

**Carin Holroyd** is Associate Professor of Political Studies, University of Saskatchewan. She has published extensively on national innovation strategies in Asia and is currently working on a study of government policy and the commercialization of environmental technologies in Japan. She is the author of *Government, International Trade, and Laissez-Faire Capitalism: Canada, Australia, and New Zealand's Relations with Japan* (McGill-Queen's University Press, 2002). Her research interests include government-business relations, Canada-Japan relations, international trade, and national innovation policies.

**Heon Joo Jung** is Assistant Professor of East Asian Languages and Cultures and Adjunct Assistant Professor of Political Science at Indiana University, Bloomington. He received his Ph.D. in political science from the University of Pennsylvania. His research interests include political economy of South Korea and Japan, East Asian regionalism, and politics of economic crisis and reform. Among his recent publications are "The Rise and Fall of Anti-American Sentiment in South Korea: Deconstructing Hegemonic Ideas and Threat Perception" in *Asian Survey* (2010); "Financial Regulatory Reform in South Korea Then and Now" in *Korea Observer* ( 2009); "Financial Regionalism in East Asia: Regional Surveillance Cooperation and Enforcement Problem" in *Pacific Focus* (2009); and "What Went Wrong with South Korea-Chile Free Trade Agreement?: Implications to Regional Economic Integration in East Asia" (coauthored) in *International Journal of Korean Studies* (2005). He is working on a book manuscript that examines financial regulatory reforms in South Korea and Japan since the late 1990s.

**Mason M. S. Kim** is Assistant Professor of Political Science at the University of Tennessee, Martin (UTM). He received his Ph.D. from the University of Pittsburgh. He teaches East Asian political economy and Chinese politics. His fields of interest are political economy and political change, particularly focusing on globalization and welfare state development. Prior to coming to UTM, he taught at Tulane University.

**Hochul Lee** is Dean of College of Social Sciences and Professor of Political Science and China Studies at University of Incheon, Korea. He is President-elect of the Korean Association of International Studies. He earned B.A. at Seoul National University in Korea and M.A. and Ph.D. in political science at Rutgers University in the United States. His primary research areas are China's political economy and foreign policy and East Asian international relations. His publications include "China in North Korean Nuclear Crises: 'Interest' and 'Identity' in Foreign Behavior", *Journal of Contemporary China* (2012), *China's Foreign Policy-Making in Post-Cold War East Asia* (Edward Elgar, 2011), "Political Institutionalization as Political Development in China," *Journal of Contemporary China* 19 (June 2010), and "Reforming China's State-Owned Commercial Banks: A 'Double Game' between 'Market' and 'Plan' "(in Korean), *Korean Journal of International Relations* 46 (2006).

**Diqing Lou** received her Ph.D. from the Department of Political Science at Texas A&M University in 2008. She is currently an Assistant Professor at the Department of Political Science at Rider University. Her main area of research is comparative politics, especially Chinese politics, with a focus on political participation, political representation, development of civil society, and political liberalization. Her publications have appeared in *Journal of Contemporary China, Asian Politics & Policies, Journal of Chinese Political Science*, among others.

**Mary M. McCarthy** is an Assistant Professor of Politics and International Relations at Drake University in Des Moines, Iowa. She received her Ph.D. in political science from Columbia University in 2007. She specializes in Japan and China's respective domestic and foreign policies. Her current research interests include cooperation and conflict between Japan and China in the East China Sea, and the historical legacies of the Asia-Pacific War on Japan–China relations.

**Carol Ann Medlicott** is Associate Professor of Geography at Northern Kentucky University. She received her Ph.D. from the University of California at Los Angeles in 2003 and completed a post-doctoral fellowship at Dartmouth College. Her research considers a range of topics in historical and cultural geography, including nationhood, memory, and symbolic landscapes. Dr. Medlicott began studying the Korean peninsula in the mid-1980s, during a 13-year career as a national security analyst within the US intelligence community. Her M.A. thesis analyzed US unofficial exchanges with North Korea between the late 1980s and mid-1990s. Her dissertation traced the evolution of national security discourse within the context of geographic thought, and considered the security tensions on the Korean peninsula as one case study. Her work has been published in numerous journals and edited volumes, including *International Journal of Intelligence and Counterintelligence, SAIS Review of International Studies, National Identities, Geopolitics, Journal of Historical Geography*, and *Terrae Incognitae*.

**Lana Obradovic** is an Assistant Professor of International Relations and Diplomacy at Mercy College in New York. She holds a Ph.D. in political science from the City University of New York. Dr. Obradovic has held teaching positions at St. John's University, CUNY Queens College and Hunter College in New York City, and most recently at Yonsei University in South Korea, where she taught East Asian international relations and conducted research on national security policymaking in the region. Dr. Obradovic's research interests are comparative defense policy, civil-military relations, international relations, and conflict resolution.

**Atsuko Sato** teaches in the Department of Political Science at California State University, Los Angeles. Dr. Sato, who received her Ph.D. from the University of Hawaii at Manoa, is also a Visiting Professor at the Graduate School of Environmental Science at Hokkaido University, located in Sapporo, Japan. In addition to her visiting position at Hokkaido University, Dr. Sato has received several fellowship and research grants from the Global COE (Centers of Excellence) Project through Hokkaido University for her research on environmental governance and sustainability. Her most recent publications include articles on Japan's climate change policy, social constructivism in International Relations theory, and social movements. Dr. Sato's areas of specialization include Japan's environmental policy, gender equality policy in Japan, and women and politics. She is working on a comparative analysis of gender politics in Japan and South Korea.

**Matthew A. Shapiro** is Assistant Professor of Political Science at Illinois Institute of Technology. He received his Ph.D. in political economy and public policy at the University of Southern California in 2008. His primary research on science and technology policies and environmental policies—especially in Northeast Asia—has been published in *International Journal of Public Policy, Scientometrics, Accounting, Auditing & Accountability Journal, Technology Analysis and Strategic Management, Korea Observer*, and a number of book chapters. He is currently examining the micro-level effects and network structures from micro-blogging and the conveying of scientific information about climate change.

**Wendy Weiqun Su** is Assistant Professor in the Media and Cultural Studies Department at the University of California, Riverside. Her research falls on the intersection of global communication, Chinese media studies, and cultural studies. Specifically, she is interested in China's cultural policy study, cultural industries research, transnational film studies, audience research, and the impact of transnational capital and American culture on China's media and cultural landscape. Her academic works can be found in the *Journal of International and Intercultural Communication, Global Media and Communication, Asian Journal of Communication*, and the *Journal of Peking University*. Prior to pursuing her Ph.D., she was a long-time journalist in mainland China and Hong Kong, and edited a book and published numerous articles in news outlets both in and outside China.

**Chunjuan Nancy Wei** is Assistant Professor and Chair of International Political Economy and Diplomacy at the University of Bridgeport (UB) in

Connecticut. She received her Ph.D. from Claremont Graduate University in California. Professor Wei teaches Political Economy of China, Political Economy of East Asia, and US foreign policy, among others. She and her students won a Distinguished Delegation Award from the Model UN Europe Conference in 2010. She is a recipient of the Chiang Ching-kuo Foundation Scholarly Exchange Research Grant which supported her research trip to Taiwan during summer 2010. Dr. Wei is also an awardee of UB's Seed Money Grant and its Center of Learning and Teaching Excellence award. She has published on US-China relations, East Asian political economy, and cross-Taiwan Strait politics. Her recent publications include "China's Anti-Secession Law and Hu Jintao's Taiwan Policy" (*Yale Journal of International Affairs,* 2010), "From Mao Back to Confucius: China's Approaches to Development and Peace" (*Journal of Global Development and Peace*, 2010), "Democratic Paradox: What Has Gone Wrong in Thailand?" (*Southeast Review of Asian Studies*, 2009), and "The U.S. and China: The Power of Illusion" (with Hilton Root, published in his book *Alliance Curse*, 2008). She is completing her monograph exploring cross-Taiwan Strait politics and its implications for global policymakers.

**Teresa Wright** received her B.A. in political science at Santa Clara University, and her M.A. and Ph.D. in political science at the University of California, Berkeley. She has been a professor of political science at California State University, Long Beach since 1996, and has been chair of the political science department since the fall of 2009. She also has worked as a Visiting Scholar at the Academia Sinica in Taiwan and the East-West Center in Honolulu. Dr. Wright's research focuses on East Asia (particularly China and Taiwan), protest and dissent, and the relationship between capitalism and democracy. Her first book, *The Perils of Protest: State Repression and Student Activism in China* (University of Hawaii Press, 2001), compares student strategy and behavior in the protest movements of 1989 in China and 1990 in Taiwan. Her second book, *Accepting Authoritarianism: State-Society Relations in China's Reform Era* (Stanford University Press, 2010), examines the impact of economic liberalization and growth on popular political attitudes in China's post-Mao era. Professor Wright also has published articles in *Comparative Politics, Communist and Post-Communist Studies, The China Quarterly*, and *Asian Survey*. In addition, she has published numerous chapters in edited volumes.

# List of Abbreviations

| | |
|---|---|
| ADB | Asian Development Bank |
| APEC | Asia Pacific Economic Cooperation |
| APT | ASEAN Plus Three |
| ARATS | Association for Relations Across the Taiwan Strait |
| ASEAN | Association of Southeast Asian Nations |
| BBSs | bulletin board systems |
| CASS | Chinese Academy of Social Sciences |
| CCGA | Chicago Council on Global Affairs |
| CCP | Chinese Communist Party |
| CCTV | China Central Television |
| CEDAW | Convention on Elimination of All Forms of Discrimination Against Women |
| CEPA | Closer Economic Partnership Arrangement |
| CFIEC | China Film Import & Export Corporation |
| CPF | Central Provident Fund |
| CSI | Container Security Initiative |
| DC | defined contribution |
| DMZ | demilitarized zone |
| DPJ | Democratic Party of Japan |
| DPP | Democratic Progressive Party |
| DPRK | Democratic People's Republic of Korea |
| EAC | East Asian Community |
| EAI | East Asia Institute (Seoul, Korea) |
| ECC | Economic Cooperation Committee |
| ECFA | Economic Cooperation Framework Agreement |
| EEOL | Equal Employment Opportunity Law |
| EEZs | exclusive economic zones |
| EIA | environmental impact assessment |
| EIS | environmental impact statements |
| EPF | Employee Provident Fund |
| FDI | foreign direct investment |
| FTAs | free trade agreements |
| G-2 | Group of Two (the United States and China) |

| | |
|---|---|
| GDP | gross domestic product |
| GHGs | greenhouse gases |
| GPR | Global Posture Review |
| GWOT | Global War on Terror |
| HAN | Highly Advanced Nation Project |
| ICT | information and communication technology |
| IFEZ | Incheon Free Economic Zone |
| IMF | International Monetary Fund |
| IPR | intellectual property rights |
| ITRI | Industrial Technology Research Institute |
| KMT | Kuomintang |
| KORUS-FTA | Korea-US Free Trade Agreement |
| KPA | Korean People's Army |
| LDP | Liberal Democratic Party |
| METI | Ministry of Economy, Trade and Industry |
| MLP | Medium to Long Term Plan (for the Development of Science and Technology) |
| MLSG | Minimum Living Standard Guarantee |
| MND | Ministry of National Defense |
| MOCIE | Ministry of Commerce, Industry and Energy |
| MOST | Ministry of Science and Technology |
| MPF | Mandatory Provident Fund |
| NEPA | National Environmental Protection Agency |
| NICs | newly industrialized countries |
| NPC | National People's Congress |
| NPS | National Pension Scheme |
| NSC | National Science Council |
| OBM | original brand manufacturer |
| ODM | original design manufacturer |
| OECD | Organization for Economic Cooperation and Development |
| OEM | original equipment manufacturer |
| OSOCA | One Side One Country Alliance |
| PAP | People's Action Party |
| PERS | Prior Environmental Review System |
| PLA | People's Liberation Army |
| PPP | purchasing power parity |
| PRC | People's Republic of China |
| PSI | Proliferation Security Initiative |

| | |
|---|---|
| R&D | research and development |
| ROC | Republic of China |
| ROK | Republic of Korea |
| ROT | Republic of Taiwan |
| SARs | Special Administrative Regions |
| SARFT | State Administration of Radio, Film and Television |
| SDF | Self-Defense Forces |
| SEF | Straits Exchange Foundation |
| SOFA | Status of Forces Agreement |
| S&T | science and technology |
| TEMM | Tripartite Environment Ministers' Meeting |
| TSU | Taiwan Solidarity Union |
| TVEs | township and village enterprises |
| USFK | US Forces in Korea |
| VOA | Voice of America |
| WBIC | Warner Bros. International Cinemas |
| WHO | World Health Organization |
| WTO | World Trade Organization |

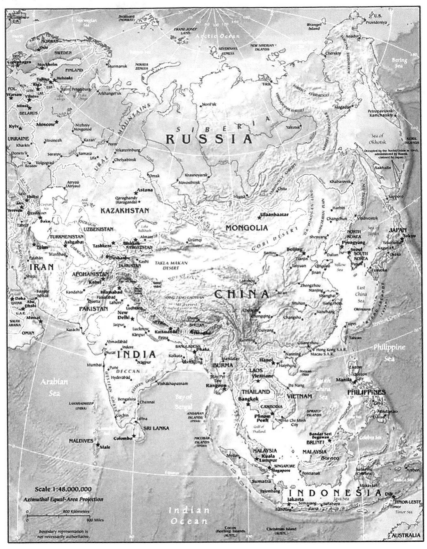

**Map 1** https://www.cia.gov/library/publications/the-world-factbook/maps/p_refmap_asia.html

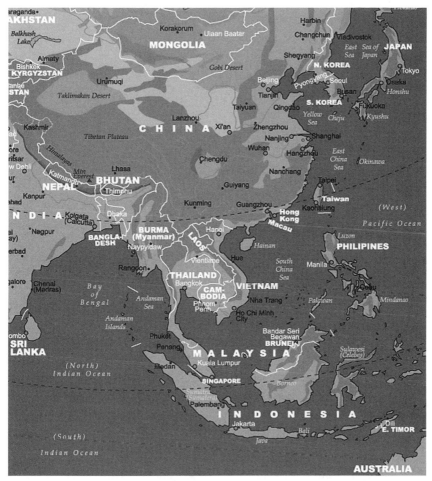

Map 2

# Useful Resources for Studying East Asia

## 1. Major News Outlets in East Asia

Asahi Shimbun (www.asahi.com/english)

Asia Times Online (www.atimes.com)

Beijing Review (www.bjreview.com.cn)

China Central Television (http://english.cntv.cn/01/index.shtml)

China Daily (www.chinadaily.com.cn)

China Post (www.chinapost.com.tw)

China Times (www.chinatimes.com)

China Youth Daily (www.cyol.net)

Chosun Ilbo (http://english.chosun.com)

Dong-A Ilbo (http://english.donga.com)

eTaiwan News (www.etaiwannews.com/etn/index_en.php)

Far Eastern Economic Review (www.feer.com)

Focus Taiwan (http://focustaiwan.tw)

Global Times (www.globaltimes.cn)

Guangming Daily (www.gmw.cn)

Hankook Ilbo (http://news.hankooki.com)

Japan Times (www.japantimes.co.jp)

Joongang Ilbo (http://joongangdaily.joins.com)

Korea Herald (www.koreaherald.com)

Korea Times (www.koreatimes.co.kr)

Korean Central News Agency of the DPRK (http://www.kcna.co.jp/index-e.htm)

Kyodo News (http://english.kyodonews.jp)

Lianhe Zaobao [Singapore] (www.zaobao.com)

Mainichi Shimbun (www.mainichi.co.jp)

NHK World (http://www3.nhk.or.jp/daily/english)

North Korea Daily (http://nkoreadaily.com)

People's Daily (http://english.peopledaily.com.cn)

People's Liberation Army Daily (http://english.chinamil.com.cn/english/pladaily)

South China Morning Post (www.scmp.com)

Straits Times [Singapore] (www.straitstimes.com)

Taipei Times (www.taipeitimes.com)

Taiwan Today (www.taiwantoday.tw)

United Daily News (http://udn.com/NEWS/mainpage.shtml)

Yomiuri Shimbun (www.yomiuri.co.jp)

Yonhap News Agency (http://english.yonhapnews.co.kr)

Xinhua News Agency (www.xinhuanet.com)

# 2. Key Government Websites

## China

The Communist Party (http://english.cpc.people.com.cn)

Ministry of Commerce (http://english.mofcom.gov.cn)

Ministry of Education (www.moe.edu.cn)

Ministry of Foreign Affairs (www.fmprc.gov.cn/eng)

Ministry of National Defense (http://eng.mod.gov.cn)

The PRC Central Government (www.gov.cn/english)

## Japan

Ministry of Defense (www.mod.go.jp/e/index.html)

Ministry of Economy, Trade, and Industry (www.meti.go.jp/english/index.html)

Ministry of Education, Culture, Sports, Science and Technology (www.mext.go.jp/english/index.htm)

Ministry of Foreign Affairs (www.mofa.go.jp)

Office of the Prime Minister (www.kantei.go.jp/foreign/index-e.html)

## Taiwan

Government Information Office (www.gio.gov.tw)

Ministry of Education (http://english.moe.gov.tw)

Ministry of Foreign Affairs (www.mofa.gov.tw)

Office of the ROC President (http://english.president.gov.tw)

Straits Exchange Foundation (www.sef.org.tw/mp1.html)

## North Korea

DPRK Government (www.korea-dpr.com)

## South Korea

Cheong Wa Dae [Office of the President] (http://english.president.go.kr/main.php)

Ministry of Education, Science and Technology (http://english.mest.go.kr)

Ministry of Foreign Affairs and Trade (www.mofat.go.kr)

Ministry of National Defense (www.mnd.go.kr)

Ministry of Unification (http://www.unikorea.go.kr)

ROK Government (www.korea.net/index.do)

# 3. Key Scholarly Journals on East Asian Affairs

American Review of China Studies

Asia-Pacific Review

Asian Affairs

Asian Affairs: An American Review

Asian Journal of Political Science

Asian Perspective

Asian Politics & Policies

Asian Profile

Asian Security

Asian Survey

Australian Journal of International Affairs

China: An International Journal

China Security

Chinese Journal of International Politics

The China Journal

The China Quarterly

Critical Asian Studies

East Asia: An International Quarterly

Electronic Journal of Contemporary Japanese Studies

International Journal of Korean Studies

Issues & Studies

Japan Focus

Japan Review of International Affairs

Japanese Studies

Journal of Asia-Pacific Affairs

Journal of Asian and African Studies

Journal of Asian Studies

Journal of Chinese Political Science

Journal of Contemporary China

Journal of East Asian Affairs

Journal of East Asian Studies

Journal of International and Area Studies

Journal of Korean Studies

Journal of Japanese Studies

Korean Journal of International Relations

Korean Studies

Modern China

Pacific Affairs

Pacific Review

Social Science Japan Journal

# 4. Other Useful Online Information

www.aei.org

www.ait.org.tw

www.amnesty.org

www.asiawind.com/hkwwwvl

http://asiasociety.org

www.bbc.co.uk/news

www.bbc.co.uk/zhongwen/simp

http://beijing.usembassy-china.org.cn

www.brookings.edu

www.businessweek.com

www.chathamhouse.org.uk

www.chinatoday.com

www.cia.gov/library/publications/the-world-factbook

http://coombs.anu.edu.au/WWWVL-AsianStudies.html

http://csis.org/region/asia

www.DemographicsNowChina.com

www.dynamic-korea.com

www.econoomist.com

www.heritage.org

www.hrw.org/en/asia

www.imf.org/external/index.htm

www.jamestown.org

http://japan.usembassy.gov

www.japantoday.com

www.lowyinstitute.org

www.ncuscr.org

www.newsweek.com

www.rfa.org/english

www.rsis.edu.sg

http://seoul.usembassy.gov

www.stimson.org

www.state.gov

http://taiwanreview.nat.gov.tw

www.time.com

www.uschina.usc.edu

www.voanews.com/chinese/news

www.voanews.com/english/news

www.whitehouse.gov

www.WorldBank.org

# Introduction: East Asian Politics Today[1]

Zhiqun Zhu

---

## Chapter Outline

## Shaping the world of the twenty-first century

East Asia remains one of the most dynamic and rapidly changing regions in the world in the first decades of the twenty-first century. It is home to two of the world's three largest economies—China and Japan, and two of the world's potentially most explosive flashpoints—the Korean Peninsula and the Taiwan Strait. In the information age, East Asia has become a major center of technological innovation, with continued heavy investment in education. In the new "green economy," East Asia has increased the share of renewable energy in power generation, leading the world in renewable energy development. While East Asian states have become deeply interdependent economically, political, territorial, and historical conflicts between and among them continue to loom large in their relations. How has rapid growth impacted domestic political development, cultural values, social structure, and gender roles in East Asian states? What are continuities and changes in their security and foreign relations? This book attempts to capture some of the contemporary political, economic, and social developments in East Asia.

It is fair to say that if not for the fast growth of rising economies like China, the world might well have descended into a real depression in 2008 when the US-triggered financial crisis struck the world economy. There is no doubt that developments in East Asia will continue to shape the future of the world. As the first decade of the twenty-first century came to an end and the second decade began, several events in East Asia attracted much global attention. These events, like many others that took place in East Asia, have significant impact on world politics and economy.

In 2010 China's aggregate gross domestic product (GDP) became the second largest in the world, replacing Japan which had held the number two position for over 40 years. While China's economic performance has been impressive, its lack of political democratization has disappointed many people both in and outside of China. The gap between China and the West on issues such as human rights and political freedom remains wide. The empty chair reserved for Chinese dissent Liu Xiaobo at the Nobel Peace Prize Award Ceremony in December 2010 was more than just an embarrassment for China. The Chinese government's stepped-up crackdown on dissidents including renowned artist Ai Weiwei (who helped to design the Bird's Nest Stadium for the 2008 Beijing Olympics) in the aftermath of popular protests in the Middle East and North Africa in spring 2011 demonstrated the Chinese Communist Party (CCP)'s determination to keep iron-clad control on a society that is becoming increasingly unstable below the surface. As the income gap widens, popular discontent is growing in China. One can also image that an ever more powerful but nondemocratic China is likely to feed the "China threat" alarm and create new tensions between China and its neighbors and other powers.

The power structure continues to evolve in East Asia as Japan struggles to step out of the economic stagnation which has plagued Japan since the bubble economy of the 1980s collapsed in 1991. In 2011 the island nation suffered the worst disasters since World War II. The March 11, 2011 massive magnitude-9.0 earthquake, the subsequent tsunami, and the nuclear calamity wreaked further havoc on Japan—a critical link in the global supply chain—and inevitably disrupted the global economy. As devastating as these triple disasters were, they reinforced unity and strength among the Japanese. The Japanese are known for their resilience, fortitude, and discipline. The composed response of the Japanese people to the tragedies evoked much respect for them worldwide. One should not doubt that Japan will recover and rebound to vitality and prosperity once again. However, in the short term, Japanese politicians have to be more responsible and create a healthy and stable political environment for economic recovery.

The 2011 catastrophes may eventually serve as a catalyst for Japan to fix its political and economic woes that were long overdue. They also offered a rare opportunity for Japan to mend its troubled relations with China and South Korea. China and South Korea were among the first countries to send search and rescue teams and aid supplies to Japan. In a message to Japanese emperor Akihito, Chinese president Hu Jintao mourned the dead and extended condolences to the Japanese people and said that the Chinese government and people stood ready to offer necessary help. Chinese Premier Wen Jiabao made special remarks during his press conference at the end of the March 2011 National People's Congress (NPC) annual session to express his condolences and sympathies to Japan. When East Asia's two leading economies put aside their disagreements over history, territory, defense, and trade, the region as well as the world at large will benefit. The question is how long they can remain friendly towards each other.

In Chinese and Japanese kanji, the word "crisis" (危机) contains two characters—danger and opportunity. After the 2008 Sichuan earthquake, the Japanese search and rescue team was the first foreign group to arrive at the scene to offer help, which generated much goodwill among the Chinese. In the aftermath of the Sendai earthquake in March 2011, the Chinese government repaid Japan's kindness by quickly dispatching a group of experienced rescue members to Japan. The Chinese public also demonstrated its sympathy to Japan. According to an online poll conducted in China, 83 percent surveyed thought that China should offer humanitarian aid to Japan.[2] The outpouring of sympathy to Japan among the Chinese public and their donations to Japan suggest that at least temporarily they were putting politics to the backseat. Disasters can bring out the best and the worst in human beings. These natural disasters in China and Japan have brought out the best in the two peoples. One can only hope that China and Japan will shift their attentions away from the unpleasant past and the current territorial disputes and endeavor to establish a more cooperative and closer relationship for the future.

At the beginning of 2010, the downward spiral of US-China relations, due to controversies over US arms sales to Taiwan, President Barack Obama's meeting with the Dalai Lama, Google's partial withdrawal from China, etc., worried many people on both sides of the Pacific. Then in April, President Obama and President Hu Jintao had a long telephone conversation and President Hu decided to attend the nuclear security summit hosted by President Obama in Washington, D.C. The relationship seemed to be back on track. In late May the two countries held the second Strategic and Economic Dialogue, with Secretary of State Hillary Clinton and Secretary of the Treasury Timothy Geithner leading the largest ever US delegation of over 200 officials to Beijing, including those from the Department of Defense and the US Pacific Command. Yet in early June, the Chinese government turned down a planned visit to Beijing by US Secretary of Defense Robert Gates, and then military officials from the two sides engaged in a tit-for-tat debate in the annual Shangri-la security conference in Singapore. In July, US Secretary of State Hilary Clinton and Chinese Foreign Minister Yang Jiechi spatted over whether the United States was taking sides on the disputed South China Sea issue between China and a few Southeast Asian countries.

The US-China relationship was not fully resumed until January 2011 when Secretary Gates eventually went to China, and President Hu Jintao paid a high-profile state visit to Washington. In March 2011, President Obama nominated Secretary of Commerce Gary Locke, a prominent Chinese-American, to be the new US ambassador to China. Locke's predecessor, the Mandarin-speaking Jon Huntsman Jr., resigned after less than two years in Beijing and entered the 2012 US presidential campaign as a Republican candidate. While US-China relations have become more mature and stable than before, conflicting domestic forces and interests will at times create tensions between the two powers.

On the Korean Peninsula, a South Korean navy warship, *Cheonan*, was allegedly torpedoed by North Korea in March 2010, with 46 South Korean sailors killed. The international team of investigators invited by the South Korean government looked into the case and published a report in May implicating North Korea. The United States and Japan voiced strong support for South Korea and condemned North Korea's recklessness. China, while expressing condolences to the South Korean government and South Korean families affected by the tragedy, refrained from openly criticizing North Korea. Instead, it emphasized the importance of maintaining stability and peace in the region. Largely due to China's strong opposition, the United Nations Security Council only passed a presidential statement, not a resolution, condemning the attack, without naming North Korea as the culprit. In November 2010, North Korea fired approximately 170 artillery shells on the Yeonpyeong Island in South Korea, killing two South Korean soldiers and two civilians. North Korea's provocation once again raised tensions on the Korean Peninsula, prompting the South Korean Defense Ministry to authorize South Korean military to retaliate immediately if provoked again. All these took place in the context in which North Korea aspires to be a nuclear power. The Six-Party Talks aimed at resolving North Korea's nuclear issue had been stalled since 2009. With a fragile Kim Jong-il busy preparing for a power transition to his youngest son Kim Jong-un and the United States struggling to pull its economy back on track, serious negotiations on North Korea's nuclear program have been put on hold.

In Japan, Prime Minister Yukio Hatoyama of the Democratic Party of Japan (DPJ), which came to power in September 2009 after a historic victory over the long-standing ruling party, the Liberal Democratic Party (LDP), resigned in June 2010 after only eight months in office, and was succeeded by fellow DPJ member Naoto Kan. Kan became the fifth Japanese prime minister in just four years. The revolving door of Japanese prime ministers has significant impact on Japan's domestic and foreign policies. Prime Minister Kan had been struggling from the very beginning with a low approval rating and slow economic recovery. Kan's top aide and foreign minister Seiji Maehara resigned in March 2011 for taking political donations from a Korean national living in Japan, further eroding Kan's political foundation. Kan's lackluster handling of the triple disasters after March 2011 led to calls from opposition parties and rival factions within his own party for his resignation. Kan was eventually forced to resign in August 2011 and was replaced by Yoshihiko Noda in September 2011. Obviously the messy and factional politics is not conducive to Japan's recovery from the catastrophe and the long recession.

As the world continued to pull itself out of economic recession at the beginning of the 2010s, many countries suffered from inflation. Rising wages for Chinese workers and the potential labor shortage contributed to the global inflation. According to a study by Credit Suisse Group in Hong Kong, demand for workers in China may soon outstrip supply, which has the potential to further push up consumer prices.[3] China's "family planning" policy is taking its tolls now. Just like Japan, China is becoming a graying society with a shrinking labor force. This may affect China's manufacturing, its exports, its social safety net, and its domestic stability. According to the 2010 Census which was released by the Chinese government in April 2011, China's population was 1.34 billion, below the 1.4 billion predicted by UN demographers. The population grew 5.84 percent from 2000 to 2010, or 0.57 percent a year. While the growth has slowed, the population has become older. People aged 60 and older now represent 13.26 percent of the population, an increase of 2.93 percentage points from 2000.[4] The changing demographic structure will have significant impact on economic, social, and political developments in China and beyond in the decades ahead.

Rapid developments in East Asia such as those mentioned above make it imperative for us to take account of how politics and society are evolving and being challenged by the ongoing transformations in East Asia.

The East Asian regional dynamic is undoubtedly dominated by the reemergence of China. China's meteoric growth, its daunting domestic challenges, and its apparently more assertive foreign policy fundamentally influence politics and policies of other states in the region, including the United States. Preoccupied with war against terror elsewhere since 2001, the United States has created a power vacuum for China to quickly expand its trade, investment, and influence in Asia and elsewhere. Though the United States had never retreated from Asia, the rapid rise of China and increasing tensions in the region, often involving China, prompted the Obama administration to declare that "the United States has returned to Asia."[5]

In addition to the many traditional political, economic, social, and security challenges, East Asian states have to deal with nontraditional ones such as natural disasters, refugees and illegal immigration, environmental degradation, demographic transformation, cyber attacks, and threat to freedom of maritime navigation. The Sichuan earthquake of 2008 that claimed 90,000 lives, the Qinghai earthquake of 2010 that claimed 3,000 lives, and the Sendai earthquake and subsequent Tsunami of 2011 that caused over 30,000 deaths and disrupted Japan's already faltering economy remind people how powerful the nature is and how vulnerable human beings are.

Deepening globalization, a burgeoning information revolution, a vibrant civil society, widespread global, political, and economic repercussions, and changing security landscape, among others, have brought about fundamental challenges to East Asian states. There is no doubt that what happens in East Asia will continue to affect international affairs and global economy. This book focuses on such significant dynamics, developments, and challenges in East Asia and aims to help readers make sense of East Asian politics and its implications for international political economy.

# About this book

There are few good textbooks on East Asian politics. Among those existing books, most follow the standard or traditional route to focus on descriptive accounts of the government, institutions, political parties, elections, interest groups, etc. Given the number of countries covered, most East Asian politics classes can only conduct a sketchy survey of the political history and society of these countries during a semester.

While the traditional focus has its merits, students today often get lost in the study of comparative politics of East Asia. What interests the young people most seems to be what is happening in East Asian countries now and what their peers there are thinking and doing in this rapidly changing world. The editor and contributors feel that there is an urgent need for such a book that reflects the latest developments in East Asian politics and society as a way to introduce students to the fascinating field of East Asian politics or to supplement their knowledge about East Asia with updated scholarship. This book attempts to fill a vacuum in the learning and teaching of East Asian politics.

Contributors to this volume are all active East Asia scholars who are teaching and researching on East Asian politics, culture, media, society, political economy, history, geography, and foreign policy at various colleges in the United States, Canada, and South Korea. Some of the chapters were originally presented at different international conferences but have been thoroughly revised and updated to meet the needs of largely undergraduate readers; others were specifically written for this volume. Together, the chapters offer an opportunity for our readers to learn more about the new dynamics in East Asian security, political economy, and society.

Not a traditional survey text, this book has the following distinctive features:

- It's interdisciplinary, covering a wide range of topics such as media politics, environmental legislation, civil society, political culture, local legislative elections, welfare state, gender, national identity, women in the military, political economy, security, and foreign policy. It goes beyond the scope of traditional textbooks on government and politics by looking at how new developments at the societal, national, and international levels challenge politics of East Asian states today. The 15 chapters are grouped into three sections: security and foreign policy, the new political economy, and changing societies, which makes the book very easy to follow. By focusing on these three main themes and examining relevant issues, the book extends the basic lessons promulgated in an East Asian politics course and generates more interest in the study of East Asia.
- Pedagogically, the book has several tools to help teaching and learning of East Asia. Some chapters address general trends in the region while others focus on individual states, with every chapter raising "Five Questions for Discussions" about the topic the chapter examines. This introductory chapter includes a list for further reading and all other chapters have a list of selected bibliography

for additional study and research. Furthermore, the book includes a section called "Useful Resources for Studying East Asia," which contains a list of major news outlets in East Asia, key websites of East Asian governments, a list of key scholarly journals on East Asian affairs, and other useful online information such as think tanks, virtual libraries, and international organizations.

– The width and depth of the book makes it especially useful as a required or supplementary reading for undergraduate and M.A.-level graduate students. Contributors include active teacher-scholars in political science, cultural studies, geography, media, environmental studies, history, and international relations. They are both scholars of their academic fields and specialists on the East Asian region. Their extensive knowledge about their respective fields helps broaden the scope of the book; their expertise on a specific East Asian state or a topic adds depth to the book.

Due to a lack of unified books on East Asian politics, most instructors usually need to pick at least three books to cover East Asia, which deal with China, Japan, and Korea separately. This book is an effort to include in a single volume major political, economic, and social developments in these countries so that readers can get a glimpse of what is happening in East Asia and how events there affect the international political economy. This is different from a standard textbook. Instead, along the three connected themes—security, political economy, and society, we are covering some of the most important issues and topics about East Asia, hoping to generate increased interest and deeper thinking among college students and other readers. However, this single volume cannot cover all topics that we wish to address. We believe it is a good starting point, from where readers may reach out to discover and study other important and interesting topics, and we encourage them to do so.

Given the unique features, strengths, and timeliness of this book, it can serve as a text for East Asian politics class. It should also be useful as supplementary readings for other East Asia-related courses in comparative politics, international relations, international political economy, Asian studies, history, sociology, geography, cultural studies, women's studies, etc.

# Contents

In Part I, Security and Foreign Policy, five chapters deal with security and foreign policy challenges in East Asia. The rapid reemergence of China as a great economic and military power dominates the political and economic landscape of East Asia and beyond. One cannot discuss East Asian politics without talking about China's rise and its implications. In Chapter 1, Hochul Lee addresses this important issue. China's rise will arguably be the most important story in the twenty-first-century international relations. However, we have contrasting prospects over China's future, either pessimistic or optimistic. To comprehensively evaluate the effects of a rising China on peace and security in East Asia, Lee suggests an integrative model of peace equation of China, which incorporates key theoretical variables at distinct levels. Major findings are first, a US-China power transition is not an imminent possibility. Second, China has been and will be more economically interdependent with its East Asian neighbors and the United States which will have pacifying effects. Third, China has been fully involved in most of major multilateral institutions and organizations, indicating likely peaceful governance of potential China-related conflicts or disputes. Finally, actor-related factors such as the imperative of continued economic development, stable leadership transitions, the CCP's enhanced confidence and competence, and a new state identity of a responsible great power will turn China into a system defender rather than a revisionist. In short, the peace equation of a rising China will be positive in the near future and China is unlikely to breed major conflicts or seek to reshape the existing regional and global orders in the years ahead.

The United States expressed a strong interest in Asia through official contacts with East Asian nations in the nineteenth century. It has been deeply involved in Asian affairs since the early twentieth century. Since the end of World War II, the United States has served as the backbone of regional stability in East Asia. The role of the United States looms large in any discussion of East Asian politics. In Chapter 2, Il Hyun Cho addresses the issue of the changing US role and the shifting regional order in East Asia in the new century. The hub-and-spokes system of the American alliances with Japan and South Korea has not only deterred challenges to the regional status quo but also dampened the security dilemma among countries in the region. Since 9/11, however, the United States has been eager to transform the regionally confined alliance structure into a global military coalition in the name of jointly addressing various global security challenges. Cho locates the role of the United States in historical perspective, highlighting the contrast between US regional strategy before and after 9/11. With the United States increasingly dwelling on the global dimension after 9/11, there is an acute sense of strategic uncertainty in East Asia, prompting regional countries to adjust to what seems to be a shifting regional order. The chapter suggests that it is crucial to renew the terms of the relationship between the United States and its regional counterparts in ways that will meet new global challenges, while not losing sight of traditional regional priorities.

China-Japan relations have been one of the most complex and difficult in East Asian politics. The relationship has been especially rocky since 2001 when Japanese prime minister Junichiro Koizumi (2001–6) began to pay his annual visit to the controversial Yasukuni Shrine. In Chapter 3, Mary M. McCarthy investigates the progress and setbacks that Japan–China relations have seen since 2006 when Koizumi left office, and where the relations seem to be heading in this new era. In the 1970s, Japan–China relations were characterized by the so-called panda diplomacy. For the Japanese, China's gift of a pair of pandas symbolized close cultural ties between the two countries, and it produced a wellspring of positive feelings toward China. This "golden age" did not last, as historical and other issues began to negatively impact relations in the mid-1980s, with a postwar low point in political relations by the early years of the twenty-first century. However, since 2006, we have seen concerted efforts to improve the relationship. In 2010 the World Expo was held in Shanghai, and Japan's pavilion focused on the theme of Japan–China friendship. One symbol of that friendship is the ibis, a bird that was brought back from the edge of extinction in Japan with the help of China. For the Japanese organizers, the ibis represents both Japan–China friendship and how bilateral cooperation is imperative in this age of transnational issues. This chapter explores what the author terms "ibis diplomacy" and the degree to which such bilateral cooperation on issues of transnational importance can sustain.

In Chapter 4, Chunjuan Nancy Wei examines the latest developments in cross-Taiwan Strait relations. Taiwan's relationship with the People's Republic of China (PRC) creates one of the most emotional, complex, and dangerous flashpoints in the world. Taiwan and the Chinese Mainland have been ruled separately after the Chinese Civil War in the 1940s. Initially a dictatorship under Chiang Kai-shek, Taiwan had achieved economic prosperity and political democratization by the late 1980s, widening the gap across the Taiwan Strait. The debate over whether Taiwan should reunify with or be independent from China has long dominated Taiwanese politics. Since President Ma Ying-jeou assumed office in 2008, replacing the pro-independence Chen Shui-bian administration of the previous eight years, reconciliation and cooperation have largely replaced recrimination and confrontation at the cross-Strait interface, though political relations between the two governments remain deadlocked. In 2010 the two sides signed the landmark Economic Cooperation Framework Agreement (ECFA), Northeast Asia's first free trade deal. Meanwhile, a set of thorny questions emerged: How can the rivals embrace each other economically when they still harbor significant political differences? Will this agreement that is economically beneficial to Taiwan come at a political cost? How will this deal influence East Asian regional economic integration, especially between Northeast Asia and Southeast Asia? This chapter not only examines changing relations between Taiwan and the PRC but also discusses political, economic, and security implications on East Asia's integration.

The Korean Peninsula is another location where security challenges are real and imminent. In Chapter 5, Heon Joo Jung discusses South Korea's foreign policy today, with a specific reference to the rise and fall of anti-Americanism in South Korea and the ways in which hegemonic ideas of anti-North Korea and pro-US have been deconstructed in South Korea. Jung suggests that a sudden rise of anti-American sentiment in South Korea in the early 2000s was a surprise to most Korea observers who worry about its impact on the bilateral relationship and beyond. Most works predict that anti-American sentiment in South Korea would be enduring because many causes are structural and irreversible. However, anti-Americanism seemed to be on the wane in the late 2000s. This chapter analyzes the rise and fall of anti-Americanism in a coherent framework by taking seriously the triangular relationship among two Koreas and the United States and the role of threat perception. It takes a closer look at the ways in which hegemonic ideas of anti-North and pro-US had been deconstructed and argues that the extent to which South Koreans perceive the North Korea threat exerts a significant influence on anti-Americanism in the South. The chapter asserts that North Korea's nuclear program has complicated the triangular relationship. The new and continuous threat the nuclear North Korea poses is an essential adhesive for an otherwise shaky relationship between South Korea and the United States.

In Part II, The New Political Economy, five chapters cover major developments in several key issues in East Asia's political economy. East Asian states such as South Korea and Taiwan have been known as equitable societies during their economic development. East Asian governments have been heavily involved in economic affairs. Now with demographic and policy changes, the income gap is widening in East Asia. In China's case, to ensure more equal and fair distribution of wealth has become a key challenge for the government. In Chapter 6, Mason M. S. Kim studies welfare states in East Asia. He examines the institutional divergence of East Asian welfare states, raising the question of whether East Asian welfare states show variations while maintaining their developmental credentials and, if so, why. This is the only chapter that also covers Singapore, Thailand, Malaysia, and Hong

Kong in addition to China, Japan, Taiwan, and Korea that are the focus of the book. Kim notes that traditionally, social policy in East Asia was regarded by government as a policy instrument to increase economic productivity. In this productivist framework, welfare beneficiaries were largely those who own skills with higher education. This pattern, however, has begun to change in recent decades, as economic globalization with increasingly competitive international markets put constraints on governments' social policy options. In response to challenges from globalization in general and the 1997 Asian financial crisis in particular, East Asian states began embarking different forms of welfare institutions. While social insurance schemes and social assistance programs are central to the welfare state in Japan, South Korea, and Taiwan, individual savings schemes play a leading role in Singapore, Malaysia, and Hong Kong. Meanwhile, China and Thailand stay between the two groups, combining both social insurance and individual savings schemes supplemented by modest public assistance programs. In explaining this institutional divergence, this chapter highlights financial system and political regime type as two mediating factors that direct the development of welfare institutions toward either "redistribution-oriented" or "efficiency-oriented" policy in the globalization era.

Global competitiveness holds the key to national prosperity in the twenty-first century. Countries around the world have devoted a great deal of time and money to national innovation strategies designed to promote what is generally called the "new economy." East Asia has entered the digital age. By 2011, for example, the number of China's Internet users had reached over 450 million, and cell phone users topped 800 million. How are East Asian nations doing in this new information revolution? In Chapter 7, Carin Holroyd and Ken Coates discuss the new digital media and innovation environment in East Asia. According to them, East Asia has been a formidable and successful competitor in digital innovation, investing heavily in science and technology, spawning numerous government-university-business partners and ramping up the post-secondary education system. Digital content—the preparation of material for distribution via digital means—has emerged as a critical part of the emerging economic order. East Asian countries, led by Japan and South Korea, have been world leaders in such fields as anime, multi-player online gaming, animation, and digital representations of national culture. National governments have been both creative and aggressive in building the new sector, which does not operate according to the standard structures and paradigms of industrial and commercial growth. Digital content relies heavily on creativity and artistic skill and requires very strong connections to youth culture and new consumer electronics. The manner in which East Asian governments have responded to the imperatives of the digital economy, both in terms of digital technologies and digital content, demonstrates the continued importance of government-led economic development in the region. The attention given to digital content also runs counter to the standard assumption that East Asian countries are more adept at technological and scientific activities and less successful with content and creative enterprises.

In Chapter 8, Mary Alice Haddad deals with how media in East Asia covers environmental issues and the "green economy." East Asia is jumping on the environmental bandwagon. In January 2009 South Korea pledged 4 percent of its GDP toward a "Green New Deal." In the fall of the same year the new Japanese prime minister pledged to cut his country's greenhouse emissions by 25 percent its 1990 level, and China became one of the largest producers of renewable energy in the world. Across East Asia, even in nondemocratic countries, citizens are organizing and advocating that their governments act against climate change. Drawing on a content analysis of major newspapers in China, South Korea, and Japan (the *Asahi Shimbun* for Japan, the *Chosun Ilbo* for Korea, and the *People's Daily* for China) from 1990–2008, this chapter investigates media coverage of environmental politics. It reveals that all three newspapers increased their coverage of environmental issues over the period, and there was an increase in coverage of civil society actors over the time period in all three papers. Haddad's study suggests that in the "green economy" media coverage of government and business has been generally positive in East Asia.

In Chapter 9, Matthew A. Shapiro studies environmental legislations in East Asia. He provides a complete overview and analysis of environmental policies in Japan, South Korea, Taiwan, and China. Given the current nature of environmental problems, such policies call for a mix of science and technology innovations which are both planned and unanticipated. This creates a degree of ambiguity in terms of identifying policy outcomes, but it is also the most promising method of addressing the potentially grave consequences of environmental degradation, particularly climate change. In all four cases Shapiro identifies connections between innovation and environmental policy through an extensive review of ministerial-level documents and white papers and sub-categorizes policies within each country according to policy stringency and policy flexibility, which are the mechanisms connecting environmental policy and innovation. The implications are significant—especially within the East Asian region. The chapter suggests that East Asia must continue to focus on demand-driven innovation for environmental protection.

Confucian traditions have profoundly influenced politics and culture of East Asian nations, which tend to be male-dominated societies. In Chapter 10, Lana Obradovic studies the women's role in East Asia's political economy, especially in the military. In the region where the Cold War has not ended yet, where defense budgets continue to grow, and where citizenship is often defined in militarized terms, analysis of women's role in the armed forces has been largely neglected by Western social scientists. Obradovic argues that the key to understanding the recent "feminization" of the military in China and North Korea and lack thereof in South Korea and Japan lies in the relationship between the military, political leadership, and society in each state, and a tragic history of militarization of the lives of women in the region. More specifically, the chapter posits that in China and North Korea, where "party controls the gun" and where women are more economically active and recognized, at least officially by both the military and political leadership as equal defenders of the socialist cause both in economics and politics, women enjoy a higher degree of inclusiveness in the military. On the other hand, in South Korea and Japan, low levels of female economic activity and often-strained civil-military relations due to the collective historical experience of victimization by colonial and neocolonial powers have led to apathy regarding political and economic integration policies at large and low levels of women's military participation in particular.

In Part III, Changing Societies, five chapters cover some of the major societal changes and challenges in East Asian states. Tens of thousands of mass, sometimes violent, protests against corruption, unfair treatment of migrant workers, arbitrary land grabs, environmental pollution, etc. take place in China every year now. What is the role of China's college-educated youth—the future leaders of China—in these social movements? In the West, many assume that economic liberalization and growth, especially when accompanied by increased access to information, will lead to strain between a society and the authoritarian regime over which it governs, ultimately eliciting popular pressures for liberal democratic change. Yet when it comes to China's college students, this has not been the case. To the contrary, relative to China's early reform period (1978–89), since 1990 individuals pursuing college degrees in China have exhibited decreased support for Western-style democracy, and less inclination to distance themselves from and challenge the ruling CCP. In Chapter 11, Teresa Wright documents the changing character of Chinese university students' political attitudes and activities in the post-Mao China, highlighting the contrast between the early period of 1978–89 and the late period of 1990–2011. This comparison suggests that economic liberalization and growth may not always be accompanied by greater public support for the type of liberal democracy found in the West. At the same time, the chapter emphasizes that some of the political attitudes and behaviors evidenced by Chinese university students have remained virtually unchanged throughout the reform period. Wright examines major factors that have contributed to these changes and continuities, including access to the Internet, the demographic characteristics of China's university student population, the degree of unity within the top CCP leadership, the content conveyed in domestic media coverage and the educational system, and China's global economic and political status.

In a related but separate study, Li Chunling of the Institute of Sociology at the Chinese Academy of Social Sciences (CASS) notes that over 50 percent of China's college graduates today prefer to work in the government, state-owned enterprises, and institutions of higher learning and research. In comparison, less than a quarter wants to work in foreign or Chinese-foreign joint ventures.[6] The Chinese youth's attraction by the "iron rice bowls" and their willingness to join China's political and economic establishment have significant impact on China's future. Since they benefit from the current system, they are less likely to challenge it or demand significant political reforms.

In Chapter 12, Carol Ann Medlicott studies the relationship between nature and nation in North Korea. Since the mid-twentieth century, Korea—like the rest of Asia—has been increasingly engulfed in the Western discourses that fuel today's processes of globalization. Among these is nationalism. The very concept of "nation-state" is a Western one, involving the assertion that all people within the boundaries of a given political territory comprise a community that shares exactly the same cultural identity. Globalization has not only universally imposed the "nation-state" ideal, but also problematized it. Migration, mobility, and global communications strain the notion of what constitutes "community" and whether cultural identity and geographic location must necessarily coincide for a "nation" to be a valid political unit. Medlicott suggests that the concept of "nation" is particularly problematic on the Korean Peninsula, whose once unitary "hermit kingdom" was divided just as the modern global community was forming. To critically engage the concept of "nation" on the Korean Peninsula, this chapter examines some of the distinctive physical and aesthetic motifs pervading the nationalist narratives of North Korea. No political community arrives at "nationhood" easily or automatically. In many cases, inscribing nationalism onto sovereign territory involves the appropriation and replication of motifs associated with formative historical moments. North Korea looks to the alleged exploits of Kim Il-sung for its nationalist narrative, specifically those exploits that unfolded in a geographically distinctive region of the Peninsula. Knowing North Korea's view of nationhood is essential to understanding its current policies.

China's rise is not just in economic and military dimensions but also on cultural front. Since the early 2000s, China has attempted to project its soft power globally through various means such as expanding trade and investment, enhancing educational and cultural exchanges, and establishing hundreds of "Confucius Institutes" to promote Chinese language learning. In Chapter 13, Wendy Weiqun Su seeks to analyze China's cultural policy and counter hegemony strategies toward global Hollywood and Hollywood-led transnational media conglomerates from 2000 to 2011. Situating China studies within the global context, this chapter investigates the impact of the cultural policy on China's domestic film industry, local and global cultural landscape. Su holds that the cultural policy of the Chinese government during this period is a revision of its previous policy from 1994 to early 2000. The policy shift is a commitment that the Chinese government had to make to meet the requirements of the World Trade Organization (WTO), and a result of the redefinition of film as a cultural industry. She argues that the Chinese government is the biggest beneficiary of its own policy. Through both the alliance and tug-of-war with global capital, and through the Greater China alliance, the Chinese government has effectively consolidated its authoritarian power. As a result of the policy shift, a strong market-oriented film industry is being established from production to distribution, and box office revenue seems to have become the sole measure to judge the success of a film. Overdone Kung Fu movies that combine both spectacular Hollywood-style special effects and traditional Chinese cultural elements become the influential genre of the domestic film industry and prime market attraction. Meanwhile, transnational, trans-regional coproductions become the major contributor to China's film revenue and a backbone force to its film industry. Such an intertwined partnership network is in the process of forming not only regionally in Asia, but globally. How will the so-called Chinawood challenge Hollywood remains to be seen.

Among developed countries, Japan probably has one of the lowest rates of women's participation in national politics, reflecting the country's slow progress in achieving genuine gender equality. In 2011, for example, women made up only 11 percent of lawmakers in the powerful lower house of the parliament.[7] In Chapter 14, Atsuko Sato looks at evolution of Japan's gender policy. The evolution of Japan's gender-based equality policy reveals a shift in concepts and strategies: from "equal opportunity" to a "gender-equal society." Sato examines the development of policy orientations in the 1980s and 1990s to the present, and their outcomes and consequences in Japanese society. Using a methodology based on frame analysis, this chapter first analyzes how gender equality and family policy were framed in the 1986 Equal Employment Opportunity Law (EEOL) and in related measures throughout the 1980s. Second, it analyzes the period after the so-called 1.57 shock in 1990 (a time when the fertility rate hit 1.57). It was at this point that the government shifted significantly the framing of gender and family policy through a series of measures, including the 1999 Basic Law for a Gender-Equal Society. The chapter reveals, however, that public policies based on the concept of "equal opportunity" were never intended to bring about actual gender equality. Further, after more than a decade from the introduction of a gender mainstreaming approach in the Basic Law, Japan has not much improved gender equality, nor has the country achieved a gender equal society. Sato argues that a lack of effective implementation of policies and the persistent social norms on appropriate gender roles and social arrangements have been the key obstacles. Obviously Japan has a long way to go to become a fully gender-equal society.

China is not a democracy, yet its leadership change has been institutionalized since Deng Xiaoping's limited political reforms in the 1980s. With the introduction of term and age limits, life-long tenure for leaders has been abolished. Top leadership transition every ten years (two terms) has been smooth so far. Most significantly, largely fair, free, and competitive elections at the village and local legislative levels have been held in China since the late 1980s. In Chapter 15, Diqing Lou examines how the local people's congress elects congressional representatives at the municipal level. She notes that the local people's congress has been playing an increasingly important role in local politics, and the electoral procedures have become more systematic and regulated. It has started to allocate some of the congressional seats to interested citizens, especially the emerging business elites who contribute to the local economy and those private entrepreneurs who seek political status and privileges. Lou argues that the changes in the local congressional politics are part of the grassroots political reform initiated by the CCP to increase public support, strengthen its governance, and provide more political space to accommodate societal changes during economic reform. These measures have brought about political liberalization in China to a certain extent and helped to build political alliances for the CCP at the grassroots level. Overall, the status and responsibilities of the local people's congress have improved significantly, and the people's congress has broadened its scope in political representation, especially for the segment of the society that possesses abundant socioeconomic resources. Many China observers wonder when such elections will be introduced at higher levels of government.

# Concluding remarks

Taken together, these chapters offer readers a great opportunity to learn about some of the key developments in security, political economy, and society of China, Japan, North Korea, South Korea, Taiwan, and the East Asian region as a whole. No book on East Asia can capture every major issue or development in these states. What we attempt to do in this book is to selectively examine a few important developments and prevailing trends and use them as cases or examples to generate more interest in East Asian politics. The "Five questions for discussions" at the end of each chapter are designed as a pedagogical tool to help readers reflect upon the issues covered and think about these issues in broad historical, cultural, and theoretical contexts.

While East Asia faces some common challenges, each of these states has to deal with its unique issues and problems. Development and peace are the common pursuits of East Asian people. All these states have been affected by the fluctuation of the world economy, global climate change, and both traditional and nontraditional security challenges. Every nation needs to address its own problems. In Japan, for example, one of the biggest problems is the slow economic recovery after the lost two decades of 1990s and 2000s. The frequent change of political leaders does not bode well for the recovery efforts. Facing a graying and declining population, Japan needs to further improve women's social status and may have to loosen its immigration policy to absorb more skilled workers from other countries. In China, decades of obsessive and narrow focus on GDP growth has led to a tremendous income inequality, rampant corruption, and sharp decline in social morality. The Chinese government has to pay more attention to the quality, not just the speed, of growth and achieve a more balanced development, especially for its vast Western region. On the Korean Peninsula, North Korea's provocative behaviors present the biggest challenge. Its leadership transition, nuclear program, extensive poverty, and refugee flows are some of the issues that its neighbors have to deal with even if they need to focus on their own domestic problems. East Asia faces an array of complex challenges. These challenges are real, but East Asian governments and people are as optimistic as ever.

In the years and decades ahead, East Asia is likely to remain a dynamic region that has the potential to significantly contribute or disrupt international political economy. For this reason alone, we need to seriously study and closely follow the political and economic developments in East Asia. If this book can help to promote learning of East Asia, the editor and contributors will be very satisfied.

## Five questions for discussions

1. Why and how do developments in East Asia shape international political economy?
2. What major obstacles does Japan need to remove in order to recover from its long economic stagnation?
3. What are major challenges the Chinese government faces today? What are the main features of the so-called China model?
4. Why is North Korea unwilling to abandon its nuclear program? What obstructs the unification of the two Koreas?
5. What is the role of the United States in East Asian politics today?

# Notes

1 Geographically, East Asia includes both Northeast Asia and Southeast Asia. However, most scholars consider Southeast Asia as a separate field of study. In this book, East Asia refers to the region that includes the People's Republic of China, Taiwan, Japan, North Korea, and South Korea. As a geo-political term, East Asia may include the United States since the United States is also an Asian power.

2 "Riben Zainan Jiehou, Lajing Zhongri Guanxi (Japan's tragedy brings Sino-Japan relations closer)," *Voice of America* (Chinese), March 16, 2011.

3 "Global inflation starts with Chinese workers," *Bloomberg Businessweek*, March 7–13, 2011, 9–10.

4 "Backgrounder: China's national population censuses," *Xinhua*, April 28, 2011.

5 Secretary of State Hillary Clinton declared "The United States is back" during her visit to Thailand while attending an East Asian regional forum in July 2009. Apparently the administration of President Obama thought it was time to show Asian nations that the United States was not distracted by its wars in Iraq and Afghanistan and intended to broaden and deepen its partnerships in Asia.

6 Li Chunling, "Employment and Wage of Chinese University Graduates," paper presented at the International Conference on China's Social Policy Reform, July 30–1, 2010, Singapore.

7 "Japan: Public Office Quota for Women Is Considered," *The Wall Street Journal*, June 24, 2011, A10.

# List for further reading

Cargill, Thomas F. and Takayuki Sakamoto. *Japan since 1980* (Cambridge: Cambridge University Press, 2008).

Carlin, Robert L. and Joel Wit. *North Korean Reform: Politics, Economics and Security* (London and New York: Routledge, 2010).

Cheek, Timothy. *Living with Reform: China since 1989* (New York: Zed Books, 2007).

Copper, John F. *Taiwan: Nation-State or Province?* 5th edn (Boulder, CO: Westview, 2008).

Demick, Barbara. *Nothing to Envy: Ordinary Lives in North Korea* (New York: Spiegel & Grau, 2010).

Dreyer, June Teufel. *China's Political System,* 7th edn (New York: Longman, 2009).

Fewsmith, Joseph. *China since Tiananmen: From Deng Xiaoping to Hu Jintao* (Cambridge: Cambridge University Press, 2008).

Gilley, Bruce. *Political Change in China: Comparisons with Taiwan* (Boulder, CO: Lynne Rienner Publishers, 2008).

Gries, Peter and Stanley Rosen, eds. *Chinese Politics: State, Society and the Market* (New York: Routledge, 2010).

Hayes, Louis D. *Introduction to Japanese Politics,* 5th edn (Armonk, NY: M.E. Sharpe, 2008).

—. *Political Systems of East Asia: China, Korea, and Japan* (Armonk, NY: M.E. Sharpe, 2012).

Heo, Uk and Terence Roehrig. *South Korea since 1980* (Cambridge: Cambridge University Press, 2010).

Hessler, Peter. *Country Driving: A Journey through China from Farm to Factory* (New York: Harper, 2010).

Huang, Xiaoming. *Politics in Pacific Asia: An Introduction* (New York: Palgrave, 2009).

Huang, Yasheng. *Capitalism with Chinese Characteristics: Entrepreneurship and the State* (Cambridge: Cambridge University Press, 2008).

Inoguchi, Takashi and Purnendra Jain, eds. *Japanese Politics Today: From Karaoke to Kabuki Democracy* (New York: Palgrave Macmillan, 2011).

Joseph, William A., ed. *Politics in China: An Introduction* (Oxford: Oxford University Press, 2010).

Kil, Soong Hoom and Chung-in Moon. *Understanding Korean Politics* (Albany: SUNY Press, 2001).

Kim, Myung Oak and Sam Jaffe. *The New Korea: An Inside Look at South Korea's Economic Rise* (New York: AMACOM, 2010).

Kingston, Jeff. *Contemporary Japan: History, Politics, and Social Change since the 1980s* (Somerset, NJ: Wiley-Blackwell, 2010).

Martin, Bradley K. *Under the Loving Care of the Fatherly Leader: North Korea and the Kim Dynasty* (New York: St. Martin's Griffin, 2006).

Myers, B. R. *The Cleanest Race: How North Koreans See Themselves and Why It Matters* (New York: Melville House, 2010).

Perry, Elizabeth J. and Merle Goldman, eds. *Grassroots Political Reform in Contemporary China* (Cambridge, MA: Harvard University Press, 2007).

Saich, Tony. *Governance and Politics of China,* 3rd edn (New York: Palgrave Macmillan, 2011).

Schafferer, Christian, ed. *Understanding Modern East Asian Politics* (Hauppauge, NY: Nova Biomedical Books, 2005).

Simone, Vera. *The Asian Pacific: Political and Economic Development in a Global Context,* 2nd edn (New York: Longman, 2001).

Snyder, Scott. *China's Rise and the Two Koreas* (Boulder, CO: Lynne Rienner, 2009).

Yahuda, Michael. *The International Politics of the Asia-Pacific,* 3rd and revised edn (New York: Routledge, 2011).

Yang, Guobin. *The Power of the Internet in China* (New York: Columbia University Press, 2009).

Zhu, Zhiqun. *Understanding East Asia's Economic "Miracles"* (Ann Arbor: Association for Asian Studies, 2009).

—. *The People's Republic of China Today: Internal and External Challenges* (Singapore: World Scientific Publishing, 2010).

—. *Global Studies: China,* 14th edn (New York: McGraw-Hill Higher Ed, 2011).

# Part I
## Security and Foreign Policy

# 1

# China's Rise and
# East Asian Security*
## Hochul Lee

## Chapter Outline

# China rising

In terms of economic capabilities, China has achieved remarkable success since the late 1970s, with a growth rate of about 10 percent annually. The sheer size of its economy had quadrupled by the end of 2000s and is estimated to double again over the next decade.[1] It has become a global manufacturing center and consumes roughly a third of the global supply of iron, steel, and coal.[2] Its trade volume expanded tremendously from 22 percent of GDP in 1980 to 65 percent in 2008 with huge trade surpluses.[3] As a result, China had accumulated the largest foreign exchange reserves of over US$3 trillion by 2011.[4]

In terms of military capabilities, China has implemented defense modernization as one of its "Four Modernizations" since the launch of the reform and opening in 1978. With an ever expanding GDP, Chinese military

*This research was supported by an Asia Research Fund 2008 grant.

expenditures have increased dramatically at a rate of over 10 percent in most years since the 1990s. The Chinese military has steadily absorbed sophisticated military technologies and developed advanced weapons in land, air, sea, and even space. As a result, China's military capabilities have been considerably transformed and significantly strengthened.[5]

With a rising China, what kind of regional order will prevail in East Asia? Will it be one of realist pessimism or liberalist optimism? Specifically, will Chinese rising power breed a power transition and cause an inevitable hegemonic conflict in the region, as realists tend to think? Or will Chinese economic growth and increasing economic interdependence bring about peace and prosperity in the region, as liberalists argue? Practically, what should be done to promote peace and prosperity in East Asia? This chapter attempts to find answers to these questions that have profound implications on peace and prosperity in East Asia.

To comprehend the effects of a rising China on peace and security in East Asia, this study suggests an integrative model of peace equation that critically incorporates existing theoretical perspectives at distinct levels. After a brief review of existing theories, this study constructs an integrative model of China's peace equation, examines key variables of dominant theories at distinct levels, aggregates findings to reach a conclusion, and finally elaborates their practical implications for peace and prosperity in East Asia. The study indicates that China's peace equation in aggregate will be positive for decades or at least a decade to come. In other words, a rising China will neither breed a hegemonic war nor seek to reshape the existing regional and global order. It also argues that China needs to convince regional countries and the United States of its peaceful intentions by committing itself more firmly to common regional economic and security interests.

# Realist pessimism or liberal optimism

The most common existing answers to the questions raised here are grouped into two contending camps: either realist pessimism or liberalist optimism.[6] On the one hand, realists are mostly pessimistic, who tend to look at politics among great powers or changing distribution of power in the international system negatively. According to them, in the last 500 years, no great power managed to avoid substantial warfare around the time of its entry into great power ranks. The ultimate goal of every rising great power is to maximize its share of world power and eventually dominate the system, which creates conflict with the current hegemon. China will not be an exception. John Mearsheimer is one of such pessimistic realists. He has clearly asserted that China will rise to be a regional hegemony and that the United States and China are likely to engage in an intense security competition with considerable potential for war.[7] Similarly, Richard Bernstein and Ross H. Munro claim that China will certainly emerge as the dominant power in the West Pacific within 10 to 20 years and that China's strategic goal to be the dominant power in Asia collides with the US goal to prevent such a power in Asia. They further argue that China and the United States will be adversaries in the major global rivalry of the first decades of the twenty-first century.[8]

Contrary to liberalist argument of the pacifying effects of economic interdependence, realists view economic interdependence rather increasing vulnerability toward trading partners[9] or actually generating economic frictions that can easily offset or overwhelm its conflict-suppressing effects.[10] Further, they argue that economic interdependence is unlikely to have much of an impact on the behavior of great powers, which have large internal markets and a wide range of trading partners.[11] In another respect, it is pointed out that economic relations, including economic interdependence, are more likely a reflection of existing political relations than a determinant of those relations.[12]

On the other hand, liberals tend to be optimistic. They particularly emphasize the pacifying effects of economic interdependence, as revealed by the classic statement of Montesquieu: "trade brings peace."[13] They find that China is also on the liberal path. Michael R. Chambers, for instance, points out that the CCP leadership needs continuous economic development to strengthen comprehensive national power, to enhance regime stability, and to attain great power status, which has resulted in increasing economic interdependence with neighboring countries, the United States and European Union. He further points out that becoming globalized and more economically interdependent with the world are very much a conscious strategy of the Chinese leadership for both economic and political purposes.[14] In short, liberalists predict that China is more likely to be constrained by increasing economic interdependence toward a peaceful and stable international environment.[15]

Many Chinese scholars argue that China's strategic goal of "peace and development" (*heping yu fazhan*) and impending domestic concerns would keep China on the track of peaceful rise. Dean of Peking University's School of International Relations Wang Jisi, for example, has stated that China is most concerned about economic prosperity and social stability domestically, which leads China to seek peace and stability in regional and global contexts and especially in its relations with the United States.[16] Similarly, Zheng Bijian, an advisor to top Chinese leaders, mentions that China faces a lot of urgent domestic issues such as raising the standards of living, reducing the widening gap in economic and social welfare between the East coast and the inner West, enforcing sustainable development, strengthening environmental protection, and so on. Consequently, China does not seem to have the capabilities to compete with the United States or other major countries in the region.[17]

# Integrative peace equation

The reality only partially verifies these theoretical perspectives. Therefore, to figure out the effects of a rising China in a comprehensive way, we need to integrate key variables of realist, liberal, and constructivist theories. As Robert Jervis pointed out, "only rarely does a single factor determine the way politics will work out."[18] Thus it is necessary to estimate the impact of key theoretical variables at distinct levels on the peace equation of China to comprehend the effects of rising China on peace and security in East Asia.

## Structure level

Structure-level variables include those related to power politics in a broad sense that would affect relative distribution of power in the interstate system such as power balancing, power transition, or power preponderance by means of military buildup and/or realignment of alliances. Neorealists attend to these structural variables more than any other theorists.

Economic interdependence is also a structural property that constrains foreign behaviors of economically interdependent states. Commercial liberals might argue that expanding trade and deepening investment among countries with increasing economic interdependence could breed the pacifying effects in international relations by either the "constraining" or "transforming" effect. If a country is more economically interdependent with others, decision makers of the country would be less likely to risk military conflict with others, for the expected costs of war rise as economic interdependence increases.[19] Or if a country is more integrated into the world economy, societal preferences are transformed toward more trade and investment. Internationalist coalition might prevail within a society which could result in potential changes in the composition of the governing body.[20] In the case of China, the reform-and-opening leaderships since the late 1970s have created internationalist societal groups and sectors who have a strong interest in preserving free and open market and therefore in maintaining peace.[21] Aaron L. Friedberg assesses that economic interdependence has already helped to create a strong mutual interest in peace in the US-China relationship.[22]

## Process level

Process-level variables here refer to those related to international political processes. Even in international relations, there are political processes where distinct actors with distinct interests interact with each other to reflect their interests in decisions made at international institutions and organizations. If we have more institutions and organizations developed and if we have more states constrained by them, we would have international political processes that work more effectively. To put it differently, the more multilateralism has evolved in international relations, the more effectively international political processes would work. The UN Security Council, for instance, is one of relatively well-institutionalized organizations primarily responsible for international security issues, while the WTO is another one for international trade-related issues. International institutions and organizations could enhance the level of governance in international relations and, consequently, interstate conflicts and disputes are more likely to be governed through international political processes. In particular, neoliberal institutionalists tend to stress the governability of international affairs through international institutions and organizations.[23]

## Actor level

Actor-level variables matter significantly. They include the nature of political leadership—revolutionary, conservative or reform-oriented, shared beliefs and values among decision makers, their perception on their own and other countries, their memories of the past, state identity, regime type, historical legacies, and so on. These actor-level variables could affect a country's foreign behavior toward either accommodative or revisionist direction independently of the configuration of structure-level and process-level variables.

## An integrative model

An integrative model of peace equation that reflects all variables mentioned above can be formulated as below.

$f$(peace) = $a$(structure-level variables) + $b$(process-level variables) + $c$(actor-level variables)

= $a_1$(power politics) + $a_2$(economic interdependence) + $b$(multilateralism) + $c$(actor-level variables)

As we have discussed, neorealists tend to argue for the decisive effect of $a_1$ either positively or negatively; commercial liberals tend to stress the pacifying effects of $a_2$; neoliberal institutionalists tend to highlight the positive effect of $b$; and constructivists tend to emphasize the independent effect of $c$ either positively or negatively.

# China's peace equation

We can apply the integrative peace equation to China. In this equation, dependent variable is peace and stability in East Asia, while independent variables are those factors associated with rising China at the three levels. For structure level, we examine the effects of power politics and economic interdependence; for process level, we consider the extent to which China is engaged in multilateralism; and for actor level, we look at the nature of China's reform-oriented leadership and its effects on the peace equation. By examining the effects of these variables at three levels together on the peace equation of China, we could estimate comprehensively potential peace and conflict in East Asia as a result of China's rise. The peace equation of a rising China will be like below. We examine the effect of each variable on the equation.

$f$(peace) = $a_1$(power politics) + $a_2$(economic interdependence) + $b$(multilateralism) + $c$(reform leadership)

## Power politics

One of the most debated issues about a rising China is a possibility of global power transition and its impact on the regional and global order. According to power transition theorists, when an ascending power overtakes the dominant power and if it is dissatisfied with the existing regional or global order, it is likely to challenge the dominant power with considerable potential for conflict or even war. Applying their theories to China, they argue that if

China continues economic growth and military modernization at the current rate, a US-China power transition is inevitable and fairly imminent, probably within a generation.[24]

If we accept power transition theories, two conditions should be met to predict any conflict or war between the United States and China: a US-China power transition *and* China's dissatisfaction with the existing regional or global order. However, both conditions are not likely to be satisfied in the imminent future.

First, a power transition between the United States and China is not likely to happen soon. In terms of economic capabilities, Chinese GDP measured at purchasing power parity (PPP) is estimated to overtake American GDP around 2020 (see Figure 1.1 below). However, as Steve Chan aptly points out, Chinese GDP tends to be exaggerated because of the huge size of the population.[25] In other words, even in 2020, Chinese GDP per capita will probably still be one-fifth of that of the United States, which implies that Chinese economic capabilities will still be limited.

In terms of military capabilities, the gap between Chinese and American defense expenditures is very wide and becoming even wider (see Figure 1.2 below). Robert S. Ross points out that economic power is not easily translated into military power that requires indigenous development of sophisticated technologies and equipments for power projection capabilities. China's defense modernization has been centered on the improvement of land-power capabilities so far. Thus, China's rise into a global economic power has not transformed China into a global or region-wide military power yet.[26]

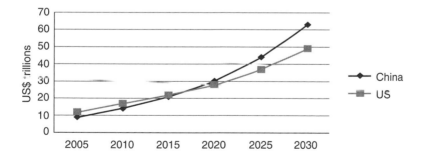

**Figure 1.1** Projected GDP at PPP

*Source*: EIU (Economist Intelligence Unit) Data Services, http://www.eiu.com; Ikenberry, "The Rise of China," 36.

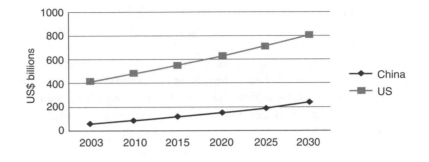

**Figure 1.2** Projected Defense Expenditures
*Source*: Ikenberry, "The Rise of China," 37.

Furthermore, as David P. Rapkin and William R. Thompson argue persuasively, the quantitative conception and measurement of power capabilities as employed by most of power transition theorists are not enough in the twenty-first-century strategic environment.[27] Not only the quantity of power capabilities such as GDP, population, and military manpower, but also their quality such as technological and organizational innovation, human capital, and strategic orientation should be taken into account in the estimation of power capabilities.[28] When we consider both quantitative and qualitative dimensions of power capabilities, a US-China power transition is not an imminent possibility.

Second, China is not dissatisfied with the current international system. It is one of the countries that have benefited most from the contemporary international order since its introduction of reform and opening in the late 1970s. The CCP leadership aims to construct a moderately prosperous society (*xiaokang shehui*) by 2020, which requires a continuous economic growth.[29] To attain this goal, China still needs to devote itself to expanding trade, attracting FDIs, and growing domestic markets, which in turn requires stable and cooperative international relations. In other words, China is unlikely to challenge the prevailing regional and global order for decades or at least a decade to come.

Even if a US-China power transition occurs combined with Chinese dissatisfaction with the regional and global order, will a hegemonic war between the United States and China be inevitable? We argue that the probability of such a war will be considerably lower than in the past centuries, because the international system of the twenty-first century has evolved substantially. As we understand, economic interdependence has increased among countries and especially between the United States and China, which would constrain state behaviors in a peaceful direction. International political processes with multilateral approaches have developed significantly with international institutions and organizations enhancing the level of regional or global governance, where both the United States and China are active participants. Structural pressure to risk war will be mitigated through international political processes and Chinese interests can be accommodated peacefully. Even if both conditions of power transition theory are satisfied in the relationship between the United States and China, a peaceful power transition is more likely to happen in the twenty-first century international system.[30]

Even if we renounce an imminent probability of power transition and related conflict or war between the United States and China, the mechanism of the security dilemma might still destabilize security in East Asia. Defensive measures of each side might raise alarm and stimulate counter-measures on the other side, resulting in arms races and downward spirals of security relations. With regard to the Taiwan issue which is most likely to be involved in the workings of the security dilemma, Beijing's military buildup in the Taiwan Strait to quail Taiwan leaders against any tendencies toward independence might provoke Washington's military assistance to Taipei to deter Beijing's military attack, with potential dangers of a crisis and an escalation into a military conflict.

However, the possibility of conflict or war between the United States and China through the workings of the security dilemma will be substantially diminished through nuclear deterrence. Furthermore, the United States and China have already developed multiple channels of communication including the annual Strategic and Economic Dialogue, which would diminish the prospects for misperception and potential dangers of conflict or war.[31]

## Economic interdependence

Since Deng Xiaoping's reform and opening policies, China has become increasingly interdependent with the global economy. In terms of trade, China's trade-to-GDP ratio has grown from 22 percent in 1980 to 65 percent in 2008.[32] As Figure 1.3 below shows, accession to the WTO in 2001 has accelerated China's total trade growth and its reliance of GDP on trade. Expanding exports and overall trade surplus have enabled the PRC to build the largest foreign exchange reserves in the world, reaching over US$ 3 trillion in 2011.

China's trade-to-GDP ratio reached its peak of 72 percent in 2006 and had fallen since then. It is partly because of Chinese leaders' political sensitivity to huge trade surplus with the United States, Japan, and EU, and partly because of shifting development strategy away from export-led growth to growth based on increasing domestic demands and consumption,[33] which was articulated into the goal of constructing a "harmonious society" (*hexie shehui*) under the Hu Jintao leadership. Nonetheless, Chinese trade will steadily expand to boost its continuous economic growth.

Chinese economic growth has also been driven by increasing FDI inflows. As Figure 1.4 demonstrates, FDI inflows increased rapidly in 1992 when the CCP leadership, in its 14th Party Congress, decided to resume reform and opening that had been temporarily suspended after the Tiananmen incident in 1989. To implement the Party's decision, the Chinese government carried out far-reaching financial reform measures, which contributed to the increase of FDI inflows. The chart also demonstrates that FDI inflows increased dramatically after China's entry into the WTO in 2001.

Chinese activities in negotiating and implementing a number of free trade agreements (FTAs) are another indicator of increasing economic interdependence. As of 2011 China had already concluded FTAs with ASEAN, Australia, New Zealand, Chile, and Pakistan and plans to negotiate FTAs with India, South Korea, and Japan.

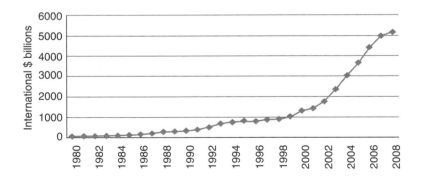

**Figure 1.3** China's trade volume

*Source*: World Bank, "World Development Indicators."

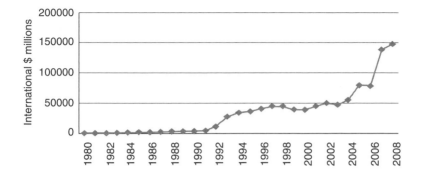

**Figure 1.4** China's FDI net inflows
*Source*: World Bank, "World Development Indicators."

All of these indicators imply increasing Chinese economic interdependence with other East Asian countries, the United States, and the EU, which would breed the pacifying effect. Indeed, we find the pacifying effect particularly in ASEAN-China relations. The Spratly Islands in South China Sea is a real flash point, where military conflict between the PRC and some of its neighbors has been likely since the 1990s with overlapping claims over the islands because of the islands' fishery, submarine energy resources, and geostrategic location. China seized and fortified Mischief Reef in 1995. However, all claimants concluded the Declaration on Conduct of Parties in the South China Sea in 2002. Furthermore, Chinese and Philippine oil companies agreed to a joint exploration project in 2004 in an area over which they have overlapping claims and the Vietnamese joined the project in 2005.[34] Though tensions may continue to rise in the region as what happened in the summer of 2011 when both Vietnam and the Philippines conducted military exercises in the disputed area, the chances for real military clashes will remain low in the near future due to China's restraint and its domestic development focus.

China also cooperates with Indonesia, Malaysia, and Singapore to protect security of the Strait of Malacca which is a crucial part of sea lane for Southeast and Northeast Asian countries.[35] In addition, Beijing employs economic interdependence strategically in its relations with Taiwan. It has tried to tie the two economies closely together so that Taiwanese leaders will not be able to declare Taiwan's formal independence from China without destroying the island's economy.[36]

## Multilateralism

Initially Chinese leaders regarded multilateral institutions and organizations negatively as interfering in the internal affairs of other countries and dominated by the United States and Western powers. However, through the experiences in the 1990s, Chinese leaders and diplomats became more and more positive about multilateral organizations and began to perceive them contributing to China's interests.[37] As David Shambaugh succinctly puts it, their views on multilateral organizations evolved from being "suspicious of" to "uncertain about" and then to "supportive of" such organizations.[38] By the turn of the millennium, China had fully involved and participated in over 80 percent of international organizations. By 2004, China-participating international treaties had increased to 233 from 34 in 1979.[39]

China's positive perception of and active participation in multilateral institutions and organizations suggest that any China-related potential conflicts or disputes are more likely to be governed through international political processes. Thus we can expect that the process-level variable, multilateralism, will positively affect the peace equation of China.

## Reform leadership

Actor-level factors are also positive in the peace equation. The Hu Jintao leadership, like previous Deng Xiaoping and Jiang Zemin leaderships, stressed the importance of continuous economic development as critical to China's grand strategy, which requires cooperative and stable international relations in East Asia. The next leadership after 2012 is likely to continue to promote economic development through reform and opening, which is crucial to the CCP's political legitimacy.

On the other hand, with decades of remarkable economic success and stable leadership transitions after Deng Xiaoping, Chinese leaders and government officials had gained much confidence. In particular, China's responses to the East Asian financial crisis in 1997–8 such as resisting devaluation pressure of the Chinese currency yuan or providing aid and low-interest loans to Southeast Asian countries were widely appreciated as having contributed to East Asia's early recovery from the crisis.[40] Since then, the idea of a "responsible great power" (*fuzeren daguo*) has become a general guideline of Chinese foreign policy. More profoundly, these experiences had led Chinese leaders and government officials to transform gradually their perception of China's identity from a state of *taoguang yanghui* to that of *fuzeren daguo*.[41]

The imperative of continuous economic development for CCP leaders and its requisite of cooperative and stable international relations, their sense of confidence and competence, and the evolution of state identity into a responsible great power are all likely to lead China to be a system defender rather than a system changer, or a constructive system manager rather than a reactive system challenger.

# Conclusion

The following is a summary of key findings of this chapter. First, a US-China power transition is not an imminent possibility when we consider both the quantity and quality of China's power capabilities. China is not dissatisfied with the existing regional and global orders. Instead, it has been the greatest beneficiary of the contemporary international system. Second, China has been and will be more economically interdependent with the United States and East Asian neighbors through expanding trade and increasing FDI flows. Increasing economic interdependence will constrain Chinese foreign behavior toward peace and stability, as demonstrated in its relations with ASEAN countries. Third, by the turn of the millennium, China had been fully involved in most of major multilateral institutions and organizations, indicating more likelihood of peaceful governance of potential China-related conflicts or disputes. Finally, actor-related factors such as the imperative of continued economic development for the CCP's legitimate rule, the Party's enhanced sense of confidence and competence as a result of economic success and stable leadership transitions, a new state identity of a responsible great power are more likely to turn China into a system defender rather than a system challenger. Based on these variables at different levels, the peace equation of a rising China is likely to be positive in the years ahead. In other words, a rising China will neither breed a major conflict nor seek to reshape the existing regional or global order in the near future.[42]

What implications do these findings suggest? First of all, to promote peace and prosperity in East Asia, it is necessary for other countries to encourage China to be more deeply engaged in both economic and security dimensions. By engaging China more extensively in economic and security areas, not only will China be able to pursue its vital interest of continued economic development, it will also become a stronger system defender. In return, East Asian countries will benefit from China's growth and China's commitment to common regional security. Indeed, China's economic development has been an opportunity for neighboring and other countries.

Second, on the part of China, it needs to convince its East Asian neighbors and other powers of its peaceful intentions. It needs to engage neighboring countries to share the benefits and costs of maintaining peace and prosperity in the region.[43] By willingly assuming its share of responsibility in maintaining peace and stability in regional and global orders, and by being firmly committed to international rules and norms, China can rise peacefully without triggering fear of the China threat.

One must note that this positive aggregation of the peace equation is based on the proviso that China will remain primarily focused on economic development and that Chinese foreign policies will be directed toward maintaining the international and regional environment conducive to its domestic growth. However, it is possible that as its power continues to rise, a nation's objectives will expand and its policies will change. In the future, if China drastically changes its policies, then the peace equation will have to be recalculated.

## Five questions for discussions

1. What are key elements of the power transition theory? To what extent do you think the theory can be applied to US-China relations in the future?
2. What challenges and opportunities are presented in East Asia with a rising China?
3. What specific interests does the United States have in East Asia and why? Do the United States and China share common interests in East Asia?
4. Despite a strong likelihood of a positive peace equation of China's rise, why are some people concerned about a more powerful China?
5. What issues do you think should be resolved most urgently from a long-term perspective to secure peace and prosperity in East Asia?

# Notes

1 EIU (Economist Intelligence Unit) Data Services at http://www.eiu.com; See also G. John Ikenberry, "The Rise of China and the Future of the West: Can the Liberal System Survive?" *Foreign Affairs* 87 (January/February 2008): 23–38.

2 Ikenberry, "The Rise of China and the Future of the West," 26.

3 World Bank, "World Development Indicators," http://data.worldbank.org/data-catalog.

4 Ibid.

5 For the analyses of the military capabilities of the PRC, see Robert S. Ross, "The Rise of Chinese Power and the Implications for the Regional Security Order," *Orbis* 54 (Fall 2010): 525–45; June

Teufel Dreyer, "China's Power and Will: The PRC's Military Strength and Grand Strategy," *Orbis* 51 (Fall 2007): 651–64.

6 Albeit a minority group, there could be also realist optimists and liberalist pessimists. Within the constructivist group, there could be also optimists and pessimists. As regards these diverse theoretical perspectives, see Aaron L. Friedberg, "The Future of U.S.-China Relations: Is Conflict Inevitable?" *International Security* 30 (Fall 2005): 7–45.

7 John J. Mearsheimer, "China's Unpeaceful Rise," *Current History* 105 (April 2006): 160–2.

8 Richard Bernstein and Ross H. Munro, "The Coming Conflict with America," *Foreign Affairs* 76 (March/April 1997): 18–32.

9 Kenneth N. Waltz, *Theory of International Politics* (Reading, MA: Addison-Wesley, 1979), pp. 143–60.

10 David P. Rapkin and William R. Thompson, "Will Economic Interdependence Encourage China's and India's Peaceful Ascent?" in *Strategic Asia 2006–2007: Trade, Interdependence, and Security,* ed. Ashley T. Tellis and Michael Wills (Seattle and Washington, D.C.: NBR, 2006), pp. 333–63.

11 John J. Mearsheimer, *The Tragedy of Great Power Politics* (New York: Norton, 2001).

12 Joanne Gowa, *Allies, Adversaries, and International Trade* (Princeton: Princeton University Press, 1994).

13 See Robert Gilpin, *The Political Economy of International Relations* (Princeton: Princeton University Press, 1987), p. 56.

14 Michael R. Chambers, "Rising China: The Search for Power and Plenty," in *Strategic Asia 2006– 2007: Trade, Interdependence, and Security,* ed. Ashley T. Tellis and Michael Wills (Seattle and Washington, D.C.: NBR, 2006), pp. 65–103.

15 See, for instance, James L. Richardson, "Asia-Pacific: The Case for Geopolitical Optimism," *National Interest* 38 (Winter 1994/5): 28–39.

16 Wang Jisi, "China's Search for Stability with America," *Foreign Affairs* 84 (September/October 2005): 39–48.

17 Zheng Bijian, "China's 'Peaceful Rise' to Great-Power Status," *Foreign Affairs* 84 (September/ October 2005): 18–24.

18 Robert Jervis, "The Future of World Politics: Will It Resemble the Past?" *International Security* 16 (Winter 1991/2): 40.

19 Scott L. Kastner, "Does Economic Integration Across the Taiwan Strait Make Military Conflict Less Likely?" *Journal of East Asian Studies* 6 (September–December 2006): 322

20 Kastner, "Economic Integration Across the Taiwan Strait," 322.

21 Hochul Lee, "Global Liberalization and Domestic Accommodation: The Case of the Chinese Socialist Market Economy," *Issues & Studies* 34 (June 1998): 117–34.

22 Friedberg, "The Future of U.S.-China Relations," 13.

23 For a typical neoliberal institutionalist approach, see Robert Keohane, *Power and Governance in a Partially Globalized World* (London: Routledge, 2002).

24 See for instance, Ronald L. Tammen, et al., *Power Transitions: Strategies for the 21st Century* (New York: Chatham House, 2000); David Rapkin and William R. Thompson, "Power Transition, Challenge and the (Re)Emergence of China," *International Interactions* 29 (2003): 315–42.

25 Steve Chan, "Is There a Power Transition between the U.S. and China?: The Different Faces of National Power," *Asian Survey* 45 (September/October 2005): 687–701.

26 Ross, "The Regional Security Order," 525–45.

27 Rapkin and Thompson, "Power Transition," pp. 315–42.

28 Rapkin and Thompson, "Power Transition"; Chan, "Is There a Power Transition?"

29 National Bureau of Statistics of China reported that China had attained 74.6 percent of the goal of building a "well-off society" by the end of 2008. http://www.gov.cn/jrzg/2009-12/21/content_1493212.htm.

30 Ikenberry also points out "the potential to turn the coming power shift into a peaceful change." Ikenberry, "The Rise of China," 33; Zhiqun Zhu also argues that the power transition between the United States and China will be peaceful, even though the author does not address whether a US-China power transition will actually occur or not. See Zhiqun Zhu, "Power Transition and U.S.-China Relations: Is War Inevitable?" *Journal of International and Area Studies* 12 (2005): 1–24.

31 For a similar assessment, see Charles Glaser, "Will China's Rise Lead to War? Why Realism Does Not Mean Pessimism," *Foreign Affairs* 90 (March/April 2011): 80–91.

32 World Bank, "World Development Indicators."

33 Chambers, "Rising China," p. 94.

34 Ibid.

35 Ibid.

36 Ming Wan, "Economics versus Security in Cross-Strait Relations: A Comment on Kastner," *Journal of East Asian Studies* 6 (September–December 2006): 347–9.

37 Susan L. Shirk, *China: Fragile Superpower* (New York: Oxford University Press, 2008), chapter 8.

38 David Shambaugh, ed. *Power Shift: China and Asia's New Dynamics* (Berkeley: University of California Press, 2005), p. 27.

39 Wang Cungang and Wang Ruiling, "Lun Zhongguo Fuzeren Daguo Shenfen de Jiangou" (Discussion on the Construction of China's Identity of Responsible Great Power), *Shijie Jingji yu Zhengzhi Luntan (Forum on Global Economy and Politics)* 1 (2008): 8.

40 Shambaugh, *Power Shift*, chapter 1; Shaun Breslin, "Understanding China's Regional Rise: Interpretations, Identities and Implications," *International Affairs* 85 (2009): 833–4; Bates Gill, *Rising Star: China's New Security Diplomacy* (Washington, D.C.: Brookings Institution Press, 2007), chapters 1 and 2.

41 *Taoguang Yanghui* roughly means "conceal capabilities and avoid limelight." It's a strategy developed by Deng Xiaoping in the early 1990s.

42 Mel Gurtov and Charles Glaser are also led to portray an "optimistic" East Asian international relations and a "positive" U.S.-China relations. Mel Gurtov, *Pacific Asia?: Prospects for Security*

and Cooperation in East Asia (Lanham: Rowman & Littlefield Publishers, Inc., 2002), chapter 8; Glaser, "Will China's Rise Lead to War?" 80–91.

43 See, for instance, David Shambaugh, "China Engages Asia: Reshaping the Regional Order," International Security 29 (Winter 2004/5): 64–99.

# Selected bibliography

Bernstein, Richard and Ross H. Munro. "The Coming Conflict with America." Foreign Affairs 76 (March/April 1997): 18–32.

Chambers, Michael R. "Rising China: The Search for Power and Plenty," in Strategic Asia 2006–2007: Trade, Interdependence, and Security, ed. Ashley T. Tellis and Michael Wills (Seattle and Washington, D.C.: NBR, 2006), pp. 65–103.

Chan, Steve. "Is There a Power Transition between the U.S. and China?: The Different Faces of National Power." Asian Survey 45 (September/October 2005): 687–701.

Friedberg, Aaron L. "The Future of U.S.-China Relations: Is Conflict Inevitable?" International Security 30 (Fall 2005): 7–45.

Glaser, Charles. "Will China's Rise Lead to War?: Why Realism Does Not Mean Pessimism." Foreign Affairs 90 (March/April 2011): 80–91.

Ikenberry, G. John. "The Rise of China and the Future of the West: Can the Liberal System Survive?" Foreign Affairs 87 (January/February 2008): 23–38.

Mearsheimer, John J. "China's Unpeaceful Rise." Current History 105 (April 2006): 160–2.

Rapkin, David P. and William R. Thompson. "Power Transition, Challenge and the (Re)Emergence of China." International Interactions 29 (2003): 315–42.

Ross, Robert S. "The Rise of Chinese Power and the Implications for the Regional Security Order." Orbis 54 (Fall 2010): 525–45.

Shambaugh, David, ed. Power Shift: China and Asia's New Dynamics (Berkeley: University of California Press, 2005).

Shirk, Susan L. China: Fragile Superpower (New York: Oxford University Press, 2008).

Tammen, Ronald L., Jacek Kugler, Douglas Lemke, Allan C. Stam III, Carole Alsharabati, Mark A. Abdollahian, Brian Efird, and A. F. K. Organski. Power Transitions: Strategies for the 21st Century (New York: Chatham House, 2000).

Zheng, Bijian. "China's 'Peaceful Rise' to Great-Power Status." Foreign Affairs 84 (September/October 2005): 18–24.

Zhu, Zhiqun. US-China Relations in the 21st Century: Power Transition and Peace (London and New York: Routledge, 2006).

# 2

# The Changing US Role and the Shifting Regional Order in East Asia

Il Hyun Cho

## Chapter Outline

## Introduction

Since the end of the Korean War, the United States has served as the backbone of regional stability in East Asia. The so-called hub-and-spokes system of US alliances with Japan and South Korea has not only deterred challenges to the regional status quo but also dampened the security dilemma among countries in the region. With the 2004 Global Posture Review (GPR) and the Global War on Terror (GWOT) launched in the wake of the September 11, 2001 terrorist attacks, however, the George W. Bush administration charted a new course in America's global strategy. As demonstrated in various US-led multilateral security measures, such as the Proliferation Security Initiative (PSI), the United States has increasingly been relying on ad hoc, fluid coalitions at the global level, rather than more traditional alliance mechanisms. Similarly, the Bush administration was eager to transform the regionally confined alliance relationship into a worldwide military coalition in the name of jointly addressing various global security challenges.

After eight years of the Bush presidency, the arrival of the Barack Obama administration animated foreign policy debates in various parts of the world. In East Asia, the stake is higher since the expected change in US foreign policy direction coincides with a perceived shift in the regional order. Despite the changes in tone and immediate priorities, however, the Obama administration has shown a remarkable degree of continuity in its approach to foreign policy, with a strong tendency to address new, global issues. It has also been relying on a variety of ad hoc global coalitions. Sensing this shift in the US strategic focus, policymakers in China, Japan, and South Korea have intensified domestic debates centered on the effects of the US global strategy on the regional order in East Asia.

The 2010 Nuclear Security Summit held in Washington, D.C. provided a unique window into the changing US role and its regional impact on East Asia. While the Obama administration zeroed in on the global proliferation issue, the three East Asian countries used the venue to address a wide variety of regionally salient issues. For instance, Chinese President Hu Jintao and Japanese Prime Minister Yukio Hatoyama discussed the formation of an East Asian Community and a gas exploration project in the East China Sea, while South Korean President Lee Myung-bak, in an interview just before leaving for the summit, stressed the importance of the speedy ratification of the Korea-US Free Trade Agreement (KORUS-FTA) as a way to ensure a "positive" role of the United States in the region.[1] These contrasting priorities highlight the central questions of this chapter: What explains the changing US roles in addressing global and regional security challenges? What are the likely effects of this transformation on the regional order in East Asia?

Answering these questions is particularly important since the changes in American priorities came amid a rapidly evolving regional order in East Asia. In this vein, the change in the role of the United States and the shifts in its global and regional priorities present East Asian countries with a difficult and unfamiliar challenge of maintaining the regional order without jeopardizing their respective relationships with the region's traditional stabilizer, the United States. To be sure, given the two ongoing wars and democratic uprisings in North Africa and the Middle East, the current US strategic focus on these regions is understandable. This reality, however, does not permit the United States to overlook East Asia, especially when new regional developments, such as the rise of China, the nuclearization of North Korea, and the ongoing process of regional economic integration, demand greater US attention to the region. Hence, it is important to renew the terms of engagement between the United States and its Asian partners in ways that are better suited to the changing dynamics of the region.

This chapter first locates the role of the United States in historical perspective, highlighting the contrast between US regional strategy before and after 9/11. It then considers several factors illuminating the causes and effects of the changing US role in the region. Next it provides an analysis of the extent to which the post-9/11 US global strategy has shaped the regional security dynamics in East Asia. By examining current alliance politics and regionalism in East Asia, this chapter aims to demonstrate the complicated effects of the changing US role on East Asia. With the United States—the traditional regional power broker—increasingly dwelling on the global dimension, there is an acute sense of strategic uncertainty in the region, prompting regional countries to adjust to what seems to be a shifting regional order. The ways in which the United States and its regional partners recast their strategic relationships will not only affect the viability of America's Asian alliances but also influence the emerging order in East Asia in the years ahead.

# The US role in East Asia in historical perspective

Throughout the post-World War II period, the United States played a predominant role in ensuring regional stability in East Asia. Along with its postwar occupation of Japan, America's involvement in the Korean War in 1950 and its forward-deployed forces since then consolidated its paramount position as a de facto regional hegemon. The image of the United States as an indisputable power broker in the region persisted even in the aftermath of the Cold War. Indeed, many scholars observed that unlike its role in Europe, the United States became more important in East Asia during the first decade of the post-Cold War era as it played a leading role in the first North Korean nuclear crisis of 1993–4 and the Taiwan Strait crisis of 1995–6. In the case of the North Korean crisis, scholars like Barry Buzan and

Ole Wæver even suggest that no meaningful deal would have been made "if the US had not taken the lead."[2]

The second North Korean nuclear crisis that began in late 2002 coincided with a dramatic decline in the US role and influence in managing regional affairs. This change reflected a larger trend in which the United States focused more on global priorities. The shift began during the Bush presidency as it utilized an ad hoc "coalitions of the willing" approach, or what Richard Haas called "a la carte multilateralism" tailored to address specific short-term global tasks at hand. Prominent examples include the Container Security Initiative (CSI) and the Proliferation Security Initiative (PSI), both aimed at preventing the transfer of sensitive technologies and weapons of mass destruction.[3]

The increasing global focus is also manifested in US defense strategy, particularly in the transformation of forward-deployed forces. Following the Future of the ROK US Alliance Policy Initiative (FOTA), for instance, US forces stationed in South Korea were not only reduced to less than 30,000 but also significantly transformed: from fixed, land-based deployments to more fluid ones that are better positioned to enhance power projection, readiness, and deterrence both on the Korean Peninsula and regionally. Although the need to address more immediate challenges in Iraq and Afghanistan is reasonable, the question is how to strike a balance between "traditional alliance politics in the region [and] the new emphasis on more fluid and diverse force capabilities."[4]

In characterizing the shift in the US role, some suggest that it is a temporary aberration in the post-9/11 context, a feature unique to the Bush presidency. Stephen Walt, for instance, argues that after 9/11 the Bush administration used its predominant military position "to mold a world that would be compatible with U.S. interests and values."[5] In his critique of the Bush administration's "aggressive unilateralism," Robert Pape contends that the strategy "is changing the United States' long-enjoyed reputation for benign intent," prompting other major powers to pursue "soft-balancing."[6] The assumption in this line of thinking is that if the United States abandons such a unilateral strategy and returns to the multilateral fold, the need for soft balancing against the United States would dramatically decrease. From this vantage point, the arrival of the Obama administration with its penchant for multilateral engagement and diplomacy promised a markedly different foreign policy stance.

In fact, initial signs were largely positive as the president himself pledged to rejuvenate America's tarnished global image and to fully engage various parts of the world, including East Asia. In fact, Secretary of State Hillary Clinton's first foreign trip was to Asia, while President Obama himself spent more than a week in his first official trip to East Asia. In its first year, a catch-phrase of the Obama administration was that the United States was "back in Asia" and intended to stay longer. In a dramatic policy shift, Secretary Clinton signed the Treaty of Amity and Cooperation with the Association of Southeast Asian Nations (ASEAN) that the Bush administration refused to sign. Along with the elevation of the G-20, which includes China, Japan, and South Korea, to a major global forum to address various global challenges, the administration increased consultation with Japan and South Korea over North Korea to assuage what the US National Security Council's Senior Asia Director Jeffrey Bader called Asian allies' "bruised feelings" caused by the Bush administration's relative lack of consultation with allied nations.[7]

Rhetoric aside, the Obama administration has thus far followed the Bush administration in its emphasis on global challenges and limited attention to East Asia's strategic dimension. President Obama's calls for a world without nuclear weapons and a renewed effort in the War in Afghanistan show that his administration is also more focused on global agendas than equally important regional tasks. Overall, in the post-9/11 context there has been a growing gap in strategic priorities between the United States and its Asian counterparts, with significant implications for the regional role of the United States and the regional order in East Asia.

# Grasping the causes and effects of the changing US role

Several competing accounts illuminate the causes of the shifting US role and its impact on the East Asian order. From a realist perspective, the material power of the United States is the single most important variable in conceptualizing the US role and its effects on the regional order in East Asia. As long as the predominant power position of the United States continues, in this power-based view, its preferences should be upheld most of the time, and it can shift priorities, be they global or regional, at will without significant security repercussions in the region. Given the mounting concerns about global terrorism and weapons of mass destruction following the 9/11 attacks, in this account, the United States is expected to turn its focus more to new, global security challenges aimed at maintaining its global dominance. This shift, however, would not provoke any meaningful regional challenges to the United States, as its power position remains unaltered in the region. Indeed, there has been no regional attempt at balancing the United States in East Asia, while its forward deployed military forces continue to serve their primary function of being prepared for regional contingencies. The 2010 Quadrennial Defense Review specifically stated that US naval forces would continue "to be capable of robust forward presence and power projection operations, even as they add capabilities and capacity for working with partner navies."[8]

Experts on US-Asia relations such as Bates Gill and Michael Green argue that despite Asia's new multilateralism, "the underlying security and well-being provided by an attentive and attuned United States" will remain as a key regional feature in the years ahead.[9] So we should expect a continuation of the US-led hub-and-spokes system in East Asia in the foreseeable future.

The main weakness of the power-based realist account, however, is its myopic focus on "the staying power of the United States and whether countries are balancing against it," at the neglect of an equally, if not more, important question as to "whether the United States is achieving its policy objectives."[10] When regional countries perceive that the United States is focused more on coping with global challenges than on meeting the regional objective of ensuring stability, Washington will face growing difficulties in maintaining its regional leadership and influence. In this vein, a recent study noted that one of the key factors behind the Bush administration's dismal record in the Middle East stemmed from its failure to "resolve long-standing tensions between its policies at the general level (national security vs. democracy promotion) and specific level (invade Iraq vs. pursue al-Qaida)."[11] This chapter argues that similar friction exists in East Asia, especially in the context of America's increasing global focus and its perceived oversight of regional priorities as it attempts to appropriate its regional assets for realizing its lofty global goals. This will have corrosive long-term effects on US leadership and influence in East Asia.

From an institutionalist perspective, the shifting US role can be explained by the changes in the global and regional contexts in which the traditional functions of security and economic institutions are no longer sufficient, thereby requiring institutional adaptation. As a wide variety of global challenges loom large in the post-Cold War context, the traditional, Cold War-type alliance system should be transformed into a flexible security mechanism akin to the post-Cold War NATO. Celeste Wallander and Robert Keohane, for instance, argue that institutional persistence hinges on how well institutions "can adapt rules and procedures devised for one set of problems to the emerging issues of the day." The effects of the changing US role in this expanded institutional structure would in turn depend on "portability"—"the ease with which the rules and practices of one institution can be adapted to other institutions" and the degree of institutionalization. Interestingly enough, Wallander and Keohane single out the US-Japan alliance as a successful case in which high level of institutionalization of the alliance can help the two nations to "guard against external threats and, increasingly, to deal with the risk that tensions on economic issues between the two countries would disrupt their security partnership."[12]

As evident in recent discord between the United States and Japan over various regional security issues, however, the optimistic institutionalist assumption is increasingly in question. In fact, successful institutional adaptation rests to a large degree on the regional understanding and acceptance of the proposed institutional change. Even if the United States has a convincing rationale for transforming regional alliances and other institutional mechanisms into broader global frameworks, unless East Asian countries accept the rationale for the change, they would refuse to go along. Simply put, institutional change depends not just on institutional efficiency but also on shared understanding.

Furthermore, the emphasis on portable, flexible arrangements may have unintended regional consequences. In fact, the relocation of US forces from the demilitarized zone (DMZ) to south of Seoul and the movement of portions of US marines stationed in Okinawa to Guam give regional countries the impression that the United States may be focusing more on pressing problems elsewhere, while deferring its role as a regional stabilizer to other countries in the region.[13] A veteran Asia watcher agrees that America's "continuing preoccupation with developments in other parts of the world will likely constrain its ability to focus clearly on the evolving debates on Asian regionalism."[14]

# The US role and legitimacy in East Asia

The overall assumption from the realist and institutionalist accounts is that the changing US role would have few, if any, regional implications. The image here is that of the United States continuing to shift its strategic focus to the global level without incurring any significant costs in its power and influence in East Asia. As shown below, however, the shifting US role has a far greater impact on the regional order than the realist and institutionalist interpretations would have us believe. It is important to bear in mind that the US power position has remained largely unchanged since the end of the Cold War. Similarly, its institutional frameworks, in particular alliance networks, continue to exist, and in some cases have even been expanded. What has changed after the United States turned to global priorities, however, is the regional perceptions of US legitimacy and influence—an ideational dimension of US leadership in the region.

The central premise of this chapter is that we cannot assume *a priori* the utility of power and institutions in achieving various political goals. A hegemonic system, be it purely power-centered or more institutionalized in form, is based on the calculation of material factors, but at its core, it is "ultimately a form of social hierarchy, based on status and recognition."[15] As such, "[having] superior military capabilities does not necessarily bring with it superior status, acceptance, or respect."[16] Without acceptance by others, hegemonic power or institutional frameworks do not translate automatically into meaningful influence. It happens only when regional actors view the hegemon's strategy as legitimate.[17] The regional perception of legitimacy in turn depends on the ways in which the hegemonic strategy is compatible with regional priorities.

It is in this context that countries in East Asia are increasingly worried about America's legitimacy. Broadly speaking, the legitimacy of US leadership and its military presence in East Asia is assured when they serve not only to "deter major powers from developing or intensifying dangerous rivalries" but also "to manage regional conflicts with the potential to escalate to local and even broader wars."[18] In the economic realm, US legitimacy stems to a large degree from its perceived role as "a market of last resort, stabilizer of financial crises, and strongest advocate of deeper interdependence and market liberalization."[19]

Based on this line of reasoning, however, recent US security and economic policies toward East Asia have been problematic at best. Specifically, the Bush administration's global focus on terrorism and nuclear proliferation often came at the cost of effectively coping with regional problems. In the security arena, for instance, countries in East Asia, in particular China and South Korea, viewed the Bush administration's confrontational approach toward North Korea as a major destabilizing factor in the region. In the economic dimension as well, US legitimacy has been questioned in the wake of the global economic recession that originated in the United States in 2008. Japan's former prime minister Yukio Hatoyama, in a manuscript circulated during his election campaign, even denounced "American-style capitalism as 'void of morals or moderation'—a blight Japan must cast aside at all costs."[20]

The US focus on the use of ad hoc global coalitions also has a damaging effect on its legitimacy by undercutting various regional institutional frameworks. As a result, there are growing doubts about the future of what John Ikenberry calls America's strategic restraint by which the United States binds itself into institutional frameworks as a major source of stability and prosperity in the postwar context.[21] The short-term benefits of utilizing institutional frameworks for America's global priorities are largely offset by its weakened legitimacy which will not only constrain the US capacity to address immediate global challenges but also undercut the long-term durability of US hegemony in East Asia and beyond.[22]

To be sure, in retrospect, the US role in regional order building has not always been effective. For instance, America's respective strategic and political relations with Israel and Saudi Arabia have often served as a major impediment to order building in the Middle East. In contrast, the United States has been largely successful in establishing and maintaining a stable regional order in Europe and Asia throughout and even after the Cold War period. Central to this remarkable achievement was America's role as a benign hegemon, helping to reassure regional countries and dampening the security dilemma among themselves. Specifically, "the political restraints that NATO, the US-Japan security treaty, and international economic institutions imposed on Germany and Japan" reassured their neighbors.[23] Now with a growing emphasis on Japan's global role facilitated by the United States, some regional actors began to raise questions about the US role as an honest power broker. In the following section, the chapter examines the regional consequences of this transformative shift.

# The impact of the changing US role on East Asian regional order

As the United States focuses on its global agenda, East Asian countries have begun to seek their own ways to address regional priorities. In fact, simply following the US lead can weaken domestic support for governments in East Asia, since the global effort is often viewed as being imposed upon by the United States. Specifically, the regional effects of the changing US role are manifested in two ways: (1) its impact on alliance politics in East Asia and (2) its influence on emerging regionalism in the region. In fact, concerns about America's role in East Asia began to surface even before the War in Iraq. Writing in 2002, Lowell Dittmer, for instance, asked whether the United States would be successful in integrating regional organizations into its global war on terror. He warned that the global campaign that comes at the neglect of regional priorities could lead to "a regional architecture that excludes Washington."[24] Although still evolving, there are various signs that the changing US role is reshaping the regional order in East Asia.

## Alliance management

The shift in focus from the regional to global dimension is most evident in the Global Posture Review (GPR). A central task of the Review is to combine immediately employable forward stationed forces with "globally available reconnaissance, strike, and command and control assets; information operations capabilities; and rapidly deployable, highly lethal and sustainable forces."[25] In short, this is an effort to realign US forces' global posture to deal with various non-state and local contingencies, rather than deterrent missions currently in place in East Asia. For US alliance partners, the real challenge is how to reshape their force structure in anticipation of this rapid transformation on a global scale. Sidestepping this thorny issue for its alliance counterparts, the Bush administration simply stated that the war on terrorism "has proven that America's alliances in Asia not only underpin regional peace and stability, but are flexible and ready to deal with new challenges."[26]

In comparison, the United States was far better at aligning global and regional alliance priorities in the 1990s. During and after the first North Korean nuclear crisis of 1993–4, for instance, the Clinton administration ensured that inter-Korean relations were not sidelined by the US proliferation concerns through "facilitating" relations between South Korean president Kim Young-sam and his North Korean counterpart.[27] During the Bush presidency, however, America's global focus raised questions about the role of US alliances in ensuring stability in East Asia, including the Korean Peninsula. It is in this context that a South Korean presidential aide was quoted as saying, "We understand the US global strategy for rapid redeployment of their forces and support it as in the case of Iraq, provided it does not adversely affect the Korean peninsula. The redeployment should be restricted if it involves conflicts in our region."[28]

Alliance management problem was most pronounced during the Roh Moo-hyun government, whose engagement policy toward North Korea was often at loggerheads with the Bush administration's hardline, counter-proliferation approach toward North Korea. The Roh government even sought to play "the role of a balancer, not only on the Korean peninsula, but throughout Northeast Asia."[29] With the arrival of the pro-American Lee Myung-bak government in 2008, the US-South Korean alliance seemed to have improved markedly. In fact, Presidents Bush and Lee announced that the US-South Korea alliance would play a greater global role.[30] In view of what seemed to be a declining North Korean threat at the time, US Secretary of Defense Robert Gates declared in June 2008 that the alliance would "[broaden] security relations beyond the Korean Peninsula to regional and global issues."[31] For its part, the South Korean government seemed determined to elevate the US-South Korean alliance to the global level. President Lee pledged that South Korea and the United States would "work together to resolve global issues like climate change, stopping the spread of nuclear materials, eradicating terrorism, poverty and so forth."[32]

The lofty rhetoric of jointly tackling global challenges, however, cannot conceal South Korea's main priority that still lies in the region. Along with lingering tensions with North Korea, the fact that Korea was divided amid great power rivalries makes South Korea very sensitive to geopolitical tensions around the Peninsula. In recent years, its growing economic cooperation with China and Southeast Asian countries also underscores the importance of regional integration. As the Lee government sought to follow its predecessors' regional community building, a South Korean analyst predicted that placing "South Korea within a hub-and-spoke alliance against China, using the North Korean nuclear crisis as a catalyst" might risk "a nationalist backlash if the United States is increasingly viewed as an impediment to Korean unification and regional security."[33]

The impact of the Bush administration's global focus has been even greater in the case of the US-Japan alliance. One scholar characterizes the Bush administration policy toward Japan as a de facto "globalization" of the alliance, which "obfuscates the clear distinction maintained in the past between support for the United States in alliance-based activity and engagement in international peacekeeping."[34] Specifically, Japan's Ministry of Foreign Affairs has expanded its bilateral ties with the United States, while its Defense Agency (now the Ministry of National Defense) has elevated its role in the security policymaking process.[35] Along with its contribution to the wars in Iraq and Afghanistan, Japan agreed to conduct joint research on missile defense, a measure that is likely to "further consolidate the US–Japan alliance and tighten technological cooperation between the two militaries." A major base realignment plan in Okinawa was also aimed at strengthening "the bilateral alliance to meet regional and global security threats," which would "make Japan a frontline command post in the projection of US military power, not only in East Asia but extending as far as to the Middle East."[36]

As the globalization of the US-Japan alliance gained momentum, however, Japan's post-9/11 security strategy, especially that of the Shinzo Abe administration (2006–7), was seen as "drawing Japan too tightly into the foreign policy objectives of the United States."[37] For instance, Kazuo Ogoura, a former high-ranking Japanese foreign ministry official, warned that "[the] globalization of the Japan-US alliance" has engendered "a subtle, negative liability: shouldering or associating itself with the negative US image that has spread worldwide, particularly in the Middle East and some parts of Asia."[38] Moreover, such a global shift in alliance politics increasingly jeopardizes Japan's "bridging role in the Pacific region and for other key non-ASEAN regional players."[39]

The Obama administration continues this trend of expanding the alliance's global role. In fact, before assuming his current position of US Assistant Secretary of State in Asia Pacific Affairs, Kurt Campbell issued a report entitled "The Power of Balance: America in Asia," which called for Japan's "active engagement in areas outside its immediate neighborhood, including Tokyo's efforts to promote peace and stability in Afghanistan and Iraq, as well as in Africa."[40] In a congressional testimony, Assistant Secretary Campbell also announced the US plan to "create a more durable and forward-looking vision for the alliance that seizes upon Japan's global leadership role on climate change and humanitarian and development assistance programs."[41]

The hope of elevating the US-Japan alliance to the global level, however, was soon dashed as the Democratic Party of Japan (DPJ) led by Prime Minister Yukio Hatoyama came to power in 2009. From the start, the DPJ government has shown a greater interest in an East Asian Community. In a dramatic policy shift, the Hatoyama government refused to extend Japan's refueling mission conducted in the Indian Ocean to support US-led antiterrorism operations.[42] The Japanese government also began to reconsider the 2006 agreement with the United States to relocate the US Marines Futenma Air Station to another location in Okinawa. As the Hatoyama government's decision over the relocation delayed, the Obama administration in turn decided to postpone bilateral security consultations aimed at "deepening the Japan-US alliance."[43] Assistant Secretary Campbell even warned that Japan's failure to resolve the dispute by May 2010 "would affect bilateral ties not only on security issues but also in other areas."[44] Although Hatoyama, faced with various domestic and external challenges, eventually agreed to move the Futenma airbase as planned, the long-running tension over the air base made regional officials worry about "the future of the US security role in the region."[45] Hatoyama's policy reversal disappointed many of his supporters, and he had to resign after less than one year in office.

All in all, the global focus of the Bush and Obama administrations made alliance management between the United States and its Asian allies increasingly difficult. Different priorities between the United States and regional countries became all the more significant during an informal talk at the Nuclear Security Summit between Prime Minister Hatoyama and President Obama in 2010. While Hatoyama sought to garner Obama's support for his efforts for the base relocation, Obama reportedly focused more on Iran's nuclear program.[46] In South Korea, too, the main focus is hardly global. Despite Obama's global agenda, the Lee Myung-bak government highlighted the relocation of US bases in South Korea and the delayed ratification of the Korea-US Free Trade Agreement as key issues in South Korea's relations with the United States.

## Regionalism

Apart from alliance politics, America's global focus has also been affecting East Asia's pursuit of community building, especially the type of regional institutional mechanisms on the horizon. Historically, East Asian countries have shown a strong preference for what is called "open regionalism," whose primary objectives were to avoid the rise of economic blocs and the disengagement of the United States from the region.[47] As the United States tilted more toward the global dimension, increasing tension between its global and regional roles, there were signs of a regional rivalry over the ideal type of regional institutional frameworks, which in turn made open regionalism exceedingly difficult to maintain.

An early warning of the friction between the global and regional roles of the United States and its negative impact on US legitimacy and influence came in the wake of the Asian financial crisis in the late 1990s. At the time, the US role as a manager of the global economy representing the International Monetary Fund (IMF) was in conflict with its regional role as an honest power broker. Since the United States was viewed in the region as "[abdicating] its leadership responsibilities," East Asian countries quickly sought alternate regional institutions such as the ASEAN Plus Three (APT) and the Asian Monetary Fund.[48] Accordingly, the scope of regionalism has been narrowed from the trans-Pacific sphere of the Asia Pacific Economic Cooperation (APEC) to the East Asia-focused APT, which emerged as what some consider "the most coherent and substantive pan-Asian grouping."[49] Overall, regional institutions that include the United States (e.g., the APEC) have been in decline, while indigenous institutions, such as the APT and the East Asia Summit, are proliferating.[50]

The changing role of the United States is also a source of concern for China, especially in the context of Japan's growing global and regional ambitions. The Chinese are particularly worried about the US strategy of utilizing regional institutions as a means to contain China. From a Chinese perspective, a regional security dilemma is not just a Cold War relic since the strengthened US-Japan alliance may "become a tool for defending an independent or permanently separated Taiwan."[51] In this context, Japan's expanded regional and global role during the Bush presidency was alarming in the minds of Japan's neighbors, and the Chinese were particularly concerned about the possibility that the expanded alliance may be directed at China.[52]

On the surface, the advent of the Obama administration and its policy of strategic cooperation with China, pronounced in the notion of the G-2, seem to have alleviated China's concern. At the 2009 meeting of the US-China Strategic and Economic Dialogue, President Obama proclaimed that the two countries' shared responsibility and close cooperation were critical in various issue areas.[53] As for the main areas for cooperation, however, the president offers a long list of global issues, including "economic recovery, climate change, clean-energy technology, nuclear nonproliferation, counterterrorism and humanitarian disasters like the one in Darfur, Sudan."[54]

In his first speech laying out his Asia policy, President Obama also stressed cooperation with China, but mainly as a means to "jumpstart economic recovery," to "[promote] security and stability in Afghanistan and Pakistan," and to strengthen the global nonproliferation regime.[55] The Obama administration's focus on the global dimension is also evident in Secretary of State Hillary Clinton's agenda during her first trip to Asia. At the time, the State Department issued a statement that "notably did not mention the nuclear impasse with North Korea," while highlighting the global recession and climate change as key issues to discuss with its Asian counterparts.[56] The Obama administration also launched the first trilateral dialogue with China and Japan. But the historic talk was focused more on short-term global issues than on long-term regional security issues. A Chinese analyst thus questioned the efficacy of such an ad hoc dialogue and instead called for addressing regional questions, including "how to change the role of the US-led military alliance, to solve the North Korean nuclear issue and build a collective security mechanism in the region."[57]

Sensing the increased Sino-American cooperation on various global issues, officials in South Korea and Japan, for their part, began to worry about "a greater US 'tilt' toward China," demanding a reassurance that improved Sino-American relations will not come at their expense.[58] Similarly, President Obama's global nonproliferation effort and the declared objective of nuclear disarmament also invited Asian allies' calls for the United States to reaffirm its commitment to their defense.[59] A growing sense of anxiety in the region is captured in the warning of an Indian politician that "the United States would leave Asia to China to run."[60]

The perceived decline of US influence in turn has led its Asian allies to promote regional institutions which exclude the United States.[61] Interestingly, Prime Minister Hatoyama reaffirmed his vision for the regional community in his first meeting with Chinese president Hu Jintao, when both sides agreed to deepen cooperation on various issues, including North Korea and a joint gas-development project in the East China Sea.[62] Similarly, China and South Korea held the first high-level strategic dialogue in December 2008, exchanging views on issues of common concern.[63]

All in all, there are increasing signs of East Asia's new regional dynamic that goes beyond the US-led hub-and-spokes system. One example is found in Japan's growing cooperation with the ASEAN in regional security. In March 2010, senior defense officials from Japan and the ten-member Southeast Asian grouping had their second annual meeting to discuss common "nontraditional" security challenges such as disaster relief, antipiracy, and international peacekeeping operations. What is particularly noteworthy is Japan's interest in expanding ties with ASEAN over traditional regional security as expressed in Japan's defense minister Toshimi Kitazawa's opening remarks:

> While ASEAN countries and Japan have developed primarily economic relationships, it is my belief that going forward, we should further deepen our cooperation in the areas of security and defense as well . . . I sincerely hope that this meeting will help deepen mutual understanding among the participating countries and strengthen cooperation in the area of regional security.[64]

# Conclusion

What emerges from the above discussions is the competition between two radically different visions for the role of the United States in East Asia. Whereas the global role of the United States is premised on an expansive definition of US strategic priorities and the contribution of East Asian allies and partners within that broader global strategic vision, East Asia's perceived role of the United States is predicated on the latter's contribution to regional stability and open regionalism. As evidenced in this chapter, the US administrations since 9/11 left an indelible imprint in the minds of East Asian policymakers that the traditional US role may now take a backseat, with negative consequences for US legitimacy in the region.

Although the Bush administration's radical experiment is over, its legacy lingers in the form of the ongoing wars in Iraq and Afghanistan, an inheritance that still consumes most of the foreign policy attention of the Obama administration. Despite the changes in overall direction and tone, therefore, there are little signs that the new president gives greater priority to America's regional role. Of course, some of the global objectives are important to East Asian countries as well, such as nuclear nonproliferation and energy security. As argued in the chapter, however, the pursuit of global priorities should not come at the expense of regional ones.

The US failure to balance its global and regional roles in turn has regional implications. At stake is America's long-term reputation as a regional stabilizer and its commitment to allies and regional partners. As questions about the US role mount, there will be a more energetic pursuit of regionalism without US participation. It is in this context that a report by the Council on Foreign Relations warns that the US-led hub-and-spokes system is "unsustainable," and there will be significant costs to "its interests, credibility, and influence unless it acts to shape multilateral trends in Asia."[65]

This is not to say, however, that the US regional influence cannot be restored. In fact, after the 2010 North Korean artillery attacks on a South Korean island, the United States sent an aircraft carrier battle group to the waters near the Korean Peninsula, reaffirming its alliance commitment. More broadly, Asian perceptions of the United States are far from negative. In a 2009 CSIS survey of Asian elites, for instance, 40 percent of respondents predicted that "the U.S. would be the greatest force for peace and stability in the region in 10 years, compared with 26 percent that cited China." The same survey also showed that 79 percent of respondents still maintained that the United States should be a member of an East Asian Community.[66] This regional view was in parallel with a 2009 Pew Global Attitudes Survey in which half of the 24 nations surveyed had "a more favorable view of the U.S. than they did of China or Russia."[67]

In conclusion, it is an opportune time to renew the terms of relationship between the United States and its regional counterparts in ways that meet a host of new global challenges together, but it is equally important to ensure that such joint global efforts do not come at the expense of both traditional regional priorities and new realities in East Asia. The trilateral dialogue between the United States, Japan, and China failed to make an impact precisely because it was geared more toward global aspects and not well integrated into a long-term, coherent set of regional agendas. Given East Asia's growing interest in regionalism, American analysts have also begun to stress the importance of "redefining how and where the United States fits into a twenty-first century Asia."[68] A genuine effort to reinvigorate the deteriorating relationship between the United States and East Asia would begin with a better realignment of America's global and regional priorities.

## Five questions for discussions

1. What have historically been the central features of the regional security structure in East Asia?
2. What has led to the changing role of the United States in East Asia?
3. What are major contributing factors and impediments to East Asian regionalism respectively?
4. What type of a regional role is appropriate for the United States in the post-Cold War context?
5. What are the likely regional effects of a rising China and what are some of the mechanisms through which other East Asian states can cope with it?

# Notes

1 "Hatoyama Asia community plan places China, Japan at the core," *Japan Times*, April 14, 2010; "Fred Hiatt interviews South Korean president Lee Myung-bak," *Washington Post*, April 12, 2010; A17.

2 Barry Buzan and Ole Wæver, *Regions and Powers: The Structure of International Security* (Cambridge University Press, 2004), p. 176.

3 The term, "a la carte multilateralism" is quoted in Lowell Dittmer, "East Asia in the 'New Era' in World Politics," *World Politics* (October 2002): 46.

4 William Tow, "Bush and Asia: The Evolving Strategic Context," in Mark Beeson, ed. *Bush and Asia: America's Evolving Relations with East Asia* (Routledge, 2005), pp. 89–90.

5 Stephen M. Walt, *Taming American Power: The Global Response to U.S. Primacy* (W.W. Norton & Company, 2005), p. 23.

6 Robert A. Pape, "Soft Balancing against the United States," *International Security* 30:1 (Summer 2005): 9–10.

7　John Pomfret, "U.S. is reaching out to East Asia's powerful nations," *Washington Post*, November 7, 2009.

8　Michael McDevitt, "The 2010 QDR and Asia: messages for the region," *PacNet*, Number 12, Pacific Forum, CSIS, March 15, 2010.

9　Green, Michael J. and Bates Gill, eds. *Asia's New Multilateralism: Cooperation, Competition, and the Search for Community* (Columbia University Press, 2009), p. 27.

10　Jeremy Pressman, "Power without Influence: The Bush Administration's Foreign Policy Failure in the Middle East," *International Security* 33:4 (Spring 2009): 150.

11　Ibid., 169.

12　Celeste A. Wallander and Robert O. Keohane, "Risk, Threat, and Security Institutions," in Helga Haftendorn, Robert O. Keohane, and Celeste A. Wallander, eds. *Imperfect Unions: Security Institutions over Time and Space* (Oxford University Press, 1999), pp. 32–4.

13　Michael Mastanduno, "Hegemonic Order, September 11, and the Consequences of the Bush Revolution," in Mark Beeson, ed. *Bush and Asia: America's Evolving Relations with East Asia* (Routledge, 2005), p. 34.

14　Ralph A. Cossa, "Evolving U.S. Views on Asia's Future Institutional Architecture," in Green and Gill, eds. *Asia's New Multilateralism*, pp. 33–4.

15　Christian Reus-Smit, *American Power and World Order* (Polity, 2004), p. 66.

16　Deborah Welch Larson and Alexei Shevchenko, "Status Seekers: Chinese and Russian Responses to U.S. Primacy," *International Security* 34:4 (Spring 2010): 63–95. Also, Mastanduno, "Hegemonic Order," pp. 25–6.

17　For a fuller discussion of US legitimacy as a factor shaping East Asian regionalism, see Il Hyun Cho, "Hegemon's awakening: America's response to East Asian regionalism," paper presented at the annual meeting of the International Studies Association, New Orleans, LA, February 17–20, 2010.

18　Mastanduno, "Hegemonic Order," p. 27.

19　G. John Ikenberry and Michael Mastanduno, "Conclusion: Images of Order in the Asia-Pacific and the Role of the United States," in G. John Ikenberry and Michael Mastanduno, eds. *International Relations Theory and the Asia-Pacific* (Columbia University Press, 2003), p. 423.

20　Hiroko Tabuchi, "Japan's victors set to abandon market reform," *New York Times*, September 1, 2009.

21　G. John Ikenberry, *After Victory: Institutions, Strategic Restraints, and the Rebuilding of Order* (Princeton University Press, 2001).

22　David A. Lake, "Beyond Anarchy: The Importance of Security Institutions," *International Security* 26:1 (Summer 2001): 160.

23　Peter J. Katzenstein, *A World of Regions: Asia and Europe in the American Imperium* (Cornell University Press, 2005), p. 3.

24　Lowell Dittmer, "East Asia in the 'New Era' in World Politics," *World Politics* (October 2002): 45.

25 *Quadrennial Defense Review Report*, Department of Defense, the United States, September 31, 2001, 20, 25.

26 *The National Security Strategy of the United States of America*, The White House, Washington, D.C., September 2002, 26.

27 Victor D. Cha, "The U.S. Role in Inter-Korean Relations," in Samuel S. Kim, ed. *Inter-Korean Relations: Problems and Prospects* (Palgrave Macmillan, 2004), pp. 146–7.

28 Lee Tee Jong, "No expanded role for US troops: Seoul: Roh's remarks seen as pre-empting any US deployment in a cross-Strait war," *Strait Times*, March 10, 2005.

29 Emanuel Pastreich, "The balancer: Roh Moo-hyun's vision of Korean politics and the future of Northeast Asia," *Japan Focus*, August 1, 2005.

30 Kurt M. Campbell, Lindsey Ford, Nirav Patel, Vikram J. Singh, "Going Global: The Future of the U.S.-South Korea Alliance," in Kurt M. Campbell, et al. eds. *Going Global: The Future of the U.S.-South Korea Alliance* (Washington, D.C.: The Center for a New American Security, 2009), p. 59.

31 Eric Schmitt, "Gates approves of 3-year tours for U.S. troops in South Korea," *New York Times*, June 4, 2008.

32 "Fred Hiatt interviews South Korean President Lee Myung-bak," A17.

33 Lim Wonhyuk, "Regional Multilateralism in Asia and the Korean Question," in Green and Gill, eds. *Asia's New Multilateralism*, pp. 95–6.

34 Aurelia George Mulgan, "Japan and the Bush Agenda: Alignment or Divergence?" in Beeson, ed. *Bush and Asia*, pp. 110–11.

35 Christopher W. Hughes, "Japan's Security Policy, the US-Japan Alliance, and the 'War on Terror'," *Australian Journal of International Affairs* 58:4 (December 2004): 442.

36 Peter J. Katzenstein, "Japan in the American Imperium: rethinking security," *Japan Focus*, October 2008.

37 Kenneth B. Pyle, "Abe Shinzo and Japan's Change of Course," *NBR Analysis* 17:4 (October 2006): 23.

38 Kazuo Ogoura, "Inscrutable, 'invisible' Japan," *Japan Times*, June 13, 2008.

39 Akiko Fukushima, "Japan's Perspective on Asian Regionalism," in Green and Gill, eds. *Asia's New Multilateralism*, p. 119.

40 "U.S. ties underscored by Russia, China factors," *Japan Times*, June 13, 2008.

41 "Campbell: stick to base relocation deal," *Japan Times*, January 23, 2010.

42 "Refueling mission will not go on: Hatoyama," *Japan Times*, September 27, 2009.

43 "U.S. puts off meetings on broader ties/PM's inaction on Futenma issue blamed," *Yomiuri Shimbun*, December 9, 2009.

44 Satoshi Ogawa, "Campbell says airfield feud could affect ties," *Yomiuri Shimbun*, March 7, 2010.

45 Blaine Harden, "Future of Okinawa base strains U.S.-Japanese alliance," *Washington Post*, January 24, 2010.

46  Kohei Kobayashi and Satoshi Ogawa, "Japan, U.S. still apart on Futenma/Hatoyama-Obama informal talks only call attention to strained ties," *Yomiuri Shimbun*, April 15, 2010.

47  Paul Evans, "Between Regionalism and Regionalization: Policy Networks and the Nascent East Asian Institutional Identity," in T. J. Pempel, ed. *Remapping East Asia: The Construction of a Region* (Cornell University Press, 2005), p. 212.

48  Green and Gill, *Asia's New Multilateralism*, p. 23.

49  Evan A. Feigenbaum and Robert A. Manning, *The United States in the New Asia*, Council Special Report No. 50, Council on Foreign Relations, November 2009, 7.

50  William Overholt, *Asia, America, and the Transformation of Geopolitics* (Cambridge University Press, 2009), p. 242.

51  Alastair Iain Johnston, "Beijing's Security Behavior in the Asia-Pacific: Is China a Dissatisfied Power?" in J. J. Suh, et al. eds. *Rethinking East Asian Security: Power, Interests, Identity* (Stanford University Press, 2004), p. 59.

52  Allen Carlson and J. J. Suh, "Conclusion," in J. J. Suh, et al., eds. *Rethinking Asian Security*, pp. 226–8.

53  Glenn Kessler, "U.S.-China meeting renews the dialogue: economic, strategic issues stressed," *Washington Post*, July 28, 2009

54  Mark Lander, "Obama opens policy talks with China," *New York Times*, July 28, 2009.

55  Remarks by President Barack Obama at Suntory Hall, Tokyo, Japan, November 14, 2009.

56  Glenn Kessler, "Clinton packs full Asia agenda for first trip as Secretary of State," *Washington Post*, February 6, 2009.

57  Jian Junbo, "Doubts over US-China-Japan talks," *Asia Times*, June 16, 2009.

58  Ralph A. Cossa and Brad Glosserman, "Secretary Clinton's No. 1 mission is to reassure allies," *Japan Times*, February 12, 2009.

59  Brad Glosserman, "Washington should not forget its Asian allies," *Japan Times*, October 1, 2009.

60  Jim Hoagland, "As Obama bets on Asia, regional players hedge," *Washington Post*, February 16, 2010.

61  Feigenbaum and Manning, *The United States in the New Asia*, 19.

62  "Hatoyama-Hu: Hatoyama proposes creating an 'Asian EU,'" *Japan Times*, September 23, 2009.

63  "China, ROK to hold first strategic dialogue between diplomatic departments," *People's Daily*, December 2, 2008.

64  "Japan, ASEAN push regional security, disaster relief cooperation," *Japan Times*, March 26, 2010.

65  Feigenbaum and Manning, *The United States in the New Asia*, 4.

66  Bates Gill, et al. "Strategic views on Asian regionalism: survey results and analysis," Pacific Forum *PacNet*, #12 (February 17, 2009).

67  Andres Martinez, "The next American century," *Time*, March 10, 2010.

68  Feigenbaum and Manning, *The United States in the New Asia*, 29.

**Author's Note**: An earlier version of this chapter was presented at the annual meeting of the Midwest Political Science Association, Chicago, IL, April 22–25, 2010. For their helpful comments and suggestions, I am grateful to participants at the MPSA panel, Seo-Hyun Park and Professor Zhiqun Zhu.

# Selected bibliography

Beeson, Mark., ed. *Bush and Asia: America's Evolving Relations with East Asia* (London, UK: Routledge, 2005).

Cha, Victor D. "The U.S. Role in Inter-Korean Relations," in Samuel S. Kim, ed. *Inter-Korean Relations: Problems and Prospects* (New York: Palgrave MacMillan, 2004), pp. 139–57.

Cho, Il Hyun, "Hegemon's Awakening: America's Response to East Asian Regionalism," paper presented at the annual meeting of the International Studies Association, New Orleans, LA, February 17–20, 2010.

Dittmer, Lowell, "East Asia in the 'New Era' in World Politics." *World Politics* (October 2002): 38–65.

Feigenbaum, Evan A. and Robert A. Manning, The United States in the New Asia, Council Special Report No. 50, Council on Foreign Relations, November 2009.

Green, Michael J. and Bates Gill, eds. *Asia's New Multilateralism: Cooperation, Competition, and the Search for Community* (New York: Columbia University Press, 2009).

Hughes, Christopher W. "Japan's Security Policy, the US-Japan Alliance, and the 'War on Terror'." *Australian Journal of International Affairs* 58:4 (December 2004): 427–45.

Ikenberry, G. John and Michael Mastanduno, eds. *International Relations Theory and the Asia-Pacific* (New York: Columbia University Press, 2003).

Katzenstein, Peter J. *A World of Regions: Asia and Europe in the American Imperium* (Ithaca, NY: Cornell University Press, 2005).

—. "Japan in the American Imperium: Rethinking Security." *Japan Focus*, October 2008.

Lake, David A. "Beyond Anarchy: The Importance of Security Institutions." *International Security* 26:1 (Summer 2001): 129–60.

Larson, Deborah Welch and Alexei Shevchenko. "Status Seekers: Chinese and Russian Responses to U.S. Primacy." *International Security* 34:4 (Spring 2010): 63–95.

Martinez, Andres. "The Next American Century." *Time*, March 10, 2010.

The National Security Strategy of the United States of America, The White House, Washington, D.C., September 2002.

Overholt, William. *Asia, America, and the Transformation of Geopolitics* (Cambridge, UK: Cambridge University Press, 2009).

Pape, Robert A. "Soft Balancing against the United States." *International Security* 30:1 (Summer 2005): 7–45.

Pempel, T. J., ed. *Remapping East Asia: The Construction of a Region* (Ithaca, NY: Cornell University Press, 2005), pp. 195–215.

Pyle, Kenneth B. "Abe Shinzo and Japan's Change of Course." *NBR Analysis* 17:4 (October 2006), *The National Bureau of Asian Research*, 5–31.

Reus-Smit, Christian. *American Power and World Order* (Cambridge, UK: Polity, 2004).

Suh, J. J., Peter J. Katzenstein, and Allen Carlson, eds. *Rethinking Asian Security: Identity, Power and Efficiency* (Stanford, CA: Stanford University Press, 2004).

Walt, Stephen M. *Taming American Power: The Global Response to U.S. Primacy* (New York: W.W. Norton & Company, 2005).

# 3

# The Era of "Ibis Diplomacy" in Japan–China Relations?[1]

Mary M. McCarthy

## Introduction

The 2010 World Expo was held in Shanghai, China. Japan's pavilion focused on the theme of Japan–China friendship. The Japanese organizers chose to represent that friendship by the symbol of the crested ibis, a bird that was brought back from extinction in Japan with the help of China. The ibis can represent both Japan–China friendship and how Japan–China cooperation is imperative in this current age of globalization.

This chapter explores what the author calls "ibis diplomacy" and to what degree we see bilateral cooperation on issues of mutual importance for

Japan and China. We will particularly focus on the "strategic relationship of mutual benefit," developed between Japan and China in 2006, and what has been called a cornerstone of that framework for bilateral cooperation, joint development and exploration of energy resources in the East China Sea. In the process, we will investigate two questions: First, is this a new era in the bilateral relationship? And second, if so, can we say this new era is characterized by "ibis diplomacy," as defined in this chapter?

As we will see, the evidence suggests that it certainly is a new age in terms of the rhetoric of political diplomacy, as the governments of both China and Japan have come to emphasize friendship and cooperation over rivalry and disputes. And this rhetoric does focus on issues that are of mutual concern to both countries and that require cooperation to solve. After years of political discord and stalemate, focused on the so-called history issues, in 2006 there was a rhetorical recommitment by the political elites of both countries to the improvement of bilateral relations and to a new vision that acknowledges the new challenges, as well as opportunities, China and Japan face in today's globalized world.

However, it is debatable to what degree rhetoric has extended to real action and substantial progress on issues. While there has been some forward movement on the issue of joint exploration and development in the East China Sea, for instance, it has not advanced to the extent of the rhetoric of the political elites. Similarly, it is questionable whether elite rhetoric has positively influenced public sentiments, the negativity of which may actually be contributing to a lack of advancement on certain issues, including the East China Sea. Furthermore, with the "history issues" unresolved, some concern remains that these issues may arise again, to the detriment of friendship and cooperation in the relationship. Finally as two great world powers, residing next to each other in East Asia, Japan and China eye each other cautiously and are likely to continue to do so in the foreseeable future.

# From the golden age of panda diplomacy to the low point of Yasukuni

In the 1970s, it can be argued that Japan–China relations were characterized by so-called panda diplomacy, as China used the gift of pandas as a diplomatic tool to foster good relationships with foreign powers. To celebrate the postwar normalization of relations between Japan and China in 1972, China presented two giant pandas to Japan. For the Japanese, this symbolized the close cultural and historical ties between the two countries, and it produced a wellspring of positive feelings toward China. It represented how much of worth had come from China to Japan, from culture to language to cuisine. It both engendered and reflected an atmosphere of friendship and cooperation, at both the state and public levels.

This "golden age" did not last, however, as issues of history, security, economics, and internal stability began to negatively impact relations in the mid and late 1980s. Yet it was not until the early years of the twenty-first century that Japan–China political relations reached their post-World War II low point, with a suspension of bilateral summit meetings (imposed by the Chinese leadership) and a profusion of anti-Japanese rhetoric in China and anti-Chinese rhetoric in Japan. Although the roots of this negativity were deep and complex, the dominant issue of dispute was differing interpretations of how the invasion and occupation of China by the Japanese in the early and mid-twentieth century should be remembered and memorialized today.

Although Japanese Prime Minister Junichiro Koizumi entered office on April 26, 2001 with the stated goal of improving Japan–China relations, his actions did not serve to further this goal. His annual visits to the Yasukuni Shrine, which enshrines the souls of Japan's war dead, including those convicted as war criminals after World War II, earned him severe and increasing criticism from China, and hurt the ability of Japan–China political relations to go forward in a positive direction during his tenure.

Prime Minister Koizumi made a total of six visits to the Yasukuni Shrine during his five years as prime minister. The Chinese leadership decried the visits as reflecting and fostering an "incorrect" interpretation of history, leading to a possible resurgence of Japanese militarism. The importance of these historical issues in the bilateral relationship was expressed by China's foreign ministry spokesperson Kong Quan in his observation that "a correct perception of and approach to that period of history, of China's early-twentieth-century war with Japan, is the political basis of the China-Japan relationship and a key for Japan to truly win trust from Asia and the world."[2] The Chinese government sees Yasukuni Shrine as a symbol of Japan's past aggression and contempt for the victims of its expansionism.[3] For the Japanese, the visits and the drama surrounding them showcase two separate issues: the internal debate and disagreement within Japan itself about how World War II should be remembered and memorialized, and political and public sentiments and viewpoints about a rising China and how Japan should best engage with this emerging power.

Although Koizumi made two official visits to China as prime minister,[4] he was never welcomed again after his second visit to the Yasukuni Shrine in 2002. Koizumi did meet with the Chinese leadership at other venues, but sustained differences on the issue of the Yasukuni Shrine in particular, and history issues more broadly, often cast a pall over these one-on-one discussions. Koizumi's continuing visits to the Shrine and statements that seemingly expressed an inability (or unwillingness) to understand the concerns of the Chinese, along with the demands of the Chinese public that its government be more assertive in its responses to Japan, would make Japan–China diplomatic ties increasingly strained. And as time passed, the Chinese leadership made it clear that a bilateral summit would depend on the Japanese prime minister not visiting Yasukuni.

Since Koizumi refused to bow to Chinese pressure and, instead, followed his own conscience and viewpoint on these issues, there were no Japanese prime minister visits to China in 2003, 2004, or 2005. In fact, there were to be no Japanese prime minister visits to China until Koizumi left office and was replaced by Shinzo Abe in 2006. Similarly, no Chinese premier or president made an official visit to Japan from 2001 through 2006. This is despite the fact that Japan and China are the greatest economic and political powers in East Asia and the state of their bilateral relationship has a tremendous impact on the stability and development of the region as a whole.

The election of a new Japanese prime minister was not going to bring about an immediate change in Japan–China relations. Therefore the forecast was not overly optimistic when Shinzo Abe was elected to succeed Koizumi in September 2006. China was cautious in its response to the new administration. This was particularly due to Abe's stated views on the Yasukuni Shrine, as Abe had supported the former prime minister's visits to Yasukuni. Still Abe began his tenure as prime minister making concerted efforts toward improving Japan–China relations, starting with the issue of the Yasukuni Shrine. Even before his election, Abe, as the front-runner, made the public decision not to visit the Yasukuni Shrine on August 15,[5] despite his normal practice of doing so each year. He then went on to ensure that China was his first overseas visit as head of state, the 2006 Japan–China Summit in Beijing coming less than a month after Abe began his term of office. Furthermore, he expressed his endorsement of former PM Tomiichi Murayama's statement of apology given on the occasion of the 50th anniversary of the end of World War II.

Thus, with the dawn of a new Japanese administration in 2006 and, especially one intent on improving relations with China and moving beyond the dominance of history issues in political discourse, there seemed to be much potential for the bilateral relationship to move in a positive direction. Yet, has it? And if so, what characterizes this new positive direction?

# Ibis diplomacy: a new era in Japan–China relations?

It has been argued that a new era began in Japan–China relations in 2006/7, after Abe succeeded Koizumi as prime minister of Japan. This chapter explores not only whether a new era has begun, but whether this new era may be symbolized by the ibis, just as an earlier era was symbolized by the panda.

In describing the crested ibis in the *Japan Times*, journalist Rowan Hooper wrote, "It doesn't get much more Japanese than this." As a "world-wide symbol of Japan," the crested ibis was declared a national treasure in 1952. However, by the 1970s, the ibis was at the point of extinction in Japan, as the result of being overhunted and the victim of the environmental degradation of its habitat.[6] In response, in the 1990s, China provided Japan with ibises, allowing the bird to reestablish itself in Japan. In 2007, during Premier Wen Jiabao's first visit to Japan as premier, he presented two ibises as a gift of friendship. And in 2010, one of the focal points of Japan's pavilion at the World Expo in Shanghai was this story of the crested ibis as an example of Japan–China friendship and exchange.

The story of the crested ibis is a story of friendship, but also a story of a problem that required (and continues to require) bilateral cooperation to solve. Today Japan and China, housing some of the few habitats world-wide where ibises live, are working together to keep the ibis from becoming extinct.[7] The current joint project was a product of President Hu Jintao's 2008 visit to Japan, when the two countries agreed to expand cooperation on a wide range of issues, including the protection of the ibis.[8] This is one issue area, among many, where Japan and China can achieve mutual benefit through cooperation. And it can also serve as a symbol of such friendship and cooperation.

In this chapter, "ibis diplomacy" is defined as an approach where governments seek to cooperate to solve a problem that neither is able to solve on its own, but that both can receive benefit from if a solution is found. It is based on a realization that one cannot isolate oneself in today's globalized world. This understanding should come with the rhetoric of friendship and cooperation, concomitant with action and progress. If ibis diplomacy exists in Japan–China relations, we should expect to see political rhetoric of friendship and cooperation, tied with actual cooperative initiatives on issues of mutual concern, where neither is able to resolve the problem on its own.

# Political rhetoric and displays of the new diplomacy

In order to determine whether we see a new era in Japan–China relations since 2006, one characterized by ibis diplomacy, we will begin by looking at the rhetoric and actions of political elites. Although rhetoric does not automatically or necessarily translate into action, not much progress can be made if the leaders are not committed to such advancements. This was seen from 2002 to 2006, when cooperation could not be achieved on many issues because "history issues," and the Yasukuni Shrine, in particular, dominated the political discourse between the leadership of Japan and China. The Chinese leadership refused to even entertain serious discussion on certain issues, as long as the Japanese prime minister continued to visit the Yasukuni Shrine. This made it difficult to create a top-down vision for bilateral relations, which would have facilitated greater cooperation on issues of mutual concern.

This changed in 2006. One can say that it began with action (the Japanese prime minister's visit to China) and was fortified by rhetoric. After years of contentious political diplomacy between Japan and China, with "history issues" at the center, in 2006 there was a rhetorical shift by the political elites of both countries. First, rhetoric changed in terms of the use of friendly language and the discussion of the start of a new era in bilateral relations. Second, it was decided that this new era would be characterized by a "mutually beneficial relationship based on common strategic interests," as agreed to during Prime Minister Abe's visit to China in October 2006. Third, this was reinforced by regular high-level visits and a specific commitment to an annual summit meeting between the leaders of Japan and China. As mentioned earlier, Prime Minister Abe visited China for a bilateral summit in October 2006, within one month of becoming head of state. This was the first official visit of a Japanese prime minister to China since April 2002. For four and a half years there had been no official visit of a Japanese leader to China or of a Chinese leader to Japan.

Abe's visit was clearly an attempt by both sides to turn a new page in Japan–China relations. During the visit, Abe proposed that bilateral relations should be characterized as a "strategic relationship of mutual benefit." In explaining what this means, Abe stated, "In the political sphere, we need to exchange views and build up shared objectives and by building these building blocks we shall be able to build a strategic relationship of mutual benefit."[9] Although this was vague in content, it showed a clear attempt to articulate a vision for Japan–China relations. And to focus on creating a foundation that could then be used as a basis for finding solutions to any problems that might arise. Yang Bojiang has argued that during Koizumi's administration there failed to be "a clear or systematic strategy to manage Japan's relations with China."[10] Abe sought to correct this and, thereby, improve Japan–China relations.

In his post-summit press conference, Abe stated, "I am convinced that this visit to China has proven to be a turning point that will lead Japan-China relations to a higher level."[11] Abe had changed the tone of the relationship to one of friendship and cooperation. And he set the stage for cooperative initiatives in many areas, calling particular attention to North Korea missile tests and the Six-Party Talks, the environment, energy, and economics, as fruitful areas for mutual benefit through cooperation.

Haikuan Gao has argued that Abe's proposal for a Japan–China strategic relationship of mutual benefit was "an important breakthrough," "a sea change in Japanese foreign policy," and "the most effective means of rectifying and improving Japan's relationship with China."[12] Takashi Hoshiyama has called this period onward a "qualitative shift in Japan–China relations."[13]

It is true that, at least at the elite political level, a new era in Japan–China relations had emerged. Despite the yearly turnover in Japanese leadership from 2006 through 2011 (see Table 3.1), including across party lines, one constant has been the commitment to the strategic relationship of mutual benefit introduced during Prime Minister Abe's 2006 visit to China. In June 2010, when Premier Wen spoke with the newly elected prime minister of Japan, Naoto Kan, five days after he officially took office, Prime Minister Kan said he "would like to place greater emphasis on the 'Mutually Beneficial Relationship based on Common Strategic Interests' and deepen it further."[14] This is despite the fact that Kan is not of the same political party as Abe, who introduced this framework for the bilateral relationship. Kan specifically mentioned issues of food safety, resource exploration in the East China Sea, and communications between the defense ministries.[15] These are all issues that his predecessors, of both the Liberal Democratic Party (LDP) and Democratic Party of Japan (DPJ) have raised.

**Table 3.1** List of Japanese prime ministers, 2006–11

| Name | Political party | Term of office |
| --- | --- | --- |
| Shinzo Abe | Liberal Democratic Party (LDP) | September 2006–September 2007 |
| Yasuo Fukuda | LDP | September 2007–September 2008 |
| Taro Aso | LDP | September 2008–September 2009 |
| Yukio Hatoyama | Democratic Party of Japan (DPJ) | September 2009–June 2010 |
| Naoto Kan | DPJ | June 2010–August 2011 |
| Yoshihiko Noda | DPJ | September 2011– |

*Source*: by the author.

There has been a similar sustained commitment to regular visits between the leaders of Japan and China to each other's country since 2006. As of September 2010, after no official visits in either direction for four and a half years, Japanese prime ministers visited China annually for four consecutive years, in 2006, 2007, 2008, and 2009. China's premier visited Japan in 2007 and 2010. And China's president visited in 2008. With each successive visit by a prime minister, premier, or president, there was a renewed commitment to the concept of a "strategic relationship of mutual benefit."

In May 2008, Chinese president Hu Jintao visited Japan for the first time since coming to office in 2003. The visit was timed to celebrate the 30th anniversary of the China-Japan Treaty of Peace and Friendship. Hu spent five days in Japan, which was the longest period he had spent on any official visit to a foreign country since becoming president. It was the first official visit of a Chinese president to Japan since Jiang Zemin's, Hu's predecessor, visit in 1998.

The Joint Statement between the Government of Japan and the Government of the People's Republic of China on Comprehensive Promotion of a "Mutually Beneficial Relationship Based on Common Strategic Interests," signed by President Hu and PM Yasuo Fukuda during Hu's visit to Japan, was only the fourth political document the two countries have signed since the post-World War II normalization of relations, setting out the vision and guidelines for the relationship.[16] The Chinese media publicized "this latest document" as "clearly indicat[ing] the [sic] China-Japan relations have entered a new phase of development. The guiding principles contained in it have pointed out the direction for the bilateral ties to proceed in the new era and expanded the horizon for cooperation."[17] Reports of the joint statement also highlighted the clause that "China speaks highly of Japan's adherence to the path of a peaceful country in the past six decades and more since World War II and its contribution, through peaceful means, to world peace and stability."[18] This is particularly important given the negative impact of historical issues on the bilateral relationship for the previous two decades, and, specifically, in the early years of the twenty-first century.

The visit was represented by the respective governments, as well as the media, as monumental. It represented real progress in the shift of policies in both countries that had begun with Abe's visit to China in 2006. In the days prior to the visit, Shi Yinhong, a scholar of foreign policy at Renmin University in Beijing, highlighted the importance of the visit, asserting that "Hu wants a lasting improvement in relations with Japan to be one of his defining foreign policy achievements."[19] While Huang Dahui, a Japan scholar at the same university, asserted that "This visit will symbolize that relations are becoming more normal. It won't solve any substantive issues. The symbolism of the visit itself will be the main substance."[20]

However, one may say that it went beyond symbolism. Some specialists on Japan–China relations have pointed out the substantive significance of the statement signed by Hu and Fukuda. For example, as expressed by Hoshiyama, "By comparison [with the 1998 declaration], . . . the 2008 joint statement sets out very clearly the facts that the strategic reciprocal relationship is not simply a bilateral affair and that the two countries are responsible powers in the Asian region and the international community."[21] Illustrating this, the joint statement declares that "China and Japan now have great influence on and bear solemn responsibilities for peace, stability and development of the Asia-Pacific region and the world" and will work "to achieve the noble objectives of peaceful coexistence, friendship for generations, mutually beneficial cooperation, and common development for their two nations."[22] This demonstrates recognition of each other as great world powers that must learn to coexist for the stability and advancement of East Asia and beyond. It also supports the idea of ibis diplomacy, Japan and China needing to cooperate for mutual benefit on issues of transnational importance, as well as for the benefit of their neighbors and other fellow states.

In April 2009, Taro Aso, who had become Japan's prime minister in September 2008, visited China. Aso emphasized in his press conference in China that he and the Chinese leaders had made concrete progress in a number of areas, based on the strategic relationship of mutual benefit. This included agreeing to curb protectionism and promote domestic demand in the face of the global economic crisis; agreeing to cooperate on energy conservation in coal-powered plants and reduction of pollution; promoting youth exchanges between the two countries; and agreeing to cooperate on promoting the resumption of the Six-Party Talks on North Korea denuclearization.[23] Yoshihiko Noda became the prime minister in September 2011 and visited China in December. He emphasized both the framework of the strategic relationship of mutual benefit and the desire to resume talks for implementation of the 2008 agreement on the East China Sea.

In all these ways, the focus in political diplomacy transitioned from moving Japan–China relations onto a new path and having a new vision for bilateral relations to illustrating that real progress had been made in areas related to this new vision. In one way this was a natural transition, from rhetoric to action, but it also required a commitment by the political elites of both countries to more than words.

To explore whether Japan and China have entered an age, not only of friendly rhetoric, but of advancement in terms of cooperative initiatives on issues of mutual concern, we will investigate a specific issue area in more depth: the case of the East China Sea.

# Actions: East China Sea as a "Sea of Peace, Cooperation, and Friendship"[24]

In discussing the strategic relationship of mutual benefit, the word "concrete" has often been used to illustrate that there is movement beyond rhetoric. In response to a reporter's question, Prime Minister Aso declared in 2009 that Japan and China had reached agreement on 70 items during President Hu's visit to Japan in 2008 and that cooperative initiatives had begun to go forward on about 80 percent of these. He mentioned an additional 505 projects in the fields of the environment and energy conservation.[25]

This section will focus on one particular agreement, the journey to that agreement, and the path forward to actual implementation of the agreement. The case of study will be joint exploration and development of energy resources in the East China Sea.[26] This case has been chosen because it is one primary area that has been highlighted in the discussions between Japan and China on the strategic relationship of mutual benefit. In fact, Christopher W. Hughes argues that "The *centerpiece* of Japan and China's 'mutually beneficial relationship' has been the attempt to resolve the dispute over gas fields in the East China Sea" [emphasis added].[27]

Joint exploration and development of energy resources in the East China Sea is an area that is ripe for mutual benefit and requires some degree of cooperation, due to the realities of competing sovereignty claims. Undersea natural gas fields and oil reserves that have been discovered (or are believed to exist) in the East China Sea potentially can be of great benefit to both countries.[28]

Japan is a resource-poor country, with heavy dependence on energy imports from volatile regions such as the Middle East. China has moved from a net exporter of energy resources to a net importer of energy resources, as its economy has grown and developed. Natural gas fields and oil reserves in the East China Sea may be able to supply the two countries with energy with minimal transport costs and dangers, enhancing the energy security of both.

However, sovereignty issues have kept China and Japan from being able to fully benefit from these resources. There have been ongoing disputes between China and Japan over their respective exclusive economic zones (EEZs) in the East China Sea. Although an agreement on fishing rights was concluded between China and Japan in 1997, an agreement on rights to energy resources has proven more difficult to negotiate. The question of who has the right to these resources has become particularly heated since 2004, when China began exploration and development activities near the disputed area. Japan's claim to the area is based on the fact that the location is within 200 nautical miles (370 km) from Japan's coast; Japan proposes a median line be drawn between the two countries. China's claim is based on its being part of the natural extension of its continental shelf; it does not accept Japan's median line proposal.[29]

China's gas exploration near the disputed area in 2004 led to heightened animosity and antagonistic rhetoric between Japan and China. To defuse the tension and work on resolving these issues, Japan and China began negotiations later that same year (in October 2004).[30] However, the early talks were impeded by the difficult political relationship between Japan and China and failed to yield any solid results. As an example of the hindrance that politics caused, after Prime Minister Koizumi visited the Yasukuni Shrine in 2005, for the fifth time while prime minister, the Chinese government delayed talks on the East China Sea for about five months as a way to show its disapproval.

Janet Xuanli Liao argues that a way forward could not be found because of a lack of "political trust" between the two countries.[31] However, once Abe came into office, and the strategic relationship of mutual benefit was put forward as a new framework for the bilateral relationship, some glimmer of progress began to be seen in negotiations on the East China Sea as well.[32]

As Kung-wing Au states, "the pace at which [the talks] were held indicates that the overall Japan-China relationship did have an impact on progress . . . When Koizumi was in office, only six rounds of talks were held within the nearly two-year period from October 24, 2004 to July 8, 2006 . . . [Yet] eight rounds of talks occurred in nine months in 2007 [under the Abe and Fukuda administrations] after Sino-Japanese relations had improved."[33] James Manicom and Andrew O'Neil agree that "as the relationship improved from April 2007, formal and informal talks on the East China Sea dispute accelerated with the aim of settling the matter by the time Hu Jintao visited Japan in spring 2008."[34]

Although an agreement was not in place by the time of Hu's visit in May, about a month later, Japan and China announced their agreement for cooperation in the East China Sea. According to the June 2008 agreement, Japan and China would shelve the sovereignty issue and jointly explore, develop, and invest in energy resources in specified areas. The specified areas cover 2700 square kilometers, extend over the median line proposed by Japan, and include the Chunxiao gas and oil field, which had been the lightning rod for much of the conflict since 2004.[35]

Although the foreign ministries of both countries emphasized the agreement as a "first step"[36] and some scholars have suggested it is a "very small step,"[37] Gao Jianjun argues that "The 2008 China-Japan Consensus on the East China Sea Issue is highly significant. It temporarily eases the maritime disputes that exist between China and Japan in the East China Sea and stabilizes the situation and, therefore, is conducive to peace and stability in the East China Sea."[38] The Chinese media described the agreement as containing "very strong symbolic meanings," even though it only covers a portion of the East China Sea, and quoted Liu Nanlai, an expert on international law at the Chinese Academy of Social Sciences, as saying that "It can be regarded as an experiment and the two countries are likely to continue the joint development scheme in other areas in the East China Sea."[39] The Japanese media declared that "the two governments' decision to put the [sovereignty] matter aside and proceed with joint development is likely to build momentum for furthering the mutually beneficial strategic relationship."[40]

Still, one cannot say that the issue of joint exploration and development of energy resources in the East China Sea has now been resolved, as the agreement has yet to be implemented. This has much to do with the reception by the respective domestic publics. While the Japanese media and public tended to applaud the agreement as an acknowledgment of the position maintained by the Japanese government, with regard to the median line and the Chunxiao gas and oil field,[41] the Chinese public expressed much criticism for a deal that they saw as one where their government gave up too much. The Chinese foreign minister had to spend the days following the announcement of the agreement in public relations crisis management, trying to clarify what "joint development" really means[42] and what role, if any, the Japanese would have in the Chunxiao field.[43] The Chinese government continues to be involved with trying to manage its own public, while imploring Japan to do the same.[44]

As a result, progress has been slow. The first round of negotiations on the implementation of the agreement began in July 2010 (more than two years after the agreement was announced) and the second round was planned for fall 2010. However, the exact timing of the second meeting is now in doubt given China's postponement of the negotiations to protest Japan's holding of the captain of a fishing boat that collided with two Japanese Coast Guard vessels in the East China Sea, near the disputed Senkakau/Diaoyutai Islands, in September 2010.

Overall, there was clear progress on negotiations over joint exploration and development of the East China Sea after the beginning of the Abe administration and the dawning of the new era in Japan–China relations. First, it was highlighted as an important part of the strategic relationship based on mutual benefit. Second, progress on the negotiations was tied to prime minister/premier/president-level meetings between the two countries, which occurred every year under the new framework. Finally, an agreement was announced in June 2008, shortly after President Hu's visit to Japan.

However, actual implementation of the agreement has not yet gone forward. The diplomatic scuffle between Japan and China over the September 2010 incident in the East China Sea is one important reason. Just as significant is the domestic criticism emanating from the Chinese side since immediately after the agreement was announced.

# Earthquake diplomacy

On March 11, 2011, the Tohoku region of Japan suffered a magnitude-9.0 earthquake and tsunami. This was followed by a nuclear crisis, as the natural disasters damaged nuclear plants. Like those around the world, the Chinese responded with sympathy and assistance, including the delivery of gasoline and heavy oil (which were in high demand and short supply after the disaster). Some have argued that this tragedy in Japan is an opportunity for the emergence of a renewed Japan–China relationship based on mutual concern and cooperation, where the past is finally, and permanently, left behind. There is precedent to support this type of optimism. After the 2008 Sichuan earthquake, Chinese impressions of Japan became increasingly favorable in response to Japan's assistance. However, as of this writing there are no clear indications that the 2011 crises have shifted public opinion, leading to greater support for a more cooperative government-to-government relationship. It is still an open question what the impact of the adversities will be on Japan–China relations, and on Japan itself.

# Conclusion

It is clear that since 2006, a new vision has been created for Japan–China relations—"a mutually beneficial relationship based on common strategic interests." This vision has been actively promoted by the political leadership in both Japan and China. It includes a plethora of transnational issues, from North Korea's denuclearization to the global economic crisis. It has been supported by an institutionalization of regular high-level visits and enhanced communication between the leaders of Japan and China. Such regular communications help in deescalating crises and force deadlines on lower-level negotiations (leaders have to make some announcement after a summit).

The political elite commitment to improving relations has created pressure for a greater degree of progress on issues of mutual concern. Joint exploration and development of energy resources in the East China Sea is one example where an improvement of the bilateral relationship, including summit meetings of the heads of state, has led to advancement. Although concrete steps forward may have been slow, there was a concerted effort to discuss, negotiate, and make progress. And as Au has asserted, "more talks mean more chances for a breakthrough"[45] and more talks are definitely something we have seen in this new era.

However, at the same time, we see obstacles to further cooperation and growth in friendly relations that will not be surmounted quickly or easily. First, the domestic populations of each country seem more cautious toward the other than do their governments. If the political elites truly seek to fully embrace this strategic relationship of mutual benefit, they must make bolder efforts to enlist the support of their citizens.

A second obstacle is the history issue. Although a Japan–China Joint History Research Committee was established and history issues are no longer at the forefront of the bilateral relationship, they have not been resolved. There is always the potential for them to resurface. This is especially true in an atmosphere where the domestic publics do not feel particular affection toward each other and do continue to list "history" as a main issue in public opinion polls.[46] And if it is useful for the political leadership of either country (whether to mobilize the public or to enhance political legitimacy) then this author predicts we will see the history card used again.

Finally, Japan and China are two great world powers who happen to be neighbors in East Asia. This provides them with tremendous opportunities, particularly in this age of globalization, to cooperate for mutual benefit. However, it also presents them with significant challenges, the most important of which is how to manage the relationship so that they can take advantage of these opportunities and not be waylaid by conflict. One example of conflict obstructing progress on an issue of mutual benefit is the postponement of negotiations over the East China Sea due to the September 2010 collision between a Chinese fishing vessel and two Japanese Coast Guard ships. Government officials must have a long-term, big-picture perspective in their responses to such crises that arise.

This chapter argues that Abe's succession to the Japanese prime ministership inaugurated a new era in Japan–China relations. Since 2006 there have been great successes in political diplomacy between Japan and China. In a sense it is a second normalization of diplomatic relations, as visits between the leaders of Japan and China have resumed, and a recommitment to improved bilateral relations under a new vision. It is also an era in which the leadership of both Japan and China has illustrated an awareness of the necessity of cooperation to achieve mutual benefit, as well as a recognition that this benefit extends beyond their two countries to the region and the world as a whole. This has been expressed through rhetoric of friendship and cooperation. It has also been demonstrated with action and progress, which the case of the 2008 agreement on joint exploration and development in the East China Sea exemplified in this chapter. Therefore, we can say there have been exercises in ibis diplomacy, but only time will tell whether the era as a whole is characterized by ibis diplomacy, or whether ibis diplomacy will be sidetracked by domestic publics, history issues, and/or great power conflict.

## Five questions for discussions

1. How and why has history impacted Japan–China relations in the twenty-first century? Can countries overcome historical rivalries and perceived injustices? If so, how?
2. What is "ibis diplomacy"? Do you think it exists between Japan and China now?
3. What factors support the argument that a new era began in Japan–China relations in 2006/7?
4. To what degree does the domestic public influence the ability of a government to implement foreign policy?
5. Do you believe that the evidence supports the likelihood for greater incidences of cooperation or conflict between Japan and China over the next decade?

# Notes

1  An earlier version of this chapter was presented at the Tenth International CISS Millennium Conference held in Venice, Italy, July 4–5, 2010. The author would like to thank all panelists and audience members for their feedback and, in particular, the discussant, Askhat Safiullin. Special thanks also to Naoko Kumagai and Michael Chiang for their comments.

2  Quoted in James Przystup, "Not Quite All About Sovereignty—But Close," *Comparative Connections* 6:2 (2004).

3  See, for example, "Vice Foreign Minister Wang Yi Expound China's Solemn Position on Yasukuni Shrine," May 19, 2001, accessed February 13, 2009. http://www.fmprc.gov.cn/eng/wjb/zygy/gyhd/t24948.htm.

4  Koizumi visited China a third time as part of the Asia Pacific Economic Cooperation (APEC) Leaders' Meeting, which took place in Shanghai in 2001. This was prior to his second Yasukuni visit in April 2002.

5  August 15 is the anniversary of Japan's surrender in World War II and is considered by the Chinese leadership to be the most sensitive date for Japanese politicians to visit the Yasukuni Shrine.

6  Rowan Hooper, "Japanese crested ibis," *The Japan Times Online*, December 10, 2008.

7  "Japan, China to step up cooperation over ibis protection," *Japan Today*, August 28, 2010.

8  "Japan inks ibis pact with China," *The Japan Times Online*, January 30, 2010.

9  Press Conference by Prime Minister Shinzo Abe Following His Visit to China, October 8, 2006.

10  Yang, "Redefining Sino-Japanese Relations after Koizumi," 129.

11  "Press Conference by Prime Minister Shinzo Abe Following His Visit to China."

12  Gao, "China-Japan Mutually Beneficial Relationship," 39.

13  Hoshiyama, "New Japan-China Relations," 69.

14  "Telephone Conversation between Prime Minister Naoto Kan and Mr. Wen Jiabao, Premier of the State Council of the People's Republic of China." June 13, 2010.

15  Ibid.

16  The previous three documents being: the Joint Communique of the Government of Japan and the Government of the People's Republic of China (1972), the Treaty of Peace and Friendship between Japan and the People's Republic of China (1978), and the Japan–China Joint Declaration (1998).

17  Tao Wenzhao, "Launching a new era in China-Japan relations," *China Daily*, May 12, 2008. (Tao is a researcher at the Chinese Academy of Social Sciences.)

18  "China, Japan sign joint statement on promoting strategic, mutually beneficial ties," *Xinhua News Agency*, May 7, 2008.

19  Quoted in Chris Buckley, "China's Hu heads to Japan seeking trust and respect," *Reuters*, May 3, 2008.

20  Ibid.

21 Hoshiyama, "New Japan-China Relations," 75. Others who have stressed the significance of the joint statement include Gao, "The China–Japan Mutually Beneficial Relationship."

22 "Joint Statement between the Government of Japan and the Government of the People's Republic of China on Comprehensive Promotion of a 'Mutually Beneficial Relationship Based on Common Strategic Interests,'" accessed September 3, 2010. http://www.mofa.go.jp/region/asia-paci/china/joint0805.html.

23 Press Conference by Prime Minister Taro Aso during his Visit to the People's Republic of China, April 30, 2009.

24 This is a phrase that gained popularity after being used by Premier Wen in 2007 to describe the potential for Japan–China relations in the East China Sea. (See "Wen: East China Sea place of 'peace, friendship, cooperation,'" *Xinhua News Agency*, April 4, 2007.)

25 Press Conference by Prime Minister Taro Aso during his Visit to the People's Republic of China, April 30, 2009.

26 This chapter only presents a general overview of Japan and China's conflict and cooperation in the East China Sea. For a more comprehensive study, see, for example, Manicom, "Sino-Japanese Cooperation in the East China Sea: Limitations and Prospects" or Au, "The East China Sea Issue: Japan-China Talks for Oil and Gas."

27 Hughes, 844.

28 There have been differing reports about the amount of energy resources available in the East China Sea. The Energy Information Agency of the US Department of Energy reports that China's unproven oil reserve estimates are between 70 and 160 billion barrels, while foreign estimates are about 100 billion barrels. China's unproven gas estimates are between 175 and 210 trillion cubic feet, but an official survey by Japan in 1970 placed it at about 7 trillion cubic feet. ("East China Sea," Energy Information Agency, US Department of Energy, March 2008. http://www.eia.doe.gov/emeu/cabs/East_China_Sea/pdf)

29 Both claims arguably can be supported by international law, particularly by different articles of the UN Convention on the Law of the Sea (1982).

30 Au, "East China Sea Issue," 224–8.

31 Liao, "Sino-Japanese Energy Security and Regional Stability: The Case of the East China Sea Gas Exploration," 58.

32 Although Liao asserts that this did not mean an immediate end to political mistrust, as Japan and China continue to be competing powers in the region.

33 Au, "East China Sea Issue," 239–40.

34 Manicom and O'Neil, "Sino-Japanese Strategic Relations: Will Rivalry Lead to Confrontation?" 222.

35 "China and Japan Reach Principled Consensus on the East China Sea Issue," June 18, 2008, accessed September 6, 2010. http://chinaembassy.org.pg/eng/fyrth/t466632.htm.

36 Ibid.; "Joint Press Conference by Minister for Foreign Affairs Masahiko Koumura and Minister of Economy, Trade and Industry Akira Amari (Regarding Cooperation between Japan and China

in the East China Sea)," June 18, 2008. http://www.mofa.go.jp/announce/fm_press/2008/6/0618. html.

37  See, for example, Manicom, "Sino-Japanese Cooperation," 471.

38  Gao, "A Note on the 2008 Cooperation Consensus," 297.

39  "East China Sea agreement 'flexible and pragmatic,'" *Xinhua News Agency*, June 18, 2008.

40  "Japan, China agree on gas exploration in East China Sea," *The Japan Times Online*, June 16, 2008.

41  For example, it was misleadingly stated that in the agreement "the border previously drawn by China was of no value. Japan's territorial assertions regarding the East China Sea were upheld" (Du Tran, "Unbalanced bargaining game with China," *The Japan Times Online*, February 24, 2009). This is despite the fact that no decision was made with regard to sovereignty issues.

42  The Chinese government prefers the term "cooperative development." ("China: 'supervise' domestic media coverage of gas drilling dispute," *The Japan Times Online*, May 13, 2010.)

43  For example, see "Foreign Ministry Spokesperson Jiang Yu's Remarks on the East China Sea Issue," June 18, 2008. http://www.chinaembassy.org/pg/eng/fyrth/t466626.htm.; Stephanie Ho, "China 'clarifies' agreement with Japan," *Voice of America*, June 19, 2008.

44  "China: 'supervise' domestic media coverage of gas drilling dispute," *The Japan Times Online*, May 13, 2010.

45  Au, "East China Sea Issue," 240.

46  For example, in a 2009 joint Japan–China poll, when asked what issues should be settled and prioritized for the betterment of Japan–China relations, the top response in both Japan and China was "history." ("Joint Japan-China public opinion poll: a gap in Japan-China perceptions, economics, China places importance on US," *Yomiuri Shimbun*, December 8, 2009.)

# Selected bibliography

Au, Kung-wing. "The East China Sea Issue: Japan-China Talks for Oil and Gas." *East Asia: An International Quarterly* 25:3 (2008): 223–41.

Buszynski, Leszek. "Sino-Japanese Relations: Interdependence, Rivalry and Regional Security." *Contemporary Southeast Asia* 31:1 (2009): 143–71.

Dreyer, June Teufel. "Sino-Japanese Rivalry and Its Implications for Developing Nations." *Asian Survey* 46:4 (2006): 538–57.

Gallicchio, Marc, ed. *The Unpredictability of the Past* (Durham, NC: Duke University Press, 2007).

Gao, Haikuan. "The China–Japan Mutually Beneficial Relationship Based on Common Strategic Interests and East Asian Peace and Stability." *Asia-Pacific Review* 15:2 (2008): 36–51.

Gao, Jianjun. "A Note on the 2008 Cooperation Consensus between China and Japan in the East China Sea." *Ocean Development & International Law* 40:3 (2009): 291–303.

Hoshiyama, Takashi. "New Japan–China Relations and the Corresponding Positioning of the United States—History, Values, Realism in a Changing World." *Asia-Pacific Review* 15:2 (2008): 68–101.

Hughes, Christopher W. "Japan's Response to China's Rise: Regional Engagement, Global Containment, Dangers of Collision." *International Affairs* 85: 4 (2009): 837–56.

Liao, Janet Xuanli. "Sino-Japanese Energy Security and Regional Stability: The Case of the East China Sea Gas Exploration." *East Asia: An International Quarterly* 25:1 (2008): 57–78.

Manicom, James. "Sino-Japanese Cooperation in the East China Sea: Limitations and Prospects." *Contemporary Southeast Asia* 30:3 (2008): 455–78.

Manicom, James and Andrew O'Neil. "Sino-Japanese Strategic Relations: Will Rivalry Lead to Confrontation?" *Australian Journal of International Affairs* 63:2 (2009): 213–32.

Men, Honghua. "East Asian Order Formation and Sino-Japanese Relations." *Indiana Journal of Global Legal Studies* 17:1 (2010): 47–82.

Mochizuki, Mike M. "Japan's Shifting Strategy toward the Rise of China." *The Journal of Strategic Studies* 30:4/5 (2007): 739–76.

Peterson, Alexander M. "Sino-Japanese Cooperation in the East China Sea: A Lasting Arrangement?" *Cornell International Law Journal* 42:3 (2009): 441–74.

Przystup, James. *Comparative Connections*. Various issues. http://csis.org/program/comparative-connections.

Roy, Denny. "China's Democratised Foreign Policy." *Survival* 51:2 (2009): 25–40.

Smith, Paul J. "China-Japan Relations and the Future Geopolitics of East Asia." *Asian Affairs: An American Review* 35:4 (2009): 230–56.

Yang, Bojiang. "Redefining Sino-Japanese Relations after Koizumi." *The Washington Quarterly* 29:4 (2006): 129–37.

Yang, Jian. "China's Security Strategy towards Japan: Perceptions, Policies, and Prospects." Centre for Strategic Studies Working Paper No. 17/01, Victoria University of Wellington (2001): 1–23.

# 4

# Cross-Strait Relations Today: Challenges and Opportunities

Chunjuan Nancy Wei

## Chapter Outline

# Introduction

Taiwan's relationship with the People's Republic of China (PRC) creates one of the most complex and dangerous flashpoints in the world. It is emotional because different state and national identities are involved in the dispute among different ethnic Chinese groups. It is convoluted because multiple partisan and national interests dictate that different rules are played at different levels of games. In addition, it has the potential to draw the United States and China, the world's two leading nuclear powers, into a head-on collision and probably ruin the fastest growing economies in East Asia. While economic interdependence has further deepened with 5–10 percent of the Taiwanese population settling on the Chinese Mainland, elite-initiated conflicts during President Chen Shui-bian's terms (2000–8) threatened to upset the cross-Taiwan Strait equilibrium and bring the dyad closer to a military show-down.

In 2002 the independence-minded Chen Shui-bian articulated the cross-Strait relationship as "one country on each side" (of the Strait) which angered Beijing. A year later, Taipei launched a campaign on a referendum law that would allow the island to conduct a plebiscite to declare its *de facto* independence from China *de jure*. Under pressure from the United States and China, only a watered-down version was passed. However, Chen seized the opportunity to hold a "defensive" referendum to coincide with his reelection bid, calling on China to remove missiles targeting Taiwan and to renounce force against the island. To counter Taiwan's moves, in 2005 Beijing passed the Anti-Secession Law (*fan fenlie guajia fa*, literally the Anti-Splitting-the-State Law) authorizing military operations if Taiwan declared *de jure* independence.[1] Chen defied by scrapping the symbolic "National Unification Guidelines" with China which was adopted by Taiwan's legislature in 1991. Having prepared for the Taiwan contingency for more than a decade via double-digit military spending and weapons modernization, Beijing responded in early 2007 by its first successful anti-satellite weapons test in space. Taiwan countered with launching a new-round of referenda to join the United Nations in the 2008 presidential elections. A frustrated and worried Washington repeatedly warned Taiwan and China that it expected "no unilateral changes to the status quo" from Taipei and no use of force by Beijing.

To distinguish from his predecessor's confrontational China policies, presidential candidate Ma Ying-jeou promised voters a warmer relationship and closer economic ties with Beijing in the backdrop of global financial crisis. With Ma's inauguration in May 2008, reconciliation and cooperation have replaced recrimination and confrontation in the cross-Strait interface. Internationally, Ma substituted his predecessor's "fire-setting diplomacy" (*fenghuo waijiao*) with the "diplomatic truce," aiming at stopping the checkbook competition with Beijing for allies. He also assured Washington, his most important supporter, a "surprise-free" promise. On cross-Strait level, the two governments renewed their interest in the "1992 consensus," a formula agreed upon in 1992 by the two sides which recognizes that Taiwan and the PRC both belong to the one and same China, but that each disagrees what that China means. Negotiations based on the formula produced rapid reconciliation and 15 agreements, including "the Economic Cooperation Framework Agreement" (ECFA) in 2010, Northeast Asia's first free trade pact.

The PRC-Taiwan relationship has been deeply influenced by path dependency, structural shifts in great power politics, and partisan struggles across the Taiwan Strait. One may wonder, what had suddenly changed between 2008 and 2010 to make such a landmark trade deal possible between the archrivals? Why was it signed despite domestic opposition? How did these rivals embrace each other economically when they still harbored significant political differences? Will this economically beneficial agreement to Taiwan come at a political cost? How will this deal influence East Asian regional economic integration, especially between Northeast Asia and ASEAN?

In the following sections, a historical context with partisan calculations of the term "China" will be introduced, followed by detailed information on the six-round negotiations that include signing of the ECFA. President Ma's diplomatic truce and its influence on East Asia regional integration is presented next, followed by a discussion of the successful resumption of the "1992 Consensus." The ECFA's implications for Taiwan's Pan-Greens (pro-independence groups) and their countermoves are also explored. The last section discusses the future direction of the Cross-Strait relationship.

# The "China" tangle

The year 2011 marked the centennial of China's October 1911 Revolution, a watershed event which ended imperial dynasties and established Asia's first democratic republic, the Republic of China (ROC). That government now survives in Taiwan but is not recognized by any major country of the world. The very title, ROC, is dearly held by some and bitterly opposed by others, even on the island itself. Meanwhile, the idea of Taiwan celebrating the centenarian birthday of the ROC reminded many on the Chinese Mainland that China remains divided. Though separated since 1949, much like their North and South Korean neighbors, tensions across the Taiwan Strait are nevertheless at the lowest ebb in some 60 years.

Older citizens on the Mainland still remember the ROC, their country's name when they were born. The nation began as a democracy, but soon disintegrated into chaotic warlordism, followed by Japanese invasion and disastrous civil wars. Then, in 1949, the ROC was relocated to Taiwan when the Communist leader Mao Zedong founded the People's Republic of China (PRC) in Beijing. Mao initially hoped to keep the ROC as the new government's designated abbreviation, but some of his colleagues did not want to have anything to do with it.[2] The PRC's creation marked the genesis of "two Chinas" across the Taiwan Strait; however, each government viewed itself as the only "legitimate" regime of China, with the other a swarm of "bandits" to be eliminated. Internationally, the ROC represented China in the United Nations until 1971 when it was unseated by the PRC. As of 2012 the PRC is recognized by 169 countries while only 23 small, impoverished countries identify with Taiwan.

The ROC's position at home is equally distressing, if not more so. Its legitimacy has been challenged for decades. Is Taiwan a province of China or a new state? Is the ROC a residual China, or an illegitimate foreign regime? What is the proper relationship between Taiwan and the ROC? These are difficult political questions. As the founder of the ROC, Ma's Kuomintang (KMT) and its splinter parties insist that the ROC has been an independent country since 1911. Generally known as the Pan-Blues because of the blue color of the ROC flag, this group tends to favor a Chinese nationalist identity, and prefers a closer economic and cultural link with the Mainland. They endorse the made-in-China constitution, believing that the ROC territory includes the Mainland, though its jurisdiction currently is limited to Taiwan. To them, the PRC is only a conditional threat.

Disparaging Pan-Blue beliefs as political myth, the opposition Democratic Progressive Party (DPP) and its more radical allies in Taiwan, attack the ROC as an illegitimate regime. Viewing Ma's KMT and the Chinese Communist Party (CCP) as a pair of evil Siamese twins, they favor a separatist identity, and want to establish a truly independent and new Republic of Taiwan (ROT) to replace the ROC. Thanks to their green flag, this group is collectively known as the Pan-Greens. Fearing that economic ties with the Mainland would diminish their hopes for a permanent separation, the Pan-Greens insist on minimum socioeconomic links. To prevent closer economic ties and cultural exchanges with China, Chen Shui-bian's DPP government forbid Mainland tourists and investments from coming to Taiwan, stifling profitable deals for the island's economy. For them, the PRC constitutes an all-weather military and economic threat.

Long hostile to the ROC regime in Taiwan, the CCP declared the demise of the ROC in 1949. Since 1971 the PRC government has used all means to block Taiwan from using its official name at any international events where it appears. In recent years, witnessing the Pan-Greens severing the island's political (and cultural) umbilical cord with the Mainland, the PRC has found that its best option in dealing with the island is not to deny the ROC institutions, which provide the legal foundation for an eventual national unification with Taiwan. To put it simply, of the two options for Taiwan's name—the ROC or ROT—Beijing prefers the lesser evil, the ROC.

Despite this preference, Mainland China faces a catch-22. Denying the ROC's existence would only strengthen the pro-independence movement in Taiwan. Recognizing the ROC would create two Chinas, possibly followed by international dual recognition, which might be exploited by the Pan-Greens if they return to power in democratic elections. There currently seems to be no satisfactory political solution. For Beijing, focusing on low-level issues such as economy and culture exchanges might be a viable way out. Straddling a mid-ground between the unification-minded Mainland and the independence-leaning Pan-Greens, the Ma Administration proved to be on the same wavelength as Beijing.

# Six rounds of negotiations

Barely three weeks in office, President Ma re-opened cross-Strait channels of talks by lifting the decade-long suspension of the semi-official Straits Exchange Foundation (SEF) and the Beijing-based Association for Relations Across the Taiwan Strait (ARATS). At this writing, six rounds of negotiations have been held, which resulted in 15 agreements and a consensus document[3] (see Table 4.1).

By focusing on functional matters, the two sides have achieved a significant thaw in their relationship. In the absence of government-to-government ties, Taiwan's SEF Chairman Chiang Pin-kung met ARATS Chairman Chen Yunlin in Beijing. Their first meeting which was held in June 2008 concluded with agreements for direct weekend charter flights and about 3,000 Chinese tourists to Taiwan each day. Previously, direct flights could only be held over four major holidays. Despite improvements, the new charter flights, though nonstop, still had to take a circuitous route through Hong Kong airspace due to Taiwan's insistence, which added an hour to the flying time.

Chiang-Chen's second talk in November 2008, and the first ever meeting in Taiwan, put an end to the unnecessary detour for cross-Strait travelers. Both sides agreed on aviation routes, direct air and sea transportation links, postal services and food safety standards. A month later on December 15, direct air and sea transportation and postal services were launched, marking the arrival of the "major three links" era. As a result of this agreement, a flight from Taipei to Shanghai now takes only 90 minutes, saving the extra hour from the Hong Kong detour, and radically improved over the 9 hours of a few years ago when layovers were required.

The third-round cross-Strait talks occurred in Nanjing, where Taiwan's ruling KMT had its last capital on the Mainland. Both sides agreed to

**Table 4.1** Cross-Strait agreements since May 2008

| Negotiation rounds (# of agreements) | Date | Place | Agreement contents |
|---|---|---|---|
| **Round 1 (2)** | Jun. 8–13, 2008 | Beijing, China | Agreement on Cross-Strait Tourism of Mainland Residents to Taiwan<br>Minutes of Talks on Cross-Strait Chartered Flights |
| **Round 2 (4)** | Nov. 4, 2008 | Taipei, Taiwan | Agreement on Cross-Strait Air Transport<br>Agreement on Cross-Strait Sea Transport<br>Agreement on Cross-Strait Postal Services<br>Agreement on Cross-Strait Food Security |
| **Round 3 (3) with 1 consensus** | Apr. 26, 2009 | Nanjing, China | Cross-Strait Financial Cooperation Agreement<br>Supplementary Agreement on Cross-Strait Air Transport<br>Agreement on Joint Cross-Strait Crime-fighting and Mutual Judicial Assistance<br>Consensus on Mainland Investment in Taiwan |
| **Round 4 (3)** | Dec. 21–5, 2009 | Taichung, Taiwan | Agreement on Cooperation of Agricultural Product Quarantine and Inspection<br>Agreement on Cooperation in Respect of Standards, Metrology, Inspection & Accreditation<br>Agreement on Cooperation in Respect of Fishing Crew Affairs |
| **Round 5 (2)** | Jun. 29, 2010 | Chongqing, China | Economic Cooperation Framework Agreement (ECFA)<br>Cross-Straits Agreement on Intellectual Property Right Protection & Cooperation |
| **Round 6 (1)** | Dec. 20–2, 2010 | Taipei, Taiwan | Medical and Health Cooperation Agreement |

*Source*: The Straits Exchange Foundation and Mainland Affairs Council websites: http://www.mac.gov.tw/np.asp?ctNode=5689&mp=1

establish a financial cooperation mechanism and to collaborate in civil and criminal fields on fighting crime, the latter being more significant to Taiwan because the travel convenience allowed more criminals from Taiwan to hide in the Mainland. The third agreement launched additional regular cross-Strait passenger and cargo flights with more destinations on the Mainland. A memorandum of understanding was also signed to promote Mainland investment in Taiwan, covering banking, securities and insurance. Prior to the meeting, President Ma instructed his delegation to mention Taiwan's desire to sign the ECFA, framing it as a "public livelihood" issue. The negotiators addressed the topic but did not set a time table.

The fourth round negotiations concluded three agreements to boost economic collaboration related to the fishing industry, agricultural quarantine inspection and also industrial product standards and certification. Since 1991, Taiwan has allowed Mainland Chinese crew members to work on its fishing boats due to labor shortages. The new agreement established a cooperative mechanism for crewmember employment of each other's citizens. New provisions for agricultural quarantine procedures and industrial product standards further guaranteed the safety of agricultural production and worker health.

Chen and Chiang's fifth talks focused on the ECFA agreement and the copyright protection agreement. The concept of a cross-Strait free trade deal was floated in February 2009. After 18 months of deliberation and negotiation, the delegates consummated the landmark Economic Cooperation Framework Agreement (ECFA) on June 29, 2010.[4] The accord promised reduction and elimination of trade barriers in goods and services, as well as protection of investments and intellectual property rights against piracy. With ratification by Taiwan's parliament in September 2010, Northeast Asia's first free trade agreement was enacted.

From a purely economic perspective, the accord helps assure Taiwan's continued economic prosperity by further opening up the massive Mainland market to the island's leading industries and business-savvy firms. With reduced tariffs on more than 800 goods and services across the Taiwan Strait, it is especially beneficial to Taiwan's economic development. The "early harvest" list, which came to effect on January 1, 2011, cleared the way for 539 Taiwanese goods worth $13.83 billion, and 267 Chinese goods worth $2.86 billion to enter each other's market with zero tariff treatment. Products and services that are not on the list will enjoy a three-phase tariff reduction in the next two years.[5]

The trade agreement is also a political move for Beijing, aimed at reincorporating Taiwan into the China orbit through economic integration. With its inclusion of 18 Taiwanese agricultural and fishery products in the trade concessions, Beijing wanted to please Taiwan's politically sensitive farmers who live in the southern Taiwan and tend to support independence. The agreement is also a political victory to President Ma's Kuomintang (KMT) party as it allows the latter to claim progress in the thorny cross-Strait relationship. Despite dissent from the Pan-Greens, Ma's Administration convinced the public that the deal would fend off Taiwan's isolation in the fast-growing East Asian economy. The regional trade agreement with China, the so-called ASEAN+1, is scheduled to include South Korea and Japan in the years ahead; accordingly, it is crucial that Taiwanese goods retain competitive in the vast Chinese market.

Due to its political sensitivity, immediately after ECFA was signed Taiwan's government asked its Mainland Affairs Council to conduct island-wide surveys on citizens' views. According to Table 4.2, a majority of respondents was pleased with the Intellectual Property Rights (IPR) agreement (73%), the zero or reduced tariff arrangements (54.8%), and the overall negotiation results (61%). While almost two-thirds (64%) of people viewed positively the inclusion of 18 agricultural and fishery products in the zero-tariff category, an even larger four-fifths of respondents were satisfied with the cross-Strait negotiation mechanism. The number of respondents not satisfied

**Table 4.2** Taiwanese views of the fifth round meeting

| Are you satisfied with these elements of the ECFA? | Very satisfied | Somewhat satisfied | Slightly unsatisfied | Very unsatisfied | Don't know |
|---|---|---|---|---|---|
| 1. Zero or reduced tariff rates | 14.2 | 40.6 | 11 | 13.8 | 20.4 |
| | | 54.8 | | 24.8 | |
| 2. 18 Agricultural & fishery products zero tariff | 19 | 44.6 | 12.2 | 14.6 | 9.5 |
| | | 63.6 | | 26.8 | |
| 3. ECFA's overall negotiation results | 15.5 | 45.6 | 12.9 | 17.1 | 8.9 |
| | | 61.1 | | 30 | |
| 4. Agreement on intellectual property rights & cooperation | 29.8 | 43.3 | 7.5 | 9.9 | 9.5 |
| | | 73.1 | | 17.4 | |
| 5. Institutionalized negotiations | 39.6 | 39.7 | 6.5 | 9.4 | 4.8 |
| | | 79.3 | | 15.9 | |
| 6. Investment protection negotiation | 37.3 | 33.7 | 8.5 | 13.9 | 6.6 |
| | | 71 | | 22.4 | |

Note: Survey Time: July 2–4, 2010; Sample: 1114; Sponsored by Taiwan's Mainland Affairs Council
Source: "民眾對第五次『江陳會談』之看法」民意調查"
http://www.mac.gov.tw/public/Attachment/07621452091.pdf

with ECFA (30%) corresponds equivalently to the size of pro-independence supporters.

To counter accusations from the opposition that Ma's government did not protect "weak" industries and was "selling off" Taiwan to Mainland China, a list of interesting questions appeared in the survey as well (Table 4.3). Taiwan's relatively disadvantaged industries comprise 17 sectors that did not appear on the "early harvest" list (those scheduled for immediate tariff reduction), including towel manufacture, household appliances, and agricultural and fishery products. Still there were 37 percent of respondents who did not think the government protected enough. In spite of the dissatisfaction, a majority of people thought Ma's government did a good job protecting Taiwan's interests (66.8%) and national sovereignty (58.9%).

At the sixth round of talks held in December 2010, a medical agreement was signed, which covers four areas: prevention of infectious diseases, management and development of new drugs, emergency rescue operations, and the study of Chinese medicine and its safety management. The new pact is expected to facilitate epidemics information exchanges on each other's jurisdiction, and to benefit Taiwan's budding biotechnology industry with a lucrative Mainland market.

It is worth noting that as a result of this latest meeting, a seven-panel Economic Cooperation Committee (ECC) was formed to handle commodities trade, service trade, financial services, intellectual property rights, economic cooperation, dispute settlement, and investment protection. Instead of having government officials wear "white gloves," pretending to be private citizens, each of these panels are headed by government bureau or department executives from both sides.[6]

**Table 4.3** Taiwanese views of the fifth round meeting

| Questions | Yes | No | Don't know |
|---|---|---|---|
| 1. Has the gov't protected Taiwan's weak industries? | 53.1 | 36.7 | 10.3 |
| 2. Will ECFA help Taiwan sign FTAs with other countries? | 62.6 | 25.9 | 11.4 |
| 3. Will ECFA have long-term positive impact? | 59.2 | 31.0* | 9.9 |
| 4. Did ECFA protect Taiwan's interests? | 66.8 | 22.5 | 10.7 |
| 5. Did ECFA hurt national sovereignty? | 29.8 | 58.9 | 11.3 |

*Combination of "No impact" and "Negative impact"

Note: Survey Time: July 2–4, 2010; Sample: 1114; Sponsored by Taiwan's Mainland Affairs Council

Source: "民眾對第五次『江陳會談』之看法」民意調查"

http://www.mac.gov.tw/public/Attachment/07621452091.pdf

# Ma's diplomatic truce

In spite of the importance of bilateral negotiations, cross-Strait harmony would be impossible to attain without both sides offering goodwill to reconcile diplomatic issues. Since the early 1990s Taiwan's three leaders—Lee Teng-hui, Chen Shui-bian, and Ma Ying-jeou—have faced the same international reality: the ROC is losing ground in its competition for diplomatic allies with the PRC. To reverse the trend, Lee campaigned for dual recognition, asking countries to recognize Taipei in addition to Beijing, which was not successful due to Beijing's firm resistance. In contrast, his checkbook diplomacy, offering generous aid to any country willing to de-recognize Beijing, proved largely effective. By the time Lee left office in 2000, Taipei had grabbed 17 of Beijing's friends. Beijing did not lose too badly, though. It managed to snatch ten of Taipei's remaining allies, some of them relatively heavy-weights in international politics, such as Saudi Arabia (1990), South Korea (1992), and South Africa (1998).[7]

President Chen inherited Lee's confrontational policy along with the dollar diplomacy, but not his luck. Chen's eight years coincided with Beijing's rise on the global stage. With more money and resources, and a resolve to compete with Taiwan for allies, Beijing more often than not took the upper hand. Accordingly, the Chen Administration's "fire-setting diplomacy" led to nine losses with only three gains.[8] Countries like Australia and New Zealand publicly condemned Beijing and Taiwan for engaging in corrupt diplomatic practices in the South Pacific.

Unfortunately for President Chen, regionalism and globalization also worked against his administration's provocative policy. When Chen came into office in 2000, East Asia had only three free trade agreements (FTAs) in effect and China had none. By the time he left, the region had seen ten times more such compacts, and China had signed six FTAs.[9] A month before ECFA was inked, an Asian Development Bank (ADB) report put the East Asia FTAs at 45, with some 85 more in the pipeline.[10] Taiwan's Southeast Asian neighbors viewed Chen's independence efforts as a "collective bad," that is, a negative externality for their relationship with China.[11] The tense cross-Strait relationship made it extremely difficult for Taiwan to initiate bilateral or multilateral trade agreements with any of its regional trading partners. Although the Chen government worked hard to push for FTAs, Taiwan was only able to sign FTAs with its five diplomatic allies in Latin America that have miniscule trading volume with the island.[12] Fearing economic marginalization, Taiwan anxiously observed the Mainland, South Korea, and Japan, three of Taiwan's top trading partners, signing FTAs with other partners. A forced trade-off between *de jure* independence and economic vitality left Taiwan internally divided.

When Ma was voted in office in 2008, he knew that his predecessors' confrontational checkbook diplomacy was not working. Understanding that the cross-Strait relationship should rank higher than most external matters, Ma proposed the diplomatic truce concept. The essence of the new policy is to freeze the current number of allies at 23, not to compete for new ones via dual recognition or foreign aid. To demonstrate his sincerity, Ma even eliminated a third of the foreign ministry's 2009 confidential diplomatic budget, which was previously used to seduce the PRC's allies. Beijing responded in kind by refusing to establish diplomatic relations with any of Taiwan's allies. For example, Beijing cold-shouldered Paraguayan president-elect Fernando Lugo's request for diplomatic ties, which allowed Taiwan to keep its only ally in South America.[13]

Another issue is Taiwan's membership in international organizations. Both sides were able to work out a deal for Taiwan's participation in the annual World Health Organization (WHO) meetings as an observer using the name "Chinese Taipei." May 2009 marked the first time that Taiwan was allowed to attend a meeting of the UN specialized agencies since 1971, a major breakthrough for the Ma government. Despite recent dispute over a leaked WHO document that listed Taiwan as a province of China, President Ma downplayed it by stressing that health ministers from both sides are working on equal footing in the organization. PRC president Hu Jintao commented on a number of occasions that Taiwan's diplomatic space can be discussed in negotiations.

# Success of ambiguity: the *Tamamushi-iro* approach

The pace and scope of the negotiations, as well as the endorsement from both governments, were unprecedented in their tortured history. As can be imagined, given the political sensitivity of Taiwan's status, negotiating and ratifying the 15 agreements between long-term adversaries encountered many roadblocks; any reckless move could derail previous efforts and set the negotiations back to square one. Was there a secret negotiation strategy? Taiwan's chief negotiator Chiang Pin-kung, who received his Ph.D. from the University of Tokyo, described his success in a familiar Japanese term, a *tamamushi-iro* approach.[14]

*Tamamushi* is the Japanese name of a jewel beetle whose color changes depending on the angle of the observer and the source of the light. The *iro* (colors) may be different but the insect is still the same. According to a Japanese scholar, the term *tamamushi-iro* bears "a positive connotation" in Japanese culture.[15] In diplomacy, *tamamushi-iro* solution refers to a deal reached through a vague, ambiguous term that is designed to please both sides. With mutual appreciation, the parties involved would not challenge each other's interpretations.

The first major block was the controversial "One China principle," which Beijing has insisted as a prerequisite for any negotiations with Taiwan. The PRC and the ROC do not formally recognize each other. They are currently at a stage of "mutual non-denial," to use President Ma's terminology. Legally, Taiwan treats the Mainland as an "area" within the ROC territory, in accordance with the *Act Governing Relations between the Peoples of the Taiwan Area and the Mainland Area*. The Mainland, on the other hand, views Taiwan as a province within the PRC.

To seek common ground while allowing each side to score points, Chiang and his Chinese counterpart reused a successful modus operandi, the "one China with different interpretations." The formula, often dubbed "the 1992 Consensus," allows both sides to read their definition of what that China actually means. The agreement allows Beijing to interpret it to mean the PRC, and Taipei to refer to it as the ROC. Former president Chen, who did not tolerate any gray areas by denying the existence of such an agreement, was partially responsible for the diplomatic stalemate with Beijing. Accepting "the 1992 Consensus" proves to be a winning move on Ma's administration.

As such, the signing parties were not the heads of state, nor foreign ministers, but Taiwan's Straits Exchange Foundation (SEF) and its Mainland equivalent, the Association for Relations Across the Taiwan Strait (ARATS), both bearing the status of quasi-governmental institutions. As Lee Ping in Hong Kong's *Apple Daily* has commented on the first round of cross-Strait negotiations, "both sides are more ambiguous about 'One China' and reunification, indicating that ideological conflicts are diminishing."[16]

As is well known, an FTA between countries of different sizes is more beneficial to the smaller economy because the latter gains valuable access to a larger market. In other words, Taiwan is set to gain much more economically in its free trade deal with Mainland China, whose market is not limited to the vast size within its borders but to include the ASEAN ten countries since January 1, 2010. The diplomatic ambiguity on the nature of cross-Strait relationship leaves ample room for Beijing to respond with sincerity, compromise, and generosity in functional cooperation.[17] To calm Taiwan's fears that ECFA could open a floodgate of cheap Chinese goods, Premier Wen Jiabao promised in March 2010 that any trade deal would not harm the island.[18] Taiwan's premier Wu Den-yih acknowledged that Beijing offered a deal "better than WTO norms." Taiwan's products that enjoy immediate tariff cuts in the Chinese market are twice as many and value nearly $11 billion more.[19] KMT honorary chairman Wu Poh-hsiung and others even referred the trade deal as Taiwan's economic "vitamins."

# Free trade or birdcage: ECFA's implications for Taiwan's Pan-Greens

Taiwan's two major political camps read Beijing's call for economic integration from different scripts and had drawn different conclusions regarding the social, cultural, and political implications for Taiwan. During each round of the cross-Strait talks, Taiwan's Pan-Greens argued that economic integration is bad for Taiwan. They believe that ECFA would lead to massive job losses and a flood of Taiwan with cheap Chinese products. Opponents to the trade deal fear that deregulation of the agricultural and financial sectors would undermine Taiwan's self-sufficiency, and would thus be detrimental to Taiwan's security. Pushing for an ECFA referendum, the extremist Taiwan Solidarity Union (TSU) painted President Ma as China's puppet, and the deals as setting the stage for an eventual Chinese takeover of Taiwan. The most radical view holds that the ECFA should be abolished once the DPP comes back to power.

Critics of the Taiwan-China deal also likened ECFA to its earlier Hong Kong version, the Closer Economic Partnership Arrangement (CEPA).[20] In an article published in the pro-independence *Taipei Times*, Woody Cheng, history professor at National Cheng Kung University, compared ECFA to a China-imposed "birdcage" that Taiwan should flee from. Using a textual analysis characterized by postmodernist thought, Cheng deconstructed ECFA in terms of timing, venue, and the expressions comparing them with CEPA. He pointed out two interesting coincidences of the signing ceremony: The same initial signing date (June 29) and the choice of Chongqing, the Mainland city where 65 years ago Mao Zedong's Communists and Chiang

Kai-shek's Nationalists held their second round of peace talks. Cheng's third interesting element lies in his interpretation of the "A" in both cases. Though he acknowledged that CEPA's "A" means "arrangement" while ECFA's "A" refers to "agreement," reflecting Taiwan's relatively larger bargaining room, Cheng suggested the Chinese phrase of framework (*kuangjia*) in ECFA "implies a greater sense of confinement" that is meant to "lock" Taiwan into the Chinese orbit.[21]

If Beijing had wanted to use the trade deal to prevent the DPP from taking office in 2012, its strategy was not successful, judging from the results of the post-ECFA municipality mayoral elections. As anticipated, the KMT retained hold of the north (Taipei, Sinbei [formerly Taipei County] and Greater Taichung), while the DPP maintained control of the south (Greater Tainan and Greater Kaohsiung). Despite the election-eve shooting violence widely believed to have benefited the KMT, the total vote-count was in favor of the DPP, the party that loathes the ECFA. The DPP won 49.9 percent of popular votes while the ruling KMT only garnered 44.5 percent, with a difference of 400,000 ballots.[22]

If ECFA had any immediate impact on Taiwan's politics, it seemed contrary to the interests of the signing parties. While all the small parties were marginalized, the newly minted One Side One Country Alliance (OSOCA), formed by the incarcerated ex-President Chen Shui-bian, has gained momentum. Established in September 2010, barely two months prior to the elections, the radical alliance ran an "anti-China abolishing-the-ECFA" campaign, with former minister of foreign affairs Mark Chen as its president. Of the 40 councilor candidates that it endorsed (35 DPP members and 5 independents), the OSOCA won 30 seats in all 5 municipalities, thus becoming the largest political pressure group, with influence expanding to every corner of the island. Notably, Chen Chih-chung, son of the former president who ran on an independent ticket, won the highest number of votes in his district in Tainan. Some of OSOCA's most infamous members include Wang Ding-yu who had mobilized supporters to violently attack the visiting Chinese envoy a year earlier. Another prominent member was Tsai Ting-kuei, a National Taiwan University professor who heads the Taiwan Referendum Alliance.[23]

Through this political maneuver, Chen has no doubt extended his grip beyond the current confinement. It was notable that the jailed former president had accurately anticipated the election results. From the Taipei Detention Center where he was held for embezzlement and money laundering, Chen managed to put together a group of candidates that covered most districts in the five municipalities. He had predicted, correctly, that the KMT would win three of the five municipalities, with the DPP winning the rest, but capturing a larger share of the electoral votes.[24] Via the *Ah-Bian's Notes* series, Chen voiced his concerns that the DPP, under Chairperson Tsai Ing-wen, might move toward the middle. Chen feared a middle road would lead his former party to nowhere. Drawing connections between his OSOCA and America's Tea Party movement, Chen urged followers not to quit their fundamental ideals for an independent Taiwan. In his most recent "*Ah-Bian's Notes 56*," the former president quoted Tea Party candidate Christie O'Donnell in cautioning the DPP's new leader not to deviate from the direction that Chen had formerly led.[25]

Despite Chen's influence, there are indications that the DPP under Chairperson Tsai Ing-wen is moving toward the middle in its China policies. In an interview with *Apple Daily* in September 2010, Tsai suggested that her party, if voted into power in 2012, would continue Ma's conciliatory cross-Strait policies. She implied that a DPP government would not make changes to cross-Strait agreements, including ECFA, unless via democratic procedures. On a separate occasion, she advocated establishing a think-tank research center to strengthen the DPP's policy capacity regarding cross-Strait development. In a sign of her breakaway from the former president's corruption allegations, Tsai did not rehabilitate Chen, nor did she take an offensive on the ECFA referendum promoted by the more radical Taiwan Solidarity Union.[26] By and large, the cross-Strait issues were basically put on the back burner during recent elections.

Another indicator that Tsai might have more policy leeway is the DPP's newly adopted nomination rules. In January 2011, the party congress replaced primaries with public polls for all future candidates—presidential, legislative, or mayoral. Though bitterly resisted by hardliners, the majority of the party members approved the motion. The professed goal was to curb factional disputes, which demoralized the last presidential race, so that the party could unite to win the presidential election in 2012. In effect, the new selection mechanism would give Tsai a freer hand by reducing the influence of radical members on her policy options related to China.

# Whither cross-Strait relations?

Two thousand years ago in a Chinese kingdom, King Xuanwang of Qi asked his advisor Mencius (Meng Zi) how to maintain a neighborly relationship. Mencius replied succinctly, "The great power should treat the small with magnanimity, and the small should respond to the great with prudence. In so doing, the great power brings peace to the world and the small power protects its kingdom."[27] Mencius teachings remain useful to today's cross-Strait relations.

In negotiations leading to the ECFA, leaders on both sides heeded the wisdom of Mencius. Mainland China treated Taiwan with goodwill and generosity, while Taiwan's government and negotiators responded in kind. Prior to the Chinese New Year in 2011, President Ma said that "patience, love and perseverance" were keys to cross-Strait breakthroughs. He further expressed his conviction that their joint culture and wisdom may guide the cross-Strait relations toward peace and prosperity.

The Taiwan Strait has never been calmer since Chiang Kai-shek's nationalist army retreated to the island in 1949. Moving away from his predecessor's confrontational China policy, President Ma broke the ice with China using a formula of "the 1992 Consensus" in which each side agrees to disagree on the meaning of One China. This *Tamamushi-iro* approach proved effective in overcoming the long-term cross-Strait dilemmas. By focusing on functional matters and diplomatic truce, the two sides have achieved a significant thaw in their economic and trade relationships. Their approach may provide a meaningful case study for future conflict resolution practices.

With rapid cross-Strait reconciliation and ECFA in effect, it is anticipated that regional integration between Northeast Asia and ASEAN will be accelerated. As of 2010, Northeast Asia has 32 FTAs in effect, with Japan having implemented 11, China 10,[28] South Korea 6, and Taiwan 5 respectively. The AFTA, East Asia's oldest trade bloc founded in 1992, has created one of the largest free trade areas by admitting all the ten Association of Southeast Asian Nations. In addition, it has established five separate FTAs with China, India, Japan, South Korea, and Australia and New Zealand respectively. ECFA is expected to facilitate Taiwan's debut in the East Asian regional trade bloc.

Despite these positive developments, structural problems remain; the cross-Strait relationship is still fraught with many uncertainties. On the triangular relationships, Taipei will continue to request US arms sales; frustrating Beijing's wishes, Washington refuses to halt the lucrative deals. The arms sales are expected to be a repeated source of friction for US-China relations. In Taiwan's domestic front, identity politics remains a potent weapon in electoral seasons, which may once again split the society. On the cross-Strait level, the Pan-Greens' unwillingness to accept the "1992 Consensus" as a prerequisite for negotiations with China may derail future cooperation should the DPP return to power. Ultimately, Beijing's national interest and its degree of tolerance of the Pan-Greens' independence agenda may determine whether the Taiwan Strait should once again be packed with tourists or regionally plugged with landmines.

## Five questions for discussions

1. What is ECFA? How did the PRC and Taiwan embrace each other economically when they still harbored significant political differences?
2. What is a *tamamushi-iro* approach? How does it help improve Taiwan-PRC relations?
3. Will this economically beneficial agreement to Taiwan come at a political cost? If so, which side bears more cost?
4. How will this deal influence East Asian regional economic integration, especially between Northeast Asia and Southeast Asia?
5. What are some of the challenges for a harmonious cross-Strait relationship? What are the major obstacles that still separate them apart?

# Notes

1  Chunjuan Nancy Wei, "China's Anti-Secession Law and Hu Jintao's Taiwan Policy," *Yale Journal of International Affairs* 5(1) (Winter 2010): 112–27.

2  See Gao Xiaolin and Qi Jun (高小林, 綦军). *Declassifying the Nation-Founding Ceremony* [解密开国大典(增订版)] (Beijing: Chinese Communist Party History Publishing House, 2006), chapter 3.

3  For information about all six rounds talks, see Taiwan's ministerial Mainland Affairs Council's website at http://www.mac.gov.tw/np.asp?ctNode=5689&mp=1

4  For a list of major events on ECFA, see Taiwan's government website at http://www.ecfa.org.tw/event.aspx?pagenum=1&; For the Chinese version of the Agreement and their English translations, see http://www.ecfa.org.tw/RelatedDoc.aspx

5  "Early harvest lists finalized at ECFA meet," *The China Post*, June 25, 2010.

6  For example, the IPR Panel is headed by Taiwan's Ministry of Economic Affairs' Intellectual Property Office director-general Wang Mei-hua.

7  Liu Shih-chung, "Seeking a cross-Strait diplomatic truce: theory and practice," *Brookings Institution* (2008): 3, accessed May 12, 2011 at http://www.brookings.edu/~/media/Files/events/2008/1030_taiwan/1030_taiwan.pdf

8  Liu, "Seeking a cross-strait diplomatic truce," 3.

9  The six FTAs include ASEAN-China FTA (November 2002); two Closer Economic Partnership Arrangements with Hong Kong (June 2003) and Macau (October 2003); and FTAs with Chile (November 2005), Pakistan (November 2006), New Zealand (April 2008). Since Ma came into office, China has signed 3 FTAs, with Singapore (October 2008), Peru (April 2009), and Costa Rica (April 2010) respectively.

10  Masahiro Kawai and Ganeshan Wignaraja, "Free Trade Agreements in East Asia: A Way toward Trade Liberalization?" *ADB Briefs* No. 1 (June 2010): 2–3.

11  For example, former Singaporean prime minister Lee Kuan Yew was vocal in his criticism of Chen and the independence movement.

12 Panama (August 2003); Guatemala (September 2005); Nicaragua (June 2006); El Salvador and Honduras (both in November 2006).

13 Liu, "Seeking a cross-strait diplomatic truce," 7–8.

14 Liling Qiu[邱 莉苓], "Chiang Pin-kung mentions tamamushi-iro in overcoming the difficult '1992 Consensus' Problem" [九二共识解套 江丙坤提玉虫色]," *Radio Taiwan International*, December 29, 2010.

15 Akihiro Yoshida, "On Tamamushi-iro Expression: A Phenomenological Explication of Tamamushi-iro-no (Intendedly Ambiguous) Expressive Acts," *Collection du Cirp*, Vol. 1 (2007): 252.

16 "Media praise China-Taiwan talks," *BBC News*, June 12, 2008.

17 Interview with Chiang Pin-kung, Taipei, July 8, 2010.

18 Wen said, "In negotiating this agreement . . . we need to keep in mind Taiwan's small businesses and ordinary people, and the interests of farmers in Taiwan. We will let the people of Taiwan benefit from tariff conditions and early harvest programs." See Ben Blanchard and Ralph Jennings, "China's Wen seeks to reassure Taiwan on trade deal," *Reuters*, March 15, 2010.

19 "Early harvest lists finalized at ECFA meet," *The China Post*, June 25, 2010.

20 Along with six annexes, the CEPA was signed by Mainland China and its Hong Kong Special Administrative Region (SAR) on June 29, 2003 and September 29, 2003 respectively. Since then seven supplements have been added to the arrangement, with one on each intervening year. The full text of the CEPA and its supplements can be found at http://www.tid.gov.hk/english/cepa/legaltext/cepa_legaltext.html

21 Woody Cheng, "Taiwan needs to flee the birdcage," trans. Julian Clegg, *Taipei Times*, July 10, 2010, 8.

22 The November 2010 elections were designed to select a total of 314 city councilors. The result shows that the DPP and the KMT each won 130 city councilor seats. The small pro-unification parties won 7 seats, with the People First Party and New Party winning 4 and 3 seats, respectively. The radical pro-independence Taiwan Solidarity Union fared worst: out of the 15 nominees it won only 2 seats and is now severely marginalized, partly because of the emergence of "One country on each side" caucus that competed for the same constituents.

23 Liu Xing-ren, "yi-bian yi guo lianxian, tai zhengzhi zuida bianshu" [One Side One Country Alliance, the greatest variable in Taiwan's Politics], *China Review News*, December 19, 2010.

24 Ko Shu-ling, "Chen warns DPP on Taipei election," *Taipei Times*, September 28, 2010, 1.

25 Vincent Y. Chao, "Chen draws from 'Tea Party' ideas," *Taipei Times*, October 15, 2010, 3.

26 Vincent Y. Chao, "DPP would maintain PRC policy: Tsai," *Taipei Times*, September 25, 2010, 3; So-Heng Chang, "The Political Implications of Taiwan's Big Five Mayoral Elections," *Foreign Policy Research Institute*, December 2010, accessed January 12, 2011 at http://www.fpri.org/enotes/201012.chang.taiwan.html

27 *Mencius: Liang Hui Wang II.* The Chinese text can be found at http://www.cycnet.com/encyclopedia/literature/ancient/collection/mengzi/mengzi002.htm

28 See China FTA Network website http://fta.mofcom.gov.cn/english/index.shtml

# Selected bibliography

Blanchard, Ben and Ralph Jennings. "China's Wen seeks to reassure Taiwan on trade deal." *Reuters*, March 15, 2010.

Chang, So-Heng. "The Political Implications of Taiwan's Big Five Mayoral Elections." *Foreign Policy Research Institute*, December 2010. Accessed January 12, 2011 at http://www.fpri.org/enotes/201012.chang.taiwan.html

Chao, Vincent Y. "DPP would maintain PRC policy: Tsai." *Taipei Times*, September 25, 2010, 3.

—. "Chen draws from 'Tea Party' ideas." *Taipei Times*, October 15, 2010, 3.

Cheng, Woody. "Taiwan needs to flee the birdcage," trans. Julian Clegg. *Taipei Times*, July 10, 2010, 8.

"Early harvest lists finalized at ECFA meet." *The China Post*, June 25, 2010.

Gao Xiaolin and Qi Jun [高小林, 綦军]. *Declassifying the Nation-Founding Ceremony* [解密开国大典(增订版)]. Beijing: Chinese Communist Party History Publishing House, 2006.

Interview with Chiang Pin-kung, Taipei, July 8, 2010.

Kawai, Masahiro and Ganeshan Wignaraja. "Free Trade Agreements in East Asia: A Way toward Trade Liberalization?" *ADB Briefs* No. 1 (June 2010): 2–3. Accessed May 12, 2010 at http://www.adb.org/documents/briefs/ADB-Briefs-2010-1-Free-Trade-Agreements.pdf

Ko, Shu-ling. "Chen warns DPP on Taipei election." *Taipei Times*, September 28, 2010.

Liu, Shih-chung. "Seeking a cross-Strait diplomatic truce: theory and practice." *Brookings Institution* (2008): 1–22. Accessed May 12, 2011 at http://www.brookings.edu/~/media/Files/events/2008/1030_taiwan/1030_taiwan.pdf

Liu, Xing-ren "yi-bian yi guo lianxian, tai zhengzhi zuida bianshu [One Side One Country Alliance, the greatest variable in Taiwan's politics]." *China Review News*, December 19, 2010.

"Media praise China-Taiwan talks." *BBC News*, June 12, 2008.

Qiu, Liling[邱莉苓]. "Chiang Pin-kung mentions tamamushi-iro in overcoming the difficult '1992 Consensus' problem" [九二共识解套 江丙坤提玉虫色]. *Radio Taiwan International*, December 29, 2010.

Wei, Chunjuan Nancy. "China's Anti-Secession Law and Hu Jintao's Taiwan Policy." *Yale Journal of International Affairs* 5:1 (Winter 2010): 112–27.

—. Dissertation, 2008. Analyzing Taiwan Strait Relationships 2002–2007: A Four-Level Nested Games Approach. Claremont Graduate University.

Yoshida, Akihiro. "On Tamamushi-iro Expression: A Phenomenological Explication of Tamamushi-iro-no (Intendedly Ambiguous) Expressive Acts." *Collection du Cirp* Vol. 1 (2007): 251–80. Accessed May 12, 2011 at http://www.cirp.uqam.ca/documents%20pdf/Collection%20vol.%201/14.Yoshida.pdf

# 5

# The Rise and Fall of Anti-Americanism in South Korea[1]

Heon Joo Jung

# Introduction

The surge of anti-American sentiment in South Korea in the early 2000s was a surprise to most Korea observers because anti-Americanism had not taken a central place in Korean politics until then. The anti-Americanism that began in the early 1980s was regarded as a minority view held mostly by young college students. As one scholar mentioned, South Korea was "one of the few places in the world where 'Yankee go home' was not supposed to be uttered."[2] Therefore, the sudden rise of anti-American sentiment beginning from 2002 made many observers in Seoul and Washington worry about its consequences. Many scholarly essays and alarmist commentaries have been written to address the sources, development, and future prospects of the rising anti-Americanism in South Korea and its adverse impacts on the US-Republic of Korea (ROK) alliance and beyond.[3]

These writings, with rare exceptions, predict that anti-American sentiment in South Korea will not easily vanish because its primary causes are structural and difficult to reverse.[4] Some emphasize democratization, national pride, and the unequal relationship with the United States, while others stress the hegemony of the United States and its arrogance and hypocrisy. Despite all these warnings, anti-American sentiment in South Korea seemed to be on the wane in the late 2000s. An explicitly pro-American president was elected in 2007 and positive views of the United States began to override negative ones.[5] A survey by the Pew Research Center in 2010 showed that South Korea was one of the most pro-American countries in the world, with 79 percent of respondents holding favorable views of the United States. The extant literature does little to explain this sudden fall in anti-American sentiment.[6]

To complement existing literature, this chapter examines anti-American sentiment in South Korea in a broader context of the triangular relationship among the two Koreas and the United States. It first shows how deconstruction of dominant ideas of anti-North and pro-United States made possible what had been unthinkable: low threat perception of North Korea. During the Cold War when the threat of North Korea was taken as ever-present and imminent, pro-North sentiment was as socially unacceptable as was anti-US sentiment among South Koreans. However, as dominant ideas of anti-North and pro-US were challenged and deconstructed, South Koreans began to view North Korea as a lesser threat than previously. The so-called *chujŏk* (main enemy) debates in the 1990s and 2000s are indicative of this reduced threat perception of North Korea. Unlike military tensions during the Cold War that had strengthened pro-US and anti-North sentiment among South Koreans, the deadly naval battle between North and South Korean navies in June 2002 did not increase positive views toward America.[7] Instead, massive anti-American demonstrations took place a few months later. This chapter, however, finds that as South Koreans came to feel more threatened by the nuclear North, they conceived more favorable attitudes toward America.

This chapter argues that the rise and fall of anti-American sentiment can be better explained by analyzing the ways in which two axes—attitudes toward the North and attitudes toward the United States—interact. Although these two attitudes are interdependent, the degree of their interdependence is strongly influenced by how threatened South Koreans feel by their brethren in the North. When South Koreans do not feel threatened, these two axes become more independent and less covariant, leaving more room for anti-Americanism to emerge if not actually determining its timing and contents. In other words, the rise of anti-Americanism becomes a possibility as the tension between the two Koreas declines.

In contrast, when South Koreans feel threatened by the North, the two axes become more tightly bound together and covariant, as they were during the Cold War. Although the circumstances are different, people locate sentiment on an anti-North/pro-US and pro-North/anti-US axis. The fall of anti-American sentiment, however, does not necessarily mean the restoration of a good relationship between South Korea and the United States in the traditional sense. Rather, positive views toward America should be seen as fragile in the absence of South Koreans' perception of the continuous "threat" from the North.

# Anti-American sentiment and threat perception

The global surge of anti-Americanism in the 2000s draws increasing scholarly attention to its causes and policy implications.[8] Similarly, many important works have been published on South Korea's anti-Americanism. With regard to sources of anti-Americanism in South Korea, most scholars have paid attention to macro-level changes in South Korean society: economic development and national pride; demographic change and generational differences; democratization and the rise of civil society; mass media and the Internet; low threat perception of North Korea; and US political and economic dominance.[9] Among other factors, most observers agree that the rise of anti-Americanism in the early 2000s reflected South Korea's changing demographic composition.[10] While senior citizens (those in their 50s and older) have favorable attitudes toward the United States, the younger generation, especially those in their 20s and 30s, tends to have unfavorable views.

It has been argued that older generations who experienced the Korean War and its consequences have strong emotional ties to the United States, an "ally tied by blood" rather than interests, based on shared Cold War experiences and *zeitgeist*. In contrast, younger people who learned about the Korean War and entered college in the 1980s and 1990s have rather different attitudes toward the United States. Given that the older generation constitutes a diminishing percentage of South Korea's population, many authors predict that the anti-Americanism in South Korea will be enduring.[11]

These works, however, cannot provide satisfactory explanations of the fall in anti-American sentiment since the mid-2000s. Moreover, most studies fail to address variations in anti-American sentiment among people of the same age group. They underestimate the ability of some to change their attitude toward America more easily than others when new information becomes available. This might be so because most analyses rely on aggregate data and are unable to take a closer look at the reasons people hold varying attitudes toward America at the individual level. This chapter analyzes the rise and fall of anti-American sentiment in a coherent framework by taking seriously the triangular relationship among the two Koreas and the United States, and the role of threat perception. It also complements existing work by testing key arguments with statistical analyses to understand how much threat perception matters in explaining anti-American sentiment, compared to other causes.

South Korea's anti-Americanism has been a subject of considerable theoretical and practical interest, especially because South Koreans had maintained a pro-American stance for decades. At least during most of the three decades after the Korean War, the "good" image of the United States as the best friend was widely shared and ideologically hegemonic.[12] South Korea had been seen as one of the most pro-American countries, to the extent that criticism and even questioning of American benevolence and goodwill were unthinkable and socially unacceptable.[13]

Critical to these pro-American attitudes and their sustainability among South Koreans was a shared (re-)construction of threat, real or imagined. How a country perceives external threats and evaluates their nature has a considerable influence on state behaviors and alliance patterns. According to International Relations scholar Stephen Walt, states ally with careful consideration of the nature of threat.[14] The identification of threat and the determination of whether and with whom to ally in response is determined by the factor of identity. Another scholar, Michael Barnett, also asserts that state identity offers "theoretical leverage over the issue of the construction of the threat and the choice of the alliance partner."[15] Rather than the simple logic of the anarchic nature of the international system, it is the "politics of identity" that could provide a better understanding of how a state or combination thereof considers other states as either threats—potential as well as immediate—or friends.

Anti-U.S.                          Pro-U.S.
Pro-North Korea              Anti-North Korea

**Figure 5.1** Attitudes toward America and North Korea: one axis
*Source*: By author.

As for South Koreans, it was the nation's division and subsequent Korean War that formed the South Korean state identity and the constructed "threat."[16] Substantiated by war atrocities and postwar armed clashes and tangible tensions, North Korea became *the* enemy from the very birth of South Korea. The image of North Korea as "bad," "evil," and "threatening" remained unaltered throughout the 1960s, 1970s, and 1980s, just as the image of America as "good" and "benevolent" did under the military-authoritarian regimes of Park Chung-hee and Chun Doo-hwan. Armed clashes and tensions with the North provided an unremitting source for constructing a "threat," sufficient to maintain and strengthen the negative image of the North and the positive image of the United States as well as their connectedness. In this regard, the "good" image of America and "bad" image of North Korea were inseparably tied together: anti-American sentiment was as socially unimaginable as was pro-North Korean sentiment (see Figure 5.1). Any deviation from being anti-North and pro-US was seen as unpatriotic.

Unlike the maintenance of the "bad" image of North Korea, however, the "good" image of America began to be questioned and problematized in the early 1980s.[17] For most observers, anti-Americanism in South Korea emerged from the 1980 Kwangju democratization movement and the radical student movements in the 1980s. These began with the intellectual articulation of anti-Americanism as an effort to present a counter-hegemonic idea against the existing hegemonic conception of *pangong, panbuk, chinmi* (anti-communism, anti-North, pro-Americanism).[18] Unlike the prevailing view of "America, on the whole, as liberator, philanthropist, and protector," this movement defined America as occupier, controller, and puppeteer.[19] The 1990s, however, witnessed the wane of anti-Americanism. This was partly because by the late 1980s, anti-American rhetoric in South Korea found it harder to explain how Korea could be democratized if the United States kept supporting authoritarian regimes. As a result of democratic transition and consolidation, both radical movements and anti-Americanism in South Korea shrank further, especially after the inauguration of the first elected civilian president in 32 years, Kim Young-sam, in 1993.

A new wave of anti-Americanism in the early 2000s, however, reveals its explosive nature. It emerged out of an accident in June 2002, when an armored vehicle of the US Forces in Korea (USFK) participating in a military exercise ran over and killed two 14-year-old schoolgirls as they walked along a narrow village road. Controversy and anger erupted over the US court martial's not-guilty verdict in December for the two US service members charged with negligent homicide. The decision prompted an eruption of anti-US demonstrations. On December 15, over 300,000 people participated in candlelight vigils mourning the two victims. The protests expanded from demands for fundamental revision of the "unequal" US-ROK Status of Forces Agreement (SOFA) to calls for the immediate withdrawal of US troops from South Korea.[20] Even though controversies on jurisdiction over crimes by US service members have long existed in South Korea, the distinctiveness of the 2002 anti-American demonstrations lay in their magnitude, popularity, and political impact.[21] In particular, the younger generation participated enthusiastically not only in street demonstrations but also in online communication as an alternative to reading conservative, pro-American major newspapers. An equal alliance with the United States became a major issue during the 2002 presidential election.

The tide of attitudes toward the United States started to turn again from the mid-2000s as the rate of favorable views of the United States began to rise rapidly.[22] In 2008, public outcry was voiced over US beef imports that allegedly risked carrying mad cow disease. Despite this and the high probability of its sparking anti-American demonstrations, the primary target of public anger was the South Korean government, not its US counterpart. Instead of a more equal relationship, restoration of traditional ties between Seoul and Washington became a key foreign policy goal.

The waxing and waning of anti-Americanism in South Korea make clear that there exist more than structural and irreversible factors behind either trend. Given the dominant status of *pangong, panbuk, chinmi* and the interconnectedness of the three elements, attitudinal changes toward North Korea and deconstruction of a hegemonic pro-Americanism should not be seen as isolated events. In other words, there is a need to examine how "bad" images of North Korea changed over time, in order to better understand the deconstruction of "good" images of America. The following section examines changing perceptions of the North in the 1990s and thereafter.

# The changing perception of North Korea and its threat: the main-enemy debate

The perception of the North as a major threat to South Korea has dramatically changed since the 1990s as the balance of power between them clearly tipped in favor of the South. One of the key changes in the 1990s was the disintegration of dominant ideas upon which South Korean state identity was built. Integrating forces and material bases that hegemonized and bound together ideas of anticommunism, anti-North, and pro-US began to be seen as socially irrelevant with the collapse of the Soviet Union, normalized diplomatic relations with China and other former communist countries, and the enlarging economic and military gap between two Koreas. People started to update their attitudes toward the North independent of their views toward America. To be anti-American was not necessarily to be pro-North. And even being pro-North was not always unacceptable, as the hegemonized "demonizing" images of the North as a whole were disaggregated into the "bad" North Korean regime and the suppressed "innocent" North Korean people.[23] The social meaning of the North as an entity was neutralized in South Korea.

Deconstruction of the "threatening" image of the North as a hegemonic idea was clearly demonstrated in the so-called *chujŏk* debate.[24] It first became politicized when the South's Ministry of National Defense (MND) published *Defense White Paper 1994*, which revised the "Defense Objectives" from defending "our state from the enemy's [the North's] military attacks" to defending "the nation from external military threats and aggression."[25] Omitting North Korea as the main enemy and replacing it with a more abstract term, "external military threats," provoked a nationwide debate. Facing strong resistance from conservative politicians, military officials, and senior citizens, North Korea was again designated the main enemy of South Korea in *Defense White Paper 1995* a year later.[26] Moreover, MND ordered military officials to strengthen the spiritual training of soldiers and to better prepare for ideological and psychological warfare against the main enemy. This episode seemed to confirm the resilience of the dominant "bad" image of the North as the main threat to South Korean state and society.

The next round of the debate, however, ended up with a quite different outcome. The turning point was the historic inter-Korea Summit between

South Korea's Kim Dae-jung and North Korea's Kim Jong-il in June 2000. This grew out of the "sunshine policy," the signature policy of President Kim in the South, which posited that the threat of war on the Korean Peninsula could be removed through benevolence and active engagement. This approach could reduce fear, mistrust, and hostility between two Koreas and eventually lead to coexistence and coprosperity. To attain this goal, Kim Dae-jung proposed an inter-Korean Summit as the most effective vehicle for this transformation on the peninsula, which contributed to the breakdown of the hegemonic construction based on the dual theme of anti-North and pro-US.

The *chujŏk* debate that followed the summit illustrated this change. South Korea's defense ministry proclaimed that it would not use demonizing and contemptuous terms such as *pukgoe* (Northern devil), *koeroe* (puppet), and *pukhan koeroe chŏngkwŏn* (North Korean puppet regime).[27] Even though this reflected attitudinal changes toward the North that had been observed in Korean civil society earlier in the 1990s, it was a symbolic change of importance. After the summit, the main-enemy concept became politicized again. Progressive lawmakers demanded that Seoul abandon or change the main-enemy concept, calling it an obstacle to inter-Korean reconciliation and cooperation. After intense political debate, in its *Defense White Paper 2000* the South's MND continued using the concept of main enemy but employed much less provocative terms.[28]

Under these circumstances, the publication of *Defense White Paper 2001* attracted widespread attention. At the last minute its release was delayed, even though MND had already printed thousands of copies. The defense minister announced that the White Paper would be published biennially from then on.[29] However, publication of *Defense White Paper 2002* was also postponed, reflecting the sharp conflict between pro-North progressive and anti-North conservative forces. Instead, the Kim Dae-jung administration published the *1998–2002 National Defense Policy*, in which the sensitive main-enemy concept was replaced by less provocative terms.[30] This controversy showed that the South was sharply divided over how to perceive the North and its threat.

A survey in November 2002 showed the dramatic attitudinal change toward the North and its threatening image. To the question of "what do you think is the probability that North Korea will initiate war in the future?" in 2002, 57.9 percent of the respondents answered "not much" (26.5%) or "not at all" (31.4%) while only 32.8 percent said a North Korean attack seemed probable (see Table 5.1). Given the deadly naval clash in June 2002, initiated

**Table 5.1** Views on the probability of North Korea's military attack or provocation (%)

| Question: To what extent do you think North Korea would initiate a war against us? | (1) Highly probable | (2) A little bit | (1) + (2) | (3) Not so much (very low prob.) | (4) Not at all | (3) + (4) | Don't know/ no answer |
|---|---|---|---|---|---|---|---|
| 2001 | 8.0 | 37.6 | 45.6 | 28.3 | 17.6 | 45.9 | 8.5 |
| 2002 | 4.7 | 28.1 | 32.8 | 26.5 | 31.4 | 57.9 | 9.3 |
| Changes | −3.3 | −9.5 | −12.8 | −1.8 | +13.8 | +12 | +0.8 |

*Source*: Gallup Korea, "Nambuk chŏngsang hoedam il-chunyŏn kwallyŏn chosa" [Public opinion survey on the first anniversary of inter-Korea summit], June 8, 2001; Gallup Korea, "Tongile kwanhan kungmin yŏron chosa" [Public opinion survey on reunification], November 2, 2002, <http://www.gallup.co.kr>.

when one of the North's patrol boats fired at a South Korean warship in disputed Yellow Sea waters, these poll results reveal a dramatic change among South Koreans in their perception of the North Korean threat.

This attitudinal change toward the North Korean threat played a key role in the 2002 presidential election. The election of progressive Roh Moo-hyun on December 19 was a clear departure from the past, given the issues favorable to conservative candidate Lee Hoi-chang just days before the vote. These included the capture of a North Korean ship carrying missiles to Yemen in the Arabian Sea on December 9 and North Korea's announcement three days later that it was reactivating nuclear facilities. The rising threat did not, however, automatically prompt more-negative views toward the North and more-positive attitudes toward America. The sudden surge of anti-American sentiment amid increasing tension over North Korea's nuclear program in late 2002 indicates that these two key issues were weighed separately, in contradistinction to the past.

This change in perception of North Korean threat, shown in the main-enemy debates, weakened the connection between anti-North and pro-American attitudes although these two were still interdependent. As South Koreans felt less threatened by the North and its "demonizing" images were deconstructed, an increasing number of people embraced unconventional combinations of attitudes such as pro-US/pro-North as well as anti-US/anti-North stances. Attitudes toward America and those toward the North that had been superimposed, inseparably forming one axis, became much less correlated (see Figure 5.2). This change, however, did not imply a rise of anti-Americanism per se but allowed room for the possibility of being

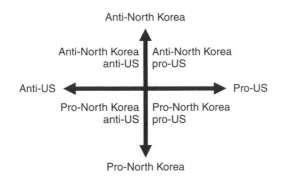

**Figure 5.2** Attitudes toward America and North Korea: two axes
*Source*: By author.

anti-American without being stigmatized as pro-North. In other words, deconstruction of the dominant ideas of anti-North and declining threat perception of the North provided favorable conditions for the emergence and spread of anti-Americanism, although the timing and content of the latter were largely influenced by specific events, political strategies, and public discourse.

In sum, the hegemonized "bad" image of North Korea as *the* enemy and "good" image of America as *the* friend based on *pangong, panbuk, chinmi* were being deconstructed, if not broken down entirely. They had been problematized since the 1980s and the change was accelerated in the early 2000s as the relationship between two Koreas improved. As unquestioned ideas were problematized, behaviors and attitudes that had been hardly imaginable became possible, leaving more room for political entrepreneurs to play with "unthinkable" issues including disputes over North Korea as the main enemy.

# The nuclear North and change of attitude toward the United States

A series of events in the 1990s and early 2000s indicated dramatic changes in South Koreans' perception of the threat posed by the North. Even the unquestionably provocative behaviors of the North did not affect this perception change. Prior to Kim Dae-jung's administration, South Korea's conservative forces had construed military confrontation as confirming evidence of North Korea's "evilness" and "belligerence," as well as the imminence of a large-scale war. This amplified the image of North Korea as the main enemy and of America and USFK as reliable friends. However, even tangible threats and armed conflicts in 2002 a few kilometers from Seoul did not produce the same effects they had in the past. Whereas the June 29 battle in the Yellow Sea left considerable casualties and damage, South Korean tourism to Mount Kumkang in North Korea was not interrupted.[31] Low threat perception made possible what had been "unthinkable" in the past.

By contrast, North Korea's nuclear program and prolonged tensions around it turned out to be frustrating enough to change South Koreans' attitudes again. Soon after admitting in October 2002 that it had a uranium enrichment program, Pyongyang withdrew from the Nuclear Nonproliferation Treaty (NPT) in January 2003. Despites efforts to resolve this nuclear crisis via Six-Party Talks among China, Japan, Russia, the United States, and the two Koreas, the threat perception among South Koreans toward the nuclear North began to grow. Pyongyang's missile tests in July 2006 and nuclear test that October strengthened negative views toward the North.

Although the hegemonized image of "bad" and "belligerent" North Korea had been challenged and deconstructed since the 1990s, South Koreans began to feel fatigued with no tangible change in the North's approach; they took seriously the danger of North Korea's nuclear program. Missile tests and diplomatic failures to denuclearize the North frustrated South Koreans who yearned for the behavioral changes promised under two consecutive progressive administrations via the "sunshine policy." In addition, some believed the North's nuclear weapons drive could make irrelevant the superiority of South Korean conventional military capabilities. Finally, the reconstruction of the "threatening" image of a nuclear North Korea was facilitated by the South's conservative forces trying to galvanize political and ideological support.

A survey result shows this attitudinal change. According to the survey by the East Asia Institute (EAI) and the newspaper *Hankook Ilbo* [Korea Daily News], the share of South Koreans who perceive a security threat has increased dramatically since 2002 (see Figure 5.3). Although less than 20 percent felt insecure toward the North in 2000, by 2006, 63.8 percent had become worried about the security environment. Most people disagreed with North Korea's contention that its nuclear weapons program was for self-defense. Another survey in 2008 showed that approximately 80 percent of respondents would feel threatened if North Korea acquired nuclear weapons.[32]

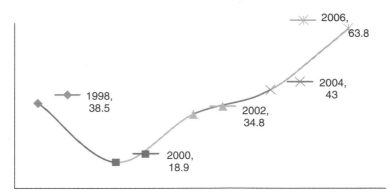

**Figure 5.3** Threat perception regarding South Korea's security environment, 1998–2006 (%)
*Note*: The value represents those who feel "very insecure" and "somewhat insecure"
regarding Korea's security environment.
*Source*: *Hankook Ilbo*, December 18, 2006, p. 5.

As more and more South Koreans grew to feel threatened by the nuclear potential of the North, they again updated their attitudes toward America. A statistical analysis shows that threat perception of the nuclear North has a significant effect on attitudes toward the United States. In order to test the causal relationship, the survey, conducted by EAI, *Joongang Ilbo*, and the Chicago Council on Global Affairs (CCGA) in 2006, is used because it includes key variables such as feelings toward the United States, threat perception of North Korea's nuclear weapons, national pride, ideological orientation, sex, age, income level, and education. Because the dependent variable, attitude toward the United States, is continuous, multiple regression analysis is employed (see Table 5.2).

First, the regression reveals that two variables—age and threat perception—have significant effects on South Koreans' attitudes toward the United States.[33] Second, interestingly, national pride, ideological orientation, and other socioeconomic variables turn out to be insignificant in explaining the dependent variable. Although existing studies expect high levels of national pride and progressive ideological orientation to positively affect anti-American sentiment, both are statistically insignificant. Third, the effect of threat perception is also significant in practical terms. According to the regression analysis, someone who feels very threatened by North Korean nuclear weapons would have more favorable feelings toward the United States by 10 points on a scale of 1–100, compared to a person who feels no threat. A 10-point increase in favorable feelings toward the United States requires a

**Table 5.2** Multiple regression analysis

| Parameter | B | Std. error | t | Sig. |
|---|---|---|---|---|
| Intercept | 33.719 | 7.103 | 4.747 | .000 |
| Age | .366 | .066 | 5.527 | .000 |
| Sex (Male) | .485 | 1.393 | .348 | .728 |
| Sex | 0ª | . | . | . |
| Income | .152 | .422 | .360 | .719 |
| Education (Middle school) | −.039 | 2.889 | −.014 | .989 |
| Education (High school) | .026 | 1.610 | .016 | .987 |
| Education (College and above) | 0ª | . | . | . |
| Threat perception (very much) | 9.578 | 1.973 | 4.854 | .000 |
| Threat perception (somewhat) | 5.758 | 1.799 | 3.202 | .001 |
| Threat perception (no threat) | 0ª | . | . | . |
| National price (very proud) | .329 | 6.293 | .052 | .958 |
| National pride (somewhat) | 1.245 | 6.278 | .198 | .843 |
| National pride (not very proud) | −1.671 | 6.491 | −.257 | .797 |
| National pride (not at all) | 0ª | . | . | . |
| Ideological orientation | .425 | .370 | 1.149 | .251 |

*Note:* Survey data are available at the Korea Social Science Data Archive (Data number: A1-2006-0068). Survey questions: Attitude toward the United States: "Please rate your feelings toward the U.S., with 100 meaning a very warm, favorable feeling, zero meaning a very cold, unfavorable feeling, and 50 meaning not particularly warm or cold"; Threat perception of North Korean nuclear weapons: "How much do you feel threatened if North Korea possesses nuclear weapons?" (1 = feel very threatened; 2 = feel somewhat threatened; 3 = feel no threat; 9 = do not know/no answer); National pride: "How proud are you of being a South Korean?" (1 = very proud; 2 = somewhat proud; 3 = not very proud; 4 = not at all proud; 9 = do not know/no answer); Ideological orientation: "Please rate your ideological orientation, with 10 meaning very conservative, zero meaning very progressive, and five meaning centrist."

a. This parameter is set to zero because it is redundant.

*Source:* EAI, Joongang Ilbo, and CCGA, "Taeoeinsike taehan kungmin yŏron chosa" [Public opinion survey on perception of foreign affairs], June 19, 2006–July 7, 2006.

26-year age difference. In short, this analysis confirms that the more South Koreans feel threatened by the nuclear North, the more favorable they feel toward the United States.

One may argue that the fall in anti-American sentiment was simply caused by the rising North Korean threat. This contention, however, cannot capture a significant aspect of attitudinal changes. Figure 5.4 compares the distribution of attitudes toward America and North Korea in 2006 and those in 2008. Although the surveys are limited and used only as a proxy, the data show that as South Koreans felt more threatened by the North,

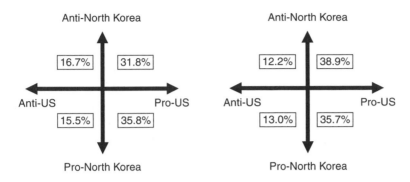

**Figure 5.4** Distribution of attitudes toward America and North Korea, 2006 and 2008

*Note*: Neutral answers are divided and placed equally into each of the four categories.
*Source*: EAI, *Joongang Ilbo*, and CCGA, "Public opinion survey on perception of foreign affairs"; EAI, *Joongang Ilbo*, and CCGA, "Tongasiaŭi sop'ŭt'ŭ p'awŏ" [Global Views 2008: Soft Power in East Asia], January, 2008–March, 2008.

they began to have more pro-American attitudes (from 67.6% in 2006 to 74.6% in 2008), especially compared to their attitudes in 2002. More interesting is that among those who were pro-US, the percentage with negative views of North Korea increased rapidly, from 31.8 in 2006 to 38.9 in 2008. The results also showed that there existed a group of people, one-third of respondents, who had pro-US/pro-North attitudes regardless of the North Korean threat.

The comparison shows that the share of people whose attitudes can be seen as conventional, located on the axis of pro-US/anti-North versus anti-US/pro-North, increased from 47.3 percent in 2006 to 51.9 percent in 2008. At the same time, unconventional combinations of attitudes (pro-US/pro-North and anti-US/anti-North) decreased from 52.5 percent to 47.9 percent. This reveals that as South Koreans feel more insecure with regard to the nuclear North Korea, the two axes—pro-US/anti-US and anti-North/pro-North—become more tightly bound together. As more people began to locate their attitudes on this conventional axis, there was less room for political entrepreneurs to manipulate otherwise more fluid attitudes for their own political goals. These analyses show that the increasing threat perception has considerable effects on the ways in which South Korean attitudes toward America and toward the North interact.

In sum, we can observe that the rising threat from the North has a significant impact on attitudes toward America and pushes two axes—attitudes toward America and those toward North Korea—more closely together.[34]

It is against this backdrop that growing threat perception leaves little room for political entrepreneurs to politicize anti-American sentiment. In 2008, when massive demonstrations occurred in the center of Seoul protesting US beef imports, many people were initially concerned lest this become another wave of anti-Americanism. However, it turned out to be an exaggeration to see this as rising anti-American sentiment, because protesters mainly criticized the South Korean government and officials rather than those in Washington. Given the high probability of this event being a source of renewed anti-Americanism, there was a surprising lack of relevant slogans despite the efforts of anti-American activists. The fall of anti-American sentiment in the late 2000s, however, could be overstated, even misleading: sentiment may be fragile in the absence of continuous threat perception of North Korea.

# Conclusion

The 2000s witnessed the waxing and waning of anti-American sentiment in South Korea. Although widespread anti-American sentiment in 2002 alarmed many decision makers in Seoul and Washington, it seemed clear that anti-Americanism in South Korea, once regarded as being on the rise, was actually on the wane as of the early 2010s. Many scholarly studies and policy briefs provided analyses of anti-Americanism's causes and prescriptions, arguing that it would not disappear easily. However, the fall of anti-American sentiment and growth of positive views toward America since the mid-2000s require us to reexamine this issue through a novel lens.

This chapter shows that the dominant ideas of anti-communism, anti-North, and pro-US have been dismantled since the 1980s. A range of factors, from the Kwangju democratization movement, the collapse of communist countries and normalization with China and the former communist states to the growing gap between the two Koreas in economic and military capabilities, all contributed to the deconstruction of these hegemonic ideas. As one of the three tenets, anticommunism, became largely irrelevant and South Koreans began to reevaluate their attitudes toward the North, the two remaining dominant ideas, though still interdependent, became less covariant than previously. It was in this context that South Koreans began to view North Korea as a lesser threat, which had been unthinkable during the Cold War era.

This changing attitude toward America and North Korea could be observed in the main-enemy debates in the early 2000s and the rising anti-Americanism during the same period. Then, threat perceptions of North Korea among South Koreans were very low, which served as an enabling factor in the sudden rise of anti-Americanism, if not dictating when and how it emerged and with what content. However, by the mid-2000s, when South Koreans felt frustrated with a prolonged nuclear crisis and threatened by the nuclear North, they expressed more positive views of the United States. A growing threat perception also forced the two axes to converge and led more South Koreans to reevaluate their attitudes on the conventional axis of pro-US/anti-North versus anti-US/pro-North. This analysis shows that the extent to which South Korean attitudes toward the North and toward America are correlated is heavily influenced by threat perception toward the North, which in turn provides a broader context in which attitudes toward the US-ROK relationship is shaped. In this sense, the new and continuous threat the nuclear North poses is an essential adhesive for an otherwise shaky ROK US relationship.

## Five questions for discussions

1. What is anti-Americanism? Do people hate what the United States does or what the United States represents?
2. In the early 2000s, the rise of anti-Americanism around the globe was observed. What do you think are the main sources of this rise?
3. What factors can explain the rise and fall of anti-Americanism in South Korea?
4. Why did South Koreans feel less threatened by North Korea in the 1990s and early 2000s and why have they felt more threatened since the mid-2000s?
5. What kind of US foreign policies do you think can help to reduce anti-Americanism and why is such an effort important?

# Notes

1 The author wishes to thank Byung-Kook Kim, Mike Robinson, Shin-Kap Han, Ian Lustick, Rogers Smith, Han-Wool Jeong, Tim Rich, Zhiqun Zhu, and an anonymous reviewer for their constructive comments on earlier versions at various stages. He is also grateful to Stephanie Dickinson for her assistance in statistical analyses. An earlier version of this chapter was published as Heon Joo Jung, "The Rise and Fall of Anti-American Sentiment in South Korea: Deconstructing Hegemonic Ideas and Threat Perception," *Asian Survey* 50:5 (September/October 2010): 946–64, © 2010 by the Regents of the University of California.

2 Katharine H. S. Moon, "Citizen Power in Korean-American Relations," in *Korean Attitudes toward the United States: Changing Dynamics*, ed. David I. Steinberg (New York: M. E. Sharpe, 2005), p. 233.

3 David I. Steinberg, ed. *Korean Attitudes Toward the United States: Changing Dynamics* (New York: M. E. Sharpe, 2005); Derek J. Mitchell, ed. *Strategy and Sentiment: South Korean Views of the United States and the U.S.-ROK Alliance* (Washington, DC: CSIS, 2004); Eric V. Larson, Norman D. Levin, Seonhae Baik, and Bogdan Savych, "Ambivalent Allies? A Study of South Korean Attitudes toward the U.S.," TR-141-SRF (Santa Monica, CA: RAND Corporation, March 2004).

4 One of the rare exceptions includes Youngshik Bong and Katherine H. S. Moon, "Rethinking Young Anti-Americanism in South Korea," in *The Anti-American Century,* ed. Ivan Krastev and Alan McPherson (Budapest and New York: Central European University Press, 2007).

5 Nae-Young Lee and Han Wool Jeong, "Fluctuating Anti-Americanism and the Korea-U.S. Alliance," *International Studies Review* 5:2 (October 2004): 23–40.

6 Pew Research Center, "Obama More Popular Abroad Than at Home, Global Image of U.S. Continues to Benefit: 22-Nation Pew Global Attitudes Survey," June 17, 2010.

7 This naval clash took place when two North Korean naval vessels crossed the Yellow Sea border and opened fire at a South Korean naval vessel on June 29, 2002. South Korean navy returned fire and forced North Korean vessels to retreat across the border. It resulted in the deaths of 6 and injuries of 18 South Korean sailors, and sinking of a South Korean patrol boat while a North Korean ship was severely damaged and more than 30 North Korean sailors were dead or wounded. See *Donga Ilbo,* July 1, 2002, 1.

8 Peter J. Katzenstein and Robert O. Keohane, eds. *Anti-Americanisms in World Politics* (Ithaca: Cornell University Press, 2007); Ivan Krastev and Alan McPherson, eds. *The Anti-American Century* (Budapest and New York: Central European University Press, 2007).

9 Chung-in Moon, "Between *Banmi* (Anti-Americanism) and *Sungmi* (Worship of the United States): Dynamics of Changing U.S. Images in South Korea," in *Korean Attitudes,* ed. Steinberg, pp. 139–52; Seung-Hwan Kim, "Anti-Americanism in Korea," *The Washington Quarterly* 26:1 (Winter 2002): 109–22; Katherine H. S. Moon, "Korean Nationalism, Anti-Americanism, and Democratic Consolidation," in *Korea's Democratization,* ed. Samuel S. Kim (New York: Cambridge University Press, 2003), pp. 135–57; Chaibong Hahm, "Anti-Americanism, Korean Style," in *Korean Attitudes,* ed. Steinberg, pp. 220–30; Chang Hun Oh and Celeste Arrington, "Democratization and Changing Anti-American Sentiments in South Korea," *Asian Survey* 47:2 (March/April 2007): 327–50; Gi-Wook Shin, "South Korean Anti-Americanism: A Comparative Perspective," *Asian Survey* 36:8 (August 1996): 787–803.

10 Kim, "Anti-Americanism in Korea," 116.

11 Mitchell, *Strategy and Sentiment*; Kim, "Anti-Americanism in Korea," 113–16.

12 Jinwung Kim, "From 'American Gentlemen' to 'Americans': Changing Perceptions of the United States in South Korea in Recent Years," *Korea Journal* 41:4 (2001): 172–98.

13 Jae-Jung Suh, *Power, Interest, and Identity in Military Alliances* (New York: Palgrave Macmillan, 2007).

14 Stephen M. Walt, *The Origins of Alliance* (Ithaca: Cornell University Press, 1987).

15 Michael N. Barnett, "Identity and Alliance in the Middle East," in *The Culture of National Security: Norms and Identity in World Politics*, ed. Peter J. Katzenstein (New York: Columbia University Press, 1996), p. 401.

16 Jang Jip Choi, "Political Cleavages in South Korea," in *State and Society in Contemporary Korea*, ed. Hagen Koo (Ithaca: Cornell University Press, 1993).

17 Manwoo Lee, "Anti-Americanism and South Korea's Changing Perception of America," in *Alliance Under Tension: The Evolution of South Korean-U.S. Relations*, ed. Manwoo Lee, R. D. McLaurin, and Chung-in Moon (Boulder: Westview Press, 1988).

18 Ibid., p. 10; For 1980 Kwangju massacre and its effect on the image of America, see Gi-Wook Shin, "Marxism, Anti-Americanism, and Democracy in South Korea: An Examination of Nationalist Intellectual Discourse," *Positions: East Asia Cultures Critique* 3:2 (1995): 509–13.

19 Sang-Dawn Lee, *Big Brother, Little Brother: The American Influence on Korean Culture in the Lyndon B. Johnson Years* (Lanham: Lexington Books, 2002), p. 22.

20 SOFA has outlined how the US servicemen in South Korea should be treated since its signing in 1966. It has been argued that US-ROK SOFA is heavily in favor of America compared with similar pacts the United States signed with other countries such as Japan and Germany.

21 Youngshik Bong, "Yongmi: Pragmatic Anti-Americanism in South Korea," *Brown Journal of World Affairs* 10:2 (Spring/Summer 2004): 153–66.

22 Pew Research Center, "Obama More Popular Abroad Than at Home," 1.

23 Roland Bleiker, *Divided Korea: Toward a Culture of Reconciliation* (Minneapolis: University of Minnesota Press, 2005), p. 4.

24 Suh, *Power, Interest, and Identity*, pp. 196–8; Chung Min Lee, "Revamping the Korean-American Alliance: New Political Forces, Paradigms, and Proses and Missions," in *Korean Attitudes*, ed. Steinberg, p. 162, fn. 16.

25 The Ministry of National Defense, *Defense White Paper 1994* (Seoul: MND, 1995), <http://www.mnd.go.kr>; *Chosun Ilbo*, September 11, 1995, 2; *Defense White Paper* had been issued every year since 1988 and the controversial concept appeared amid high tension over North Korea's nuclear weapons program.

26 The Ministry of National Defense, *Defense White Paper 1995* (Seoul: MND, 1996).

27 *Donga Ilbo*, July 1, 2000, 1.

28 *Chosun Ilbo*, June, 23, 2000, 9; December 5, 2000, 2.

29 *Donga Ilbo*, November 23, 2001, 2.

30 *Joongang Ilbo* [Central Daily News], December 28, 2002, 2.

31 *Donga Ilbo*, June 30, 2002, 5.

32 EAI, *Joongang Ilbo*, and CCGA, "Taeoeinsike taehan kungmin yŏron chosa" [Public opinion survey on perception of foreign affairs], June 19, 2006–July 7, 2006.

33 In a similar analysis, Chae finds no significant relationship between threat perception and attitudes toward the United States. This difference may result from the fact that Chae uses survey data of South Korean college students in 2004. See Haesook Chae, "Understanding

Anti-Americanism among South Korean College Students," *International Journal of Korean Studies* 9:1 (Fall/Winter 2005).

34  It is noteworthy that after the sinking of the *Cheonan*, a South Korean warship, near the disputed Yellow Sea waters on March 26, 2010, the Lee Myung-bak administration reportedly considered resuming the use of the main-enemy concept that had not been used since the mid-2000s. On May 20, 2010, South Korean government officially announced that the *Cheonan* was sunk by a torpedo attack from a North Korean submarine. In response to this latest threat, South Korea conducted one of the largest joint military exercises with the United States in July. Moreover, the North's shelling of Yeonpyeong Island of the South on November 23, 2010 that caused civilian casualties strengthened pro-American and anti-North sentiments among South Koreans.

# Selected bibliography

Barnett, Michael N. "Identity and Alliance in the Middle East," in *The Culture of National Security: Norms and Identity in World Politics*, ed. Peter J. Katzenstein (New York: Columbia University Press, 1996), p. 401.

Bleiker, Roland. *Divided Korea: Toward a Culture of Reconciliation* (Minneapolis: University of Minnesota Press, 2005), p. 4.

Bong, Youngshik. "Yongmi: Pragmatic Anti-Americanism in South Korea." *Brown Journal of World Affairs* 10:2 (Spring/Summer 2004): 153–66.

Bong, Youngshik and Katharine H. S. Moon. "Rethinking Young Anti-Americanism in South Korea," in *The Anti-American Century*, ed. Ivan Krastev and Alan McPherson (Budapest: Central European University Press, 2007).

Cha, Victor D. "Anti-Americanism and the U.S. Role in Inter-Korean Relations," in *Korean Attitudes toward the United States: Changing Dynamics*, ed. David I. Steinberg (New York: M. E. Sharpe, 2005), pp. 116–38.

Chae, Haesook. "Understanding Anti-Americanism among South Korean College Students." *International Journal of Korean Studies* 9:1 (Fall/Winter 2005).

Hahm, Chaibong. "Anti-Americanism, Korean Style," in *Korean Attitudes toward the United States: Changing Dynamics*, ed. David I. Steinberg (New York: M. E. Sharpe, 2005), pp. 220–30.

Katzenstein, Peter J. and Robert O. Keohane, eds. *Anti-Americanisms in World Politics* (Ithaca, NY: Cornell University Press, 2007).

Kim, Jinwung. "From 'American Gentlemen' to 'Americans': Changing Perceptions of the United States in South Korea in Recent Years." *Korea Journal* 41:4 (2001): 172–98.

Kim, Seung-Hwan. "Anti-Americanism in Korea." *Washington Quarterly* 26:1 (Winter 2002): 109–22.

Krastev, Ivan and Alan McPherson, eds. *The Anti-American Century* (Budapest: Central European University Press, 2007).

Larson, Eric V., Norman D. Levin, Seonhae Baik, and Bogdan Savych. "Ambivalent Allies? A Study of South Korean Attitudes toward the U.S." TR-141-SRF (Santa Monica, CA: RAND Corporation, March 2004).

Lee, Manwoo. "Anti-Americanism and South Korea's Changing Perception of America," in *Alliance under Tension: The Evolution of South Korean-U.S. Relations*, ed. Manwoo Lee, R. D. McLaurin, and Chung-in Moon (Boulder: Westview Press, 1988).

Lee, Nae-Young and Han Wool Jeong. "Fluctuating Anti-Americanism and the Korea-U.S. Alliance." *International Studies Review* 5:2 (October 2004): 23–40.

Lee, Sang-Dawn. *Big Brother, Little Brother: The American Influence on Korean Culture in the Lyndon B. Johnson Years* (Lanham, MD.: Lexington Books, 2002).

Mitchell, Derek J., ed. *Strategy and Sentiment: South Korean Views of the United States and the U.S.-ROK Alliance* (Washington, D.C.: Center for Strategic and International Studies, 2004).

Moon, Katharine H. S. "Korean Nationalism, Anti-Americanism, and Democratic Consolidation," in *Korea's Democratization*, ed. Samuel S. Kim (New York: Cambridge University Press, 2003), pp. 135–57.

Oh, Chang Hun and Celeste Arrington. "Democratization and Changing Anti-American Sentiments in South Korea." *Asian Survey* 47:2 (March/April 2007): 327–50.

Shin, Gi-Wook. "Marxism, Anti-Americanism, and Democracy in South Korea: An Examination of Nationalist Intellectual Discourse." *Positions: East Asia Cultures Critique* 3:2 (1995): 509–13.

—. "South Korean Anti-Americanism: A Comparative Perspective." *Asian Survey* 36:8 (August 1996): 787–803.

Snyder, Scott. "The Role of the Media and the U.S.-ROK Relationship," in *Strategy and Sentiment: South Korean Views of the United States and the U.S.-ROK Alliance*, ed. Derek J. Mitchell (Washington, D.C.: Center for Strategic and International Studies, 2004), pp. 73–81.

Steinberg, David I., ed. *Korean Attitudes toward the United States: Changing Dynamics* (New York: M. E. Sharpe, 2005).

Suh, Jae-Jung. *Power, Interest, and Identity in Military Alliances* (New York: Palgrave Macmillan, 2007).

# Part II
## The New Political Economy

# 6

# Economic Globalization, Democracy, and Social Protection: Welfare Capitalism in East Asia

Mason M. S. Kim

## Introduction

Sociocultural factors derived from Confucianism is one of the reasons why East Asian states have long been regarded as "less developed" welfare regimes.[1] A more fundamental reason is the belief that the increase of public expenditures on social welfare would undermine economic growth.[2] Indeed, throughout the entire period of industrialization in East Asia, state-led economic strategies based on the export of labor-intensive manufactures put a priority on labor market flexibility and made governments and enterprises strongly resistant to any forms of social welfare expansion that would increase labor costs.[3] At the same time, export-oriented economic strategies provided incentives to expand access to public education, since human capital formation is crucial for economic development.[4] Thus, social policy in East Asia was not intended for social protection or redistribution itself, but rather for the promotion of economic productivity. The financial crisis in 1997 became a momentous watershed, not only because the crisis hit the region hard and wide but also because it led East Asian countries to pay more attention to the importance of social protection.

However, East Asian countries have shown significant variation in social policy methods in coping with challenges arising from economic globalization in general and the financial crisis in particular. Indeed, despite their similar export-oriented economic strategies and similar challenges from globalization, East Asian welfare states have been showing a diverging pattern of social security programs. While social insurance schemes and social assistance programs are central to the welfare state in Japan, South Korea (henceforth, Korea), and Taiwan, compulsory savings schemes play a leading role in Singapore, Malaysia and, to a lesser degree, Hong Kong. China and Thailand are between the two groups, combining both social insurance and individual savings schemes supplemented by modest public assistance programs.[5] In response to pressures of economic globalization, why have some countries expanded social insurance and public assistance programs that are expected to have redistributive functions, whereas others have chosen to develop compulsory individual savings schemes that emphasize the self-help principle? What drives East Asian welfare states to adopt different types of social security institutions in the globalization era?

This study examines the institutional divergence of East Asian welfare states. First, we argue that there is a diverging pattern of East Asian welfare states corresponding to the extent to which their financial systems are vulnerable to foreign investment and international economic conditions. A country with a financial system that is highly exposed to foreign investors tends to adopt and expand "efficient" and "competitive" welfarism (i.e., individual savings schemes and a minimum spending of government revenue on social security). By contrast, "redistributive" and "compensatory" welfarism (i.e., governments' social spending and social insurance programs) is more prominent in countries where financial market is less vulnerable to foreign investors' interests.

Second, the impact of a set of preexisting economic conditions on the institutional divergence is significant, but it does not necessarily mean that the economic-welfare nexus is automatic. Political factors should be considered as mediators because, as many studies have found, democratic regimes tend to respond to economic globalization by supporting "redistributive" and "compensatory" welfare programs. This political-welfare linkage is based on the observation that political competition makes politicians more sensitive to the demand of the people for redistribution and social protection and, accordingly, democratic states are more likely to approve social policies that might require the financial responsibility of the government.[6]

# Divergence of East Asian welfare states

## Productivist welfare capitalism in East Asia

Political and economic changes that occurred in the developing world throughout the 1980s and 1990s called scholarly attention to welfare state development in East Asia, Latin America, and Eastern Europe.[7] Such interest was based on the prevailing view that welfare state development requires industrialization and/or democratization as a necessary condition.[8] However, despite their remarkable economic development over the past decades, East Asian states have not been among those spending a considerable portion of revenues on social security and welfare.

As seen in Figure 6.1, East Asian nations spend much less on social policy as a whole than countries of the Organization for Economic Cooperation and Development (OECD) as well as Eastern European and Latin American countries between the 1970s and the 2000s. While the average level of social expenditure ranged from 8.7 percent to 18.9 percent of GDP and 37.6 percent to 52.6 percent of total government spending in other parts of the world, East Asia spent only 2.1 percent and 9.9 percent, respectively. This trend has prompted scholars to raise a question of why welfare spending in East Asia is not as significant as in other regions.

Earlier studies that examined East Asian welfare states can be divided into two groups. One group of scholars focused on the cultural factor derived from Confucianism. Dixon and Kim and others attributed the most remarkable difference between Western and Asian approaches to social welfare to Confucian "familialism" and its aversion to public social services.[9] The other group focused on the role of the state. Of particular importance was Deyo's argument that East Asia's social welfare is used as a policy tool for economic development. According to him, social policy in East Asia—particularly

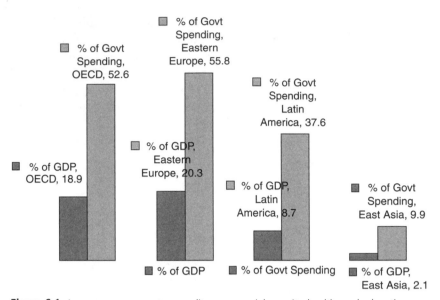

**Figure 6.1** Average government expenditures on social security, health, and education (1970s to 2000s)

*Notes*: a. Average central government expenditures (except China that includes both central and local governments). b. Selected countries: OECD–19 countries, Eastern Europe–6 countries, Latin America–14 countries, and East Asia–11 countries. c. Data for OECD and Latin America cover the 1973–2000 period. d. Data for Eastern Europe are from the 1990s only. e. Data for East Asia are from the 1980s to the 2000s.
*Source*: IMF, *Government Finance Statistics*; Asian Development Bank, *Key Indicators*. Data are also from various national statistical yearbooks.

Japan, Korea, Taiwan, Hong Kong, and Singapore—was "driven primarily by the requirements and outcomes of economic development policy."[10]

Scholars like Holliday attempted to theorize this pattern, presenting a model called "productivist welfare capitalism."[11] This model is predicated on the claim that, unlike advanced capitalist societies where social welfare generally embodies the successes of social democratic politics, East Asia's social policy is strictly subordinate to the overriding policy objective of economic growth. Unlike OECD, Eastern European, and Latin American countries in which social welfare is by far the biggest spending sector, East Asian states spend substantially more on economic development programs (22.7% of total government spending) and education (14.9%) than on health (5.9%) and social welfare (8.8%) throughout the 1980s–2000s period (see Table 6.1). The expansion of education has featured prominently as a

Table 6.1 Government expenditure on social and economic policies in East Asia as a percentage of total government expenditure

| | Education | | | | Health | | | | Social welfare | | | | Economic affairs | | | |
|---|---|---|---|---|---|---|---|---|---|---|---|---|---|---|---|---|
| | 80s | 90s | 00s | Avg. | 80s | 90s | 00s | Avg. | 80s | 90s | 00s | Avg. | 80s | 90s | 00s | Avg. |
| China | 11.5 | 14.9 | 13.3 | **13.2** | 9.7 | 4.8 | 3.1 | **5.9** | 1.7 | 2.3 | 7.9 | **4.0** | 53.8 | 41.0 | 30.1 | **41.6** |
| Japan | 9.3 | 15.0 | 12.4 | **12.2** | 13.6 | 20.6 | 22.2 | **18.8** | 18.8 | 13.6 | 23.6 | **20.3** | 7.4 | 8.9 | 9.3 | **8.5** |
| Korea | 18.5 | 17.9 | 14.9 | **17.1** | 1.7 | 1.1 | 0.8 | **1.2** | 7.0 | 9.6 | 17.1 | **11.2** | 19.3 | 22.0 | 21.9 | **21.1** |
| Taiwan | 5.2 | 9.2 | 11.5 | **8.6** | 1.6 | 0.6 | 1.3 | **1.1** | 15.2 | 22.3 | 23.8 | **20.5** | 16.7 | 18.4 | 19.2 | **18.1** |
| Hong Kong | 16.4 | 17.9 | 20.7 | **18.3** | 8.4 | 11.3 | 12.4 | **10.7** | 5.3 | 7.4 | 12.4 | **8.3** | 22.3 | 18.6 | 18.6 | **19.8** |
| Singapore | 17.0 | 20.3 | 20.9 | **19.4** | 4.8 | 6.4 | 6.0 | **5.7** | 1.2 | 3.3 | 5.8 | **3.4** | 16.6 | 13.4 | 13.1 | **14.3** |
| Indonesia | 11.7 | 8.7 | 4.3 | **8.2** | 3.3 | 2.5 | 1.4 | **2.4** | . | 5.9 | 6.5 | **6.2** | 60.9 | 22.7 | 5.7 | **29.8** |
| Malaysia | 16.7 | 20.5 | 23.3 | **20.2** | 4.3 | 5.8 | 6.8 | **5.6** | 4.0 | 3.7 | 4.2 | **3.9** | 24.7 | 19.9 | 18.3 | **21.0** |
| Philippines | 12.4 | 15.6 | 15.3 | **14.5** | 3.7 | 2.7 | 1.8 | **2.7** | 0.8 | 2.3 | 5.0 | **2.7** | 27.6 | 24.0 | 22.6 | **24.7** |
| Thailand | 19.6 | 20.9 | 21.0 | **20.5** | 5.4 | 7.1 | 8.3 | **6.9** | 3.7 | 3.5 | 8.5 | **5.2** | 16.0 | 29.8 | 20.6 | **22.1** |
| Vietnam | . | 11.7 | 12.5 | **12.1** | . | 4.2 | 3.3 | **3.7** | . | 12.4 | 9.0 | **10.7** | . | 27.2 | 29.9 | **28.6** |
| Average | 13.8 | 15.7 | 15.5 | **14.9** | 5.6 | 6.1 | 6.1 | **5.9** | 6.4 | 8.3 | 11.3 | **8.8** | 26.5 | 22.4 | 19.0 | **22.7** |

Source: IMF, Government Finance Statistics; World Bank, World Development Indicators; Asian Development Bank, Key Indicators; Statistical Bureau, Japan Statistical Yearbook; National Bureau of Statistics, Statistical Yearbook of China; General Statistical Office, Statistical Yearbook of Vietnam.

leading socioeconomic policy thrust, while welfare benefits have remained marginal in East Asia. This pattern of government spending reflects the productivist strategy of social policy. As seen in the expansion of primary education and vocational training, the role of human capital formation has been the center of the productivist welfare state in East Asia. Of course, increases of welfare programs occurred sometimes, but it was only when closely linked to economic productivity. Again, this pattern of social spending was deeply rooted in the export-oriented developmental strategy.

However, there are also significant differences among East Asian states that challenge the widespread perception that East Asian welfare regimes are broadly homogeneous. If we go over government expenditure statistics carefully, we can find that there exists an intriguing combination of deep-rooted similarities and emerging differences (Table 6.1). Economy-related affairs and education account for the largest portion of government expenditures in all these countries except for Japan and Taiwan. Also, most East Asian countries have increased social welfare expenditures since the 1990s, but the speed and magnitude of the increase vary across the region.

Some countries like China, Singapore, Indonesia, Malaysia, Philippines, and Thailand display a substantial increase of social welfare and health spending, but the overall amount is much less than 10 percent of total government spending. In the case of Singapore and Malaysia, reluctance to the expansion of social welfare continues to exist, coupled with rather strong support for public education and vocational training. To date, there remains a strong resistance to unemployment benefits of any sort and a tightly conditioned system of social assistance.[12] Others like Japan, Korea, Taiwan, and Hong Kong have consistently increased government expenditure on social welfare. Moreover, since the 1980s the level of social welfare spending has been considerably higher in these countries. Nonfinancial indicators also show that their progressive development of social welfare is remarkably impressive. For example, Korea has enacted a series of legislation to consolidate the foundation of social safety net since the 1997 financial crisis.[13] The Korean government had designed the National Pension Scheme (NPS) as a policy tool for capital mobilization in 1972.[14] When the NPS was implemented in 1988, it aimed to cover only large-firm employees and skilled workers, but during the 1990s, the scheme was substantially extended to farmers, fishermen, and the self-employed. Korea adopted an unemployment insurance program in 1995 and extended the benefits to all workers during the 1990s and the 2000s. Moreover, hundreds of social health insurance programs that had been occupationally segregated became unified in a single and nationwide health insurance program in 2000. In addition, a new social assistance system—that is, the Minimum Living Standard Guarantee (MLSG)—was enacted for those who were in need but not entitled to public assistance under the previous scheme. The type of institutional development of social welfare in Japan, Korea, and Taiwan seems to be a significant leap away from the traditional mode of productivist welfare states.[15]

## Measuring the divergence of East Asian productivist welfare states

How can we measure the extent of institutional changes in productivist welfarism? Government expenditure is frequently and sometimes solely used as a "consistent" and "comparative" *measurement* of welfare state development because data of government spending on social welfare is easily available and also useful for a clear comparison. However, a critical problem occurs if we solely rely on expenditure data as a proxy of social welfare development. In general, the public expenditure approach assumes that the financial source of social welfare is the government account only.[16] But the establishment of a social safety net is also an issue of how to design the institutional platform. Indeed, a number of less-developed countries frequently use less resource-intensive methods rather than relying on government spending in constructing their social security system.[17] Challenging the orthodoxy of welfare state studies, Estevez-Abe emphasizes institutional formats and "functional equivalents" like active labor market policies and argues that "we cannot understand the real scope and full nature of social protection in a country unless we look at the way different policy tools are combined."[18] In this sense, it is required to approach the issue of measuring welfare state development with not only government spending on social welfare but also institutional formats of social protection. By doing so, we can see how political leaders transform the seemingly zero-sum relationship between economic growth and social welfare into a positive-sum game.

Indeed, to cope with five broad social insecurities—that is old age, health, unemployment, work injuries, and poverty, East Asian productivist welfare states have sought social policies in combination with varied sets of welfare instruments. It means different choices have been made by governments during the process of institutional selection of social welfare. Table 6.2 compares the distinctive characteristics of the main welfare institutions chosen in East Asia. First, regarding institutional formats of social protection, we can think of two broad patterns: social insurance schemes and individual

**Table 6.2** Social security institutions in East Asia

|  | Old age | Health | Unemployment | Work injury |
|---|---|---|---|---|
| **Japan** | Social insurance | Social insurance | Social insurance | Social insurance |
| **Korea** | Social insurance | Social insurance | Social insurance | Social insurance |
| **Taiwan** | Social insurance | Social insurance | Social insurance | Social insurance |
| **P. R. China** | Social insurance & savings scheme | Social insurance & savings scheme | Social insurance | Social insurance & employer liability |
| **Hong Kong** | Allowance & savings scheme | Public assistance | Public assistance | Employer liability |
| **Singapore** | Savings scheme | Savings scheme | n/a | Employer liability |
| **Thailand** | Social insurance & savings scheme | Social insurance | Social insurance | Employer liability |
| **Malaysia** | Saving scheme | Saving scheme | n/a | Employer liability |
| **Indonesia** | Savings scheme | Social insurance | n/a | Social insurance |
| **Philippines** | Social insurance | Social insurance | n/a | Social insurance |
| **Vietnam** | Social insurance | Social insurance | Social insurance | Social insurance |

*Source*: US Social Security Administration, *Social Security Programs Throughout the World* (http://www.ssa.gov/policy/docs/progdesc/ssptw/index.html). This table does not specify institutional forms of the "poverty" area because social assistance is largely determined by the amount of government expenditure.

savings schemes. In general, savings-based systems assume more individual responsibility than social insurance systems in which risks and financial resources are pooled across contributors and generations. Of course, both social insurance and individual savings do not necessitate governments to bear financial responsibility directly. However, because insurers receive different amounts of benefits depending on their income level, governments supporting social insurance schemes are not free from financial responsibility for any possible deficits in public insurance funds.

By contrast, individual savings schemes are based on the principle of defined contribution (DC), which means eligible citizens only receive what they have saved during their working life. In this system, all the financial responsibilities belong to each individual and his or her employer, and therefore, governments do not have any financial burdens. However, the problem is that individual savings schemes are less effective in protecting those who do not have enough income to save during their working life.

Second, public assistance and allowance programs require more state involvement in their financing and regulation, though both are generally regarded as welfare instruments with an emphasis on selectivity. With respect to social assistance, the government is clearly the major, sometimes even the only, agency to provide basic social protection for the people in need.[19]

Unlike most other scholarly works that employ spending data exclusively, we use both "government spending on social welfare" and "institutional platforms" as indicators of welfare state development. Based upon these two dimensions, two sets of welfare trajectories can be presented: (a) social insurance schemes associated with relatively higher government spending and (b) individual savings scheme underlying minimal government involvement. As often examined in the literature on globalization and welfare state development, the former can be referred to as a "redistribution-oriented" welfare system, while the latter can be defined as an "efficiency-oriented" welfare system. To see if there is truly systematic variation in East Asian productivist welfare states, we created a redistribution-efficiency index of productivist welfarism, including 11 East Asian states in the sample.[20] The findings are illustrated in Figure 6.2.

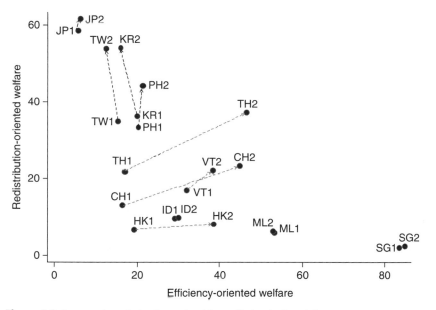

**Figure 6.2** Systematic variation in productivist welfarism in East Asia

*Note:* The number 1 indicates an average value for the period of 1987–92, while the number 2 is for the period of 2003–7.

*Source:* Asian Development Bank, *Key Indicators*; IMF, *Government Finance Statistics*; OECD, *Social Expenditure Database* (SOCX); US Social Security Administration, *Social Security Programs Throughout the World: Asia and the Pacific* (http://www.ssa.gov/policy/docs/progdesc/ssptw/2008-2009/asia/index.html); and other various domestic statistical yearbooks.

The moves of scatter plots in Figure 6.2 demonstrate how productivist welfare states in East Asia have evolved over time from the late 1980s to the late 2000s. The figure suggests that there is a clear pattern of divergence between redistribution-oriented welfarism and efficiency-oriented welfarism, although some of them have not changed drastically.

Japan maintains its tradition of redistributive social policy, thus spending relatively more on social welfare than others. Korea, Taiwan, and, to a lesser extent, the Philippines are another set of cases that have moved in the same line, showing a drastic change to the direction of "redistribution." Just like Korea, Taiwan has witnessed a remarkable development of social welfare, especially since the Democratic Progressive Party (DPP) came to power in 2000. In particular, the increase of social welfare budget and the adoption of newly designed national health insurance system have led all the citizens to access to health care that is financed by the pooled health insurance fund.[21]

In contrast, those countries with compulsory savings schemes also continue to demonstrate their tradition of minimum government spending and efficiency-oriented welfare system. Singapore's Central Provident Fund (CPF), Malaysia's Employee Provident Fund (EPF), and Indonesia's JAMSOTEK, are all compulsory savings programs that were launched to encourage savings while constructing "self-help based" social security net. Hong Kong also adopted a savings-based scheme, Mandatory Provident Fund (MPF), in the early 2000s with the hope to reduce government budget deficits.[22] Countries like China, Thailand, and Vietnam have pursued a dual strategy that embraces both social insurance and savings schemes with moderate government spending on social welfare. For example, the basic pension insurance system designed by the Chinese government consists of three different pillars of financing. The mandatory first pillar includes two tiers— social pool and individual account. Employers contribute 17 percent of the employee's wages to social pool and 3 percent to individual accounts, while employees save 8 percent of wage in their individual account as a compulsory retirement plan. The second and third pillars are voluntary schemes associated with fully funded individual accounts.[23] This type of multi-pillar system represents China's call for balancing between redistribution and efficiency in constructing a social security system. The social pool in the first pillar aims at poverty reduction and compensatory redistribution, while individual savings play an important role in all of the three pillars. In a similar way, Thailand has also developed social insurance and provident fund schemes as its dualist strategy.

# Explaining the divergence

Given the variation in productivist welfare states, how can we understand what has affected the institutional divergence of social welfare in East Asia? What induces the growth of social insurance programs and social spending? What is behind the expansion of savings schemes that call for individuals to bear financial burdens for social security? There are a series of competing theories of social policy that explain the origin and development of state welfare in advanced industrial countries. However, there are few coherent theories and empirical tests that shed light on non-Western, especially productivist, social contexts.[24] Hence, it is desirable to test contending theories against the East Asian context and thereby pave the way for further research on the productivist welfare state.

## Financial system

The concept of productivist welfare capitalism is a product of "developmental state" where government authorities have acted to guide markets and modulate the competitive process of industrialization.[25] Needless to say, the financial system is one of the most critical terrains of this strategy. It is also the channel through which the impact of globalization is transmitted. Indeed, the developmental strategy and its corresponding productivist welfare programs are largely influenced by the structure of financial market—particularly the extent and form of their reliance on foreign investment.

According to Zysman, there are two broad types of financial market: "bank credit-based" and "capital market-based."[26] In the credit-based financial system, banks play a leading role in mobilizing savings, allocating capital, overseeing the investment decisions of corporate managers, and providing risk management vehicles; while in the market-based financial system, capital markets share center stage with banks, thus getting society's savings to firms, exerting corporate control, and easing risk management.[27] East Asian states are not an exception. During the industrialization period, they intervened intensively the operations of the financial markets, either directing credit to some industries through banks or creating a more attractive financial market for foreign investment.

In a capital market-based financial system, the economies highly rely on funds they raise from individual investors in stock markets. For instance, Singapore and Hong Kong successfully built an entrepôt economy, where international capital was given better infrastructure with less state regulation, and later they became key centers of international finance, commerce, and trade in East Asia. They are greatly constrained by those shareholders who generally seek to maximize the short-term profits of business. Particularly, in a system where the accumulation of capital in the form of FDI and portfolio investment is significant, both inside and outside pressures bearing down upon states constrain the range of policy choices available to decision makers. Welfare spending is regarded as a fiscal burden that cannot be sustained in the competitive global economy and, accordingly, productivist welfare states with this type of financial system are more likely to adopt the "efficiency-oriented" welfare system—for example, provident funds in Singapore, Hong Kong, and Malaysia—that is conducive to the construction of a social security system with less fiscal burden. Thus, the higher the ratio of market capitalization and foreign investment, the higher the possibility of an individual savings-based social security system.

In contrast, the economies with a credit-based financial system are not as vulnerable to the interests of shareholders as their market-based counterparts. Because bank loans are relatively "patient" and "less liquid," investments tend to be long-term oriented. Financial intermediaries like banks enable both the government and companies to establish long-term development strategies and invest in industries without being overly concerned with short-run fluctuations in the capital market. The main concern is rather to uphold cooperative links between industries and banks so that the government can maintain its full-employment strategy.[28] Japan, Korea, and Taiwan are typical examples of this approach. The aim of their economic policy was to build a vertical integrated economy where some of the strategic industries and banking sectors were controlled by a strong state. In this system, social insurance schemes are more likely to be chosen since a long-term economic growth strategy requires solid social safety nets as a compensatory bumper to protect skilled labors from possible social risks.[29]

Table 6.3 provides empirical evidence that there is a close correlation between financial system and welfare institution. According to Demirguc-Kunt and Levine, Singapore, Hong Kong, and Malaysia—which have pursued savings-based welfare institutions—are classified as countries with a higher level of market-based financial system (FSI ≥ 1).[30] By contrast, social insurance-based programs are more popular and important among countries with the bank-based financial system (FSI <1). To be sure, the financial system is one of the conditions that influenced policymakers' exploration of options for welfare institution between social insurance and individual savings. While East Asian economies share many characteristics, they differ in

**Table 6.3** Financial structure and welfare institution in East Asia

| Countries | Financial Structure Index (FSI) | Welfare institution |
|---|---|---|
| Japan | − 0.19 | |
| Philippines | 0.71 | Redistribution-oriented |
| Korea | 0.89 | |
| Indonesia | − 0.50 | Mixed |
| Thailand | 0.39 | |
| Singapore | 1.18 | |
| Hong Kong | 2.10 | Efficiency-oriented |
| Malaysia | 2.93 | |

*Note*: Adapted from Demirguc-Kunt & Levine (2001). The FSI is constructed in terms of size, activity, and efficiency of the financial system to gauge the relative importance of banks and capital markets. The index is an average of three indicator series, including the ratio of market capitalization to bank assets (size), the ratio of total value of equities traded to bank credit (activity), and total value of equities traded/GDP multiplied by overhead cost (efficiency).

their economic policy strategies, depending on how they have constructed their financial systems. This difference in turn influenced their social policy trajectories.

# Economic globalization

Whereas financial system is an important factor in shaping institutional divergence of productivist welfarism in East Asia, the expansion of divergence is driven by economic globalization. Regarding the interaction between globalization and social protection regime, there has been a continuing debate over whether governments respond to globalization with social policies that are oriented more toward compensating "economic losers" (redistribution) or cutting costs (efficiency) to maintain market competitiveness.[31] The efficiency approach argues that, in Western capitalist societies, "redistributive" welfare provision was taken for granted as basic social rights during the 1960s and 1970s, when prosperity, equality, and full employment seemed to be in perfect harmony. However, responding to the increasing integration of international markets, economic efficiency— which used to be a secondary concern—has emerged as one of top agenda items since the 1980s. Because generous welfare benefits were thought to bring about an increase of nonwage labor costs and government budget deficits and as a result endanger market competitiveness, pressures to cut welfare programs became intense.[32] In Western developed countries, many welfare reforms aiming at improving economic efficiency is believed to have adversely affected traditional practices of social service and progressive systems of taxation for distributional equality.

Proponents of the efficiency hypothesis argue that redistributive welfarism has faced serious challenges from market competition and economic efficiency. This is particularly true in the case of East Asia where FDI inflow—one of the indicators of economic globalization—has been an important reason for industrialization. Among others, FDI has been so important in Hong Kong, Singapore, Malaysia, and China since the 1980s. Thus, East Asia—except Japan, Korea, and Taiwan—is relatively more vulnerable than OECD countries to pressures of economic globalization due to their intense need for foreign capital. Not surprisingly, those countries with a higher level of FDI inflow have a capital market-based financial system, and globalization drives them to have little choice but to expand individual savings schemes as a nationwide social security system.

However, an effort has been made to advance a counterargument regarding the impact of globalization. The compensation perspective also acknowledges the presence of constraint effects from economic globalization, but it focuses on the political condition that presses policymakers to protect and compensate those who lose jobs or fall in difficult situations as a consequence of globalization.[33] According to the compensation school, policy makers understand that social instability resulting from increased exposure to the international market could endanger the neoliberal economic model as well as their own positions in government. Governments respond to pressures by putting into place various social policy programs to protect the domestic economy, prevent political unrest, and raise the skills of the labor force and make it more competitive in the international market.[34] Supported by a substantial body of empirical research, the compensation hypothesis appears to have stronger explanatory power.

It is dubious whether the experiences of Western democracies can explain the divergence of East Asian welfare institutions. Universalistic social insurance programs in Japan, Korea, and Taiwan challenge the proposition advocated by those who argue that strong and encompassing trade unions and social democratic political parties are a necessary precondition of redistributive and compensatory welfarism, because labor unions or left-wing parties in these countries have been insignificant in shaping and expanding social protection programs. Therefore, it is logical to assume that political factors other than ideological terrains motivated the expansion of "redistributive" productivist welfarism in Japan, Korea, Taiwan, and the Philippines.

## Regime type

The impact of economic globalization does not always result in welfare retrenchment and budget cut. In the case of East Asia, the incentive to expand entitlements and services of redistributive welfare was significantly strengthened by the advent of democracy.[35] In general, politicians in democratic regimes allocate greater government revenue to social welfare than authoritarian counterparts. Of course, democracy is not the only condition for welfare state development. Many social welfare policies in the developing world including East Asia were implemented under authoritarian regimes (e.g., China).[36] But there is no doubt that democratic governments have greater incentives to respond to demands for social security and services than authoritarian regimes. The growing divergence of productivist welfare capitalism in East Asia is an outcome of democratic political processes.

In most East Asian countries, only a few in the population had benefited from social protection programs, leaving vulnerable sections of the population such as unskilled workers and farmers outside the system. But democratization has led political leaders to be more attentive to the constituents' demands. Consequently, democratic states became more likely to approve social policies that might impose financial burdens on the government.[37] This observation is more robust when political parties are under pressure from electoral competition. Such competition provides incentives for politicians to act in the interests of voters by expanding redistribution-oriented welfare programs, that is social insurance and public assistance.

The development of Korea's National Pension Scheme (NPS) well illustrates this point. In the early 1970s, the shift of economic dynamism from light industries to heavy and chemical industries led the Korean government to seek mobilization of a substantial amount of domestic capital. Although the implement was postponed due to the first oil shock, the NPS emerged again in 1987 as a political instrument to gain votes in the presidential election. Since Korea was democratized in 1987, electoral competitions have played a leading role in the expansion of social insurance programs which are popular electoral pledges. As seen in Figure 6.3, the rates of popular votes between presidential election candidates were quite close. The margin has been about 6 to 8 percent, except the 2007 election. Democratic transition and subsequent electoral competition play a critical role in the expansion of social security programs in Korea. Although the initial design and implementation of the NPS was carried out under the conservative governments

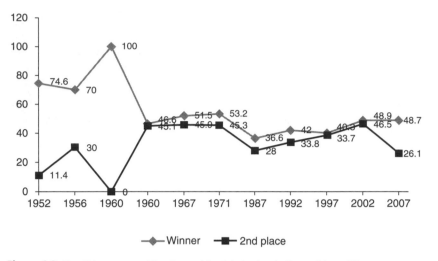

**Figure 6.3** Candidate competition in presidential election in Korea (Votes %)
*Source*: National Election Commission, Korea (http://www.nec.go.kr).

of Roh Tae-woo (1988–92) and Kim Young-sam (1993–7) in the middle of electoral competition, it was largely unequal in coverage. A substantial expansion of the NPS has been made under the Kim Dae-Jung (1998–2002) and Roh Mu-hyun (2003–7) governments in the wake of the 1997 Asian financial crisis that brought Korea to the brink of insolvency pushing the unemployment rate up to about 7 percent and increasing income inequality and poverty.

At the other extreme, by contrast, is Singapore. Even though there are some democratic procedures, Singapore is obviously less than democratic.[38] Singapore has open and competitive elections, but electoral and other rules tend to be political tools for securing the hegemony of the People's Action Party (PAP)—the ruling party. The government placed clear limits on the opposition and labor unions. Civil society activities are also tightly restrained. The index of democratic governance in Figure 6.4 illustrates the contrasting feature between democratic countries and authoritarian regimes with some electoral constraints. While Japan, Taiwan, Korea have highly developed democratic institutions up to almost the highest level (20), Singapore, Malaysia, Thailand, and transition economies have been staying at a lower level of democratic governance ranging from 3 to 10. As expected, the former countries implement social insurance-based welfare system, whereas the latter countries adopt individual savings-based schemes.

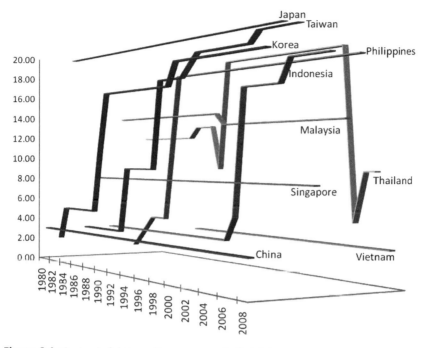

**Figure 6.4** The level of democratic governance in East Asia

*Source*: Polity IV Database (http://www.cidcm.umd.edu/inscr/polity/index.htm).

Noteworthy in this analysis is the case of China where both social insurance and individual savings schemes have been developed simultaneously (see Figure 6.2). Since the late 1970s, China has become the fastest-growing major economy in world, and its high level of FDI and trade is one of the reasons for its economic success. This is a good reason to lead us to expect that such international transactions could influence the design and development of the Chinese welfare institutions in an "efficiency-oriented" way. Indeed, China's market-oriented economic reforms in 1978 came along with severe criticism of the socialist egalitarian welfare policies such as lifelong employment, free healthcare, and generous pension benefits that are all regarded as an impediment to the promotion of economic productivity and work incentives. The egalitarian welfare system was finally removed and, the individual family now has to bear the financial burden for protecting against social risks such as unemployment, disease, and poverty. Healthcare expenditures and effectiveness have declined dramatically since the 1980s, and the healthcare system has undergone de facto privatization.[39]

However, political challenge arose from employed urban workers to the Chinese Communist Party (CCP), undermining the party's legitimacy. Between 1996 and 2001, the total number of officially reported labor disputes increased more than tripled. In a survey conducted in 1997, Chinese workers replied that the most common reasons of disputes and protests were delayed pay (61%), welfare benefits (58%), and job contracts (18%).[40] Protests by jobless workers became a commonplace occurrence, especially in rust-belt areas that used to be the old industrial centers. To deal with social unrests and political instability, China's policymakers began introducing new laws and plans—for example, the 1994 Labor Law that specified minimum wage, working hours, pensions, and unemployment insurance. Since then, China has taken a distinct course that expands social insurance-based welfare institutions on the one hand and liberalizes labor markets on the other hand. In sum, the dismantling of egalitarian socialism in the 1980s and the 1990s led the contemporary Chinese welfare regime to reveal a dualist trajectory including both welfare retrenchment and welfare expansion. Needless to say, the major function of this dualist strategy is to support market-oriented economic reform through mitigating social tensions.

# Conclusion

Is there systemic variation in the productivist welfare regime in East Asia? If so, what is the driving force behind the variation? This chapter has attempted to answer these questions by focusing on the impact of economic globalization and political liberalization on the traditional developmental economic and social policies in East Asia. As many studies show East Asian economies have long benefited from state-led developmental strategies, and the traditional pattern of welfare states was also shaped in this economic context. Social policy in East Asia was embarked on by governments for economic growth and political legitimization.

The acceleration of globalization with increasingly competitive international markets put constraints on governments' social policy options. Particularly, the 1997 financial crisis generated great pressures for retrenchment of social policy commitments. In response to challenges from globalization and demographic changes, a divergence of distinct clusters has increased since the mid-1990s. Among others, this study highlights financial system and political regime type as two mediating factors that direct the development of welfare institutions toward being either "redistribution-oriented" or "efficiency-oriented." First, those productivist countries with more open financial markets are likely to choose and expand individual savings schemes as an institutional backbone of social security. Second, electoral competitions in democratic regimes produce political incentives that politicians cannot ignore. In sum, financial structure, globalization, and domestic political conditions are the major factors driving the institutional divergence of East Asian productivist welfarism, and this trend is likely to continue in the near future.

## Five questions for discussions

1. What is "developmental state"? Discuss the post-World War II context in which the East Asian "developmental state" emerged.
2. What are the main characteristics of the East Asian welfare regime? Why is welfare in East Asia defined as "productivist"? How is it different from welfare regimes of the Western world?
3. How can we explain the divergence of productivist welfare states in East Asia? What conditions generate variation?
4. What are the differences between the Korean welfare system and Singapore's approach to social policy? Why are they different?
5. Welfare policy in China exhibits traits of both redistributive and efficient thrusts. Why does China's welfare system reveal a dualist format?

# Notes

1  John Dixon and Hung-Shik Kim, *Social Welfare in Asia* (London: Croom Helm, 1985).

2  The welfare state refers to state measures for meeting key welfare needs, often confined to old-age pension, health, education, social assistance, social services. Christopher Pierson, *Beyond the Welfare State? The New Political Economy of Welfare* (Pennsylvania State University Press, 2007), p. 10.

3  East Asia's newly industrialized countries (NICs) are well-known as the "developmental state" model. It means that a state plays a strategic role in economic development with a competent bureaucracy that is given sufficient policy measures to take initiatives and operate effectively. For a general study of the developmental state, see Chalmers Johnson, *MITI and the Japanese Economic Miracle: The Growth of Industrial Policy, 1925–1975* (Stanford University Press, 1982); and Robert Wade, *Governing the Market: Economic Theory and the Role of Government in East Asian Industrialization* (Princeton University Press, 1990).

4  Stephan Haggard and Robert R. Kaufman, *Development, Democracy, and Welfare States: Latin American, East Asia, and Eastern Europe* (Princeton University Press, 2008), pp. 8–10.

5 Huck-ju Kwon, "The Reform of the Developmental Welfare State in East Asia," *International Journal of Social Welfare* 18 (2009): 12–21.

6 Geoffrey Garrett and David Nickerson, "Globalization, Democratization, and Government Spending in Middle-Income Countries," in *Globalization and the Future of the Welfare State,* ed. Miguel Glatzer and Dietrich Rueschemeyer (University of Pittsburgh Press, 2005), pp. 23–48.

7 Among others, see Evelyne Huber, "Options for Social Policy in Latin America: Neoliberal versus Social Democratic Models," in *Welfare States in Transition,* ed. Gøsta Esping-Andersen (Sage Publications, 1996), pp. 141–91; Robert R. Kaufman and Alex Segura-Ubiergo, "Globalization, Domestic Politics, and Social Spending in Latin America: A Time-Series Cross-Section Analysis, 1973–97," *World Politics* 53 (2001): 553–87; and Alex Segura-Ubiergo, *The Political Economy of the Welfare State in Latin America: Globalization, Democracy, and Development* (Cambridge University Press, 2007).

8 Pierson, *Beyond the Welfare State?* pp. 9–40.

9 Dixon and Kim, *Social Welfare in Asia*; Catherine Jones, "Hong Kong, Singapore, South Korea and Taiwan: Oikonomic Welfare States," *Government and Opposition* 25 (1990): 446–62; Catherine Jones, "Pacific Challenges: Confucian Welfare State," in *New Perspectives on the Welfare State in Europe,* ed. Catherine Jones (New York: Routlege, 1993), pp. 198–217; Elmar Rieger and Stephen Leibfried, "Welfare State Limits to Globalization," *Politics and Society* 26 (1998): 363–90.

10 Frederic C. Deyo, "Political Economy of Social Policy Formation: East Asia's Newly Industrialized Countries," in *States and Development in the Asian Pacific Rim,* ed. Richard P. Appelbaum and Jeffrey Henderson (Sage Publications, 1992), pp. 289–90.

11 Ian Holliday, "Productivist Welfare Capitalism: Social Policy in East Asia," *Political Studies* 48 (2000): 706–23.

12 M. Ramesh and Mukul G. Asher, *Welfare Capitalism in Southeast Asia: Social Security, Health, and Education Policies* (St. Martin's Press, 2000); Ian Holliday and Paul Wilding, eds. *Welfare Capitalism in East Asia: Social Policy in the Tiger Economies* (Palgrave Macmillan, 2003).

13 Huck-ju Kwon, "Welfare Reform and Future Challenges in the Republic of Korea: Beyond the Developmental Welfare State?" *International Social Security Review* 55 (2002): 23–38; Gyu-Jin Hwang, "The Rules of the Game: The Politics of National Pensions in Korea," *Social Policy & Administration* 41 (2007): 132–47.

14 The NPS was postponed due to the oil crisis in the early 1970s and finally implemented in 1988.

15 Huck-ju Kwon, "Welfare Reform and Future Challenges in the Republic of Korea: Beyond the Developmental Welfare State?"; Stein Kuhnle, "Productive Welfare in Korea: Moving towards a European Welfare State Type?" ECPR Joint Sessions of Workshops: The Welfare State—Pros and Cons. Torino, Italy, March 22–27, 2002; M. Ramesh, "Globalization and Social Security Expansion in East Asia," in *States in the Global Economy: Bringing Domestic Institutions Back In,* ed. Linda Weiss (Cambridge University Press, 2003), pp. 83–98; Yeon-Myung Kim, "Beyond East Asian Welfare Productivism in South Korea," *Policy and Politics* 36 (2008): 109–25.

16 Huck-ju Kwon, "Democracy and the Politics of Social Welfare: A Comparative Analysis of Welfare Systems in East Asia," in *The East Asian Welfare Model: Welfare Orientalism and the State*, ed. Roger Goodman, Gordon White, and Huck-ju Kwon (Routledge, 1998).

17 Nita Rudra, "Welfare State in Developing Countries: Unique or Universal?" *Journal of Politics* 69 (2007): 378–96.

18 Margarita Estevez-Abe, *Welfare and Capitalism in Postwar Japan* (Cambridge University Press, 2008), p. 4.

19 Yeun-Wen Ku, "Comparative Welfare Policy Instruments in East Asia," in *Changing Governance and Public Policy in East Asia*, ed. Ka-Ho Mok and Forest Ray (New York: Taylor & Francis, 2009), p. 144.

20 To create the redistribution-efficiency index, I used scales that are constructed from four social policy areas—that is, government spending on social welfare, old-age insurance (or savings), health insurance (or savings), unemployment insurance (or savings). Each policy area was measured in terms of its coverage rate, the scope of eligibility.

21 Ramesh, "Globalization and Social Security Expansion in East Asia."

22 Tung Chee-Hwa, Chief Executive of the Hong Kong SAR, announced several welfare programs in 1997. In terms of the financial needs of older people, he enhanced the Comprehensive Social Security Assistance (CSSA) scheme monthly payment for older claimants by HK$380. He also suggested to change all primary schools from half-day education to whole-day schooling, and introduced a loans program to benefit 50,000 full-time tertiary students. However, the Hong Kong government abandoned its social policy plans all of a sudden when the Asian financial crisis hit the region in 1997. Chak-Kwan Chan, "Managing Welfare in Post-Colonial Hong Kong," in *East Asian Welfare Regimes in Transition: From Confucianism to Globalization*, ed. Alan Walker and Chack-kie Wong (Bristol, UK: The Policy Press, 2005), pp. 95–115.

23 Felix Salditt, Peter Whiteford, and Willem Adema, "Pension Reform in China," *International Social Security Review* 61 (2008): 55.

24 Yeun-Wen Ku and Catherine Jones Finer, "Developments in East Asian Welfare Studies," *Social Policy & Administration* 41 (2007): 115–31.

25 Gordon White, *Developmental States in East Asia* (New York: St. Martin's Press, 1988); Meredith Woo-Cumings, *The Developmental State* (Cornell University Press, 1999).

26 John Zysman, *Governments, Markets, and Growth: Financial Systems and the Politics of Industrial Change* (Cornell University Press, 1983). In comparative institutional studies, the difference in the relative importance of banks and capital markets is a general criterion to draw a distinction between two types of financial system. More recently, similar attempts have been made at classifying systems along similar dimensions like "debt-based vs. equity-based," "intermediated vs. securities-based," and "insider vs. outsider" financial systems.

27 Erik Berglof, "A Note on the Typology of Financial System," in *Comparative Corporate Governance: Essays and Materials*, ed. Klaus J. Hopt and Eddy Wymeersch (New York: Walter de Gruyter, 1997), pp. 151–4.

28 Huber, Evelyn and John D. Stephens, *Development and Crisis of the Welfare State: Parties and Policies in Global Markets* (University of Chicago Press, 2001).

29 Estevez-Abe, Margarita, "The Forgotten Link: The Financial Regulation of Japanese Pension Funds in Comparative Perspective," in *Comparing Welfare Capitalism: Social Policy and Political Economy in Europe, Japan and the USA*, ed. Bernhard Ebbinghaus and Philip Manow (Routledge, 2001), pp. 190–214.

30 Asli Demirguc-Kunt and Ross Levine, *Financial Structure and Economic Growth: A Cross-Country Comparison of Banks, Markets, and Development* (MIT Press, 2001).

31 George Avelino, David S. Brown, and Wendy Hunter, "The Effects of Capital Mobility, Trade Openness, and Democracy on Social Spending in Latin America, 1980–1999," *American Journal of Political Science* 49 (2005): 625–41.

32 Philip Cerny G. and Mark Evans, "New Labour, Globalization, and the Competition State," Working Paper Series 70 (Center for European Studies, Harvard University, 1999); Ramesh Mishra, *Globalization and the Welfare State* (Northampton, MA: Edward Elgar, 1999).

33 The traditional explanation of "compensation" is based on Ruggie's notion of embedded liberalism that governments attempt to neutralize the negative effects of economic openness by increasing spending on social welfare. See John Ruggie, "International Regimes, Transactions and Change: Embedded Liberalism in the Postwar Economic Order," *International Organization* 36 (1982): 379–415.

34 Segura-Ubiergo, *The Political Economy of the Welfare State in Latin America: Globalization, Democracy, and Development*, 8–9.

35 Haggard and Kaufman, *Development, Democracy, and Welfare States: Latin American, East Asia, and Eastern Europe*.

36 Mary Gallagher and Jonathan K. Hanson, "Coalitions, Carrots, and Sticks: Economic Inequality and Authoritarian States," *Political Science & Politics* 42 (2009): 667–72.

37 Paul Pierson, *The New Politics of the Welfare State* (Oxford University Press, 2001).

38 Beng-Huat Chua, "Welfare Developmentalism in Singapore and Malaysia," in *Transforming the Developmental Welfare State in East Asia*, ed. Huck-ju Kwon (Palgrave Macmillan, 2005).

39 Mark Frazier, *Socialist Insecurity: Pensions and the Politics of Uneven Development in China* (Cornell University Press, 2010).

40 Wenfang Tang, *Public Opinion and Political Change in China* (Stanford University Press, 2005), 150.

# Selected bibliography

Ebbinghaus, Bernhard and Philip Manow, eds. *Comparing Welfare Capitalism: Social Policy and Political Economy in Europe, Japan and the USA* (New York: Routledge, 2001).

Esping-Anderson, Gøsta. *The Three Worlds of Welfare Capitalism* (Cambridge: Polity, 1990).

Frazier, Mark. *Socialist Insecurity: Pensions and the Politics of Uneven Development in China* (Ithaca, NY: Cornell University Press, 2010).

Garrett, Geoffrey. *Partisan Politics in the Global Economy* (New York: Cambridge University Press, 1998).

Goodman, Roger and Ito Peng. "The East Asian Welfare States: Peripatetic Learning, Adaptive Change and Nation Building," in *Welfare States in Transition: National Adaptations in Global Economies*, ed. Gøsta Esping-Anderson (Thousand Oaks, CA: Sage Publications, 1996), pp. 192–224.

Haggard, Stephan and Robert R. Kaufman. *Development, Democracy, and Welfare States: Latin America, East Asia, and Eastern Europe* (Princeton, NJ: Princeton University Press, 2008).

Hall, Peter A. and David Soskice, eds. *Varieties of Capitalism: The Institutional Foundations of Comparative Advantage* (New York: Oxford University Press, 2001).

Holliday, Ian. "Productivist Welfare Capitalism: Social Policy in East Asia." *Political Studies* 48 (2000): 706–23.

Holliday, Ian and Paul Wilding, eds. *Welfare Capitalism in East Asia: Social Policy in the Tiger Economies* (New York: Palgrave Macmillan, 2003).

Kwon, Huck-Ju, ed. *Transforming the Developmental Welfare State in East Asia* (New York: Palgrave Macmillan, 2005).

Mares, Isabela and Matthew E. Carnes. "Social Policy in Developing Countries." *Annual Review of Political Science* 12 (2009): 93–113.

Mishra, Ramesh. *Globalizaton and the Welfare State* (Northampton, MA: E. Elgar, 1999).

Ramesh, M. and Mukul G. Asher. *Welfare Capitalism in Southeast Asia: Social Security, Health, and Education Policies* (New York: St. Martin's Press, Inc., 2000).

Rodrik, Dani. "Why Do More Open Economies Have Bigger Government?" *Journal of Political Economy* 106:5 (1998): 997–1032.

Rudra, Nita. *Globalization and the Race to the Bottom in Developing Countries: Who Really Gets Hurt?* (New York: Cambridge University Press, 2008).

Tang, Kwong-Leung. *Social Welfare Development in East Asia* (New York: Palgrave, 2000).

# 7

# East Asia in the Digital Age: National Innovation Strategies of Japan, Taiwan, South Korea, and China

Carin Holroyd and Ken Coates

## Chapter Outline

## Introduction

The development of information and communication technologies has been a central element in national innovation strategies in countries around the world since the early 1990s. The advent of readily available and inexpensive broadband and wireless systems has provided the infrastructure for the digital revolution, the emergence of e-commerce, e-health, e-government, and e-entertainment applications. This chapter reviews the expansion of the digital media sector in the context of national innovation strategies in Japan, Taiwan, South Korea, and China.

National innovation strategies have become the centerpieces of national economic development planning. They emphasize creativity, design, art, and digital mediation. The rapid spread of the Internet, accelerated by the global introduction of wireless systems, has transformed many key economic processes and created diverse commercial opportunities.

The early foundations of the Asian digital economy—the development of the digital infrastructure and hardware—followed fairly traditional models. Japan, followed by Korea and Taiwan, developed globally competitive industrial capacity in the production of semi-conductors, routers, switches, printed circuit boards, liquid crystal displays, and other equipment associated with the computer revolution. East Asian countries performed well in this phase of the new economy, dominating the sector through product and process innovations. By the first years of the twenty-first century, East Asian companies had dominated almost all key elements in digital equipment manufacture, albeit with step-wise shifts in design and manufacturing from Japan to South Korea, Taiwan and now China. South Korea's IT exports are now valued at over US$144 billion and constitute 35 percent of its total exports. Taiwan controls the market for a large number of computer and telecommunication components. Its excellence, even dominance, of the production of component parts—aptly nicknamed Taiwan Inside—is not widely known (see Table 7.1).

Indeed, East Asian digital manufacturing is one of the best illustrations of the effectiveness of national innovation strategies, including the mobilization of government, industry and research to produce economic opportunity and prosperity. The emergence of the region as the dominant player in digital technologies demonstrates that targeted investment, carefully constructed policies, and deliberate and collaborative research engagement can produce substantial economic results.

**Table 7.1** Taiwan's Information and Communications Technology (ICT) global market share, 2008–9

| Netbook PC | 99% | Cable CPE | 95% |
|---|---|---|---|
| Motherboard | 92% | WLAN NIC | 91% |
| Notebook PC | 92% | VoIP router | 75% |
| LCD monitor | 70% | VoIP TA | 70% |
| DSC | 40% | IP phone | 48% |

*Source*: Presentation by Taiwan's Institute for Information Industry, September 2009.

Digital media defies ready definition. One description of the field (by Digital Media Alliance Florida or DMAF) defines digital media as "the creative convergence of digital arts, science, technology and business for human expression, communication, social interaction and education."[1] More specifically, digital media refers to the development, transmission, sale and use of information and content by way of digital technologies. Until the early part of the twenty-first century, commercial attention focused on developing digital capacity, putting computers and other digital tools in as many hands as possible, and improving the technological backbone (security, dependability, maintenance, upgrading, and expansion capacity) of the personal, corporate, national, and international digital systems. Beginning in the early 2000s, the balance shifted from digital technologies to digital content, from tool makers to tool users, with related requirements for changes in national innovation systems.

There are four key elements in the digital economy:

1. **Digital Infrastructure:** The technical backbone of the digital economy consists of the Internet, digital cable services, satellite communications, digital storage systems, mobile communication networks, and new digital broadcasting capabilities.
2. **Digital Management Systems:** Digital material is transmitted through the Internet by way of content management systems, digital bandwidth, intellectual property rights systems, e-commerce payment arrangements, and technologies designed to deliver content over the Internet.
3. **Digital Production and Formatting:** Digital content production consists of the computer animation, audio and visual production, gaming, educational material, mobile applications and services, content management software, and archival and retrieval systems. Creative material is transformed into usable forms by way of digital processing technologies.
4. **Creation:** Content creation involves the work of creative personnel in such diverse fields as entertainment, art, performance, education, and culture.

Digital content creation and production has emerged as one of the fastest growth sectors of the modern economy, producing new companies, jobs and economic opportunity at a rapid pace around the world. An evaluation of the national innovation environments and the specific attention given to digital media of Japan, Taiwan, South Korea, and China illustrate both the growing importance and the uncertain approaches that reflect the uneasy fit of digital media within national innovation systems.

# Japan's national innovation strategy

Japan has long been a proponent of national innovation. The recovery from World War II emerged from a collective commitment to economic growth, a high level of collaboration between government and business, typically described as Japan Inc., and a willingness to explore new industrial and commercial sectors. The country's impressive accomplishments in manufacturing were followed, in the late twentieth century, by efforts in new economic sectors like robotics, nanotechnology, and life sciences. The long struggle to restore economic vitality after the collapse of the Japanese "bubble economy" in the 1990s focused on these new areas, with the government seeking to ensure Japan maintained a position of international economic leadership. A focus on high level performance—more Nobel Prize winners, a sharp increase in the number of patents, more attention to the commercialization of scientific and technological innovations—are seen as fundamental to success in the twenty-first century.

The foundation of this effort, which started in the mid-1990s, was a series of Science and Technology Basic Laws that sought to convert Japan into a "science and technology based nation." The first two plans (1996–2005), with a total investment of ¥17 trillion (approximately US$180 billion), focused on improving scientific research capacity and improving business-university partnerships. The Second Plan (2001–5) called for a major reform of Japan's public research-intensive universities. The national effort included more protection for intellectual property rights, a Council for Science and Technology Policy chaired by the prime minister), and an ambitious plan to produce 30 Nobel Laureates by 2050.[2]

The Third Science and Technology Basic Plan, covering the period 2006–10, promised ¥25 trillion (or about US$254 billion). This strategy focused on the life sciences, information technology, environmental research, and nanotechnology/material science. Secondary priority fields included energy, manufacturing technology, scientific and technological infrastructure, and frontier (space and oceans) science. A strong emphasis on using science and technology to improve the quality of life for Japan's citizens, scientific and technological literacy and an emphasis on the development of commercializable products demonstrated the government's desire to build innovation into the core of Japanese life. Specific elements include promoting science among youth and women, attracting more foreign researchers to Japan, supporting patenting efforts, and continuing to change national universities to make them globally competitive.

Japan made a concerted and sustained commitment to national innovation, particularly under Prime Minister Koizumi. An OECD study (2002) revealed that Japan had the highest rate of Research and Development spending in the OECD (3.12% of GDP against an OECD average of 1.83%) and the highest rate of corporate spending on R&D as well (2.32% against 1.17%). The new Japanese economy was clearly intended to be built around science and technology. With billions of dollars available to support the initiative, Japan saw a major expansion of its S&T capacity, major reforms of its national universities, more international connections and improved competitiveness. The country worked, even through a prolonged recession, to enhance its capacity in nanotechnology, biotechnology, information technology and the health sciences, focusing on building the capacity to transform laboratory discoveries into viable commercial products and services.

Ministry of Economy, Trade and Industry (METI)'s Science and Technology Policy Committee launched its work on Japan's Fourth Science and Technology Basic Plan 2011–17 in 2009. The effort focused on narrowing the list of priorities and producing more specific targets. The new strategy retained its emphasis on energy, with additional commitments to environmental technologies. The plan identified the need to attract more foreign researchers, especially from China and Korea and collaborate more with other nations (particularly in Asia). More generally, the plan called for a greater connection between S&T planning and the social, environmental, and economic needs of Japan, with science and technology touted as the best means of addressing these concerns.[3]

Due to Japan's use of culture as a government tool during and before World War II, the Japanese government did little to promote Japanese cultural products and ideas until the mid-1980s. Gradually Japan's relations with its Asian neighbors improved and at the same time Japanese television dramas, music, games, and anime began to develop a global audience. The government began to realize that these multimedia and culture-related industries were extremely lucrative. It began by subsidizing the export of television programs to, mainly, Asian countries and gradually moved toward the promotion of cultural exports more generally. Unfortunately there were soon problems with illegal copying of Japanese materials. In 2002, the Strategic Council on Intellectual Property was formed to promote the growth of all of the various aspects of Japan's intellectual property including the multimedia and culture-related industries.[4]

At the beginning of the twenty-first century, the global popularity of Japanese pop culture soared. Anime, manga, and video games had a particularly global reach but Japanese music, fashion, television, and movies also had tremendous appeal throughout Asia. During 2002–4, a digital content policy was launched as a national strategy. The Strategic Council on Intellectual Property launched its Japan Brand Strategy under the slogan of Cool Japan and the Content Industry Promotion Law was designed and passed.

Companies and researchers remain active in the field, as shown by the recent display of 4G ultra high definition video systems. Conversely, there is evidence that the government has failed to embrace new digital economic models. A March 2010 conflict between online drug stores and national bureaucrats—criticized for being too supportive of the existing drug retailers—has been cited to illustrate the complaint that the Government of Japan does not understand and does not support the full implementation of the digital economy.[5]

Japan's strengths in key digital hardware and software initiatives, particularly in animation, video games, and mobile content, have offset substantial losses in business to South Korea, Taiwan, and China on the manufacturing side. Kyoto has emerged as a major center for the digital arts and animation, challenging Tokyo for national leadership. There, is as well, an extensive digital culture environment in Japan, focusing on digital archiving and digital representations of historical settings and traditional cultural activities. Significantly much of the Japanese software developed is designed almost exclusively for the Japanese market.

The Democratic Party of Japan (DPJ) government, elected in September 2009, has reduced the commercial focus on science and technology. The cabinet proposed substantial (5%) cuts in many key areas of scientific activity, including a freeze on the budget for the Spring 9 synchrotron. The government backed off these initial proposals but only after a strong and harsh reaction from scientists and business leaders.[6] The new administration has now moved forwarded on the Fourth Basic Science and Technology Plan planning process. The top priority is "green innovation" encompassing everything from climate change mitigation (observing, monitoring, and simulating) to green industries and businesses.[7]

Japan appears to be placing its primary emphasis on its Clean-Tech initiatives, clearly believing that this sector has substantial and sustainable growth potential. IT and digital media elements remain important, particularly on the wireless side and with growing attention to health and e-government applications.

# Taiwan's national innovation strategy

Taiwan's industrial and economic structure has been remarkably adaptive and responsive to market pressures. Taiwan responded to the post-World War II environment by emphasizing low cost manufacturing, focusing initially on food and textiles in the 1950s, shifting to labor intensive manufacturing and, in the 1980s, seizing the opportunity to grow in strategic high technology industries, including semiconductors. The strategy paid off. Taiwan developed a global reputation for IT manufacturing and captured a substantial market share of core computing components. The key to its planning success lay with the Institute for Information Industry (Triple I), founded by government in 1979 to help Taiwan develop a world class ICT industry. As of 2010, the Taiwanese ICT industry was the fourth largest in the world (behind the United States, Japan, and South Korea) and Taiwan ranked first worldwide in global market share of twenty ICT high tech components (including motherboards, wireless LAN, analog modems, and LCD monitors), number two in six other items and number three in two others. (Examples are shown in Table 7.1.)

While these strategic investments served Taiwan well, market pressures have been impinging on the industry. Financial margins have shrunk, forcing it to search for higher value added products.[8] Taiwan wishes to shift its current OEM (original equipment manufacturer) and ODM (original design manufacturer) arrangements and become an OBM (original brand manufacturer). Few of Taiwan's major IT companies are known outside the country, save for Acer. Companies, therefore, have little direct connection to consumers, with Taiwan's firms serving other manufacturers rather than creating new products and services of their own. The national challenge is to assist domestic industries, which are mainly small and medium-sized enterprises, to become solution providers and technological leaders. As a Canadian government report on Taiwan indicated, "Recognizing Taiwan's weaknesses on both ends of the industrial development spectrum—innovative R&D and branding, Taiwan's government stresses the importance of controlling the whole product/service life cycle from idea through production to consumption."[9] It now supports the development of IT applications and is encouraging expanded activity in such fields as automobiles, travel (intelligent infrastructure), health care and medical devices, and environmental technologies, particularly photovoltaic devices.

The Taiwanese government has also launched "Brand Taiwan" to assist in corporate branding initiatives. This work is orchestrated by the Ministry of Economic Affairs, and its Department of Industrial Technology and Industrial Technology Research Institute (ITRI), and the National Science Council (NSC), which manages the S&T budget for the country. The NSC collaborates with the Science and Technology Advisory Group on the preparation of four-year policy statements. The main policy statement is summarized as *$2 trillion* (which refers to an emphasis on Taiwan's current success areas of semiconductors and display panels) and *Two Stars* (which describes programs for future success in which biotechnology and digital content have been thus identified).

While much of Taiwan's efforts have focused on traditional areas, there is a fast-growing recognition of the importance of digital media. In the information technology field, the government has had a series of multi-year projects, including:

- e-Taiwan (2002–7) (focusing on information technology)
- m-Taiwan (2005 on) (focusing on mobile technologies)
- u-Taiwan (2008 on) (focusing on ubiquitous computing)

Beginning in 2002, the government also began to highlight the digital content industry. After a few years, Taiwan decided to focus on animation, games, archiving, and e-learning. Much of Taiwan's hardware manufacturing may move to Mainland China, so it needs to be sure there is an industry to support employment in Taiwan. It would like to be the digital content leader for the Chinese world, now the second largest language group on the Internet.

Taiwan's emphasis on digital content emerged with the Enhance Digital Content Industry Promotion Plan, 2002–7, and developed logically into a more comprehensive Digital Content Industry Promotion Plan, launched in 2008. It has made major investments in digital architecture—the m-Taiwan initiative is comprehensive in scale and impact—and has followed that with the active promotion of e-commerce and digital content. The development of Taipei Wireless City, Nankang Software Park, Southern Software Park, Kaohsiung Cyber City, and Taichung Software Park are tangible illustrations of the high priority assigned to the area. Taiwan has perhaps the best-developed digital media components of a national innovation strategy and clearly sees the sector as pivotal to its economic success.[10] The Institute for Information Industry has maintained a high profile through the last three decades, building connections from manufacturing through to social media. The development of a clearly articulated Intelligent Taiwan strategy is not, as in many countries, a late addition to the science and technology file but rather a considered and logical outgrowth of earlier initiatives.

The government of Taiwan has provided considered and engaged leadership to the digital content initiatives. There has been a strong commitment to IT-related education, with substantial emphasis on design and content creation. Government investments specifically focused on digital content have helped spur development, as has the leadership of the Digital Content Industry Promotion Office within the Ministry of Economic Affairs. The active development of digital content industry promotion, digital content institutes, digital content market promotion, e-learning, and digital archives demonstrates Taiwan's comprehensive approach to the sector. Taiwan seeks to enhance its presence in animation, gaming, education, audio-visual, mobile content delivery and digital publication, and anticipates solid and sustained growth in the area. In particular, it promotes its digital content sector aggressively in Asia and further afield, realizing the global appeal and impact of Asian digital content.

# South Korea's national innovation strategy

The state has long been the leader in defining Korea's economic priorities and investments. Throughout the 1960s and 1970s, the government collaborated with the *chaebol* or family-owned industrial conglomerates (e.g., Hyundai, Samsung, and Daewoo) on the identification of areas of opportunity for the country, which lacked natural resources, sponsored little research, and had an underdeveloped university system. Most of the economic activity involved either imitative work or serving as suppliers for US and Japanese firms. Research activity expanded slowly, prodded and shaped by government.[11] South Korea expanded its research presence dramatically; in 2005, it spent 3 percent of its GDP on research and development, with 75 percent of the funding provided by the private sector. Much of the development in S&T capability has been internal. Foreign companies and foreign direct investment have played a lesser role than, for example, in China. Korean nationalism—and foreign firms' concerns about state interference, has made growth in this sector largely Korean-focused.

The foundation for South Korea's S&T policy lies in the Basic Research Promotion Law of 1989, which sought to improve university research and produce more scientists. The law specifically encouraged the development of more science and engineering research centers.[12] The president leads the National Science and Technology Council, which sets science and technology policy which is then coordinated and implemented by the Ministry of Science and Technology (MOST). South Korea launched a Highly Advanced Nation Project (HAN, also called G-7), designed to make it an elite S&T nation. The plan focused on several areas of product technology (including new drugs and new agrochemicals, development of next generation vehicle technology, and the development of advanced technologies for flat panel displays) and fundamental technologies (including next generation semiconductors and new functional biomaterials). The government invested US$2.7 billion on these projects between 1982 and 1995.[13]

The government refined its strategy in 1999, announcing the 21st Century Frontier R&D National Project, which focused on Korea's competitive situation, improving the quality of life for people, and developing core and leading edge technologies. The government established Biotech 2000 with the goal of achieving technological competitiveness in the field by 2010. A rapid rise in the number of biotech firms suggested that the effort had had considerable impact. MOST also selected projects in superconductivity technologies, biotechnology, information technology, conventional industrial technologies, and environmental technologies, each funded at close to US$100 million for ten years.[14]

South Korea's investments appeared to work, although only a few of the developments are known outside Asia. The country has made particular inroads into the crucial Chinese market and has made less of an effort to cultivate Western industrial nations. It is now ranked 15th globally in scientific publications, has the top broadband infrastructure in the world, has the highest annual growth in US patents and the 6th highest rate of research and development investment.[15] Private industry is a major player, contributing 75 percent of total Research and Development funding, with the *chaebol* more open and international than in the past and with a surge of small- and medium-sized companies in non-*chaebol* dominated sectors like biotech and computer games. Equally important, the country has produced a technically literate and highly skilled population.

South Korea's science and technology sector has its challenges. It has moved quickly without, some observers claim, enough attention to global developments. The *chaebol* play a very dominant a role in the Korean economy. Government involvement has been complex and widely dispersed across government agencies; in science and technology development and promotion, particularly the relationship between the main two ministries the Ministry of Science and Technology (MOST) and Ministry of Commerce, Industry and Energy (MOCIE) and 16 other ministries bear some responsibility for science and technology. More generally, as one observer argued, "the culture of hard work, deference and consensus that enabled Korea to prosper in the 1960s and 1970s may be, in part at least, an obstacle to innovation in the decades to come."[16]

South Korea is not short of big dreams and ambitious plans when it comes to science and technology, including digital media elements. Recent initiatives include U-Korea (Ubiquitous Korea), a strategy designed to develop a digitally rich e-government system and the Korean IT industry's desire to make South Korea an international software powerhouse through the promotion of open source operating systems.[17] The government is also creating the Incheon Free Economic Zone (IFEZ) in the city of Songdo, 40 kilometres from Seoul. The goal is to attract both foreign and domestic companies to the IFEZ and develop the area as a high technology business hub for northeast Asia, with a special focus on ubiquitous communications.[18] Most significant, perhaps, is the massive Digital Media City initiative underway in Sangam-dong, near Seoul, which promises to bring together researchers, companies, and digital content creators in one of the most impressive physical settings in the country.

South Korea has been a world leader in the social and commercial aspects of digital media and has been among the earliest adopters in the world in terms of e-commerce models, social networking, and digital convergence.[19] South Korea's Asian popular culture developments have tracked and facilitated expansion in animation and gaming, with Korean companies and creators using strong national markets as a launching pad into East Asia. It is a world leader in multi-player online games, attracting hundreds of thousands of users, and many site developers. Particularly popular are the new "freemium" sites, which provide basic services for free (thereby attracting players) and offering special game accelerators or other information for additional cost. The much-used game StarCraft initially had close to half of its purchasers from South Korea. Korean-made and hosted multi-player games, including Fly for Fun and Silkroad Online, the latter of which offers a game based on seventh-century AD trade connections between Asia and Europe and which has been extremely popular around the world.

South Korea's efforts to promote digital media and information technology originated in 1987 with legislation on "Informization Promotion," which focused primarily in the development of network infrastructure. The build-out continued in other years, up to the point where South Korea has one of the best broadband and wireless services in the world. The creation of such organizations as KADO (Digital Opportunity), Korea Information

Security Agency, and the Korea Internet Safety Commission demonstrated the government's growing commitment. The investments on infrastructure far outstripped national commitments to digital content production and commercialization—following a familiar global pattern—but the enthusiasm of Korean youth for new technologies provided a ready market for content providers and offered an underpinning for the rapid emergence of a digital media industry.

Two Korean economists summarized the country's emphasis on the sector succinctly:

> It is a very strategic and efficient policy for Korea, a small country with few natural resources, to develop information and communication technology (ICT) as an alternative source of development. The surprisingly rapid development of the ICT industry is a result of long term and optimal R&D investment and also due to the national uniqueness of this industry field. Specially, the fast diffusion of super-highway internet has enabled the advanced foundation for this industry. With the development of ICT, a new type of industry has emerged. The digital content industry has enjoyed the benefits of the ICT industry development and has . . . distinct characteristics compared to traditional industries.[20]

# The PRC's national innovation strategies

China's rapid emergence as a manufacturing superpower has shielded awareness of the country's emergence as a formidable presence in science and technology.[21] China clearly understands that science and technology have the potential to bring substantial economic and social benefits. Its commitment, wrote one analysis, is "the most ambitious program of research investment since John F. Kennedy embarked on the moon race."[22]

China's goal is to move beyond its manufacturing base and to find economic opportunities that will lead the country beyond its existing low-wage manufacturing base and into a level of permanent international competitiveness. Indeed, as Yifei Sun has argued, the performance of China's national innovation system is one of the more compelling illustrations of the power and ability of state governments to direct and sustain economic transition.[23] A series of scientific strategies, reaching back into the 1950s, established the foundation for China's modern science programs. Much of the momentum was lost during the Cultural Revolution, and what scientific research was being conducted had weak connections to industry.

Major reforms began in the 1970s, under the direction of Deng Xiaoping. China made major investments in academic research and training, and a solid commitment to basic science. The emphasis in government activities shifted from military to civilian priorities, with academics encouraged to cooperate more fully with industry. The "Decision on Reforms of the Science and Technology System" (1985) accelerated the process, spurring greater industrial competitiveness. The initial effort did not work very well, and China continued to lag well behind other Asian nations in innovation and research. Major initiatives continued, however. China launched the "863 Program" in 1987, focusing on automation, biotechnology, energy, information technology, lasers, new materials, and space technologies, with the important innovation that applicants had to bid for funding rather than having the funding assigned to the specific laboratories or projects.[24] It even launched spin-off ventures, called the "China Torch Program," to encourage the development of new companies and high-technology clusters near Beijing University and Tsinghua University.

An aggressive marriage of S&T and commercialization commenced in the 1990s. The Decision on Accelerating Scientific and Technological Development (1995) and the Decision to Further Reform the S&T System during the Ninth Five Year Plan (1996), changed the Chinese development paradigm by reducing state control over industrial activity, expanding commercial activity, and placing a greater emphasis on industry-based research. Perhaps the most significant change in China's national innovation system is the attitude toward R&D and innovation. During the pre-reform era, technology and innovation were in the public domain, whereas after the reform, technologies began to be viewed by an increasing number of governmental leaders and entrepreneurs as valuable commodities, whose value is determined by the market. It is also increasingly realized that intellectual property rights should be protected in order to promote innovation for the benefit of economic development.

The effort continues in 2006, with the establishment of the Medium to Long Term Plan for the Development of Science and Technology (MLP), a 15-year science and technology development initiative which highlighted eleven broad national needs areas and eight areas of cutting-edge technology including biotech, IT, new materials, advanced manufacturing, advanced energy, marine technologies, lasers and aerospace, and four new large research programs in nanoscience, growth and reproduction, protein research, and quantum modulation research. The MLP targeted the development of "indigenous" or homegrown innovation and a lessening of the country's dependence on foreign technology.[25] Following patterns developed in other East Asian countries, the MLP emphasized funding for basic research, the creation of high tech zones, expanding the scientific base in the country, expanding the university system and bringing China's intellectual property laws in line with other leading nations.[26]

The Chinese initiative worked, contributing to the remarkable expansion of the national economy. The innovation effort continues to be slowed by significant issues, however, ranging from the dominance of government research laboratories, the distance between academic research and commercialization, and the continued reliance on the government to target sectors and lead investment. Government priorities, more than entrepreneurial insight, drive S&T research, a mixing of effort that has slowed economic growth in several high tech sectors.

Still, China has done well on the innovation front. A 2007 OECD report on China's national innovation acknowledged the contributions of government policy and indicated that China could well play a major global role in extending the innovation economy.[27] The report concluded by suggesting that China had to:

- Retain openness to new S&T developments, personnel and companies
- Learn from international best practices in national innovation
- Strengthen internal capabilities in science, technology and innovation
- Re-enforce the country's "absorptive capacities" for new technologies
- Improve the "framework conditions" for innovation, including corporate governance, tax, legal systems, intellectual property rights protection, and a competitive regulatory regime
- Expand attention to the responsiveness of Chinese business, improved management of publicly funded research, expanding innovation beyond research parks
- Reduce the regulatory control by government, placing more emphasis on the framework for innovation rather than the regulation of S&T spending
- Increase the number and improve the quality and efficiency of S&T researchers
- Improve evaluation systems and ensure more effective use of resources
- Develop "competence centers" to entrench and expand the innovation culture and economy in the country.

China's national innovation system has much strength, including the size of its scientific and technological workforce, the early success of several of the country's research parks, and an emerging high tech entrepreneurial sector. Problems remain, including governmental and regulatory barriers, particularly questions about intellectual property rights, the distribution of innovative activity across the country, and the security of business transactions.

Government investment in research and development has grown 20 percent per year since 1999; in 2006, China surpassed Japan as the second largest spender on R&D in the world.[28] Its researchers are having more of an impact than ever before and their top universities are contributing significantly to the advancement of science. They are becoming better known; and China's percentage share of world scientific publications jumped from 2.1 percent in 1995 to 6.5 percent in 2004. The scale of China's commitment is simply stunning in global terms. China has the world's largest scientific workforce, with 6.5 million undergrads and 500,000 postgraduates studying science, medicine, or engineering. The Zhongguancun Science Park, northwest of Beijing, is one of the most formidable impressive engines of the commercialization of science and technology in the world.

As Mei-Chih Hu and John A. Mathews observed:

> China has achieved a remarkable transformation over the past two and a half decades, with superlative rates of growth driven largely by high levels of investment, both domestic and foreign-sourced. Its openness to investment and trade, combined with its latecomer advantages in low costs, has made it the world's export platform for manufactured goods. But the real question for its future concerns its capacity to move from imitation to innovation, since it is through an economy's capacity to sustain innovation that its future prosperity is secured. In China's case . . . the foundations of national innovative capacity are already being laid.[29]

**Table 7.2** Top 10 languages in the Internet (millions of users as of June 30, 2010)

| | |
|---|---|
| English | 537 million |
| **Chinese** | **445 million** |
| Spanish | 153 million |
| **Japanese** | **99 million** |
| Portuguese | 86 million |
| German | 75 million |
| Arabic | 65 million |
| French | 60 million |
| Russian | 60 million |
| **Korean** | **39 million** |
| All others | 351 million |

*Source*: http://www.internetworldstats.com/stats7.htm

China is a relative latecomer to the digital media field, although the rapid adoption of the Internet by Chinese users once the government lifted some of the restrictions and oversight of worldwide web use, resulted in rapid expansion in Internet content production. Indeed, by 2009, Chinese had become the second most common language on the Internet, providing an excellent entre for those countries—China/Hong Kong and Taiwan—with the technological and cultural expertise necessary to tap into the growing demand. (It is worth noting that 38% of English speakers have access to the Internet, largely due to challenges in India, and 28% of Chinese speakers make use of the Internet. For the Japanese, the number soars to 75% of the total, with slightly more than 50% of Koreans having access to the Internet.) The development of digital content and digital media in China was slowed by the need to catch up on the availability of the Internet, a process aided greatly by the expansion of the wireless Internet services in the country. As well, tight restrictions and censorship by the Government of China limited the dynamism of the digital media sector in the country, although creative and sustainable strategies have been developed. Much of China's digital content use is driven through mobile phones and the wireless Internet, generating widespread development of social networking sites and systems and sparking substantial China-centric Internet activity. The Chinese national innovation system, quite the reverse of the situation in Taiwan, has yet to embrace the digital content side of the Internet and wireless economy, with government and business priorities remaining firmly focused on manufacturing and infrastructure investments. See Table 7.2.

This said, Chinese site developers, companies, and consumers have been moving aggressively into the digital media space, actively using international multiplayer games. Happy Farm, a Chinese variant of the popular Farmville program, attracts some 20 million users a day. In contrast to the cooperative and cheerful Farmville, Happy Farm has some particular Chinese innovations, including the ability to raid other people's farms or otherwise engage in disruptive behavior. Chinese website use parallels East Asian patterns, with several globally popular sites (Google, Craigslist, Amazon, and MySpace) in the top 20 most popular sites, but with locally produced content and e-commerce sites (chinadaily, sina, tianya, people, chinavision, china, dict, chinanews, and others) dominating the list. Significantly, the number one site based in China—based on total Internet traffic—is www.made-in-china.com, a business to business website providing global purchasers with ready access to Chinese manufacturers.[30]

China is moving with considerable speed to catch up with other East Asian nations on the infrastructure side, although it faces formidable challenges.

The largest cities are competitive with other regional urban areas, but rural areas remain poorly served. The government has emphasized IT development for over a decade, and the past five years has seen a sharp spike in Internet usage and digital content development. The global Chinese diaspora provides a ready and substantially wealth market for Chinese digital content, just as the vast and growing Chinese market offers commercial opportunities for Taiwan, Hong Korea, South Korea, and Japan. China continues to wrestle with the intellectual property rights and intellectual freedom issues exemplified by its drawn-out conflict with Google over Internet regulation, putting a break on the evolution of certain aspects of the Internet.

# Insights into innovation in the East Asian digital media

There is global awareness of the current and future importance of the digital media sector, with intense government, commercial, and research interest around the world. There is much less awareness of the rapidly increasing importance of the digital creation and digital content sector—the creative and commercial activities that are capitalizing on the presence and capabilities of the Internet to forge a markedly different innovation environment. The scale and intensity of the digital content revolution has the potential to transform the East Asian economy. Digital content has already emerged as a major economic force in the region, and has the potential to continue expanding. To this point, in East Asia and elsewhere, the creative and content-based elements of the digital economy have been seen as peripheral to the main manufacturing and science-based enterprises that have arisen around the Internet. There is growing evidence, particularly in East Asia that the creative and content portion of the digital economy is expanding at a dramatic pace and may soon emerge as the primary focus for employment and corporate expansion in the digital space.

Digital content is an enormous sector which encompasses everything from computer animation, gaming software, and audio and video content to educational applications, mobile content, content management (searching and archiving). Within this broad range of content possibilities, different countries are emphasizing different areas. Taiwan has decided to focus on computer animation, digital games, archiving, and e-learning. It hopes to leverage its strength in hardware by focusing on hardware-based applications. It would also like to be the digital content leader for the Chinese world, now the second largest language group on the Internet.[31] Japan's strengths are in applications for the mobile Internet, interactive digital gaming and animation, supplementing its earlier and innovative work on digital gaming and mobile Internet. South Korea has caught up with Japan in terms of the quality of its digital manufacturing and digital applications and is poised to be intensely competitive in the coming years. China, for its part, will be largely preoccupied with its global manufacturing and exporting activities and, equally important, the development of digital application and digital content aimed at its domestic market. Importantly, the digital elements will have only a limited impact on Western and global consumers, for a great deal of the work is focused on East Asia.

The emergence of digital creativity and digital content as key elements in the Internet economy presents significant challenges for both the theory and practices of national innovation systems. The sector does not lend itself to easy integration into the policy structures and framework of the existing national innovation strategies, for it taps into a very different set of skills, markets, companies, and policies. The dynamics of trade, investment, regulation, product innovation, competition, and global market shares are markedly different from many industrial and manufacturing sectors. Governments, as a consequence, have faced considerable challenges in shifting attention and resources from the traditional industrial economy to the digital content field.

The creative sector, so central to the success of the digital content industry, has typically been promoted by different and noncommercial agencies of government, celebrated for their contributions to national culture more than economic development. The conceptualizing of national innovation systems has typically sparked questions of creativity and cultural activity as side elements in the construction of regional and national economies, not as central elements. The debates about national innovation have, almost uniformly, been dominated by scientists and manufacturers, not designers, artists, and producers.

There is growing evidence that East Asian states, particularly Taiwan and South Korea, understand the potential of digital content creation and, indeed, see the content enterprise as an integral part of national innovation. Throughout the region, there is a realization that national language and culture need to be represented on the Internet, convincing governments to invest significantly in the creation and retention of digital materials. Across East Asia, led by Japan's formidable presence in animation and video games, countries have recognized the commercial importance of creation-based enterprises, and are finding ways to support the sector, albeit it much less forcefully than other industrial fields, particularly environmental technologies. Growing cultural ties, in popular culture if not in officially sanctioned areas of endeavor, throughout East Asia are likewise creating new and expanding commercial opportunities for Asian-based creators, who have found sizeable markets that rarely extend beyond Asia. The emergence of an Asia-first digital content enterprise has meant that few Western observers are fully aware of developments in the field, leading to an underestimation of the scale, quality, and profitability of the digital media sector.

The rapid and comparatively recent development of the East Asia digital media and digital content sector highlights a series of potential important elements in the evolution of the national innovation economies in the region.

- Digital content is language and culture rich, if not specific, thus producing large and viable national markets with growing regional spill-over.
- The digital content sector is largely East Asian focused and is attracting relatively little attention from Western companies and observers, despite its considerable recent growth and explosive potential. With some exceptions—anime and animation, most of the markets are within East Asia.
- Digital content presents significant challenges for national innovation systems as it requires government and the business sector to coordinate with new and unique enterprises, including cultural producers, artists, and content providers. These companies, in turn, have markedly different entrepreneurial cultures, development profiles, and technology and creative requirements.

National economic development strategies used to be dominated by manufacturing and production industries, with support from the service and facilitating businesses that surround them. Digital content is changing the policy environment, the development profile, and the political requirements dramatically. Even more importantly, the unique elements of digital media, which link infrastructure and content creation and which bridge traditionally disparate economic and entrepreneurial environments have the potential to transform some of the core strategies built into national innovation systems.

South Korea and Taiwan have made major strides in bridging the commercial gaps and incorporating cultural and content production into the policy environment of national innovation. China still lags behind the other economies—although it is more active than typically assumed—largely because the creative and commercial imperatives of digital content production fly in the face of government controls and regulations. Cumulatively, digital media has emerged as a major economic and innovation force in East Asia, and presents a significant challenge for national governments, business associations, and the country as a whole as the world adjusts to a global economy that increasingly highlights cultural production and the commercialization of creativity atop a scientific and technological foundation.

## Five questions for discussions

1. How important are national innovation strategies in the development of twenty-first-century economies?
2. How do you evaluate East Asian nations' performance in the global technological competition? What is the appropriate role for the national government in an economic and creative field like digital content development?
3. Does the success of cultural-based economic activity, like digital content, suggest that East Asia is beginning to develop economic strategies that focus largely on East Asia and are less connected to the rest of the world?
4. Is the East Asian model of state-led economic development the appropriate strategy for the global and highly competitive economy of the twenty-first century?
5. The digital content experience suggests that the leading countries in East Asia have some clear economic advantages in terms of the development of new commercial sectors. If so, what are these advantages? If not, what are the shortcomings of this approach?

# Notes

1 See the definition at http://www.dmaflorida.org/dmaf/digital_media_is.html. In a wonderful example of digital circularity, the DMAF cites the Wikipedia entry, which in turn cites the DMAF information.

2 This section is drawn from Carin Holroyd and Ken Coates, *Innovation Nation: Science and Technology in 21st Century Japan* (London: Palgrave Macmillan, 2007); Carin Holroyd, "Reinventing Japan Inc.: Twenty-First Century Innovation Strategies in Japan," *Prometheus*, Volume 26, Number 1, March 2008.

3 Drawn from the minutes of METI Science and Technology Planning meetings.

4 Nissim Otmazgin, "Japanese Government Support for Cultural Exports," *Kyoto Review of Southeast Asia*, Vol. 4, accessible at http://kyotoreview.cseas,kyoto-u.ac.jp/issue/issue3/article_296_p.html

5 David Meerman Scott, "Japanese bureaucrats crush digital economy innovators," *Huffington Post*, April 2, 2010.

6  "New supercomputer project under fire," *Nikkei Weekly*, December 28, 2009 and January 4, 2010; Paul Guinnessy, "Japan cuts budget while France's rises," *Physics Today*, December 22, 2009.

7  Masuo Aizawa, "Science and Technology Policy for Innovating Japan," Council for Science and Technology Policy, Powerpoint Presentation.

8  Shin-Horng Chen, "Global Production Networks and Information Technology: The Case of Taiwan," *Industry and Innovation*, 9:3 (2002): 249–65.

9  "Taiwan: An S&T Powerhouse at the Crossroads," unpublished background document produced by the Canadian Trade Office in Taipei.

10  Extended briefings provided by the Institute for Information Industry and the Digital Content Industry Promotion Office in September 2009 provided excellent introductions to the shape of current government efforts in the field.

11  Webb, Molly, *Korea: Mass Innovation Comes of Age* (London: Demos, 2007).

12  Eriksson, Soren, "Innovation Policies in South Korea & Taiwan," *Vinnova Analysis*, 2005.

13  National R&D Projects at http://park.org/Korea/Pavilions/PublicPavilions/Government/most/policye2.html

14  Presentation by Jeonwook Cho, Symposium on HTS Cable Application, Kunming, June 24, 2004.

15  Webb, *Korea: Mass Innovation Comes of Age*.

16  Ibid., p. 46.

17  Ibid., p. 8.

18  Incheon Free Economic Zone at http://eng.ifez.go.kr/menu01/background.asp

19  Tomi Ahonen and J. O'Reilly, *Digital Korea* (Futuretext, 2007).

20  D. O. Choi and J. E. Oh, "Efficiency Analysis of the Digital Content Industry in Korea: An Application of Order-m Frontier Mode," Jeong-Dong Lee and Almas Heshmati, *Contributions to Economics Productivity, Efficiency, and Economic Growth in the Asia-Pacific Region* (Physica-Verlag HD, 2009).

21  James Wilsdon and James Kelley, *China: The Next Science Superpower* (London: Demos, 2007), p. 5.

22  Ibid., p. 6.

23  Yiefi Sun, "China's National Innovation System in Transition," *Eurasian Geography and Economics* 43:6 (2002): 476–92.

24  Cong Cao, Richard P. Suttmeier, and Denis Fred Simon, "China's 15-year science and technology plan," *Physics Today*, December 2006, 40.

25  Ibid., 38–9.

26  Ibid., 41.

27  OECD Reviews of Innovation Policy. *China Synthesis Report* (OECD, 2007).

28  James Wilsdon and James Kelley, *China: The Next Science Superpower* (London: Demos, 2007), p. 6.

29  Mei-Chih Hu and John A. Mathews, "China's National Innovative Capacity," *Research Policy* 37 (2008), 1467.

30  Ranking.com provides statistical information on website usage. For the report on China, see http://scripts.ranking.com/data/report_country.aspx

31  Interviews with staff at Taiwan's Digital Content Industry Promotion Office and Institute for Information Industry.

# Selected bibliography

Ahonen, Tomi and J. O'Reilly. *Digital Korea* (Futuretext, 2007).

Cao, Cong, Richard P. Suttmeier, and Denis Fred Simon. "China's 15-year science and technology plan." *Physics Today*, December 2006, 40.

Chen, Shin-Horng. "Global Production Networks and Information Technology: The Case of Taiwan." *Industry and Innovation*, 9:3 (2002): 249–65.

Choi, D. O. and J. E. Oh. "Efficiency Analysis of the Digital Content Industry in Korea. An Application of Order-m Frontier Mode," in Jeong-Dong Lee and Almas Heshmati, *Contributions to Economics Productivity, Efficiency, and Economic Growth in the Asia-Pacific Region* (Physica-Verlag HD, 2009).

Eriksson, Soren. "Innovation Policies in South Korea & Taiwan." *Vinnova Analysis*, 2005.

Holroyd, Carin. "Reinventing Japan Inc.: Twenty-First Century Innovation Strategies in Japan." *Prometheus* 26:1, March 2008.

Holroyd, Carin and Ken Coates. *Innovation Nation: Science and Technology in 21ˢᵗ Century Japan* (London: Palgrave Macmillan, 2007).

Hu, Mei-Chih Hu and John A. Mathews. "China's National Innovative Capacity." *Research Policy* 37 (2008): 1467.

OECD Reviews of Innovation Policy. *China Synthesis Report* (OECD, 2007).

Scoot, David Meerman. "Japanese Bureaucrats Crush Digital Economy Innovators." *Huffington Post*, April 2, 2010.

Sun, Yiefi. "China's National Innovation System in Transition." *Eurasian Geography and Economics* 43:6 (2002): 476–92.

Webb, Molly. *Korea: Mass Innovation Comes of Age* (London: Demos, 2007).

Wilsdon, James and James Kelley. *China: The Next Science Superpower* (London: Demos, 2007).

# 8

# Media and Environmental Politics in East Asia[1]

Mary Alice Haddad

## Introduction

East Asia has jumped onto the environmental bandwagon. In January 2009 South Korea announced an economic stimulus package that pledged US\$38.1 billion (equivalent to 4% of total GDP) on a "Green New Deal." Immediately after his election in August 2009, Japanese Prime Minister Yukio Hatoyama committed to slashing his country's greenhouse emissions by 25 percent of its 1990 levels by 2020, and in the same year China became the largest producer of photovoltaic panels in the world and the second largest producer of wind energy.[2]

These events are particularly remarkable because East Asia has a long history of exploiting the environment, and has often justified its exploitation using Confucian traditions that emphasized the importance of man's control and dominance over nature.[3] All three countries have strong states with close ties to business, and none of them has a large, professional, environmental organization that lobbies the government on environmental policies, and their memberships of international environmental organizations remain very small.[4]

Through an analysis of newspaper coverage about the environment in each country this chapter seeks insights into the nature of environmental politics in East Asia. The first section will outline the methodology used to gather and analyze the newspaper articles. The next three sections will discuss the findings for each country—Japan, South Korea (Korea hereafter), and China. A discussion of the significance of the findings and conclusion will follow.

# Methods

The three newspapers selected—the *Asahi Shimbun* for Japan, the *Chosun Ilbo* for Korea, and the *People's Daily* for China—were chosen for two main reasons: (1) they had digital databases that were keyword searchable, and (2) they have the largest or nearly the largest circulation of the papers in their respective countries. All three newspapers have among the largest circulations in the world. The circulation for the *Asahi Shimbun* is 14.1 million; the *Chosun Ilbo's* is 2.4 million; and the *People's Daily's* is 2.5 million (for comparative purposes, the *New York Times* has a daily circulation of 1.1 million).[5] My goal in this project is not to pick up radical or fringe reporting, which is found in abundance in all three countries either in niche papers or through Internet blogs, etc., but rather try to capture something close to mainstream media coverage of environmental politics. Thus, the results discussed here likely under-report environmental political coverage in the respective countries. This will be particularly true in China because the *People's Daily* is an official newspaper of the Chinese Communist Party (CCP).

In each paper we searched for the word "environment" (環境 huanjing; 環境 kankyou; and 환경 hwan-gyeong). We selected this very general word because we wanted to capture a wide range of political behavior that would likely not have the word "politics" anywhere in the article. For example, we wanted to include articles reporting on community efforts to improve local environments that would likely discuss grassroots political activity but may not contain the word "politics." We preferred to have a larger number of irrelevant articles in my results than to miss important grassroots activity that would likely be excluded by a narrower search. As it turned out, a preliminary search of both "environment" and "politics" in all three papers yielded fewer relevant articles and many more irrelevant articles than the more general "environment" keyword search did.[6]

For the time period under study, 1990–2008, the number of hits ranged from a low of 861 in 1990 Korea to a high of 22,665 in 1998 Japan (see Table 8.1 below for exact counts). The *Chosun Ilbo* and the *People's Daily* databases sorted the keyword search by relevance, with the most relevant articles coming first in the list and the least relevant articles coming last. For both of those papers we downloaded the text of the first 100 articles generated by the search. The *Asahi Shimbun* database sorted the articles by date rather than relevance. For that paper we selected every Nth article in a given year's search results such that the total articles collected were about one hundred.[7]

The articles were then coded by native speakers for a number of characteristics. Four areas in particular are relevant for this chapter: Relevance

**Table 8.1** Word hits for "Environment"[1]

|  | Asahi Shimbun[2] | Chosun Ilbo | People's Daily |
|---|---|---|---|
| 1950 | 3 | 2 | 568 |
| 1955 | 8 | 1 | 424 |
| 1960 | 12 | 15 | 528 |
| 1965 | 65 | 11 | 309 |
| 1970 | 219 | 49 | 231 |
| 1975 | 467 | 50 | 308 |
| 1980 | 467 | 75 | 1,059 |
| 1985 | 1,944 | 60 | 1,637 |
| 1990 | 9,309 | 861 | 2,275 |
| 1992 | 11,834 | 1,391 | 2,895 |
| 1994 | 11,320 | 1,870 | 2,789 |
| 1995 | 10,991 | 2,163 | 3,219 |
| 1996 | 11,283 | 2,297 | 3,400 |
| 1998 | 22,016 | 2,668 | 3,691 |
| 2000 | 22,665 | 3,723 | 4,812 |
| 2002 | 19,591 | 4,074 | 4,918 |
| 2004 | 17,759 | 4,035 | 6,046 |
| 2005 | 18,605 | 3,716 | 5,631 |
| 2006 | 17,288 | 4,107 | 5,950 |
| 2008 | 19,271 | 6,326 | 5,208 |

1. Japanese: 環境 *kankyou;* Chinese 環境 *huanjing;* and Korean 환경 *hwan-gyeong.*

2. The Asahi database switches from a keyword search of catalogued keywords prior to 1985 (and pdf files of the articles) to keyword full text searches (and digital files of the articles) from 1985 through to the present. It is likely that this difference in the search mechanism, rather than a dramatic change in the interest in the topic of the environment, accounts for the four-fold jump in the number of hits between 1985 and 1990.
*Source*: by the author.

to environmental politics broadly construed, so articles that discussed the highly competitive "environment" of an upcoming sports event were discarded, but articles related to a local clean-the-river effort were included. Tone toward a number of actors was ranked on a 5-point scale—highly negative (–2), negative (–1), neutral (0), positive (+1), and highly positive (+2): government (local and national), civil society (local, national, and international), and business (local and national). The number of civil society actors discussed in an article was also recorded.

## Japan

Japan had by far the most coverage of the environment of the three countries. This extensive coverage of the issue is in keeping with its long history of engaging in grassroots political activity related to the environment.[8] Furthermore, it was the host of the important COP3 meeting and a key signatory of what is now called the Kyoto Protocol, which has served as the benchmark for national policy initiatives related to climate change.[9] It is likely that the excitement around this international conference, which was held in December of 1997, is partially responsible for the doubling of environment-related articles between 1996 and 1998.

Because of the difference in the search mechanism of the database (sorting by date rather than by relevance), the collected articles yielded significantly fewer articles relevant to our topic of study than those collected from the other two papers (30–40% compared to more than 90% for most years in the other two papers). All of the analyses below for all papers discuss only the relevant articles.

Research on television media suggests that Japanese media spends a considerable time covering national government, particularly the bureaucracy.[10] Therefore, it was somewhat surprising to find that there was very little coverage of national or local government with respect to the environment, and there were twice as many articles discussing local government than national government. Articles that did discuss national or local government actors were usually neutral or slightly positive.

This finding suggests that press coverage is strongly related to patterns of civil society organization. Recent research on Japan's civil society has found that Japanese civil society tends to be more active at the local, grassroots level than at the national or international levels.[11] Furthermore, Japanese nonprofit organizations tend to work in areas such as social welfare and community development (75% of registered NPOs work in these areas) in cooperation with the government, while only about 30 percent of registered

NPOs list environmental protection as one of their key mission areas.[12] This organizational context, where more environmental groups tend to be active at the local rather than national level and organizations tend to be more cooperative rather than confrontational with the government may help explain the disproportionate coverage of environmental issues at the local level and its generally positive tone toward the government.

Coverage of civil society was on par in terms of volume with coverage of government, but its distribution was much less even. Perhaps not surprising given the explosion of civil society organizations in Japan through the 1990s and 2000s,[13] there was a rise in coverage of civil society over the period. Articles related to local civil society more than doubled between 1990 and 2008, and the tone of all of the articles was positive with the proportion of positive articles increasing over the period. There was considerably more coverage (about 100 articles) of local civil society than of national (11 articles) or international (22 articles) civil society. Articles discussing civil society did not portray a diverse civil society but rather covered only one civil society actor at a time.

The most remarkable aspect of newspaper coverage in Japan about environmental issues was how much coverage there was of business and how generally positive it was. There were 365 total articles related to the environmental politics that discussed business (more than all of the articles discussing government and civil society combined), and while most were neutral in their coverage, to the extent that there was a tone, it was overwhelmingly positive (only 5 negative articles compared to 71 positive articles).

Articles tended to discuss positive environmental innovations by Japanese businesses, focusing on Japanese companies as important global leaders in "green" business. Many of these articles take the form of special interest articles or science articles that discuss a particular technological development effort (e.g., fuel cell cars, etc.). See Table 8.2.

This coverage stands in stark contrast with coverage of environmental politics in the United States, which tend to blame industry for environmental

**Table 8.2** Tone towards business

|  | Japan | | | Korea | | | China | | |
|---|---|---|---|---|---|---|---|---|---|
|  | **Negative** | **Neutral** | **Positive** | **Negative** | **Neutral** | **Positive** | **Negative** | **Neutral** | **Positive** |
| Local | 21 | 15 | 28 | 8 | 1 | 11 | 50 | 58 | 41 |
| National | 0 | 267 | 67 | 15 | 18 | 58 | 10 | 53 | 43 |

*Source:* by the author.

pollution and generally portray business as uniformly antienvironment.[14] This trend may have begun shifting very recently with more coverage of "green industry" and "green innovation," but newspaper coverage often still portrays business' role in environmental politics as obstructionist and antienvironment.

Thus, newspaper coverage of environmental politics in Japan reflects a high level of social interest in the subject. The pattern of coverage about the issue also mirrors the broader civil society context of the country: it tends to focus on the local level and cover stories that portray civic organization, government, and business in a positive light. The most surprising feature of coverage of environmental politics in Japan was the disproportionately high level of coverage granted to business and its overwhelmingly positive tone. While this finding was perhaps stronger than expected, it too is consistent with other research on the Japanese media.

## Korea

Although the *Chosun Ilbo* is usually considered to be a conservative news-paper, it was far more critical of its government than either of the other two papers. It was the only paper that carried any highly negative stories about the central government, and it had 20 of them. Although most of its coverage about government at all levels was neutral, it had nearly twice as many negative stories (78) as positive ones (44). See Table 8.3.

The newspaper's critical tone toward the government is consistent with the role that the press has played in promoting democracy in Korea. Fights against censorship have been a common theme throughout Korean history, and the press has played an important role in supporting civil society's effort to bring about democratic transitions in that country.[15]

The *Chosun Ilbo* also had much greater variation in tone than the other two papers in its coverage of civil society. It was the only paper to have any strongly negative articles about local civil society (2 articles), and it also

**Table 8.3** Tone towards government

| Gov't | Japan | | | Korea | | | China | | |
|---|---|---|---|---|---|---|---|---|---|
| | Negative | Neutral | Positive | Negative | Neutral | Positive | Negative | Neutral | Positive |
| Local | 29 | 56 | 20 | 20 | 86 | 26 | 50 | 136 | 165 |
| National | 14 | 24 | 8 | 58 | 219 | 18 | 16 | 167 | 207 |

*Source*: by the author.

had many more articles that strongly supported local civil society than the other papers (22 articles compared to 4 for China and 0 for Japan). A similar pattern also existed at the national and international levels, with Korea having the only strongly negative articles about national civil society of the three countries and many more strongly positive articles about national and international civil society than either Japan or China.[16]

Compared to the other two papers, the *Chosun Ilbo* had less coverage of business involvement in the environment, but as was the case with Japan, the coverage that did exist was much more positive than negative (69 positive articles compared to only 23 negative ones). This generally positive coverage of business is consistent with Korea's history of close business-government-press relations.[17]

In addition to its more polarized coverage of government and civil society, an additional item of note was the emphasis on education, which did not show up very much in the other papers. Articles from throughout the period discuss environmental education efforts in schools, eco-friendly summer camps, adult education, etc. These were discussed both at the local level, for example, highlighting a particular school or region, as well as at the national level, for example, discussing the adoption of environment-related textbooks and curriculum.

This pattern also reflects broader trends in Korean civil society. Building off a Confucian culture that reveres scholars, educators have long played important roles in Korean politics. While they were often appointed by the state and served in advisory roles, they also functioned to deliberate and criticize government policy.[18] More recently, Korean NGOs have been very active in democracy education programs, promoting democratic values and skills.[19]

The environment is one of the greatest issues for contemporary Korean politics. Arguably, the issue has greater prominence in Korea than in either of the other two countries under examination in this chapter. The current Korean government views itself as a global leader in "green growth" and is promoting environmentally responsible development and industry as a key domestic and international political strategy.[20] Furthermore, the environment is a key area of citizen engagement and organization, with more NGOs reporting a mission related to the environment than to any other purpose.[21]

Given the high level of interest in the subject and the intensity of the public debate about the issue, it becomes less surprising that newspaper coverage of the environment is as dynamic as it is. Reflecting other trends in Korean civil society, the coverage tended to focus more at national level politics, was generally positive in tone with respect to business, and had significant discussion of environmental education efforts across the country.

# China

Of the three countries, perhaps the most interesting results of this analysis of newspaper coverage of environmental politics emerged from the *People's Daily*. Not surprisingly, since it is an official CCP paper, the paper was overwhelmingly positive about China's government at both the national and local levels. It had far more coverage of governmental involvement in the environment than the other two papers (741 total articles compared to 151 in Japan, and 427 in Korea). And, again not surprisingly, many, many more positive articles (372 compared to 28 in Japan and 44 in Korea), and as expected the positive bias was even stronger with respect to articles discussing the central government. Only 4 percent of the articles discussing the central government contained any kind of negative tone, (16 negative articles compared to 207 positive ones), and none of them were highly negative.

There was one aspect of all of this positive coverage that was a bit surprising. Recent research on the Chinese media has suggested that there has been an increase in the negative coverage of the local government with the liberalization (and quasi-privatization) of the media in the 2000s. Yuezhi Zhou argues that the more critical media serve the dual function of exposing corruption and other local problems as well as to legitimize central government policies and reinforce a public perception that the central government is working to solve local problems faced by the people.[22] Indeed, one of the articles in the sample, from May 2000, articulated exactly this argument, claiming that the media was forcing the local government to be more responsible on the environment.[23]

Many of the articles that were critical of the local government did follow a general pattern consistent with that interpretation: Ministry XX calls on local government YY to be more responsible when implementing the new ZZ policy. While the number of negative articles did rise over time (21 articles in 1990–8 to 30 articles in 2000–8), they were still dwarfed by the number of positively valenced articles, which also increased in number (80 articles in 1990–8 to 85 articles in 2000–8). The positive articles also took on a similar, almost formulaic character. The headline would read: "City (or Province) XX should serve as an example for their excellent efforts in sustainable development," and the article would describe the efforts that the various government organizations were taking to promote positive environmental activity.

In looking at the articles in more detail, one could see that newspaper coverage was being used both to highlight problems and to publicize their successful resolution by the government. For example, an article in May of

1990 calls for the formation of a local environmental protection effort to investigate problems with the construction of a dam by a foreign company. An article in September of the same year announces that the local government had successfully resolved the problem.[24]

Several articles were quite blatant in their efforts to show how attentive the central government was to local environmental problems. A particularly inspiring one from May 1990 discussed how a middle school student had written Li Peng (Premier at the time) about local pollution problems. The government then solved the problem and recruited the student to become an "environmental protection" supervisor of the Provincial government.[25]

Two strong reporting trends about the local government became apparent over the time period: first was the rise in "rural environment" issues, and the second was somewhat subtle shift from the idea that environmental problems could be solved and the government should play a "leading role" to one where the government should play a leading role combined with the public and the media. The rise in the focus on the rural environment becomes apparent starting in 2004 and becomes stronger over time. The early articles emphasize the problems and the importance of both pollution control as well as especially clean energy development. The later articles become more technocratic in their language and discuss national policies directed toward solving these problems, including coverage of the First Rural Environment Conference held in Beijing in July 2008.

Similarly, throughout the entire time period there is an emphasis on the important role that government can play in developing solutions to environmental problems. In the earlier articles this is usually done by highlighting the accomplishments of particular cities or provinces that have done well with environmental protection or sustainable development. One article from 1996 discusses the positive outcomes in Benxi and encourages everyone to work together for a better environment, emphasizing that government should play a "leading role" in improving the environment.[26] By January 2002, editorials are calling for the government to encourage "public participation," "media supervision," and "market mechanisms" in their efforts to improve the environment, and articles report on expert panels that recommend an increasing role for the market in solving environmental problems.[27] That same year, the first government seminar on "Public Participation and Environment Policy Making" is held in Beijing with representatives from both government and civil society.[28] A National Party Congress member submits a bill that recommends the following roles in environmental policymaking: government to lead, market to function/promote, public to participate.[29] By 2008 there is regular coverage of nongovernmental efforts related to the environment, including coverage of legal and NGO efforts and the adoption of "green insurance" and other market-oriented incentives to improve the environment.[30]

Supporting this trend toward more diverse coverage of actors related to the environment, there was a rise in the coverage of civil society, especially at the national level. Somewhat surprisingly, it was positive throughout the period, and became more so. See Table 8.4.

The most striking difference in the coverage of civil society was the diversification of civil society actors discussed. While only 12 articles in the 1990s discussed more than 1 civil society actor, from 2000–8 there were 22 that did so. In the latter period it became increasingly common to portray civil society actors as numerous and diverse. Across the time period, and increasingly so as mentioned above, civil society organizations were discussed as working positively in cooperation with the government to solve environmental problems.

What exactly constitutes civil society in China is the subject of growing scholarly literature since it is very difficult to operate in China without some kind of government approval or connection.[31] For the purposes of coding these articles, organizations that were not explicitly part of the government or a profit-making enterprise (government or private) were considered civil society.

There was a moderate level of coverage about business involvement about the environment. Overall, the coverage was positive (60 negative articles compared to 83 positive ones). The form of the articles largely mimicked those concerning local government—negative articles criticized the businesses for failing to conform to government policies and positive articles praised them for their eco-friendly innovations. While the tone of the

**Table 8.4** Civil society articles in China

| Tone | 1990–8 | | | 2000–8 | | |
|---|---|---|---|---|---|---|
| Level | Local | National | International | Local | National | International |
| −2 | 0 | 0 | 0 | 0 | 0 | 0 |
| −1 | 2 | 1 | 0 | 0 | 1 | 0 |
| 0 | 19 | 17 | 0 | 13 | 16 | 4 |
| 1 | 37 | 45 | 51 | 35 | 103 | 52 |
| 2 | 2 | 0 | 0 | 2 | 3 | 1 |

*Source*: by the author.

articles did not change appreciably over the period, the overall coverage of business involvement, especially national level business, jumped over the period (36 articles discussed national businesses in the 1990s compared to 70 for the 2000–8 period).

# Discussion

The evidence gathered here through a content analysis of the *Asahi Shimbun* in Japan, the *Chosun Ilbo* in Korea, and the *People's Daily* in China, demonstrates that there has been a dramatic increase in newspaper coverage about the environment in all three countries. There has also be an emphasis on government efforts toward the environment and an increasing in the volume and diversity of civil society as well as more positive reporting about civil society actors involved in environmental issues.

There were several surprising findings to emerge from this analysis. Japan's coverage of the government was much less than expected while its coverage of business was much higher than expected. Korea's newspaper had by far the biggest range in the tone of its articles, including the most negative and the most positive coverage of both government and civil society.

The findings emerging from the analysis of the *People's Daily* were perhaps the most interesting of the three. Unexpectedly, given the recent scholarly attention to the rising levels of press criticism of local government, we did not find a dramatic rise in the criticism of local government, and positive reporting on the local government far outweighed any negative reporting. However, there was a clear trend toward greater coverage of a more diverse set of civil society actors, and the coverage of civil society was highly positive throughout the period. Unexpectedly, coverage of civil society in China was greater in volume and more positive in tone than in either of the other two countries. See Table 8.5.

**Table 8.5** Tone towards civil society in Japan, Korea, and China

| Civil society | Japan | | | Korea | | | China | | |
|---|---|---|---|---|---|---|---|---|---|
| | Negative | Neutral | Positive | Negative | Neutral | Positive | Negative | Neutral | Positive |
| Local | 0 | 50 | 62 | 3 | 31 | 65 | 1 | 32 | 76 |
| National | 4 | 4 | 3 | 13 | 64 | 66 | 2 | 33 | 151 |
| Int'l | 1 | 16 | 6 | 0 | 18 | 21 | 0 | 4 | 104 |

*Source:* by the author.

The *People's Daily* coverage highlights the value of newspapers, even state-sponsored ones, for simultaneously exposing environmental problems and demonstrating that the government is attentive to those problems. Of particular interest were hints of a pattern where citizens or activists working at the local level would raise an issue, press coverage would draw the attention of national policymakers, who would then begin efforts to solve the problem. This trend was especially visible in the recent discussion of problems related to "rural environment."

In looking at all three countries, we can see a common orientation toward environmental policymaking as portrayed in the three newspapers where, as suggested by the Chinese NPC member, the government leads, the market promotes, and the citizens participate. In all three countries there has been an increase in the volume and diversity of newspaper coverage. Coverage of all three sectors—government, business, and civil society—has all increased in volume, and the share of stories related to business and especially civil society has also increased. The rise of coverage about the nongovernmental actors does not appear to indicate, in any of the three countries, that the central governments are losing authority or legitimacy. To the contrary, the governments are enabling and facilitating nongovernmental efforts, so greater coverage of the efforts of nongovernmental actors about the environment suggests a corresponding expansion of the government's role in dealing with environmental issues rather than a contraction or withdrawal.

These results are only based on the newspaper reports of a single newspaper in each country, so they do not represent all media coverage in the countries. Nor should it be assumed that they are accurately reporting the actual policymaking processes in their countries. However, these results do uncover some remarkable similarities as well as some notable differences in the ways that these three countries appear to be grappling with environmental issues, and they should provide ample seeds for future research on the subject.

# Conclusion

Concern with climate change and other environmental issues has been growing around the world in the past two decades, and the issue area has been a particularly dynamic one in East Asia. In a region known for its strong states and not known for its activist civil society, environmental politics seems to be an area where we can see how a rising and increasingly assertive civil society can interact in positive ways with strong states. While no country showed evidence of a large antigovernment environmental movement, all three countries showed rising civic activism as well as greater government willingness to cooperate with civic organizations to solve environmental policies.

As the previous chapter has demonstrated, the spread of digital technology, especially the Internet and cell phone use, has dramatically increased the ability of individual citizens to coordinate among one another around issues that they care about and share information—both information provided by the state as well as information that they gather themselves. Furthermore, the Internet facilitates greater international cooperation and collaboration. The environment is a policy area where this is perhaps at its most advanced across the region. Furthermore, East Asian governments (as well as a number of international actors) are not just listening to these civic actors, they are making dramatic policy changes.

Although a comprehensive discussion of East Asian environmental policy lies outside the scope of this chapter, it is clear from the dramatic recent policy initiatives undertaken by the governments of Japan, Korea, and China that these countries are not just listening and then ignoring activism concerning environmental issues; they are taking the issues seriously and making real changes to their domestic and international policies.

One somewhat surprising finding emerging from this research is that business actors (both domestic and international) have played important roles in raising the issue of the environment to the national policy agenda, and, at least in terms of what was covered in the newspapers, much of their pressure has been to improve rather than to fight pro-environmental policy. Forward-looking businesses and policymakers in East Asia do not see the environment as merely a "feel good" issue area for local residents, increasingly they see it as a key strategy to give East Asian businesses a competitive advantage in a globalized market place.

All three governments have recently issued top-level policy documents and made key speeches articulating their strategies for promoting economic growth. All three governments place "green growth" as a primary mechanism to promote economic growth in a global marketplace, promote national energy security, take a leadership role in international relations, as well as combat climate change.[32] As the newspaper coverage discussed in this chapter indicates, this issue also attracts a high level of citizen and international interest. Environmental policy is sure to be one of the most dynamic areas of East Asian politics for the next several decades.

## Five questions for discussions

1. How is newspaper coverage of environmental politics in East Asia different than that in the United States?
2. What are some of the problems related to newspaper coverage as a source of information about environmental politics?
3. What are some of the main differences between press coverage in democratic and nondemocratic countries?
4. How are government-business relations related to environmental policy in East Asia?
5. What are some important research questions that emerge from the findings in this chapter?

# Notes

1 I would like to thank Charlie Chung, Haruhiko Mitani, and Guangshuo Yang for their research assistance on this project, and Zhiqun Zhu, Pierre F. Landry, and Min-Hua Huang for comments on earlier drafts.

2 United Nations Environmental Program (UNEP), *Global Green New Deal: An Update for the G20 Pittsburgh Summit* (2009); Hatoyama speech at http://www.kantei.go.jp/foreign/hatoyama/statement/200909/ehat_0922_e.html; REN21 report http://www.ren21.net/forum/forum.asp?id=12.

3 Elizabeth Economy, *The River Runs Black: The Environmental Challenge to China's Future* (Cornell University Press, 2004), p. 55.

4 For example, Greenpeace has 20,000 supporters in China, 5,000 members in Japan, and no members in Korea (Greenpeace China, "2008 Annual Report," p. 16 at http://www.greenpeace.or.jp/info/), compared to more than 250,00 supporters in the United States and more than 500,000 members in Germany at http://www.greenpeace.de/ (German, accessed October 4, 2010).

5 Data from the World Association of Newspapers at http://www.wan-press.org/article2825.html.

6 Articles using both terms tended to be about the "political environment" of particular local political campaigns or, for some reason, about soccer games, neither of which was related to the kind of "environment" that is of interest here.

7 For example, in 2000 there were 22,665 hits and I selected every 200th article for a total of 114.

8 For an excellent background on the environmental movement in Japan, see Margaret McKean, *Environmental Protest and Citizen Politics in Japan* (University of California Berkeley, 1981); and Jeffrey Broadbent, *Environmental Politics in Japan: Networks of Power and Protest* (Cambridge University Press, 1998).

9 The UN framework Convention on Climate Change meeting held in Kyoto in December 1997. For the text of the Kyoto Protocol see http://www.cop3.org/ (accessed July 29, 2010). For more about Japan's role in this meeting, and especially the civic environmental activism associated with it, see Kim Reimann, "Building Global Civil Society from the Outside In? Japanese International Development Ngos, the State, and International Norms," *The State of Civil Society in Japan*, ed. Frank Schwartz and Susan Pharr (Cambridge University Press, 2003).

10 Ellis Krauss, *Broadcasting Politics in Japan: NHK and Television News* (Cornell University Press, 2000).

11 Mary Alice Haddad, *Politics and Volunteering in Japan: A Global Perspective* (Cambridge University Press, 2007); Robert Pekkanen, *Japan's Dual Civil Society: Members without Advocates* (Stanford: Stanford University Press, 2006); Yasuo Takao, *Reinventing Japan: From Merchant Nation to Civic Nation* (Palgrave Macmillan, 2007).

12 In 1998 a new law governing nonprofit organizations went into force, making it much easier for organizations to gain nonprofit legal status. A "registered NPO" is an organization that has incorporated under this legal framework. Information about all the registered NPOs is available on a searchable database at http://www.npo-hiroba.or.jp/search/ (accessed July 28, 2010). Of the 10, 375 organizations that listed an organizational mission, 75 percent listed health, social welfare, or community development as a mission while 30 percent listed environmental protection. For more explanation about the types of NPOs see Mary Alice Haddad, "Civic Responsibility and Patterns of Voluntary Participation Around the World," *Comparative Political Studies* 39:10 (2006); Mary Alice Haddad, "Transformation of Japan's Civil Society Landscape," *Journal of East Asian Studies* 7:3 (2007); Mary Alice Haddad, "A State-in-Society Approach to the Nonprofit Sector: Welfare Services in Japan," *Voluntas: International Journal of Voluntary and Nonprofit Organization* online (2010).

13 See Haddad, "Transformation of Japan's Civil Society Landscape" for an explanation for the rise in these organizations, and Takako Amemiya, "The Nonprofit Sector: Legal Background," in *The Nonprofit Sector in Japan*, ed. Tadashi Yamamoto (Manchester University Press, 1998); Haddad, *Politics and Volunteering in Japan: A Global Perspective*; Jeff Kingston, *Japan's Quiet Transformation: Social Change and Civil Society in the Twenty-First Century* (RoutledgeCurzon, 2004); Stephen Osborne, ed. *The Voluntary and Non-Profit Sector in Japan* (RoutledgeCurzon, 2003); Pekkanen, *Japan's Dual Civil Society: Members without Advocates*, Frank Schwartz and Susan Pharr, eds. *The State of Civil Society in Japan* (Cambridge University Press, 2003) for books on Japan's contemporary civil society.

14 See, for example Jacob Bendix and Carol Liebler, "Place, Distance, and Environmental News: Geographic Variation in Newspaper Coverage of the Spotted Owl Conflict," *Annals of the Association of American Geographers* 89:4 (1999) for evidence of an anti-business bias; for evidence of a pro-business bias see Moti Nissani, "Media Coverage of the Greenhouse Effect," *Population and Environment* 21:1 (1999).

15 For an excellent overview of Korea's democratization and especially civil society's role see Sunhyuk Kim, *Politics of Democratization in Korea: The Role of Civil Society* (University of Pittsburgh Press, 2000).

16 It must be noted that some of the greater degree of variation may be due to differences in coding of the articles across the different papers. Although the author made great efforts to ensure inter-coder reliability among the three coders, they were all working in different languages, making it difficult to ensure that what was considered "strongly positive" in Korean was similar to what was coded as "strongly positive" article in the other two newspapers.

17 For an excellent political history of Korea see Bruce Cummings, *Korea's Place in the Sun* (W.W. Norton, 2005). For more about the media industry in particular see Doobo Shin, "South Korean Media Industry in the 1990s and the Economic Crisis," *Prometheus* 20:4 (2002).

18 Jeong-Woo Koo, "The Origins of the Public Sphere and Civil Society: Private Academies and Petitions in Korea 1506–1800," *Social Science History* 31:3 (2007); Jongryn Mo, "The Challenge of Accountability: Implications of the Censorate," *Confucianism for the Modern World*, ed. Daniel Bell and Hahm Chaibong (New York, NY: Cambridge University Press, 1998).

19 See Kim, *Politics of Democratization in Korea: The Role of Civil Society*; Euiyong Kim, "The Limits of Ngo-Government Relations in South Korea," *Asian Survey* 49:5 (2009) for more details.

20 The White Paper that explains Korea's new green growth strategy is available online at http://eng.me.go.kr/file.do?method=fileDownloader&attachSeq=1812. For criticism of this strategy see Jon Herskovitz, "South Korea green growth to hurt environment: report" *Reuters*, March 18, 2010 at http://www.reuters.com/article/idUSTRE62H0CC20100318.

21 According to Kim, "The Limits of Ngo-Government Relations in South Korea," p. 875; 88 percent of NGOs in the *2000 Directory of Korean NGOs* were concerned with the environment; this was followed by local community (86%) and civil society (62%).

22 For example Yuezhi Zhou, "Watchdogs on Party Leashes? Contexts and Implications of Investigative Journalism in Post-Deng China," *Journalism Studies* 1:2 (2000); Yuezhi Zhou and Sun Wusan, "Public Opinion Supervision: Possibilities and Limits of the Media in Constraining Local Officials," *Grassroots Political Reform in Contemporary China*, ed. Elizabeth Perry and Merle Goldman (Harvard University Press, 2007).

23 For example Ding Ming, "Valuable environmental awareness" (可贵的环保意识), *People's Daily*, May 8, 2000; and Bai Jianfeng, "Exposing and solving environmental protection problems, Shanxi strengthens public opinion supervision" (正视问题，揭 露 解 决，山 西 强化 與论监督), *People's Daily*, January 28, 2000.

24 Xu Jun, "Protection of ecological environment in Lubuge power reservoir" (保护鲁布革电站水库生态环境 ), *People's Daily*, May 5, 1990; and "Improving ecological environment in Lubuge" (改善鲁布革的生态环境), *People's Daily*, September 25, 1990.

25 Tan Youzhi, "On the decision to further strengthen environmental protection work" (关于进一步加强环境保护工作的决定), *People's Daily*, July 18, 1990.

26  Kong Xiaoning, "Pollution control in Benxi," (宋健在本溪污染治理验收会上指出加快老工业城市环境治理), *People's Daily*, August 18, 1996.

27  "A new situation for environmental protection in the new century" (开创新世纪环境保护工作的新局面), *People's Daily*, January 10, 2002.

28  Fu Xu Zhao, "China environmental economics and management senior seminar to promote environmental protection with economic leverage" (中国环境经济与管理高级研讨会提出用经济杠杆促环保), *People's Daily*, March 24, 2002.

29  Wang Jirong, "Adhere to the environmental and economic 'Win-Win'" (坚持环境与经济"双赢"), *People's Daily*, March 8, 2002.

30  For example, Zhao, "ASEM environment ministers meeting ready" (亚欧环境部长会议准备就绪), *People's Daily*, January 11, 2002; Sun Xiuyan, "The country's first environmental pollution liability insurance compensated" (全国首例环境污染责任险获赔), *People's Daily*, December 04, 2008; and Hou Fengqi, "The value of three levels in building an ecological compensation mechanism" (企业、流域、区域三个层次相结合—构建生态环境资源价值补偿机制), *People's Daily*, February 29, 2008.

31  See for example, Richard Madsen, "The Public Sphere, Civil Society and Moral Community: A Research Agenda for Contemporary China Studies," *Modern China* 19:2 (1993); Barrett L. McCormick, Su Shaozhi, and Xiao Xiaoming, "The 1989 Democracy Movement: A Review of the Prospects for Civil Society in China," *Pacific Affairs* 65:2 (1992); Andrew Mertha, *China's Water Warriors: Citizen Action and Policy Change* (Cornell University Press, 2008); Kevin O'Brien, "Rightful Resistance," *World Politics* 49:1 (1996); Kevin O'Brien and Lianjiang Li, "Accommodating 'Democracy' in a One-Party State: Introducing Village Elections in China," *The China Quarterly* 162 (2000); and Perry and Goldman, eds. *Grassroots Political Reform in Contemporary China*.

32  For Japan see the "New Growth Strategy" Cabinet decision issued on June 18, 2010—English translation available online at http://www.meti.go.jp/english/policy/economy/growth/report20100618.pdf; for Korea see the Global Korea Keynote speech by Minister Yoon, February 25, 2010—English translation available online at http://english.mosf.go.kr/news/dpm/interviews_view.php?sect=news_interview&pmode=&sn=6816&page=1&SK=&SW; for an English summary of China's 12th Five-Year Plan for National Economic and Social Development see http://chinaviews.files.wordpress.com/2011/01/chinas_12th_five-year_plan_email.pdf(accessed May 6, 2011).

# Selected bibliography

Amemiya, Takako. "The Nonprofit Sector: Legal Background." *The Nonprofit Sector in Japan.* ed. Tadashi Yamamoto (New York, NY: Manchester University Press, 1998), pp. 59–98.

Bendix, Jacob and Carol Liebler. "Place, Distance, and Environmental News: Geographic Variation in Newspaper Coverage of the Spotted Owl Conflict." *Annals of the Association of American Geographers* 89:4 (1999): 658–76.

Broadbent, Jeffrey. *Environmental Politics in Japan: Networks of Power and Protest* (New York, NY: Cambridge University Press, 1998).

China, Greenpeace. "2008 Annual Report." (2009).

Cummings, Bruce. *Korea's Place in the Sun* (New York, NY: W.W. Norton, 2005).

Economy, Elizabeth. *The River Runs Black: The Environmental Challenge to China's Future* (Ithaca, NY: Cornell University Press, 2004).

Haddad, Mary Alice. "Civic Responsibility and Patterns of Voluntary Participation Around the World." *Comparative Political Studies* 39:10 (2006): 1220–42.

—. *Politics and Volunteering in Japan: A Global Perspective* (New York: Cambridge University Press, 2007).

—. "Transformation of Japan's Civil Society Landscape." *Journal of East Asian Studies* 7:3 (2007): 413–37.

—. "The State-in-Society Approach to the Study of Democratization with Examples from Japan." *Democratization* 17:5 (2010): 997–1023.

Kalland, Arne, ed. *Environmental Movements in Asia* (New York, NY: RoutledgeCurzon, 1999).

Kim, Euiyong. "The Limits of Ngo-Government Relations in South Korea." *Asian Survey* 49:5 (2009): 873–94.

Kim, Sunhyuk. *Politics of Democratization in Korea: The Role of Civil Society* (Pittsburgh, PA: University of Pittsburgh Press, 2000).

Kingston, Jeff. *Japan's Quiet Transformation: Social Change and Civil Society in the Twenty-First Century* (New York: RoutledgeCurzon, 2004).

Koo, Jeong-Woo. "The Origins of the Public Sphere and Civil Society: Private Academies and Petitions in Korea 1506–1800." *Social Science History* 31:3 (2007): 381–409.

Krauss, Ellis. *Broadcasting Politics in Japan: NHK and Television News* (Ithaca, NY: Cornell University Press, 2000).

Madsen, Richard. "The Public Sphere, Civil Society and Moral Community: A Research Agenda for Contemporary China Studies." *Modern China* 19:2 (1993): 183–98.

McCormick, Barrett L., Su Shaozhi, and Xiao Xiaoming. "The 1989 Democracy Movement: A Review of the Prospects for Civil Society in China." *Pacific Affairs* 65:2 (1992): 182–202.

McKean, Margaret. *Environmental Protest and Citizen Politics in Japan* (Berkeley: University of California, 1981).

Mertha, Andrew. *China's Water Warriors: Citizen Action and Policy Change* (Ithaca, NY: Cornell University Press, 2008).

Mo, Jongryn. "The Challenge of Accountability: Implications of the Censorate." *Confucianism for the Modern World,* ed. Daniel Bell and Hahm Chaibong (New York, NY: Cambridge University Press, 1998): 54–68.

Nissani, Moti. "Media Coverage of the Greenhouse Effect." *Population and Environment* 21:1 (1999): 27–43.

O'Brien, Kevin. "Rightful Resistance." *World Politics* 49:1 (1996): 31–55.

O'Brien, Kevin and Lianjiang Li. "Accommodating 'Democracy' in a One-Party State: Introducing Village Elections in China." *The China Quarterly* 162 (2000): 465–89.

Osborne, Stephen, ed. *The Voluntary and Non-Profit Sector in Japan* (New York: RoutledgeCurzon, 2003).

Pekkanen, Robert. *Japan's Dual Civil Society: Members without Advocates* (Stanford: Stanford University Press, 2006).

Perry, Elizabeth. "Casting a Chinese 'Democracy' Movement: Legacies of Social Fragmentation." *Challenging the Mandate of Heaven: Social Protest and State Power in China*, ed. Elizabeth Perry (New York: M.E. Sharpe, 2002).

Perry, Elizabeth and Merle Goldman, eds. *Grassroots Political Reform in Contemporary China* (Cambridge: Harvard University Press, 2007).

Reimann, Kim. "Building Global Civil Society from the Outside In? Japanese International Development Ngos, the State, and International Norms." *The State of Civil Society in Japan*, ed. Frank Schwartz and Susan Pharr (New York, NY: Cambridge University Press, 2003), pp. 298–315.

Schwartz, Frank and Susan Pharr, eds. *The State of Civil Society in Japan* (New York, NY: Cambridge University Press, 2003).

Shin, Doobo. "South Korean Media Industry in the 1990s and the Economic Crisis." *Prometheus* 20:4 (2002): 337–50.

Takao, Yasuo. *Reinventing Japan: From Merchant Nation to Civic Nation* (New York, NY: Palgrave Macmillan, 2007).

Tiberghien, Yves. "The Battle for the Global Governance of Genetically Modified Organisms: The Roles of the European Union, Japan, Korea, and China in a Comparative Context." *Les Etudes du CERI* 124 (2006): 1–49.

Tsai, Lily. *Accountability without Democracy: How Solidary Groups Provide Public Goods in Rural China* (New York, NY: Cambridge University Press, 2007).

United Nations Environmental Program (UNEP). *Global Green New Deal: An Update for the G20 Pittsburgh Summit*, 2009.

Zhou, Yuezhi. "Watchdogs on Party Leashes? Contexts and Implications of Investigative Journalism in Post-Deng China." *Journalism Studies* 1:2 (2000): 577–95.

Zhou, Yuezhi and Sun Wusan. "Public Opinion Supervision: Possibilities and Limits of the Media in Constraining Local Officials." *Grassroots Political Reform in Contemporary China*, ed. Elizabeth Perry and Merle Goldman (Cambridge, MA: Harvard University Press, 2007), pp. 300–24.

# 9

# Environmental Legislation in East Asia: Rationale and Significance

Matthew A. Shapiro

## Chapter Outline

# Introduction

This chapter presents an overview of environmental legislation in Japan, South Korea, Taiwan, and China, which share a regional affiliation and have the ability to influence each other's environmental policies, limit cross-border pollution spillovers, and reduce the costs of environmental degradation by clearly assigning responsibility. At the core of such positive outcomes are domestic environmental policies and the ability to respond to new environmental problems with advanced technology. Levels of environmental pollution are high in these East Asian states, especially greenhouse gases (GHGs), as are technological capabilities to treat pollution. The overarching goal of this chapter is to identify the relationship between environmental legislation and science and technology (S&T) policies in East Asia.

We scrutinize environmental legislation in these East Asian states according to stringency and flexibility, which are ideal constructs for identifying environmental and S&T policy connections. Policy stringency encourages innovation to reduce pollution, while policy flexibility permits unanticipated innovations. Both are necessary to deal with the most current wave of environmental problems; however, in the existing literature, innovation is commonly induced through pollution taxes and tradable permits, which have a stringency focus.[1] As well, policy instruments like taxes and permits do not account for demand for innovation, so we attempt to correlate demand-related factors of environmental policies with policy flexibility.

Ultimately, it will be shown that there is an increasing trend in East Asia toward policy stringency based on environmental impact assessment (EIA) legislation. EIA-related institutions legitimize the use of innovations to reduce environmental degradation and complement legislation which encourages S&T innovation. The existing call for simultaneous application of S&T and environmental policies, thus, is well heeded in East Asia, but policy flexibility can still be improved.

# Domestic environmental policymaking overview

This section provides a rough sketch of domestic environmental policy efforts in Japan, South Korea, Taiwan, and China, paying particular attention to the shift toward integrated environmental-S&T goals. From the 1940s to the early 2010s, there have been a total of over 326 environmental policies enacted by these East Asian governments. There is an overall emphasis on sustainability and environmental protection in all four states, although there remain a number of differences, particularly between China and the other three. In China, air regulations are geared primarily toward the reduction of sulfur dioxide emissions, which is the cause of acid precipitation, rather than GHGs and their long-term effects. This is, however, not necessarily surprising, given that $SO_2$ emissions in China have increased by 27 percent from 2000 to 2005. There is no viable standard to measure the effect of acid rain on industry, utilities, and automobiles, so a broad-based regulation may be among the most effective. In China, especially, the accelerated corrosion produced by acid rain is a clear threat to the country's continued industrialization, representing a significant cost if train rails, metal bridges, shipping containers, etc. require replacement twice or thrice as fast as normal.

A number of attempts have been made to incorporate environmental legislation and S&T innovation in East Asia. In China, the Decision of the State Council on Several Issues Concerning Environmental Protection (1996) gives priority to S&T which targets environmental quality-related solutions. This effort was subsequently developed through the Law of the PRC on the Promotion of Clean Production (2002) and the Decision of the State Council on Implementing Scientific Outlook on Development and Strengthening Environmental Protection (2005), both of which emphasized the dual priorities of science and development. The 2005 Decision, however, was made in response to the rapid degradation of China's environment over the previous 20 years. The model to be applied is "balanced development" through cautious application of S&T output and environmental monitoring. In Taiwan, the Resource Recycling Act (2002) promotes the establishment of environmental S&T parks which specialize in recycling renewable resources, using market-pull awards for excellence in recycling technological developments. In South Korea, development of and support for Environmental Technology Act (1994) facilitate product innovation through the efforts of the Korea Environmental Industry and Technology Institute.

Patent data is becoming increasingly reliable and accessible as a measure of innovation output. We present here the time trends of GHG-related output, given the environmental policy-S&T output connection in these four East Asian economies. There are many aspects of GHG patent output which must be detailed, especially as this specific patenting area has been given virtually no attention in the existing literature. Publications, as well, have been given scant attention in the literature in terms of their GHG focus.[2] Within the region, presented in Figure 9.1, Taiwan has shown the most dramatic increase in GHG-related patents when comparing the pre- and post-2004 periods. GHG-related publications are a very different story, with China producing nearly as many as Japan over the 2000–8 period and taking on exponential proportions (see Figure 9.2). The trends described in this section indicate that production of GHG-related technologies is emphasized in South Korea, as well as Taiwan and China, albeit still trailing far behind Japan in terms of patents.

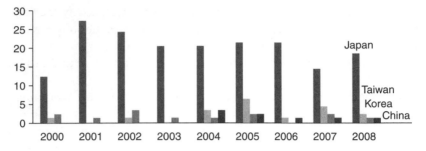

**Figure 9.1** GHG-related patents by assignment date
*Source*: Author's calculations using USPTO (2008) data

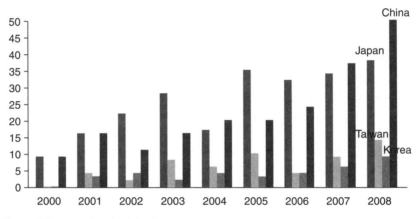

**Figure 9.2** GHG-related publications
*Source*: Author's calculations using Web of Science (2009) data.

# Case-specific observations and analysis

Data are drawn from a number of primary sources of legislation for Japan, South Korea, Taiwan, and China.[3] When the actual text of the policy was not always readily available—in either the native language or English—secondary sources were used to gather specifics about these policies. Making comparisons of policies across countries leads to weighting challenges. A "circular" is not readily comparable to an "enforcement rule", nor is a "standard" to an "act" or "law." Thus, the fact that these states are engaging in white paper-level discussions on these matters is significant, but it does not speak to the legislative impact of each document or capture the impact each policy may have had. A careful reading of each policy is necessary, thus, to discern each one's relative magnitude.

Environmental policies cover a range of subjects, shown below with the breadth of the policies enacted by these four countries over the last 50–60 years. To narrow our focus, the following analysis is based on a sub-categorization of these policies based on the following four groups: large/ instrumental frameworks, direct or indirect effects on GHG emissions, market-related, and EIAs, coded in Figures 9.3–9.6, respectively, by dash border with light gray fill, solid border with light gray fill, dashed border with dark gray fill, and solid border with dark gray fill.[4] These groups represent policy stringency and flexibility in terms of domestic policymaking of East Asian nations.

## Japan

The Air Pollution Control Law (1968) is designed to control for emissions of soot and airborne particulates and establish standards which are enforced through regulations. While there are observable results in terms of reductions in emissions from gasoline and diesel vehicles, and there have been efforts to amend the bill to address volatile organic compounds, this law is the precursor for other policies addressing GHGs and global warming. For example, the Law Concerning the Protection of the Ozone Layer through the Control of Specified Substance and Other Measures (1988, and revised in 1991 and 1994 in response to Montreal Protocol amendments in 1990 and 1992, respectively) aims to protect the ozone layer through international cooperation and implement the Vienna Convention for the Protection of the Ozone Layer. Other relevant laws include the Systematic Diagram of Automobile NOx Law (1992) that focuses on reductions of nitrogen oxides (NOx), and the Law Concerning Special Measures for Total Emission Reduction of NOx from Automobiles in Specified Areas (1992), which called for prefectural governors to establish plans to reduce NOx emissions.

The Basic Environmental Law (1993) initially was designed to promote policies for environmental conservation, outline the responsibilities of all actors (state and local governments, corporations, and citizens), and promote the EIA system. The EIA was formalized through the establishment of procedures to conduct assessments, outlined in the Environmental Impact Assessment Law (1997).

Global warming legislation arose from the Law Concerning the Promotion of Measures to Cope with Global Warming (1998), which defined GHGs,

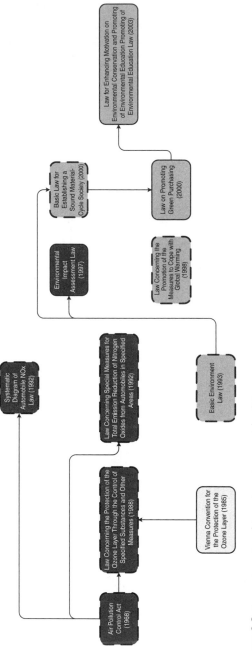

**Figure 9.3** Four categories of Japan's environmental policies

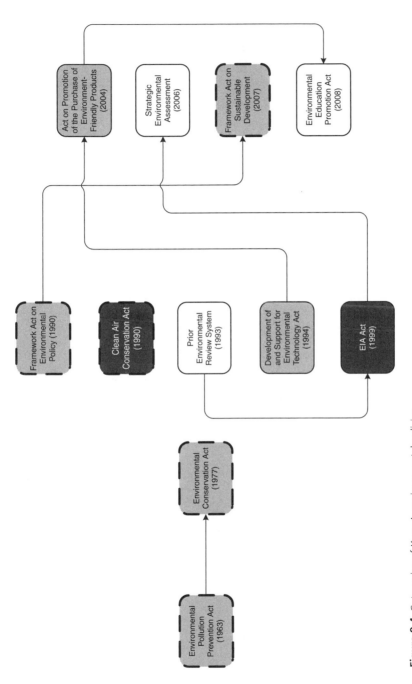

**Figure 9.4** Categories of Korea's environmental policies

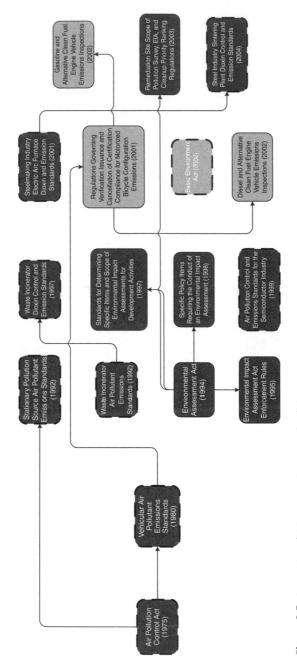

**Figure 9.5** Categories of Taiwan's environmental policies

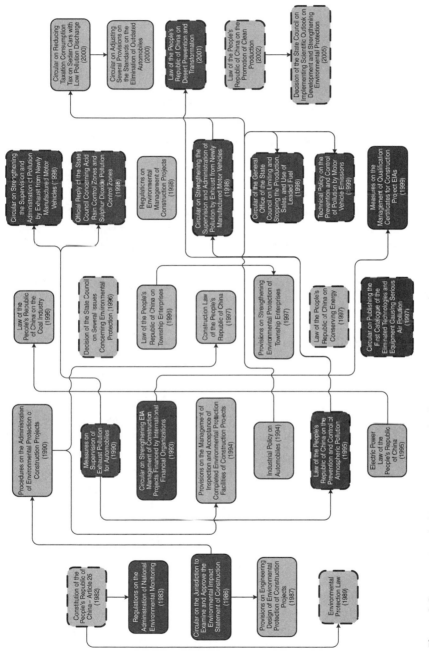

**Figure 9.6** Categories of China's environmental policies

outlined the responsibilities of the relevant actors, and established centers at multiple levels to mitigate global warming through education. Impacts of this law are intended to manifest in high levels of energy efficiency, high usage of renewable energy, and reductions in GHGs.

Building on the broad framework of the Basic Environmental Law (1993), the Basic Law for Establishing a Sound-Material Cycle Society (2000) addresses resource consumption with goals of conservation, reduction of waste, and product recycling.[5] The Law on Promoting Green Purchasing (2000) operates under a similar set of guidelines, particularly to provide information and encourage a shift in demand to eco-friendly goods. From 2001 to 2006, in fact, the number of designated "green" products increased from 100 to 214, and green product purchases by the national, prefecture, and large city governments accounted for 95 percent of all purchases, although the number is considerably lower for smaller municipalities. Attempting to influence citizen behavior along these lines, the Law for Enhancing Motivation on Environmental Conservation and Promoting of Environmental Education (2003) utilizes educational tools as well as monetary penalties for people that do not follow parts of the law.

## South Korea

South Korea's environmental public policies were initially broad in scope, beginning with the Environmental Pollution Prevention Act (1963). The Act was ultimately repealed and replaced with the Environmental Conservation Act (1977), but it was not until the Framework Act on Environmental Policy (1990) that the focus encompassed pollution prevention, environmental standards, EIAs, and responsibilities across different levels of governments, businesses, and the citizenry. Similarly, the Framework Act on Sustainable Development (2007) outlined the country's legal basis for sustainable development and established the means through which sustainable development is to be achieved.

Regarding air pollution-related policies in Korea, the Clean Air Conservation Act (1990) was designed to prevent air pollution in a sustainable manner, manage GHG emissions, focus on the Yellow Wind from China, and treat pollutants from both stationary and mobile sources. This has resulted in the installation of the CleanSys system to streamline data transmission with regard to emission facilities producing air pollution.

Development of and Support for Environmental Technology Act (1994) created a shift in the available products through the establishment of the

Korea Institute of Environment Industry and Technology (now the Korea Environmental Industry and Technology Institute). The Act also set up guidelines for new technologies, the promotion of international joint ventures, and the creation of human capital along these lines. This was later coupled with the Act on Promotion of the Purchase of Environment-Friendly Products (2004), which promotes the consumption of such products. Targets are set on the long-term development of Korea's economy, so it is a tangential goal for the Environmental Education Promotion Act (2008) to create a willing base of support to purchase these products, primarily through youth education about the environment.

The EIA structure in Korea has not been viewed as being entirely effective. Legislation began with the creation of the Prior Environmental Review System (PERS) in 1993, followed by the EIA Act (1999), which laid out guidelines so that the process is standardized with comparable impacts, followed by the Strategic Environmental Assessment (SEA) in 2006, which accounted for strategic- and project-level assessments.

## Taiwan

The public policy timeline in Taiwan begins with the Air Pollution Control Act (1975), which was put forth through presidential order to maintain public health and improve the quality of life through controls on air pollution. Based on Fang and Chen's overview of changes in air pollution legislation, it has been found that there have been consistent improvements in Taiwan's air quality over time, particularly since the mid-1990s.[6] In line with the clean-air goals of the Air Pollution Control Act, the Vehicular Air Pollutant Emissions Standards (1980) breaks down the standards for all types of fuel, although alternative/renewable fuels are not listed explicitly, even in later revisions of the Standards. The Stationary Pollution Source Air Pollutant Emissions Standards (1992) establishes criteria for the testing and classification of pollution sources, particularly with regard to air pollution of older units. Air pollution is also treated by the Waste Incinerator Air Pollutant Emissions Standards (1992) and the Waste Incinerator Dioxin Control and Emission Standards (1997), not to mention the Air Pollution Control and Emissions Standards for the Semiconductor Industry (1999).

With the Steelmaking Industry Electric Arc Furnace Dioxin and Emission Standards (2001), industry associations, environmental protect groups, and academic and government researchers were able to provide input on the dioxin emission policy. The Steel Industry Sintering Plant Dioxin Control and Emission Standards (2004) builds on this legislation, establishing a system for testing dioxin emissions based on international toxicity equivalency factor values for pollutants. Related policies, albeit more oriented toward market incentives, include Regulations Governing Verification Issuance and Cancellation of Certification Compliance for Motorized Bicycle Configuration Emissions (2001), for Diesel and Alternative Clean Fuel Engine Vehicle Emissions Inspections (2002), and for Gasoline and Alternative Clean Fuel Engine Vehicle Emissions Inspections (2002).

Broad environmental legislation was finally initiated in Taiwan with the Basic Environment Act (2002), which has goals of increasing the quality of the environment, preserving environmental resources, and sustainable development. The legislation was not easily passed, having been under consideration since 1988, when first proposed by the EPA.

EIAs in Taiwan were initiated with the Environmental Assessment Act (1994), to deal with the adverse affects of development on the environment. The process is based on the submission of an application, a public explanation meeting, and the tracking of a project's progress in accordance with the EIA report. Further details about the Act are provided in the Environmental Impact Assessment Act Enforcement Rules (1995), the Standards for Determining Specific Items and Scope of Environmental Impact Assessments for Development Activities (1997), the Specific Policy Items Requiring the Conduct of an Environmental Impact Assessment (1998), and Remediation Site Scope of Pollution Survey, EIA, and Cleanup Priority Ranking Regulations (2003). Despite the number of regulations supporting and outlining EIAs and their function, there is a sense among researchers that the EPA does not exercise supervisory duties and that the EIA is nothing more than a rubber stamp.[7]

## China

Our focus on Chinese legislation begins with the Constitution of the PRC (1982), particularly Article 26, which states that protection and improvement of the environment, prevention and control of pollution, and forest protection and afforestation are all a function of Chinese state protection. The Regulations on the Administration of National Environmental Monitoring (1983) subsequently established the various departments, their duties and functions, and procedures and regulations for reporting data. The 1980s in China culminated with the Environmental Protection Law (1989), which was designed to protect the environment, prevent pollution, facilitate socialist modernization, encourage education in the science of environmental protection, establish national standards of monitoring and inspection, and establish regulations.

The mid-1980s provided initial evidence of the connection between environmental policy and development, particularly in the form of construction.[8] Indeed, the focus on construction is emblematic of much of China's environmental policies in this early period, given the rapid growth and development which the country experienced and the environmental hazards which are likely to arise without sufficient governmental oversight. Construction and environmental protection remained a focus of Chinese environmental legislation in the early 1990s, beginning with the Procedures on the Administration of Environmental Protection of Construction Projects (1990), which formalized the procedures to be followed by construction entities, particularly the fact that environmental impact statements (EIS) are to be submitted to and reviewed by the National Environmental Protection Agency (NEPA).

The Circular on Strengthening EIA Management of Construction Projects Financed by International Financial Organizations (1993) represented a strong effort to bring the EIAs of China up to par with the rest of the world and in Asia, given requirements by the World Bank and the Asian Development Bank. The Provisions on the Management of Inspection and Acceptance of Completed Environmental Protection Facilities of Construction Projects (1994), and the Construction Law of the PRC (1997) additionally strengthened the management of environmental protection, while the Regulations on Environmental Management of Construction Projects (1998) targeted low energy consumption, low materials consumption, and low pollutant generation, detailing the processes for EISs. EIAs were further formalized through the Measures on the Management of Qualification Certificates for Construction Project EIAs (1999), which improved the quality of EIAs and added an additional layer to the evaluation process.

Air pollution was addressed in the Law of the PRC on the Prevention and Control of Atmospheric Pollution (1995) as well as the Measures on Supervision of Exhaust Pollution for Automobiles (1990).[9] This was followed by laws which specifically treated acid rain and automobile pollution.[10] These laws also functioned as precursors to later laws dealing specifically with desertification, such as the Law of the PRC on Desert Prevention and Transformation (2001), whose proposals include the use of plant forests, perennial bushes, and anti-wind/sand forest nets to limit the blowing of the yellow winds from the Gobi Desert and Inner Mongolia.[11]

The late 1990s witnessed more robust efforts by the Ministry of Environmental Protection, beginning with the Decision of the State Council on Several Issues Concerning Environmental Protection (1996), which emphasized the problems of ecological deterioration. This was followed by the Law of the PRC on Conserving Energy (1997), which promotes energy conservation, energy efficiency, and environmental protection. Within this policy, there is a statement which prohibits new industrial construction using outdated and high energy consuming-methods and technologies, which offers a connection to later calls for S&T improvements.

The Electric Power Law of the PRC (1995) and the Law of the PRC on the Coal Industry (1996) represent efforts to preempt market-led, negative effects on environmental quality in China. While the letter of these laws does not convey a sense of environmental protection, oversight of these sectors is likely to limit abuses which might lead to environmental degradation. Similarly, the Industrial Policy on Automobiles (1994) creates guidelines for the types of gasoline to be used by different types of cars, focusing on the technologies which enable low pollution and consumption. Eventually, policies would be instituted to ban leaded fuel,[12] clean-up GHGs from diesel, and replace Freon.[13]

Specifically addressing autos, the Circular on Strengthening the Supervision and Administration of Pollution by Exhaust from Newly Manufactured Motor Vehicles (1998) sought to improve air quality by having auto manufacturers inform the government about pollutant discharge. Local EPA offices then test for pollution discharges of individual vehicles and create a directory of acceptable vehicles that can be manufactured. If pollution discharge is reduced by 30 percent, there is then an added incentive for consumers to purchase these less polluting vehicles, under the Circular on Reducing Taxation Consumption Tax on Sedan Cars with Low Pollution Discharge (2000).[14]

From the late 1990s, there was also a focus on dealing with the combined economic and environmental effects of township and village enterprises (TVEs). The Law of the PRC on Township Enterprises (1996) supported such enterprises and encouraged their development and monitoring, particularly given that the number of workers absorbed by TVEs increased from 96.1 million in 1991 to 130.5 million in 1996.[15] It was not until the Provisions on Strengthening Environmental Protection of Township Enterprises (1997) were adopted that pollution discharge limits, sustainable development, and the involvement of local governments were mandated.

The Decision of the State Council on Implementing Scientific Outlook on Development and Strengthening Environmental Protection (2005) and the preceding Law of the PRC on the Promotion of Clean Production (2002) further institutionalize environmental legislation, but there is an underlying emphasis on sustainability. The 2002 law, for example, emphasizes clean production, sustainable development, and EIAs. The 2005 Decision, as well, focuses on balanced development between economic and environmental goals and greater coordination among regions. Of greater significance, though, is the emphasis on S&T output in pursuit of these goals. The 2002 Law, for example, is to be funded with "Special Technological Development Funds" and the "Small- and Medium-Sized Enterprise Development Fund," both of which target clean production R&D. In this way, the fulcrum on which balanced development rests is R&D to address economically feasible environmental improvements.

# Key observations

Several observations can be made with regard to the above presentation of environmental policies in East Asia. First, policy stringency is bolstered through the institutionalization of EIAs across East Asia. Second, policy flexibility seems to be increasing, measured by changes in demand structures for environmental innovation. Policy emphases on GHG-related S&T output complement these changes. These observations are common across East Asia, while China alone is experiencing coordination problems between the central and local governments.

EIAs have been emphasized in East Asia primarily from the early 1990s. To recapitulate, EIAs were promoted through Japan's Basic Environmental Law (1993), although it was not until 1997 that the EIA Law was formally established. Legislation in South Korea began with the creation of the Prior Environmental Review System (PERS) in 1993, followed by the EIA Act (1999). The basic framework for EIAs in Taiwan is represented by the Environmental Impact Assessment (1994). In South Korea and Taiwan, though, the efficacy of EIAs has been questioned.[16] In China, EIAs were largely focused on the construction industry, such as the Circular on Strengthening EIA Management of Construction Projects Financed by International Financial Organizations (1993) and the Measures on the Management of Qualification Certificates for Construction Project EIAs (1999). In China, EIAs are also conflated with preventative measures like Measures on Supervision of Exhaust Pollution for Automobiles (1990). Testing of emissions standards parallels the function of EIAs, the latter of which targets ex ante impacts rather than ex post effects (e.g., auto emissions).

Policy flexibility has been impacted by attempts to influence the marketability, cost, and demand structures for environmental innovations, primarily in the 2000s. Such legislation includes Japan's Law for Enhancing Motivation on Environmental Conservation and Promoting of Environmental Education (2003), which affects consumers' decisions and preferences over time. This is likely to have a significant impact on the efficacy of business-related environmental policies as is the Law on Promoting Green Purchasing (2000),[17] which is particularly affected by educational efforts. Similarly, in Korea, there is a strong drive to educate and change consumption patterns through the Act on Promotion of the Purchase of Environment-Friendly Products (2004). Also affecting incentives, the Environmental Education Promotion Act (2008) focuses explicitly on environmental education for youth, ultimately creating a more informed public interested in pursuing careers in the green sector and purchasing related goods. Across Japan, Korea, and China, the Tripartite Environment Ministers' Meeting (TEMM) attempts to formalize environmental education across these three countries.

In Taiwan and China, our reading of environmental policies indicates that policy flexibility was influenced from the 1990s. In Taiwan, the Air Pollution Control Fee Collection Regulations (1995) affected the payment structure and, thus, the market incentives with regard to construction projects. The collection of air pollution control fees based on actual emission volumes has generated a major source of revenue for the government while reducing sulfur dioxide and nitrous oxide emissions, although there are still some reporting errors by certain industries. China's Environmental Protection Law (1989) encouraged the development of education in the science of environmental protection, and the Law of the PRC on Conserving Energy (1997) discussed the rational use of energy, education, and the fostering of responsibility systems. In Taiwan, the Resource Recycling Act (2002) charged citizens with the responsibility to abide by the principles of reducing consumption and controlling waste management.

In China, the pace of economic growth presents its own set of challenges. Environmental protection efforts in China can be viewed in the presence of economic reforms, which both expand environmental institutions and increase development. Environmental quality can be sacrificed, at the same time. The close relationship between economic reforms and environmental policy seems to occur in cycles, later arising following Deng's post-1992 economic reforms. An updated approach, though, must account for the relationships between the market, civil society, and the state in the context of openness to other countries, as we have done here. The ability to avoid environmental degradation while increasing economic growth in China, claimed by Brajer, et al., is facilitated through incoming technology transfers.[18] Politically, China is also faced with the challenge of balancing environmental regulations and decentralization. Excessive decentralization of enforcement regulations is bound to result in coordination problems. For example, local government officials are responsible for environmental quality and enforcement, detailed in the Provisions on Strengthening Environmental Protection of Township Enterprises (1997).

# Conclusion

In this chapter, we have shown that environmental policymaking in East Asia has been steadily transformed from a strict focus on domestic concerns to those which account for shared environmental hazards such as climate change. There is also a strong propensity for combined effects between S&T policies and environmental policies. A careful analysis of environmental policies in Japan, South Korea, Taiwan, and China indicates that EIAs and market-related environmental policies are focusing on stringency and flexibility.

For China and other developing countries which benefit from inflows of technology to treat environmental degradation, additional institutions should be identified and analyzed. The fostering and encouragement of Intellectual Property Rights (IPR) in China, for example, are more likely to bolster inflows of technology. Indeed, IPRs are much more important than simply providing foreign aid. Given the lack of physical equipment and knowledge being transferred through aid structures like the United Nation's Clean Development Mechanism, stronger IPRs accelerate China's receipt of actual physical technology and training from abroad.

There are also a number of unresolved and/or unmentioned points which should be addressed, based on the descriptive analysis of policies provided above. For example, Taiwan's environmental policies are heavily import oriented. This is undoubtedly because of its island status, but analyses of environmental policymaking must acknowledge the international political economy and how this impacts, for example, steel imports and quality. As well, there are some major differences in terms of policy design, as shown in the elegant structure of South Korea's environmental policies in contrast to those of Taiwan and China. We must explore the reasons for broad plans in South Korea and more detailed plans used in Taiwan.

There are some clear efforts to counter climate change and other environmental problems. Yet, given the lack of tangible evidence that policy flexibility is effectively shifting demand, we recommend that additional demand-centered actions be taken. This makes sense, as demand for energy and products will continue to grow, especially in China, and any countering effort to generate and utilized planned (stringency) and unanticipated (flexibility) innovation is encouraged.

## Five questions for discussions

1. East Asia has often been studied in terms of its transferable lessons for other regions. What are the core ingredients for East Asia's success in environmental policymaking?
2. China is on track to producing the largest amount of GHGs in the world. What are the environmental policies which can allow it to continue to experience economic growth without environmental degradation?
3. The Western world has been largely omitted from this chapter. What role can Europe and the United States play in facilitating environmental policymaking in East Asia, if any?
4. What role can interest groups and environmental nongovernmental organizations play in the environmental policymaking process?
5. What are your predictions for the future of environmental policymaking in East Asia? Will S&T policies and environmental policies be consistently and simultaneously designed?

# Notes

1 See OECD, *Compedium of Patent Statistics* (2008) and "Impacts of Environmental Policy Instruments on Technological Change: Joint Meetings of Tax and Environment Experts" (2007). Also Nick Johnstone and Ivan Haščič, "Environmental Policy Design and the Fragmentation of International Markets for Innovation," CESifo Working Paper Series No. 2630, 2009.

2 Data collection for patents and publications has been done through the online patent and publications search functions of the USPTO and the Web of Science, respectively. The parameters of this search are based on two criteria: inclusion of either "greenhouse effect" or "greenhouse gas" in the patent description or the article's topic. These keywords are by no means all-inclusive parameters to capture the degree of GHG-oriented innovation, but a cursory analysis of a number of keywords over the relevant time period confirms that these two terms are greatest in number and cover the widest area of industry classes. For patents, the issue date is distinct from the filing (or priority) date in that the former typically occurs from one to four years after the

latter. Also drawn from the USPTO search function are the issue date-ordered patent numbers, the assignee's country of origin, and the inventor's country of origin.

3   Japan: Ministry of Environment, the Ministry of Environmental Protection. China: the National People's Congress, the National Environmental Protection Agency, the Ministry of Urban and Rural Construction and Environmental Protection, the State Planning Commission/Environmental Protection Commission, and the State Council. South Korea: Ministry of Environment, Presidential Commission on Sustainable Development. Taiwan: Ministry of Environment, Environmental Protection Administration, Department of Comprehensive Planning, Environmental Protection Administration, Ministry of Transportation and Communications.

4   Other policy sub-groups which may be used in future analyses include manure- and methane, recycling, international/extra-national concerns, and import/export concerns. Energy policies which treat next-generation renewable energy sources such as biomass, solar, wind, and nuclear energy should also be addressed.

5   Japan's Law Concerning the Protection of the Ozone Layer through the Control of Specified Substance and Other Measures specifically targeted proper recycling methods for ozone depleting substance (ODS)-generating machines, such as air conditioners and refrigerators. Recycling is also emphasized in Japan's Basic Law for Establishing a Sound-Material Cycle Society, although recycling and reuse is couched within a framework which also targets waste reductions and sustainable consumption of natural resources.

6   Fang, Shu-Hwei and Hsiung-Wen Chen, "Air Quality and Pollution Control in Taiwan," *Atmospheric Environment* 30:5 (1996): 735–41.

7   Tsai, June, "System Vetting Development Plans Criticized," *Taiwan Today* (2008).

8   See, for example, the Circular on the Jurisdiction to Examine and Approve the Environmental Impact Statement of Construction (1986), which correlates with the Provisions on Engineering Design of Environmental Protection of Construction Projects (1987).

9   Subsequent, related legislation includes the Circular on Publishing the First Catalogue of the Eliminated Technologies and Equipment Causing Serious Air Pollution (1997), which outlines penalties for those who sell high air polluting machines, particularly for construction.

10  See, for example, the Official Reply of the State Council Concerning Acid Rain Control Zones and Sulphur Dioxide Pollution Control Zones (1998) and the Circular on Strengthening the Supervision and Administration of Pollution by Exhaust from Newly Manufactured Motor Vehicles (1998).

11  Sandstorms in March 2010 confirm that desertification, along with overgrazing and urban sprawl, contribute to the loose dust and dirt, which is then mixed with industrial pollution. These sandstorms affected areas beyond northern China, including Hong Kong (school's outdoor activities were cancelled), Taiwan (flights cancelled due to low visibility), and South Korea (a rare nationwide dust advisory) (Bodeen 2010).

12  Specifically, the Circular of the General Office of the State Council on Limiting and Stopping the Production, Sales, and Use of Leaded Fuel (1998).

13 These last two changes are represented by the Technical Policy on the Prevention and Control of Pollution by Motor Vehicle Emissions (1999).

14 The Circular on Adjusting Several Provisions on the Standards on the Elimination of Outdated Automobiles (2000) also showed considerable foresight, given that it distinguishes between different types of cars with expectations that the Chinese citizenry will increase their auto purchases over time.

15 Wang, Zhonghai, "Transfer of Rural Surplus Labour in China: Institutional Reform and Policy Evaluation," in *Agriculture in China and Oecd Countries: Past Policies and Future Challenges*, ed. OECD (Paris: OECD, 1999).

16 Chang, Shuen-Chin, Tzu-Yi Pai, Hsin-Hsien Ho, Horng-Guang Leu, and Yein-Rui Shieh, "Evaluating Taiwan's Air Quality Variation Trends Using Grey System Theory," *Journal of the Chinese Institute of Engineers* 30:2 (2007): 361–7.

17 This law is also known as the "Law Concerning the Promotion of Procurement of Eco-Friendly Goods and Services by the State and Other Entities."

18 Brajer, Victor, Robert W. Mead, and Feng Xiao, "Health Benefits of Tunneling through the Chinese Environmental Kuznets Curve (Ekc)," *Ecological Economics* 66:4 (2008): 674–86.

# Selected bibliography

Bodeen, Christopher. "China's Sandstorms Blast Beijing with Dust, Sand." *Seattle Times*, March 22, 2010.

Carter, Neil T. and Arthur P. J. Mol, eds. *Environmental Governance in China* (London: Routledge, 2007).

Edahiro, Junko. "The Law on Promoting Green Purchasing Five Years Later—Progress and Future Tasks." *Japan for Sustainability Newsletter* (2007) at http://www.japanfs.org/en_/newsletter/200706-1.html.

Hitoshi, Nozawa. "Overview of the Air Pollution Control Law (Suppression Vocs Emissions): Optimum Combination of Regulatory and Voluntary Measures." *Journal of Japan Air Cleaning Association* 44:3 (2006): 144–50.

Jaffe, Adam B., Richard G. Newell, and Robert N. Stavins. "Technological Change and the Environment," in *Handbook of Environmental Economics: Volume 1*, ed. Karl-Goran Maler and Jeffrey R. Vincent (Amsterdam: Elsevier, 2003).

Jahiel, Abigail R. "The Contradictory Impact of Reform on Environmental Protection in China." *The China Quarterly* 149 (1997): 81–103.

Japan Petroleum Energy Center (JPEC). "The Status of Vehicle Emission Control and Air Quality in Japan." (2010) at http://www.pecj.or.jp/english/jcap/jcap1/jcap1_01.html.

Johnstone, Nick and Ivan Haš i. "Environmental Policy Design and the Fragmentation of International Markets for Innovation." CESifo Working Paper Series No. 2630, 2009.

*Korea IT Times*. "Korea Cleaning Up Its Environmental Act." (2006) at http://www.koreaittimes.com/story/2745/korea-cleaning-its-environmental-act.

Mol, Arthur P. J. and Neil T. Carter. "China's Environmental Governance in Transition." *Environmental Politics* 15:2 (2006): 149–70.

OECD. 2008. *Compedium of Patent Statistics,* http://www.oecd.org/dataoecd/5/19/37569377.pdf.

—. "Environmental Policy Framework Conditions, Innovation and Technology Transfer." (2009).

Skinner, Mark W., Alun E. Joseph, and Richard G. Kuhn. "Social and Environmental Regulation in Rural China: Bringing the Changing Role of Local Government into Focus." *Geoforum* 34:2 (2003): 267–81.

Song, Young-Il and John Glasson. "A New Paradigm for Environmental Assessment (Ea) in Korea." *Environmental Impact Assessment Review* 30:2 (2009): 90–9.

Sonnenfeld, David A. "Environmental Reform in Asia." *Journal of Environment and Development* 15:2 (2006): 112–37.

Taiwan EPA, "Air Pollution Control Fee Collection Regulations Revised." 2007.

Tsai, June. "System Vetting Development Plans Criticized." *Taiwan Today* (2008) at http://www.taiwantoday.tw/ct.asp?xItem=41705&CtNode=428.

Ueno, Takahiro. "Technology Transfer to China to Address Climate Change Mitigation, Resources for the Future Issue Brief #09-09." (2009) at http://www.rff.org/RFF/Documents/RFF-IB-09-09.pdf.

USAID and Asian Environmental Compliance and Enforcement Network (AECEN). "Strengthening Legal and Policy Frameworks for Addressing Climate Change in Asia" (Bangkok: AECEN Secretariat, 2008).

Web-of-Science, ISI. "Isi Web-of-Science Database." isiknowledge.com, 2009.

Wild at Heart Legal Defense Association (WHLDA). "Ideologically Based Development: What's the Point of Environmental Impact Assessment?" (2009) at http://en.wildatheart.org.tw/archives/ideologically_based_development_whatas_the_point_of_environmental_impact_assessment.html.

Williams, Jack F. and Ch'ang-yi David Chang. *Taiwan's Environmental Struggle: Toward a Green Silicon Island* (New York: Routledge, 2008).

# 10

# East Asian Women and the Military: Victors and Victims

Lana Obradovic

---

# Introduction

According to Western authors studying women's participation in the military, women are more likely to be integrated and enjoy a higher degree of participation in democratic and developed states, where military forces are civilian-led, technologically advanced, not conscripted, and primarily defensive in nature; where birth and unemployment are low; and where women's household responsibilities are less and their political and labor force participation are greater.[1] What about East Asia, the only region where the Cold War is still raging and where citizenship in both democratic and nondemocratic regimes is often defined in militarized terms? Are women participating in the military, and how well do Western theories capture the dynamics of their integration and role?

Only a handful of works have explored the subject of women in the armed forces of the East Asian states and although they offer an incredible amount of detailed information, none of these works are concerned with the factors behind the degree to which states integrate women into the armed forces nor do they attempt a comparative analysis.[2] Indeed, the only section of literature where security studies intersect gender studies in East Asia are those discussing the Japanese Imperial Army's sexual exploitation of some 200,000 "comfort women" during World War II as a form of both colonialism and gender stratification in Confucian societies.[3]

We know little besides what an occasional news report from the region tells us. During the 60th anniversary celebration of the PRC at the Tiananmen Square on October 1, 2009, analysts hurried to examine the newest ominous weaponry, while the largest all-female formation ever assembled for a military parade in modern times, including 378 woman soldiers of the People's Liberation Army (PLA), was noted largely for its short hot-pink skirts and knee-high leather boots. No observers mentioned that the Chinese military has the same number of women as its US counterpart, and is estimated to be up to 8 percent of China's total forces. Similarly, the media overplay the colorful images of dancing and sword-wielding female soldiers at the Arirang Mass Games in North Korea, but fail to mention that women guard North Korea's coasts, tunnels, and bridges and make up about 10 percent of the North Korean People's Army. By contrast, surprisingly lower percentages of the women in the armed forces in Japan and South Korea, 4.7 percent and 3 percent respectively, and their often-limited role do not even earn a footnote in most news stories and Western scholarly works. Yet they are crucial in helping us understand civil-military and gender relations in these two Asian democracies. Most importantly, even the little information that we have tells us that East Asia does not fit neatly within Western theoretical explanations of women's participation in the military.

In China and North Korea, the two authoritarian states where militaries are commanded by the ruling party, women's participation in the military is much higher than in democratic Japan and South Korea, where armed forces are led by the elected civilian regimes. Only Japan has an all-volunteer and primarily defensive force; the other three states' military services rely on conscription and possess both defensive and offensive capabilities. In terms of levels of threat, the East Asian states are known for military stand-offs, including North Korea's 2010 attack on South Korea's Yeonpyeong Island, and in the continued Senkaku/Diaoyu islands dispute between China and Japan. However, the levels of threat fail to explain the significant difference in the degree to which these states have integrated women into their military services.

A cursory look at the level of economic development measured by the GDP per capita demonstrates that the evidence contradicts the Western argument that highly developed and wealthy states accept more women. Both Japan and South Korea's GDP per capita is much higher than that of China. North Korea is not ranked by the World Bank due to lack of reliable information, but we know that it is among the poorest nations, and an estimated 3 to 5 percent of the population has starved to death since the early 1990s.

Manpower shortage due to low unemployment and fertility rates has not forced governments to enlist more women, either. In 2010–11, unemployment rates were all low and almost identical: China at 4.2 percent, South Korea 4 percent, and Japan 4.9 percent.[4] Unfortunately, no data are available for North Korea. Similarly, Japan and South Korea have among the lowest fertility rates in the world, with 1.27 and 1.22 children per woman, respectively, while China and North Korea are ahead with 1.77 and 1.86, respectively.[5]

When it comes to women's political status and participation, according to the Inter Parliamentary Union data, as of 2011, China had 21 percent, North Korea 15.7 percent, South Korea 14.77 percent, and Japan 11.3 percent of women holding seats in national parliaments. However, their quantitative presence in China and North Korea does not grant women any substantive power as they are largely absent from the real loci of power, such as the Central and Standing Committees of the ruling party. Most women were handpicked as "exemplary workers" rather than true political actors. For example, in North Korea, only 6 out of 260 ministers from 1948 until 2000 were women.[6] Therefore, it is difficult to argue that political participation or equality in the political sphere has had much effect on women's military status.

Moreover, there is no evidence that cultural variables such as religion or strength of religiosity have any impact. Inglehart and Norris's study of religiosity in 75 states finds East Asians among the least religious in the world; China ranks 75th, South Korea 72nd, and Japan 63rd. Again, although North Korea is not included in their study, it is common knowledge that worshiping anything besides the Kim dynasty is forbidden and punishable. Although gender equality is institutionalized in these states, in all four, women's status at home continues to be shaped by the patriarchal Confucian teachings that proscribe strict gender division of labor and define a woman as a primary child- and household-caretaker.

However, as this chapter argues, communist emancipation of women and eradication of Confucianism in the public sphere in China and North Korea in order to ensure the full participation of all citizens in economic and defense sectors has, over time, led to higher female participation in labor and the military. There are no current data for North Korea as they have not been collected since the mid-1990s due to famine, but in 1970 women accounted for 70 percent of the workforce in light industries and 60 percent of agricultural workers. China is ranked 38th by the World Economic Forum in terms of economic opportunities and participation for women while Japan and South Korea are 110th and 113th respectively. These data demonstrate that regardless of the rights bestowed upon women by these democratic governments, economic institutions are still considered male domains. China and North Korea characterize women as victors and defenders of the socialist cause and have employed them in economics for more than six decades. In South Korea and Japan, extraordinary yet gendered economic industrialization did not necessarily produce a considerable growth of opportunities for women, but has rather led to hegemonic masculinity in the workplace by creating a complex system of hierarchy similar to the traditional military structure, where subordination and sexualization of women are a norm, and the high-ranking and high-paid jobs are reserved for men.

Therefore, although Western theories seem unable to fully explain women's military participation in East Asia, they are not entirely wrong in their assumption that high economic participation and presence of women in technical and professional fields in the civilian market will "spill over" into the military labor market. This glorification of women as a worker combined with a long and rich history of being active participants in the armed forces in China and North Korea led to the higher inclusiveness in the military. On the other hand, the Japanese and Korean women's continued portrayal as mothers, caretakers, and victims of institutionalized militarism, Japanese colonialism and US neocolonialism, and the often-strained civil-military relations, have led to apathy regarding the policy of integration and low levels of participation.

This chapter is by no means an exhaustive study that can fully capture the dynamics of women's military participation, but rather an exploratory attempt to conduct research on this understudied subject in China, Japan, North Korea, and South Korea.

# Gender and security in East Asia

Each study case is a brief narrative of the historical involvement of women in the military in order to trace the factors that affect their current level of participation. Before delving into the examination of individual states, it is important to address the issue of access to information and availability of reliable sources. Collecting data regarding East Asian military services can be an arduous and, at times, an impossible task, particularly in the cases of China and North Korea. Much of the data coming from these two is difficult to verify and therefore highly suspect. Although it was much easier to obtain information regarding the Japanese SDF and South Korean forces, even official sources were often unclear what was public domain information and what was not. Therefore, data used are a combination of military press releases, Ministry of Defense white papers, recruitment and policy change public announcements, and secondary sources addressing the recruitment of women in all four states.

## China

Of all four states, China has the longest and richest history, with over 3,000 years of women's participation in the ranks. To this day, the Chinese praise the ancient heroines who fought for their families, rulers, and peasant causes such as the first-known Chinese female general, Hao Fu (1250–1192 B.C.), who commanded more than 13,000 soldiers; the Song Dynasty General Mu Guiying and soldier Hua Mulan. Sun Tzu turned the 300 concubines of King Wu into his loyal soldiers. Women's participation in the ranks continued during the peasant uprising of the Tai Ping Tian Guo Movement/Taiping Rebellion (1850–68), the overthrow of the Qing dynasty in 1911, and through the early years of the Chinese Communist movement (1927–35) that sought to reject traditional Confucian ideas regarding gender relations. Three-thousand women joined Mao on the 12,500-kilometer Long March (1934–5) in a wide range of combat and noncombat military positions, including direct guerrilla combat. Others performed on stage, including Mao's wife, He Zhizhen, promising equality and escape from poverty to the peasants and masses they encountered along the way. The Fourth Front Army from Sichuan Province boasted thousands of women, recruited because men's opium addiction had left the Army inadequate and weak. Most of these women were killed or became Kuomintang spoils of war. Only 149 survived.

Women joined the anti-Japanese movement in their thousands during the Yan An period (1935–45), but their roles were now reduced to solely noncombat positions in nursing, logistics, communications, propaganda, and administration. This new auxiliary and supporting role continued after the establishment of the PRC in 1949, and through the Korean War (1950–3), with 150,000 Chinese women serving in medical, cultural, and communications units. Their participation abruptly ended in 1955 as the PLA adopted a Soviet model of military organization, and 764,000 women were demobilized.

It was not until 1967 that they returned to the ranks, when the PLA began to recruit women again, this time at a rate of 7,500 per year. Only girls from the revolutionary "Five Reds" families—workers, peasants, soldiers, staff, and small merchants—were eligible to serve in the military, although women scientists, doctors, and engineers who did not come from such families were able to join when their skills were deemed necessary. From 1966–76, becoming a woman soldier was "regarded as a privilege," and girls, inspired by the achievements of ancient heroines and Party doctrine, had to compete fiercely to obtain a commission. This policy change coincides with the Great Proletarian Cultural Revolution (1966–76), during which Confucian values and ideas regarding societal hierarchy, women's "natural place" at home, and as a male subordinate were rejected once again by both Mao and the Party, and new gender roles were promoted. Women sought to shed the image of "bourgeois" gentle femininity and feminism by donning men's military combat clothes, cutting their hair like boys, and using belts to interrogate and beat the "enemies of the state." This militarization of the women of China did not happen overnight. Already in 1961, Mao himself had written "Militia Women," a poem glorifying women in uniform. Roughly translated, the lyrics are:

> Early rays of sun illumine the parade grounds,
> And these handsome girls heroic in the wind,
> With rifles five feet long,
> Daughters of China with a marvelous will,
> You prefer hardy uniforms to colorful silk.

In the early 1960s, a film titled *Red Detachment of Women*, and later a ballet, based on true events, lionized a group of female guerrillas who fought an abusive local landlord. By the time the Cultural Revolution began, militarism and gender-neutrality replaced feminism and femininity in the public discourse of China. This new version of gender discourse really meant that women's political identity was going to be defined by the state and party, and implemented by the All-China Women's Federation. In addition, former political criteria expressing preference for "Five Reds" women were abandoned, and more female professionals educated in the civilian sectors were able to enter the military and pursue job security and stable careers.

The policy remained unchanged until the 60th Anniversary parade in October 2009.[7] Eleven days after the women's exceptional performance had attracted much attention in China and abroad, the PLA set new regulations for the recruitment of women, including raising the maximum age to include more college graduates particularly those with technical degrees. Prior to the most recent changes, the PLA largely relied on unemployed men with limited education from rural areas who lacked other sources of income and opportunity. But as market forces are reaching deep into the Chinese Mainland, and as the PLA attempts to sharpen its image as a sophisticated and technologically advanced armed force, it is beginning to tap into the pool of talented and highly educated young women willing to join as the service offers privileges such as reimbursement for tuition fees and employment opportunities at a time of global economic and financial downturn. Besides high female labor participation, it is also important to point out that 52 percent of female workers are in professional and technical fields, therefore allowing for the spillover from the civilian labor market into military service. It remains difficult to understand the precise role that women will play in the military given that entrance exams require them to demonstrate their artistic skills and even show off their physical appearance. While many female soldiers will be working in communications, health care, and entertainment, today PLA women are sent to escort missions in the Gulf of Aden, operate submarines, and as astronauts taking part in manned docking of China's future space lab. The latest trends are primarily explained by the PLA's search for manpower with technical expertise, and the availability of such experts in the labor market. As Xiaolin Li argues,

> Women's presence in the regular armed forces of China . . . remains constant due both to the Party's ideology of equal status between genders and to the dual commitment of women to labor and family. It also derives from a tradition of using women in unconventional warfare and irregular military formations . . . to be a Chinese woman soldier in peacetime is a privilege offering job security, opportunities for education and training and better social status.[8]

Women would not have been able to participate in such numbers and extent without being given opportunities in the economic sphere first by the Communist regime, without the extensive history of women in the ranks, and a manpower need for specialized knowledge and expertise.

## South Korea

Unlike in China, there is very little evidence of ancient women warriors on the Korean peninsula. The Neo-Confucian philosophy adopted by the Chosun dynasty (July 1392–October 1897) prescribed a very strict and limited role for women as wives serving husbands, in-laws, and male heirs whereas loyalty and sacrifice for the country were virtues attributed strictly to men.

Women were admitted first in 1948 as a part of the Nursing Corps, but in 1950 the Women's Army Corps was officially established and during the Korean War most women served as surgeons, dentists, and nurses. The regulations limiting their status based on age, marital status, and motherhood were eliminated in 1987 after the first democratic elections. In 1990, a separate women's branch of the military was abolished and fully integrated into the services in the name of gender equality. Throughout the 1990s, and particularly after the election of Kim Young-sam, who proposed the change, military academies opened their doors to women, starting with the Air Force in 1997, and followed by the Army in 1998, and the Navy in 1999 and in each, 10 percent of seats are reserved for women. By 2001, first commissioned and noncommissioned officers entered both the Air Force and the Navy, and a first woman was promoted to the rank of general. Although allowed to join South Korea's infantry troops, women are not allowed in combat, which means that they would have to relinquish their positions in the event of war. Other combat positions such as fighter pilots or combat vessel crew are open to women. But it was only in December 2010 that Song Myung-soon became South Korea's first woman combat general. Until her appointment, all five female generals were in the nurse corps.

Women's numbers remain incredibly low compared to other democratic societies and are tightly controlled by the government. This is particularly surprising given the looming demographic crisis that will provide an insufficient number of young men to sustain the current force. According to the Korean National Statistical Office, 20-year-old men numbered generally more than 400,000 from 1977 to 2003, a figure entirely sufficient to sustain the 690,000 active-duty military population that had been maintained in the 1990s. But this number is projected to fall to 233,000 in 2025, and to fall below 200,000 in 2036. Yet, as of November 2009, the number of women serving in the Korean military as commissioned and noncommissioned officers is 5,560, or 3 percent of the nation's total military forces. By 2010, that number was supposed to rise to 6,340, and by 2020 to only 11,606, to make up a meager 5.6 percent of all forces.[9]

Although South Korea's glass ceiling seems to have cracked, discrimination and low participation and recruitment, as predicted, seem to reflect fairly well women's status in the economic sector of the country where female labor participation is still very low with 42 percent of the total. The numbers are slightly better in professional and technical fields, where women occupy 40 percent of positions but 37 percent of women with tertiary education being unemployed. In fact, South Korea is the only country in the OECD where the more educated the woman, the less likely she is to be employed. Women account for only 10 percent of all executives, and only 1.1 percent out of 710 executives in 140 financial firms are women.[10] In 1980, women earned 45 percent of what men made, peaking at about 65 percent in 2011.

This low participation in labor is often blamed on Confucian values constricting women to home once married and with children. It is the same values that influence the discourse regarding the association of women and the military that for most Korean nationals, regardless of their gender, will be of "military comfort women." It really refers to the sexual slavery and institutionalized and systematic rape by the Japanese Imperial Army. Most Korean victims of this crime were silent for almost 50 years primarily for the sake of self-preservation and protection of their dignity, as chastity continued to be a priority of these Confucian women. It is the Confucian philosophy of subordination of women that has allowed for both brutal recruitment and imprisonment, as well as the collective silence of the nation on this sensitive subject for more than half a century. Neo-Confucian beliefs regarding loyalty and sacrifice were manipulated and used to serve the militaristic purposes of imperial Japan, and later contributed to the failure to acknowledge the forceful conscription of female sex slaves until 1992 when Chuo University Professor Yoshiaki Yoshimi uncovered documents in the library of the Japanese SDF implicating the government. While some scholars sought to justify the recruitment of comfort women in Korea by arguing that this was a necessary evil to protect respectable women from sexual abuse by Japanese soldiers, others, such as Watanabe, see this double standards of Confucian thought, trapping the women as sexual slaves not only during the war, but for a full half century by not allowing them to speak of the violence they endured. But most importantly this commodification of the woman's body in Korea by the Japanese has created a gendered perspective on the military; on the one hand, the man's loyalty to the state, his citizenship and even economic future are inherently tied to his military service, while women are only to be used by militaries to dehumanize, humiliate, and victimize the nation. In reality, the official discourse is based on the militarized manhood through conscription and masculine national pride in Korean women's chastity, which promotes the control of women's sexuality by the state and, as Hyunah Yang points out, it "perpetuates rather than seeks to understand or overcome the colonial legacy."[11] In addition, the Korean government officially sanctioned prostitution and the sex industries to cater to American soldiers, educated its women in English and etiquette, and sent them into military camp towns to earn hard currency, and it continues to do so unofficially. As a 71-year-old former prostitute turned activist argued, "women like me were the biggest sacrifice for my country's alliance with the Americans."[12]

Although one can speculate on the future of the reform to modernize South Korea's military and abolish compulsory service, today Korean all-male conscription not only continues to be central to both construction of the anticommunist rhetoric and organization of its economic and industrial development, but it promotes gendered construction of political and economic spheres of this industrialized and modern democratic state. Only once masculinity is no longer a chief component of the official construction of Korean national identity and citizenship, we might see the expansion of the roles and numbers of South Korean women entering military forces as true equals.

## North Korea

The Sex Equality Law passed on July 31, 1946 erased all Chosun dynasty patriarchal relations and granted women equal rights in labor, politics, pay, education, and society in general. Women's participation in every sector was not a question of equality but rather, as some argue, a necessity to cope with the postwar economic recovery. Due to manpower shortage, the government required all citizens to participate in production, and women were particularly encouraged to join the workforce to revolutionize themselves but were also expected to fulfill traditional Confucian female roles such as child-rearing and taking care of the household. Unlike in China, Confucianism remained strong, and as Halliday suggests "there may be powerful links between this Confucian past and the manifestly patriarchal present under the 'Great Leader' Kim Il-sung and the 'Dear leader' Kim Jong-il, his son."[13] Both men and women were to follow their Oboi Suryongnim, or the leader who is both father and mother, thereby erasing the question of gender from the official discourse, and today there is no adequate word for gender at all in the North Korean dialect.

From the beginning, this legislation directly affected women's participation in the military forces. Unlike South Korean women, who mainly served in the medical corps during the Korean War, North Korean women performed a variety of functions, including hit-and-run operations, combat with guerrilla units, and sabotage, as well as perform surveillance, collect intelligence, and kill UN troops by disguising themselves as refugees. The Mansudae Grand Monument in Pyongyang, or the infamous holy shrine of Kim Il-sung, reveals a handful of women bearing weapons standing shoulder to shoulder with men. Kim Jong-suk, Kim's wife, and the North's most famous war heroine, is a symbol of this equality thanks to her guerrilla exploits battling the Japanese and her excellent marksmanship. She often declared proudly that her son Kim Jong-il learned to walk with her rifle in his hand.

After the war, women were recruited on a limited scale for rear-area duties: psychological warfare units, hospitals, administration, and antiaircraft units. Most women were assigned to units defending fixed installations near their workplaces.

The real change in women's military status came with the fall of the Soviet Union and the leadership of Kim Jong-il. North Korean armed forces were faced with a serious manpower shortage after the estimated 2 percent of the North Korean population, and particularly able-bodied men, fled to China to find work, and 5 percent died of starvation during the mid-1990s. The government was forced to adapt by passing the "*Songun*" (military-first) policies, giving the military supremacy in ruling the state over the Worker's Party, and the military's role was expanded across every aspect of socioeconomic life. This policy only further militarized the state, creating one of the largest armies in the world, with an estimated 1.2 million active duty personnel. Conscription never really existed in North Korea, and the government never really needed it because men seeking the perks and privileges military service provided joined in large numbers. However, now that the state was unable to recruit enough men, conscription began in 2002 and women were recruited in much higher numbers. Joining the military meant having a meal, clothes, education, elevated social status, expressing adoration for the Kim dynasty, and thus women started to fill the positions of men who increasingly were ducking the draft to make money in small businesses.

We also know Kim Jong-il continues to keep calling on skilled women to "more dynamically wage the all-out charge to build a thriving nation full of faith in sure victory and optimism and demonstrate the revolutionary spirit of the Korean women."[14] This "rational use of manpower," as Kim Il-sung referred to the recruitment of female workers seems to have been simply extended by Kim Jong-il to include talented and skilled women in the military. Although there are no current data on women's labor participation, the number of female professional and technical workers increased 10.6 times between 1963 and 1989.[15]

Today, we estimate that women make up more than 10 percent of the North Korean People's Army soldiers. The government has even specific propaganda songs to attract women into coastal artillery units and female soldiers armed with 14.5-mm automatic artillery guard most of the state's tunnels and bridges.[16] In 2002, of the 36 units that Kim Jong-il visited, "at least one-third were female units."[17] Women serve for seven years, and are most generally dispatched to antiaircraft artillery units, signal corps, or machine gun corps in the rear.

A member of the female elite artillery unit who defected to South Korea in 2003 claims that the military did not allow her to speak to her family and other ordinary citizens to ensure she did not go "soft" and lose discipline and mental and ideological strength the way the Soviets had done. She explained that every day involves two hours of political indoctrination, and two hours of military strategy, equipment training and tactics instruction. She also admitted that the promise of better opportunities and glorious heroism has faded in the last few years, as she was forced to scour fields for withered cabbage leaves to survive.[18]

The survival of its military force, industrial and agricultural sectors, and to a large extent the maintenance of the regime itself today increasingly depends on North Korean women. It is clear that the current status, high percentages, and extensive role that women play in the North Korean military were directly and primarily influenced by the communist emancipation, elimination of Confucianism from the public sphere, and labor mobilization to sustain this isolated dictatorship. There is no doubt that these have liberated but also brought new forms of oppression to the women of North Korea, by demanding they produce, reproduce, and defend. Although women have been champions of economic mobilization and the defense of the nation, the revolutionary equality so eloquently articulated by the despotic regime remains elusive in the light of continued discrimination in the social, familial, and cultural life of the state. Yet, there is a hope that their increased participation in the economy, particularly with the emerging small-scale market activity, and their continued military service might start to challenge the loci of power and traditional societal relations they stand for.

## Japan

Similar to the Koreas, there is an almost complete absence of historical records, with the exception of a great Japanese epic, *Heike Monogatari*, which glorifies female samurai, even though the Confucian-influenced Bushido code of ancient Japanese warriors and training was really meant to teach self-sacrifice to home and family rather than the country.

During World War II, while men were conscripted, all single women between ages 14 and 25 were obliged to work in factories to solve the serious labor shortage in factories. Yet, even though by the end of the war, military service itself suffered tremendous shortages, the Japanese government failed to conscript women. It is not clear, however, if this was due to patriarchal attitudes within the state or among the public at large, but, as some argue, it does speak of "static psychocultural views about the place of women in society."[19] Finally, in June 1945, the Volunteer Army Military Service Code was enacted to organize women into army combat troops, although this code was never implemented.

After the war, women were first admitted only as nurses into the new SDF. In 1967 they were allowed to take up clerical positions in the Ground Forces, and in 1974 in the Maritime and Air SDF. In addition, as the abundant economic opportunities in the private sector reduced the number of young Japanese men willing to join the SDF, Prime Minister Tanaka Kakuei initiated legislation that was to open other positions away from the combat lines for women, "to fit their nature."[20] This first opening to women was largely motivated by the manpower shortage, and given the complex realities of Cold War civil-military relations in a state where the military as an institution was discredited, and soldiers treated with contempt and distrust, military policies were largely ignored and seen as irrelevant by society. In fact, no activists from the civil society, including feminist movements, were involved due to what some term "customary contradiction between feminism and militarism in postwar Japan."[21]

But what initiated the current policies of the SDF regarding women was the civilian Equal Employment Opportunity Law (EEOL) of 1986. Before the passage of this law, Japanese society was characterized by the extreme gender inequality largely determined by the cultural values influenced by Confucian teaching and gender-proper personality beliefs, according to which women's place is at home while men are primary earners in positions of power.[22] However, after the passage of the 1986 EEOL, gender relations and traditions have been altered, and have increased the percentages and status of women in Japanese economic sector, forcing the SDF to open its doors and expand the role and numbers of *josei jieikan,* or female soldiers. By 1993, all three branches started recruiting women, and they were enrolled in the National Defense Academy in 1992. Their international debut in 1996 was as members of the transportation unit of the peacekeeping operations in the Golan Heights and have also participated in East Timor and, recently, in Iraq.

Women are allowed in all positions but there are restrictions on assignments. They are not to be assigned to a long list of positions, including infantry companies, tank companies, reconnaissance units, engineer companies, antitank helicopter sections, chemical protection units, tunnel companies, landing ships, submarines, patrol guided missile boats, special guard units, fighter aircraft, and reconnaissance aircraft. These measures are "in comprehensive consideration of protection of maternity, possibility of direct combat, security securing privacy between men and women, and economical efficiency."[23] The SDF reserves the right to revoke or suspend any other assignments if these conditions are not met. The last restrictions lifted by the Defense Ministry Office for the Promotion of Gender Equality opened positions on destroyers, minesweeper tenders, and patrol helicopters.

As in South Korea, demographic composition is changing and although the number of eligible males between ages 18 and 26 was 900,000 in 1994, it will drop to about 600,000 in the next few years. Conscription will not be a possible solution to the problem due to Constitutional restrictions, general apathy toward the military services, and political upheaval through fear of its resurrection as a source of power might create. Yet, of the 240,000 uniformed personnel serving in Japan's SDF, only 11,000 are women (about 4.3%) and their role clearly remains rather limited. In addition, although considerably reduced, a Ministry of Defense's 2007 survey shows sexual harassment is rampant within the SDF, with 3,704 servicewomen reported having experienced some form, including "forced sex" (3.4%), and "unwanted touching" (20%).[24] Unfortunately, most popular media in Japan recognize the exceptional conditions of these women soldiers, but articles and stories describe them as "female beauties in uniforms," focusing on their sex appeal by displaying them clad in bikinis and short sports outfits.[25]

In fact, what seems to continue to plague the discourse regarding women's military participation is almost the unapologetic focus on the femininity of Japanese women, their purity and their traditional obligation to procreate rather than defend. The Ministry of Defense explicitly invokes "maternity" as a mean of limiting jobs available to women. Yet, this is not new. Since World War II, Japanese government and policies sanctified motherhood and encouraged traditional supportive activities by home-front women's groups and not participation in the military.[26] The government has continued to promote pro-natalist politics and the duty of loyal women to bear "pure Japanese offspring," while men's duty was to protect their women and families.[27]

In addition, while Japanese women were largely protected from the wrath of the Imperial Army by recruiting "comfort women" elsewhere, the same cannot be said of their interaction with the postwar occupying Allied troops. But to say that Japanese women were victimized by the Allied Forces alone unjustly absolves the Japanese government of any responsibility. It is true that while the Tokyo trials were trying to punish Japanese leadership for their war crimes and militarism, the victimization of Korean and other

East Asian women during the war went unacknowledged by the court even though all the necessary evidence was collected by the US military intelligence unit. This blatant disregard for victims' rights by the tribunal and lack of punishment eventually led to a complex situation in which Japan's lack of redress, acknowledgment, and apology for the woes of comfort women to this day are key factors to the understanding of the interaction between women and the military in Japan and South Korea.

But as John Lie argues, the control of the bodies of Japanese women, and their sexuality, only started after the war ended.[28] The Japanese state, just like the Korean postwar state, became a pimp for America's occupying forces. The Japanese government resuscitated "comfort divisions" as the Recreation and Amusement Association for the US occupation forces right after the war ended. This Act was one of Prime Minister Higashikuni cabinet's first decisions and it was executed by the mastermind of the Japanese economic miracle, Hayato Ikeda. It was meant to prevent Japanese women suffering the horrors the Imperial Army had inflicted upon the women of Korea and China.[29] However, Okinawan historian Oshiro Masayasu claims there had been as many as 10,000 rapes of Japanese women by American troops during the battle for Okinawa, which some argue "does not seem unlikely when one realizes that during the first 10 days of the occupation of Japan there were 1,336 reported cases of rape of Japanese women by American soldiers in Kanagawa prefecture alone."[30]

Although disbanded in 1946, regulated and unregulated prostitution continues to exist with the tacit approval of the state, as it does in Korea. Moreover, crimes and rapes committed by US military personnel against Japanese as well as Korean women to this day are out of the jurisdiction of these two states, as they gave up that right after the war. It remains to be seen if the government will seek to remove both social and institutional barriers for women in the SDF or if it will continue to emphasize gender-appropriate roles and promote the image of a woman as a weak victim in need of a male protector.

# "Feminization" of the military: the new great leap forward in East Asia?

This narrative is the first comparative attempt to analyze military participation of women in East Asia. It sought to verify the application of previous theoretical models based on Western democracies, and it showed that most variables, with the exception of female labor participation, do not seem useful in explaining the degree to which women have been integrated.

While limited data and access to the information regarding women in the ranks of all four states significantly affect the ability to generalize, it is possible to draw certain conclusions regarding the factors that can help explain the reasons behind women's numbers and role in the militaries of East Asia. While in all four states women's status at home continues to be shaped by the patriarchal Confucian teachings that proscribe strict gender division of labor and define a woman as a main child- and household-caretaker, all four claim that the same is not true in the public sphere. However, this assertion is questionable. Although highly developed and democratized, South Korea and Japan continue to have considerably low levels of women's participation in both the economic and political spheres as governments continue to emphasize women's primary duty as a mother and a homemaker. This might help explain the small numbers of women in their military ranks. In addition, what might explain the lack of interest by the public in the lack of progress regarding women's integration into the military and expansion of their role is the tragic history of militarization of women's lives for the sake of the greater good of the society. Continued focus on the negative imagery in both South Korea and Japan of women as sexual victims of military forces affects the way the society associates gender with military, and how it debates integration of a "victim" into the ranks of their violators. In fact, discussions in both are rare, albeit heated.

On the other hand, without the stigma attached as in South Korea and Japan, in China and North Korea young women are increasingly joining the military in search of economic opportunities, perks, and benefits that service can bring them. Both governments have integrated women to solve the manpower shortage under the guise of revolutionary equality and women's emancipation. Equality in East Asian communist terms will not neatly fit the Western definitions as it is often a way of corrupting women's lives. Yet, regardless of how twisted this version of equality might be, it has allowed for better integration and wider participation of women in the military than in democratic states of the region. What might have initially been lip service paid to the Marxist ideas on which modern Chinese and North Korean states were established, women were allowed as active participants in revolutionary movements and have thereafter been portrayed as champions of the socialist cause. This has allowed for a more positive image of a female soldier that continues to influence young women in the quest to become new and popular socialist heroines fighting for the people of their land.

## Five questions for discussions

1. Is it possible for Chinese and North Korean women to be emancipated within the framework of the communist system? Do they need to live in a democratic system to consider themselves fully liberated?
2. Will demographic changes, such as low fertility rates and aging population, in Japan and South Korea lead to more women participating in the military?
3. To what extent has Japan addressed the damning legacy of "comfort women" in East Asia? How can Japan and its neighbors deal with this historical issue?
4. How are women's roles defined by Confucian teachings? How does globalization challenge such roles?
5. How does China's growing military power relate to its political and economic rise? Is there an arms race in East Asia?

# Notes

1  See Segal 1995; Iskra et al., 2000.

2  See Li Xiaolin 1993; Frühstück 2007; Goh 2003; Hong 2002; Moon 2002.

3  See Choi 1997; Hicks 1997; Tanaka 2000; Min 2003; Soh 2008.

4  For China see "China's unemployment down to 4.2% at the end of Q3," Xinhua Agency, October 22, 2010; Statistics Korea Report "Economically Active Population Survey in February 2011"; Statistics Bureau of Japan Labor Force Survey January 2011.

5  United Nations Population Division, UNdata, Total Fertility Rates (per woman), 2005–10.

6  Andreï Nikolaevich Lan'kov, p. 75.

7  "First three-service women formation debutes in military parade," *Xinhua News*, October 1, 2009.

8  Li, 1993, p. 81.

9  "Military mulls recruiting female rank-and-file soldiers," *Chosun Ilbo*, November 13, 2009.

10  "UNDP Human Development Report data on professional and technical workers (% female), 1999–2007"; World Bank Gender Statistics, labor force, female (% age of total) 2007.

11  Yang, 1998, pp. 129–30.

12  Sanghun Choi, "Ex-prostitutes say South Korea and U.S. enabled sex trade near bases," *The New York Times*, January 7, 2009.

13  Halliday, 47.

14  "N. Korea calls for women's increased role in economic campaign," *Yonhap News Agency*, July 30, 2009.

15  Park, 1992, 537.

16  "North Korean forces increasingly manned by women soldiers," *World Tribune*, January 4, 2007.

17  James Brooke, "As North Korean men turn to business, women join the army," *The New York Times*, August 17, 2003.

18 Robert Marquand, "Bleak tales of army life in N. Korea: a defector from an elite women's unit speaks of tight control and fear of 'going soft'," *Christian Science Monitor*, May 13, 2003.

19 Havens, 1975, 916.

20 Frühstück, 2007, pp. 88–9.

21 Frühstück, p. 3.

22 Lebra, Takie Sugiyama, *Japanese Women: Constraint and Fulfillment* (Honolulu, HI: University of Hawaii Press, 1985), p. 137.

23 Review of Restriction on Assignment of Female SDF Personnel, Ministry of Defense of Japan, September 22, 2008.

24 "Sexual harassment rampant in SDF," *Japan Today*, January 13, 2010.

25 Frühstück, p. 111.

26 Havens, 918.

27 Lie, 1997, 54.

28 Lie, 252.

29 Lie, 256.

30 Peter Schrijvers, 2002, p. 212.

# Selected bibliography

Andreï Nikolaevich Lan'kov. *North of the DMZ: Essays on Daily Life in North Korea* (Jefferson, NC: McFarland & Company, 2007).

Bennett, Bruce W. "A Brief Analysis of the Republic of Korea's Defense Reform Plan." Report Prepared for Republic of Korea, Ministry of National Defense (RAND Corporation, 2006).

Choi, Chungmoo, ed. *The Comfort Women: Colonialism, War, and Sex* (Durham NC: Duke University Press, 1997).

Frühstück, Sabine. *Uneasy Warriors: Gender, Memory and Pop Culture in the Japanese Army* (Berkeley, CA: University of California Press, 2007).

Goh, Dohk. "Attitudes toward Female Integration in the Korean Military." *The Korean Journal of Defense Analysis* XV:1 (Spring 2003): 275–91.

Halliday, Jon. "Women in North Korea: An Interview with the Korean Democratic Women's Union." *Bulletin of Concerned Asian Scholars* 17:3 (1985): 46–56.

Havens, Thomas R. H. "Women and War in Japan 1937–1945." *The American Historical Review* 80:4 (October 1975): 913–34.

Hong, Doo-Seung. "Women in the South Korean Military." *Current Sociology* 50:5 (2002): 729–43.

Honig, Emily. "Maoist Mapping of Gender: Reassessing the Red Guards," in Susan Brownell and Jeffrey Wasserstrom, eds. *Chinese Femininities/Chinese Masculinities: A Reader* (Berkeley: University of California Press, 2002), pp. 255–68.

Inglehart, Ronald and Pippa Norris. *Rising Tide: Gender Equality and Cultural Change Around the World* (Cambridge, UK: Cambridge University Press, 2003).

Iskra Darlene, Marcia Leithauser, Stephen Trainor, and Mady Wechsler Segal. "Women's Participation in Armed Forces Cross-Nationally: Expanding Segal's Model." *Current Sociology* 50:5 (2002): 771–97.

Kang, Hye Ryung and Chris Rowley. "Women in Management in South Korea: Advancement or Retrenchment?" in *Women in Asian Management,* ed. Vimolwan Yukongdi and John Benson (New York, NY: Routledge, 2006), pp. 73–91.

Kim, Il-sung, "Reminiscences with the Century." Volume 4, Chapter 12, To Hasten The Liberation Of The Country, 1. The Birth of A New Division.

Lebra, Takie Sugiyama. *Japanese Women: Constraint and Fulfillment* (Honolulu, HI: University of Hawaii Press, 1985).

Li, Xiaobing. *A History of the Modern Chinese Army* (Lexington, KY: University of Kentucky Press, 2007).

Li, Xiaolin. "Chinese Women in the People's Liberation Army: Professionals or Quasi-Professionals?" *Armed Forces and Society* 20:1 (1993): 69–83.

—. "Chinese Women Soldiers: A History of 5,000 Years." *Social Education* 58:2 (1994): 67–71.

Lie, John "The State as a Pimp: Prostitution and the Patriarchal State in Japan in the 1940s." *The Sociological Quarterly* 38:2 (Spring 1997): 251–63.

Min, Pyong Gap. "Korean 'Comfort Women': The Intersection of Colonial Power, Gender, and Class." *Gender and Society* 7:6 (December 2003): 938–57.

Moon, Seungsook. "Beyond Equality versus Difference: Professional Women Soldiers in the South Korean Army." *Social Politics* 9:2 (2002): 212–47.

Park, Kyung Ae. "Women and Revolution in North Korea." *Pacific Affairs* 65:4 (Winter 1992–3): 527–45.

Schrijvers, Peter. The GI War against Japan: American Soldiers in Asia and the Pacific during World War II (New York: New York University Press, 2002).

Segal, Mady Wechsler. "Women's Military Roles Cross-Nationally: Past, Present, and Future." *Gender and Society* 9:6 (1995): 757–75.

Soh, Chunghee Sarah. *The Comfort Women: Sexual Violence and Postcolonial Memory in Korea and Japan* (Chicago, Ill: University of Chicago Press, 2008).

Sugiyama Lebra, Takie. *Japanese Women: Constraint and Fulfillment* (Honolulu, HI: University of Hawaii Press, 1985).

Tanaka, Toshiyuki. *Japanese Comfort Women: Sexual Slavery during WWII and US Occupation* (London, UK: Routledge, 2001).

Watanabe, Kazuko. "Trafficking in Women's Bodies, Then and Now." *Peace and Change* 20:4 (October 1995): 501–14.

Yang, Hyunah. "Re-membering the Korean Military Comfort Women: Nationalism, Sexuality, and Silencing," in *Dangerous Women: Gender and Korean Nationalism,* ed. Elaine H. Kim and Chungmoo Choi (New York: Routledge, 1998), pp. 129–30.

# Part III
## Changing Societies

# 11

# China's Rising Generation: College-Educated Youth in the Reform Era

Teresa Wright

---

## Chapter Outline

# Introduction

In the West and particularly in the United States, many assume that economic liberalization and growth—especially when accompanied by increased access to information—will lead to strain between a society and the authoritarian regime over which it governs, ultimately eliciting popular pressures for liberal democratic change. Yet when it comes to China's college students, this has not been the case. To the contrary, relative to China's early reform period (1978–89), since 1990 individuals pursuing college degrees in China have exhibited decreased support for Western-style democracy, and less inclination to distance themselves from and challenge the ruling Chinese Communist Party (CCP). In the 1980s, relations between college-educated youths and the state were increasingly attenuated, and at times flared into outright confrontation. In the spring of 1989, it appeared that China's university students might be the vanguard of liberal democratic change. More generally, from 1978–89 students showed great admiration for the politics, philosophical ideas, and mass media of the West. Yet since the early 1990s, college students have exhibited a much more positive view of the CCP-led political system and a much more negative view of the West—including its liberal democratic governments and mass media outlets. Indeed, when college students took to the streets between 1990 and 2011, they did not press for political liberalization, but rather defended China and the Chinese government against foreign and domestic detractors.

This chapter documents the changing character of Chinese university students' political attitudes and activities in the post-Mao period, highlighting the contrast between the periods of 1978–89 and 1990–2011. This comparison of the early and late post-Mao eras suggests that economic liberalization and growth may not always be accompanied by greater public support for the type of liberal democracy found in the West. At the same time, the chapter emphasizes that some of the political attitudes and behaviors evidenced by Chinese university students have remained virtually unchanged throughout the reform period. The chapter also examines the major factors that have contributed to these changes and continuities, including access to the Internet, the demographic characteristics of China's university student population, the degree of unity within the top CCP leadership, the content conveyed in domestic media coverage and the educational system, and China's global economic and political status.

# University student attitudes, behavior, and context, 1978–89

From 1978 to 1989, China's university students displayed high regard for Western mass media outlets, philosophy, and liberal democratic forms of political rule. Simultaneously, college-educated youths showed disdain for China's communist and pre-communist characteristics, and little interest in joining the Party. At times—most notably in the winter of 1986–7 and spring of 1989—students boldly took to the streets to call for greater freedom of expression and association, and an end to political corruption. Although many factors contributed to these political attitudes and behaviors, some of the most important were: (1) the elite social status yet mediocre economic conditions of university students; (2) divisions within the top ranks of the CCP regarding economic and political reform; and (3) China's tenuous international economic and political status.

During the last ten years of Mao's rule—China's Cultural Revolution of 1966–76—China's universities were almost entirely shut down, as they were viewed as bastions of "bourgeois" thought. By the end of 1978, the universities had been reopened and the CCP was firmly in the hands of a new leader, Deng Xiaoping—a pragmatist committed to China's scientific and technological modernization. A merit-based university admissions policy was put in place, featuring a national university entrance exam that emphasized academic knowledge rather than Maoist ideology.[1] Through 1989, access to universities was determined almost exclusively by a student's score on this examination. Because admission slots were extremely limited, typically less than 5 percent of all exam-takers were able to enter a university.[2] Within the population as a whole from 1978 to 1989, roughly one-tenth of one percent of the Chinese citizenry was a university student, and just over 1 percent was a university graduate.[3] Throughout this period, university tuition and fees were extremely low, such that financial concerns rarely deterred an admitted student from enrolling.

Upon graduation, most university students were assigned to jobs by the government. As economic reforms allowed for the development of the private sector, those with college degrees enjoyed some alternative employment options. Because the number of university graduates was exceedingly small, the employment "demand" for college degree holders outstripped the "supply" by a ratio of three to one, guaranteeing fairly desirable jobs for virtually all.[4] Yet even so, for the vast majority of university graduates who became state sector employees, incomes and living standards were only marginally higher than those of their uneducated coworkers. Meanwhile, in the private sector, individuals without college degrees increasingly were earning more than university graduates with state sector jobs.

University students in the early post-Mao period also were affected by conflicts among CCP elites over the proper pace and extent of political and economic reform. Through 1989, the Party's top tier included eight "first generation" CCP elders who held few formal positions yet were extremely influential. Among them, Deng Xiaoping was the most powerful.[5] While

Deng was committed to expanding China's economy through marketization and opening to the global capitalist economy, others had deep reservations about economic reform and insisted on continuing with a planned economy.[6] Concomitantly, Deng exhibited only tenuous and lukewarm support for political liberalization. Within the second and third tiers of the CCP, factional conflict revolved around both power and policy: each faction wished to become the heir to the first-generation leadership, and each held different views regarding the proper pace and extent of reform. For most of the 1980s, the more pro-reform faction was led by CCP General Secretary Hu Yaobang and Premier Zhao Ziyang, both of whom had been placed in their positions by Deng. The more conservative (or in Chinese parlance, "leftist") faction within the CCP leadership's second tier was led by Li Peng.

Throughout the 1980s, conflict between these two groups caused CCP policy to move fitfully and uncertainly between reform and retrenchment in the economic sphere, and opening and constriction in the political sphere. As economic reform policies fluctuated, real income grew slightly from 1980 to 1982, rose fairly substantially from 1983 to 1985, and then flattened and slightly declined from 1986 to 1989. Concomitantly, urban economic inequality rose sharply from 1983 to 1984 and even more dramatically from 1987 to 1989.[7] When this occurred, the financial position of most university students—the vast majority of whom did not come from wealthy families— declined in both absolute and relative terms.

From the time of Mao's death through the student demonstrations of 1989, China's ruling elites swung between policies that ceded greater autonomy and power to university students and administrators, and policies that repressed and constricted their freedom.[8] During 1978–80, a period of loosening spurred the "Democracy Wall" movement, which was spearheaded by youths who had been deprived of a college education during the Cultural Revolution. After initially expressing support for the movement, Deng turned against it by late 1979, and key movement activists were jailed. Following a degree of renewed political relaxation and economic reform in the early 1980s, in 1983 the Party waged an "anti-spiritual pollution" campaign to combat what some top leaders perceived to be the corrupting influence of Western values and practices. Subsequently, in the mid-1980s some key CCP elites signalled their support for liberalization. Yet in 1987, political constriction reemerged in the Party's "anti-bourgeois liberalization" campaign. Shortly thereafter, China's ruling authorities again indicated their openness to reform. In 1988, for example, a CCP-affiliated China Central Television (CCTV) documentary series entitled "River Elegy" (Heshang) aired across China. Supported by CCP General Secretary Zhao Ziyang, River Elegy portrayed China's Yellow River (known as the heart of China's traditional civilization) as stagnant and yellow, contrasting it with the "blueness" of Western civilization. The film quite overtly suggested that in order for China to modernize and prosper, it must cast off its backward and inferior "Chinese" values and practices and adopt those of the West. In mid-1989, this period of loosening ended with the Party's violent suppression of the massive student demonstrations.

On the global stage, although China was on the economic rise from 1978 to 1989, it remained a struggling and uncertain economic and political player in a world still unquestionably dominated by the economies of the advanced industrial West and Japan. Further, in the late 1980s, budding anticommunist movements in Poland and other Eastern and Central European states reinforced the perception that communism could no longer persist in its existing form.

These factors fueled skepticism among university students regarding China's political, economic, and social status quo, and stimulated their admiration for alternative—and particularly Western—systems. As summed up by Stanley Rosen, university students in the 1980s "dismissed much of Chinese culture and government policy and adopted a naïve, pro-Western outlook, ranging from almost total belief in Western media reports from the BBC and Voice of America to a fascination with Western philosophers such as Jean-Paul Sartre, Friedrich Nietzsche, and Sigmund Freud."[9] Similarly, the River Elegy series was extremely popular among university students.

Concomitantly, college students in the early post-Mao period had an increasingly attenuated relationship with the ruling CCP. When China's universities reopened at the end of the Cultural Revolution, over 26 percent of university enrollees were CCP members. By 1978, this portion had dropped to less than 11 percent, and by early 1989 it had fallen below 1 percent.[10]

At times, college students in the early post-Mao period engaged in outright protest directed at the central political system. The most notable cases occurred in the winter of 1986–7 and spring of 1989. In 1986, Party General Secretary Hu Yaobang publicly argued for further educational, political, and administrative reforms. Encouraged, students at one of China's premier technical universities gathered to protest their inability to nominate candidates for the local People's Congress. Campus protest activities quickly spread across the country, including roughly 40,000 students at 150 higher education institutions in 17 cities. Students also complained about their poor living conditions and expressed indignation at the relative affluence enjoyed by those with lesser academic credentials but greater connections to representatives of the party-state. Yet the students' criticisms generally did not challenge the legitimacy of the central government. As Julia Kwong notes, "there is little to suggest that they were rejecting communist rule in favor of a multiparty system."[11]

Although General Secretary Hu quietly indicated his support for the students, Deng Xiaoping issued instructions to bring the movement to an end.[12] Hu was forced to resign and Zhao Ziyang became the new General Secretary. In official media outlets, the protestors' demands were criticized as "bourgeois liberalism," and participants were described as having been led by a "handful of lawbreakers who disguised themselves as students," bent on fomenting nationwide chaos and disrupting stability and unity. Still, the student participants generally were not punished, and central authorities did respond to some of the protestors' grievances.[13]

By mid-1988, inflation had spiraled out of control, leading to widespread public dissatisfaction. Within the upper echelons of the CCP, Zhao fell under severe criticism, and his economic decision-making powers were taken over by Li Peng.[14] Thus, by the spring of 1989, Zhao was in a precarious position.

When Hu Yaobang died on April 15, 1989, students put up "big character" posters and presented memorial wreaths for Hu on campus and at Beijing's Tiananmen Square. Their posters and speeches quickly took on a political tone. Along with castigating "corrupt" cadres (such as Deng Xiaoping's son) who used their political connections to profit from market reforms, students demanded democratic rights such as freedom of association and speech. On April 27, despite warnings by Party authorities, over one hundred thousand students from virtually every tertiary school in Beijing marched for hours to Tiananmen Square. Buoyed by their success, over one hundred thousand students held a second mass gathering on May 4. On May 13 a group of students marched to Tiananmen Square and initiated a hunger strike. They remained in the Square from this point forward, forcing the CCP to scrap a planned gala event to welcome then Soviet president Mikhail Gorbachev to Beijing on May 15. Immediately following Gorbachev's departure from China on May 19, regime divisions became publicly apparent. Under the direction of Deng Xiaoping, martial law was declared and military units were ordered to clear the Square. In high-level discussions, Zhao Ziyang voiced his disagreement. Subsequently, he visited the students at the Square, apologizing for coming "too late." As the soldiers moved from the outskirts of the city to the center, they were met by hundreds of thousands of city residents who spontaneously poured into the streets to block them.

On June 3–4, 1989, the regime's now dominant "conservative" elites moved to finally end the protests. Soldiers used violent force against anyone who stood in their way. An estimated 2,000 were killed, and many thousands more were injured. A few days later, Zhao was dismissed from his post and placed under house arrest, where he remained until his death in 2005. The official verdict in the government-controlled media was similar to that employed against the student-led protests of 1986–7, but its language was much more vehement: a "small handful" had incited "chaos" and "pandemonium," resulting in a "shocking counter-revolutionary rebellion"—a "struggle involving the life and death of the party and the state."[15]

In the minds of some key CCP leaders and many foreign observers, university students had become a dissident force bent on fundamental political change. This interpretation buttressed prevalent assumptions in the West that China's economic liberalization was leading inevitably to a rise in public pressure for political liberalization. Although in reality most protesting students desired reform rather than wholesale political transformation, the perceptions of observers, scholars, and policymakers at the time were not entirely off the mark. For as economic reform proceeded in the 1980s, it was undeniably the case that China's college students held the West and its attendant governmental structures, cultural values, and media outlets in increasingly high esteem.

# University student attitudes, behavior, and context, 1990–2011

However, from the early 1990s through the time of this writing, Chinese university students have exhibited very different political attitudes and behaviors. In marked contrast to their adulation of the West from 1978 to 1989, students since 1990 have displayed great skepticism and even suspicion toward Western governments, ideals, and media outlets. And when they have taken to the streets in protest, rather than challenging the ruling CCP and its policies, China's university students have criticized foreign governments, media outlets, and citizens that have been perceived to slight or harm China and its government. Interestingly, this has been true even though the Internet (and with it, outside information) has been much more widely available in China in the post-1989 period than was the case from 1978 to 1989. Along with this contextual development, four additional changes have had an important impact on China's university students since

1990: the commercialization and "massification" of higher education in China; greater unity among the top CCP leadership; a new emphasis on nationalism in the Chinese media and educational system; and the rise of China as a global economic power.

Since the late 1990s, Chinese university students have enjoyed an exponential increase in access to international media outlets and information. During 1978–89, Internet access was unheard of in China. In the early 1990s, the Internet was considered by CCP leaders to be "experimental," and was "restricted to China's top universities."[16] Although commercial Internet accounts appeared in 1995, through 1997 the per capita percentage of Internet users in China was infinitesimal. Since 1998, Internet usage has skyrocketed. As of 2011, China had more Internet users than any country in the world—amounting to about 30 percent of China's population. As of 2007, China had an estimated 100 million blogs.[17] Nearly 83 percent of the country's Internet users are under the age of 35, and roughly 60 percent are under 30.[18] Virtually all of China's university students now use the Internet with regularity, and virtually all universities operate electronic bulletin board systems (BBSs) that serve as a platform for online student discussion and communication.

Concerned about the potential of the Internet to spur criticism of and opposition to the ruling regime, CCP elites have worked hard to control online communication and access to content that governing authorities find threatening. Among a multitude of policies, regulations, and practices designed to pursue this official aim, some of the most important include: (1) a mandate that all news-providing websites register with the government and relay news only from official news units; (2) a requirement that anyone accessing the Internet at a public location (which is the case for most Chinese Internet users) show their national identity card; (3) the use of state-of-the-art firewall and surveillance software to block access to "unsuitable" sites, remove "offensive" content from sites, and filter all domestic e-mail messages for "sensitive" content; and (4) the use of human monitors, closed-circuit television cameras, threatening warning signs, and online "police" characters that automatically appear on computer screens to give Internet users a feeling that they are being "watched." At Chinese universities, nearly all computers with an Internet connection block access to many foreign sites.[19] Even so, most savvy and determined Internet users—including a preponderance of university students—are able to find ways around these controls and access censored sites and content.[20]

Somewhat relatedly, in the post-1989 period Chinese authorities had undertaken wide-ranging efforts to promote nationalism and "selective anti-foreignism" in domestic mass media outlets and the Chinese educational system. Since the early 1990s, the Party has invested in patriotic monuments and museums, and has directed China's domestic media outlets to avoid stories that might "harm social stability," and to cover domestic problems only when they have obvious solutions and do not question the governing regime's legitimacy.[21] Simultaneously, "patriotic education" has been emphasized in China's schools, with a focus on historical harms suffered by China at the hands of foreign powers.[22]

A third major contextual change in the post-1989 era has been the marketization of China's higher education system. As Rosen reports, in 1992, universities were allowed to "determine their own fee structures," and in 1993, universities were told to "move gradually from a system under which the government guaranteed education and employment to a system in which students were held responsible for both."[23] Meanwhile, the government contribution to education funding fell dramatically, dropping to less than 48 percent at the high school and university levels. The balance has been made up by an increase in tuition and ad hoc fees.[24]

With these changes, money has come to play a key role in university enrollment.[25] Since attendance of key high schools helps scores on the national university entrance examination that enable college admission, those who cannot afford to attend an elite high school have a greatly diminished probability of gaining a university education. Moreover, those with money are more likely to attend the leading middle and primary schools that feed prominent high schools. Further, even if one is accepted to university, the required tuition and fees have become prohibitive for most families. In 2000, the average annual expense for a college student was estimated at 8,000 to 10,000 yuan, while the average annual per capita income in China was only slightly more than 7,000 yuan.[26] Consequently, fewer qualified students from average and low-income homes have been admitted, and fewer have had the financial capacity to enroll.[27] The overall result has been that college students now largely come from China's economic elite—a status that many enjoy due to their close ties to the CCP. Unlike college students in the 1980s, they have been the beneficiaries of economic reform.

Concomitantly, central authorities have expanded the number of college admittees. In the early 1990s, the number of university students in China was around 2 million; by 1998 the total had risen to 6.4 million; and by the middle of the first decade of the 2000s it had grown to 20 million. Whereas in the first half of the reform era less than 5 percent of those who took the national exam gained university admission, by 2003 this proportion had reached 60 percent.[28] Within the population as a whole, the percentage of people with college degrees has more than tripled as compared with the early reform era.[29]

This expansion in university admissions has intensified the competition for jobs among college graduates—especially since 1997, when the government ceased to assign jobs upon graduation.[30] Whereas in the first half of the post-Mao period the ratio of the "demand" to the "supply" of university degree-holders was 3:1, by 2008 it had fallen to 7:1. As of late 2008, the unemployment rate of recent college graduates stood at more than 30 percent.[31]

A fourth key shift since the early 1990s is that the CCP's top leadership has been remarkably united. As a result, the economic and political policy swings of the early post-Mao era have disappeared. In terms of economics, the progression of reform has been consistent and smooth, resulting in very effective management of the economy and stunningly high growth rates. When challenges arose—such as the spike in food prices in 2007, the massive winter storms of early 2008, and the global economic meltdown that began in the fall of 2008—the CCP has responded quickly and effectively. Meanwhile, in the political realm, uniform opposition to liberalizing reforms among CCP elites since the early 1990s has meant that citizens who support greater political liberalization have not enjoyed the sympathy or support of top CCP leaders. Unlike the early reform era, when Hu Yaobang and Zhao Ziyang played this role, since 1989, there have been no obvious proponents of political reform within the top echelons of the CCP.

Fifth, in the late post-Mao era China's global status has been transformed. No longer a struggling economy amidst a world of prosperous and stable advanced industrial democracies, China has taken a seat alongside, and in some respects even ahead of, the world's most powerful players. This is why the 2008 Beijing Olympics were so important to so many Chinese—the games marked the ascendance of China as a modern country, worthy of the highest respect. Meanwhile, the global economic crisis that started in the United States in 2008 has diminished the appeal of the Western economic and political model.

These changes have coincided with the emergence of political attitudes and behavior among Chinese college students that are quite different than those exhibited in the 1980s. Perhaps most obviously, since 1989 there have been virtually no university student-led protests directed at or against the CCP, or calling for greater political reform. When opportunities have arisen for pro-democracy political activism directed at the central state, students have not mobilized. For example, when an opposition political party was formed (and later crushed) in 1998, 41 of its top 151 leaders had a college education, but only 2 of these individuals had entered college in 1990 or later.[32] Further, when important events have occurred—such as the death of Zhao Ziyang in 2005 and the 20th anniversary of the 1989 protests in 2009—China's university students have been virtually silent. In February 2011 when Internet posts called on Chinese citizens to gather in major cities to foment a pro-democracy "Jasmine Revolution" like that sweeping the Middle East and North Africa, Chinese university students stayed home.

While it might seem that this quiescence is simply the result of fear, the record since the early 1990s indicates otherwise. For despite the real and widely acknowledged risk of repression in the late post-Mao era, Chinese university students have at times taken to the streets without official permission, and in some cases have persisted with their public protests despite official warnings and threats. Though not as extensive as the student-led protests of the 1980s, there have been at least three such instances of note since the early 1990s—in 1999, 2005, and 2008. Unlike in the 1980s, demonstrating students from 1990–2011 have not called for greater political reform. Instead, they have raised nationalistic defenses of China and the Chinese government that entail criticism of Western governments and mass media outlets.

The student protests of May 1999 were sparked by the American military's bombing of the Chinese embassy in Belgrade. When news of the event reached the Chinese public, students on many campuses put up "big-character" wall posters featuring anti-US slogans.[33] For three days, tens of thousands of students marched through the diplomatic districts of major cities and gathered in front of the embassy compounds of the United States and other NATO countries in Beijing. Their slogans—such as "down with the Yankees" and "sovereignty and peace"—echoed the CCP-controlled media's castigation of NATO countries, particularly the United States. Though most of the student protesters remained orderly and peaceful, in Beijing some in the crowd threw chunks of concrete and ink bottles at the US embassy, and other unidentified individuals attacked American businesses such as McDonald's and Kentucky Fried Chicken.[34]

Along with providing buses for transit to and from rallies, CCP-controlled media outlets endorsed the students' complaints.[35] Perhaps for this reason, Western media outlets and politicians decried the protests as having been orchestrated by the CCP.[36] Yet by and large, CCP involvement in the protests amounted to a rear-guard effort to guide and control what were at base autonomous student actions. At Renmin University in Beijing, for example, students organized and gathered spontaneously. Student leaders of the CCP-affiliated student union attempted but ultimately failed to control and direct the protestors. When roughly a thousand students gathered on campus to march to the embassy district, student union leaders insisted that the students first garner permission from the Public Security Bureau. Ignoring these warnings, the demonstrators walked to the embassy district, some 15 miles away. When the university sent buses to transport the students the remaining distance, many students boarded, but dozens insisted on walking.[37]

Meanwhile, at Beijing University students and student union leaders worked in unison to initiate and organize protest activities, and student union leaders often clashed with school/government authorities. On May 11, for example, Beijing University student union leaders sparked a spontaneous on-campus march when they went to the campus' central meeting area with banners reading "Down with NATO" and "Sovereignty." Emboldened, the group decided to travel to the US embassy. After walking a few miles, the students tried to take the subway to cover the remaining distance, but found that the day's last train had departed. Shortly thereafter, they were approached by police officers, who told them that a special train had been added for them. After the students boarded the train, it did not move. After some time, the voice of Beijing University's Communist Youth League Secretary—Guan Chenghua—came over the loudspeaker, stating, "the demonstration you are in has not applied for permission from the Beijing Public Security Bureau. If you insist on going to protest at the US embassy, you are going to take all the consequences. However if you want to return to school . . . we will send you by our buses." As reported by Zhao,

> The students sat there and listened carefully, but nobody left the train. After a while, Guan Chenghua spoke again with a harsher tone. He said that this demonstration was illegal, and that the university was going to take disciplinary action against those who took part in it. At this moment, several leaders of the official student union . . . stood up solemnly . . . and asked the students not to listen to what Guan had said. The loudspeakers continuously broadcast warnings with even harsher tones . . . about three hundred students refused to leave the train. After quite some time, the train started to move.

The train continued only to the next station. There, Beijing University's Communist Party Secretary "spoke very seriously and demanded that the students return to school." Most refused. The train eventually continued to the next station, where a high-level official from the Beijing municipal government "told the students that the situation at the US embassy was very

chaotic and requested that the students return to school for their own safety."
Again, most students refused. Ultimately, the train took the students to the
station nearest the embassy.[38] As this anecdote shows, university students in
the late post-Mao era are not necessarily afraid of flouting the threats and
dictates of China's ruling authorities.

Even so, the students' slogans, criticisms, and demands were almost identical to those found in the official media. Probing the source of the students'
public statements, Dingxin Zhao found that student views had very little
correlation with their level of access to Chinese or foreign media outlets. In
interviews and surveys shortly after the 1999 protests, Chinese university
students reported that they were quite familiar with foreign news through
sources such as Voice of America (VOA) and the BBC (via the Internet).
Only about 15 percent of the respondents had "no access to any kind of
Western media for news during the entire incident." More than half had
listened to VOA or the BBC, and less than half believed that "the Chinese
media's account of the Kosovo crisis [was] impartial." Yet even so, over
75 percent of respondents "agreed" or "strongly agreed" that "the embassy
bombing was a deliberate act of the US government"; nearly 71 percent
agreed or strongly agreed that "the Chinese embassy was attacked because
China was not strong enough"; and over 54 percent agreed or strongly
agreed that "the embassy bombing was aimed to induce political instability
in China."[39] Thus, contrary to the expectations of most outside observers,
increased access to "outside" information via the Internet does not appear
to have made China's university students more critical of China's governing
authorities and more supportive of Western governments, media outlets, or
political ideals.

Similar features characterized the anti-Japan protests of 2005. These
demonstrations arose in the context of Japan's push for permanent membership on the UN Security Council that spring. Within China, a massive online petition campaign led by university graduate Lu Yunfei's
"China918.net" site collected more than 40 million signatures to oppose
Japan's bid.[40] In April, street protests were sparked when the Japanese government approved a new middle school history textbook that diminished
Japanese atrocities in China during World War II and portrayed Japan as
a "benevolent liberator." University students in Beijing excoriated Japan's
decision on campus electronic BBSs, and called for street demonstrations.
On university BBSs, Internet chat rooms, and other Internet sites, students
spread word about the demonstrations, including the protest routes in particular cities, slogans, and precautions.[41] The protests began as planned
on April 9, with approximately 10,000 taking to the streets in Beijing and

large demonstrations in Guangzhou and Shenzhen. Protests continued for weeks, with growing numbers of participants and activity in cities across China. Although, as in 1999, most were orderly and peaceful, in Beijing and Shanghai some threw bottles and rocks at the Japanese embassy and consulate, and in Shanghai a number of Japanese businesses were vandalized. When several anti-Japanese websites called for mass demonstrations in early May, government officials announced that future "unauthorized marches" would be illegal, and warned that police "would mete out tough blows" to those caught vandalizing property.[42] Shortly thereafter, the protests ended.

The demonstrations of 2005 shared many features with those of 1999. In both cases the demonstrators' slogans echoed the vitriol that was expressed in the CCP-controlled official media. Participants in both protests voiced their disgust and anger at a foreign country through statements of patriotic indignation. Further, their slogans evidenced no hint of dissatisfaction with the CCP.

The third major instance of student-led protests exhibited basic commonalities with those of 1999 and 2005. The demonstrations of Spring 2008 were also a response to actions undertaken by foreign governments that were perceived as harmful to China. This perceived "harm" had its roots in a clash that occurred in Tibet on March 14, wherein Tibetan street demonstrators calling for greater autonomy were linked to the destruction of Han Chinese businesses, and CCP authorities responded with force. At the time of this occurrence, the Olympic torch was making its way around the globe in anticipation of the Beijing Olympics. As the torch traveled its route, foreign protestors criticized China's ruling elites and interfered with the progress of the relay. In China, students erupted in protest—defending China's integrity, and castigating foreign media outlets, groups, and individuals critical of China's response to the demonstrators in Tibet. When the French government did not intervene to block protestors from disturbing the progress of the Olympic torch relay in France, students joined a boycott of the French "Carrefour" stores in China. Overseas Chinese students in Japan, Europe, and the United States rose up as well—at times leading to angry confrontations with pro-Tibet activists. As with the other student protests since the 1990s, participants voiced no criticism of China's governing authorities or political system; rather, they amplified the stance of the official media. When China's Sichuan province was struck with a massive earthquake in May, the student protests ended and foreign criticism of China became subdued.

Overall, these cases of student-led protest since the 1990s show that, relative to the early reform period, college-educated youths have displayed little interest in pressing for liberal democratic reform but a strong desire to defend China against its foreign detractors. Concurrently, Chinese university students have exhibited deep suspicion of Western media outlets and governments—viewing them as unfairly critical of China, and even worse, as quasi-imperialistic agents working to thwart China's rise as a global power. In this sense, the political attitudes and behavior of college-educated youth seem to have made a complete about-face since 1989.

Nationalistic sentiments and suspicions also have abounded in the on-line postings of Chinese university students and many of the sites that are most popular among them. A prime example is the video, "2008! China Stand Up!" (*Zhongguo Zhanqilai*), which appeared on April 15, 2008 on Sina.com. In the first ten days after its initial posting, the six-minute film drew more than one million hits and tens of thousands of positive comments. It quickly rose to Sina.com's fourth-most-popular rating, attracting nearly two clicks per second. As described by Evan Osnos, the film opens "with a Technicolor portrait of Chairman Mao, sunbeams radiating from his head," followed by Mao's mantra, "Imperialism will never abandon its intention to destroy us." After warning that "the West intends to 'make the Chinese people foot the bill' for America's financial woes," the film shows ostensibly Tibetan "rioters looting stores and brawling" in Lhasa, flashing the words, "so-called peaceful protest!"[43] Displaying foreign press clippings and the logos of CNN and the BBC, the film decries these "reports from distorted Western media," saying blatantly, "they lie, they lie, . . . lie again and again." The film calls on viewers to "Wake up! Wake up!" asking, "What are objectivity, justice, freedom, and democracy so-claimed by the Western media?" The film responds with Mao's words: they are "all reactionaries, paper tigers."[44] As described by Osnos, "the film ends with the image of a Chinese flag, aglow in the sunlight, and a solemn promise: 'We will stand up and hold together always as one family in harmony.'"[45]

The film's creator is Tang Jie, a 28-year-old graduate student at one of China's top universities, Fudan (in Shanghai). At the time of the video's production, Tang was writing his dissertation on Western philosophy. He reads and speaks English and German, and is working on Latin and ancient Greek. In his residence, "books cover every surface, and great mounds list from the shelves above his desk. His collections encompass, more or less, the span of human thought: Plato leans against Lao-tzu, Wittgenstein, Bacon, Fustel de

Coulanges, Heidegger, the Koran."[46] In other words, Tang is far from intellectually insulated.

The views expressed by Tang have been echoed on two popular politically related websites among college students: "anti-CNN.org" and "fenqing.net" (angry/indignant youth). Founded by a 24-year-old graduate of Qinghua University and owner of a successful Internet company in the wake of the March 2008 clashes in Tibet, "Anti-CNN" was devoted to "expos[ing] the lies and distortions in the Western media." The site was extremely popular over the course of the next year. When "anti-CNN" posted a 2009 UN Human Rights Council report on China, a substantial majority of the user comments "criticized the West for meddling in China's affairs and defended the standard Chinese government line that development must come before expanding personal freedom."[47] One representative comment stated that "China, in a state of freedom, stably developed its economy [and] government; sixty years of development demonstrates that we are correct. Foreigners always force their ideology on [other] countries' governments and people." Another user commented that "currently a lot of so-called major powers are afraid of China's power; they are always commanding us to create internal disorder whenever they have the chance. I really don't have any problems regarding my rights."[48]

"Fenqing.net" is more clearly directed toward and consulted by those who are attracted to the site's self-identification as "angry" or "indignant" youth. Although many parts of the site are not political or particularly "angry" or "indignant" in tone or content, its "Angry Youth Forum"—which appears to be the most frequented—is. This section includes a "Fenqing Manifesto" that presents an account of Chinese history that emphasizes its oppression by foreign nations such as Japan and the United States; calls on readers to expose the West's hypocrisy in calling for greater human rights and democracy in China; declares that "angry youth" should let the world know of China's strength (which is not necessarily belligerent, but can be if provoked); glorifies the merits of nationalism; and urges readers to uphold their nationalism despite the West's criticism of it. All of the user comments below the manifesto express support.[49]

Meanwhile, since the early 1990s Chinese university students have displayed a heightened interest in joining the CCP and working for the state. The portion of university students who are CCP members has risen exponentially—from 0.8 percent in 1990 to nearly 8 percent in 2001. In 2001, an estimated 33 percent of those attending college had applied to join the Party. Other surveys in the early 2000s have found that "40 percent of students expressed interest in joining the Party, with the number increasing to 50 percent for new students." Among graduate students, by 2000, over 28 percent were Party members.[50] In 2007, the official Xinhua news agency proudly proclaimed that between 2002 and 2007, nearly a third of new CCP members were college graduates.[51]

Surveys demonstrate that university students' desire for Party membership does not derive from a belief in communism. Rather, in the context of intense job competition among college graduates, it is "considered to be valuable for one's future success, most notably in finding a well-paying job and good housing in a major city."[52] Also reflecting university students' concerns about finding stable work, many have reported "a strong desire" to be employed as a government or Party official.[53]

Thus, in many respects, the political attitudes and behavior of China's college-educated youths seem to have fundamentally changed relative to the early reform era. Instead of acting as a democratic vanguard, university students often have defended and sought closer connections with China's CCP-led party-state. And whereas they once idealistically believed that Western governments and media outlets were honest and worthy of emulation, they now find lies and distortions designed to thwart China's rightful enjoyment of power, prosperity, and respect.

# Continuities in university student attitudes and behavior, 1978–2011

Despite these real changes in Chinese university students' attitudes and behavior, some continuities are apparent across the entirety of China's reform era. To begin, even though they often feel unjustly slighted, maligned, and threatened by Western media outlets and foreign powers, college-educated youths in the late reform period are not knee-jerk apologists for the CCP. To the contrary, like their predecessors in the 1980s, they are outspoken critics of corruption within China's ruling regime. Indeed, in the video, "2008! China Stand Up!", castigation of CNN and pro-Tibetan foreign protestors is interspersed with scathing criticism of the CCP's top leader, Hu Jintao. Similarly, fenqing.net features multitudinous stories about government corruption. In fact, generally speaking, younger Chinese appear less supportive of the CCP than older Chinese. In Jie Chen's 1995–9 Beijing surveys, for example, nearly 100 percent of respondents aged 56 or older expressed a "medium" or "high" level of support for the regime, but among respondents aged 18 to 25, the corresponding figure was 65 to 70 percent.[54]

In addition, along with displaying great love of country (*aiguo*, or patriotism) and nationalism (*minzuzhuyi*), college-educated youths since 1990 have continued to be vocal advocates of "liberal" values such as freedom of expression. Most prominently, they are opposed to censorship, especially of the Internet. In a 2007 survey of history students at 33 universities, for example, "even though more than 82 percent agreed that Western video products propagate Western political ideas and Western lifestyles, fewer than 12 percent expressed a willingness to negate such products."[55] Similarly, Zhao's 1999 survey finds a strong and positive correlation between nationalistic and pro-democracy views. China's contemporary college-educated youth do not appear to see these views as contradictory or mutually exclusive; they value both deeply and simultaneously. Moreover a 1999 six-city survey by Wenfang Tang finds that younger Chinese display more acceptance of liberalization and democratization than older citizens.[56]

Further, it is important to remember that although university students in the 1980s raised the banner of "democracy," they did not call for multiparty elections, mass political enfranchisement, or an end to CCP rule. Instead, they called for greater freedom of speech and association, and an end to official corruption. Like students since the early 1990s, they sought reform within the existing system, and emphasized that the rights that they were calling for were already enshrined in China's constitution.

# Conclusion

What do these continuities and changes in Chinese university students' political attitudes and behavior tell us? Generally speaking, they demonstrate that economic liberalization and growth as well as access to information do not directly or inevitably lead to greater public support for multiparty democracy. Whereas in the 1980s China's university students did exhibit increasing admiration for Western political systems, philosophies, and mass media outlets, since the early 1990s they have displayed increasing skepticism toward many Western values and practices. Importantly, this development has occurred at the same time that economic privatization, opening to the global capitalist system, and growth—and also public access to the Internet—have accelerated.

This reality suggests that outside observers need to rethink their assumptions about the universal appeal of the political, economic, and cultural values and practices of the West. While China's university students throughout the reform era have desired greater freedom of expression and access to information, and have railed against political corruption, they have shown no sign of wanting to end CCP rule or of desiring multiparty elections or universal political enfranchisement. Since the early 1990s, foreign governments and individuals have continued to criticize China and its governing system, which has appeared to only reinforce Chinese university students' suspicions about foreign motives and spur students' nationalistic defense of China's non-Western developmental trajectory and aspirations. Given this, outside observers may be well-advised to stop expressing frustration and dismay toward China, and to accept that China's rise may not lead its citizenry to emulate the West.

## Five questions for discussions

1. Does economic liberalization inevitably lead to political liberalization? Provide evidence from the Chinese case to support your argument.
2. What concerns and desires have Chinese university students exhibited throughout the post-Mao period? How have their concerns and desires changed over time?
3. Given the growing nationalism of Chinese university students today, what should be the goal of US foreign policy toward China, and how can the United States best pursue this goal?
4. Has the Internet made college students in China more supportive of liberal democracy? If not, why?
5. What factors differentiate college-educated students in China today from their counterparts in the Middle East and North Africa, who in 2011 took to the streets to press for an end to authoritarian rule? How can we explain the lack of interest among Chinese college students in participating in a "Jasmine revolution" to support democratic change in China?

# Notes

1 Stig Thorgersen, "Through the Sheep's Intestines—Selection and Elitism in Chinese Schools," *Australian Journal of Chinese Affairs* 21 (January 1989): 33. The exam still includes an ideological component.
2 "Education Finance: Pay to Play," *China Economic Quarterly* Q4 (2005): 27.
3 Gang Guo, "Party Recruitment of College Students in China," *Journal of Contemporary China* 14:43 (May 2005): 373; *China Statistical Yearbook* (Beijing, 1998), p. 105.
4 Guo, "Party Recruitment," 386.
5 The other Party elders were Chen Yun, Yang Shangkun, Wang Zhen, Li Xiannian, Peng Zhen, Bo Yibo, and Song Renqiong.
6 Zhao Ziyang, translated and edited by Bao Pu, Renee Chiang, and Adi Ignatius, *Prisoner of the State: The Secret Journal of Zhao Ziyang* (NY: Simon and Schuster, 2009), p. 91.

7  http://ageconsearch.umn.edu/bitstream/21767/1/sp00wa03.pdf, accessed March 21, 2010.

8  Merle Goldman, *Sowing the Seeds of Democracy in China: Political Reform in the Deng Xiaoping Era* (Harvard University Press, 1994).

9  Stanley Rosen, "Contemporary Chinese Youth and the State," *Journal of Asian Studies* 68:2 (May 2009): 316, referencing Shi Zhong, "Chinese Nationalism and the Future of China," translated in Stanley Rosen, ed. "Nationalism and Neoconservatism in China in the 1990s," *Chinese Law and Government* 30:6 (November–December 1997): 8–27.

10  Guo, "Party Recruitment," 373–4.

11  Julia Kwong, "The 1986 Student Demonstrations in China: A Democratic Movement?" *Asian Survey* 28:9 (September 1988): 977.

12  Ibid.; Stanley Rosen, "China in 1987: The Year of the Thirteenth Party Congress," *Asian Survey* 28:1 (January 1988): 36.

13  Kwong, "The 1986 Student Demonstrations," 981–983.

14  Zhao Ziyang, *Prisoner of the State*, pp. 68–9.

15  "Recognize the Essence of Turmoil and the Necessity of Martial Law," *Renmin Ribao*, June 3, 1989; Yuan Mu (news conference), Beijing Television Service, June 6, 1989 (FBIS, June 7, 1989, 12); Chen Xitong, *Report on Checking the Turmoil and Quelling the Counter-Revolutionary Rebellion* (Beijing: New Star Publishers, 1989).

16  Anne-Marie Brady, *Marketing Dictatorship: Propaganda and Thought Work in Contemporary China* (Roman and Littlefield, 2008), p. 127.

17  Ibid., p. 130.

18  China Internet Network Information Center, "25th Statistical Survey Report of Internet Development in China" (January 2010).

19  Brady, *Marketing Dictatorship*, pp. 128–33.

20  Personal communication with college-educated informants in China. See also Zhao, "An Angle on Nationalism."

21  Brady, *Marketing Dictatorship*, pp. 46–50, 80–3.

22  Stanley Rosen, "Contemporary Chinese Youth and the State," *Journal of Asian Studies* 68:2 (May 2009): 367.

23  Stanley Rosen, "The State of Youth/Youth and the State in Early 21st-century China: The Triumph of the Urban Rich?" in Peter Gries and Stanley Rosen, eds. *State and Society in 21st Century China: Contention, Crisis, and Legitimation* (Routledge, 2004), p. 164.

24  "Education Finance," 25–6.

25  Rosen, "The State of Youth," p. 166.

26  Huang Zhijian, "Qingnian xiaofei wu da qushi" (Five major trends in consumption patterns of youth), *Liaowang xinwen zhoukan (Outlook Weekly)* 35 (August 27, 2001).

27  Stanley Rosen, "The Victory of Materialism: Aspirations to Join China's Urban Moneyed Classes and the Commercialization of Education," *The China Journal* 51 (January 2004): 35.

28  "Education Finance," 27.

29  Guo, "Party Recruitment," p. 374.

30  Ibid., 386–7.

31  Peter Ford, "China's Ant Tribe: Millions of Unemployed College Grads," *Christian Science Monitor*, December 21, 2009.

32  Teresa Wright, "The China Democracy Party and the Politics of Protest in the 1980's–1990's," *China Quarterly* (December 2002).

33  Dingxin Zhao, "Nationalism and Authoritarianism: Student-Government Conflicts during the 1999 Beijing Student Protests," *Asian Perspective* 27:1 (2003): 14–15.

34  John Leicester, "Chinese attack US, Brit embassies," *Associated Press online*, May 8, 1999. Jeffrey Wasserstrom, "Chinese Students and Anti-Japanese Protests, Past and Present," *World Policy Journal* 22:2 (Summer 2005): 61 and Peter Hayes Gries, "Popular Nationalism and State Legitimation," in Gries and Rosen, eds. *State and Society*, pp. 189–90.

35  Jeffrey Wasserstrom, "Student Protests in Fin-de-Siecle China," *New Left Review* 237 (September–October 1999): 55. See also Zhao, "Nationalism and Authoritarianism," 5–34.

36  See Bruce Ramsey, "Little Remains of the Debate over the Bombing of the Chinese Embassy but to Agree to Disagree," *Seattle Post-Intelligencer*, July 25, 1999, E1.

37  Zhao, "Nationalism and Authoritarianism," 16, note 26; 18–20.

38  Ibid., 24–5.

39  Dingxin Zhao, "An Angle on Nationalism in China Today: Attitudes among Beijing Students after Belgrade 1999," *China Quarterly* 172 (December 2002): 894–5.

40  The "918" in "China 918.net" refers to Japan's September 18, 1937 invasion of China.

41  Xu Wu, *Chinese Cyber-Nationalism: Evolution, Characteristics, and Implications* (Rowman and Littlefield, 2007), pp. 83–4.

42  Jim Yardley, "China bans anti-Japan protest," *New York Times*, April 23, 2005, 1.

43  Evan Osnos, "Angry youth: the new generation's neocon nationalists," *The New Yorker*, July 28, 2008.

44  "2008 China Stand Up," Youtube.com.

45  Osnos, "Angry youth."

46  Ibid.

47  Patricia Kim research report to the author, July 2009.

48  http://www.anti-cnn.com/archives/5760.html, accessed July 7, 2009.

49  Patricia Kim research report to the author, July 2009.

50  Rosen, "The State of Youth," 168–9; fns. 52 and 56. See Li Zhidong, "Dangdai daxuesheng zheng-zhiguan, daodeguan, jiazhiguan diaocha yanjiu" [Investigation and Study of Contemporary University Students' Political Views, Ethics, and Values], Guangxi shifan daxue xuebao (zhexue shehui kexue ban) [*Journal of Guangxi Normal University (Philosophy and Social Sciences)*] 38:3 (July 2002): 52.

51  "Number of CPC members increases by 6.4 million over 2002," *Xinhua*, October 8, 2007.

52  Rosen, "Contemporary Chinese Youth," p. 365.

53  Rosen, "The State of Youth," p. 170.

54  Jie Chen, *Popular Political Support in Urban China* (Stanford University Press, 2004), p. 79.

55 Rosen, "Contemporary Chinese Youth," pp. 365–6, citing CASS Institute of World History Special Topics Group, "A Brief Analysis of a Survey of Young Students with Regard to Belief Systems on 21 Important Questions," *Lingdao canyue* (Reference reading for leaders), July 5, 2007, 24–8.

56 Wenfang Tang, *Public Opinion and Political Change in China* (Stanford University Press, 2005), p. 78.

# Selected bibliography

Brady, Anne-Marie. *Marketing Dictatorship: Propaganda and Thought Work in Contemporary China* (NY: Roman and Littlefield, 2008).

Fewsmith, Joseph. *China since Tiananmen: From Deng Xiaoping to Hu Jintao* (Cambridge: Cambridge University Press, 2008).

Goldman, Merle. *China's Intellectuals: Advise and Dissent* (Cambridge: Harvard University Press, 1988).

Goldman, Merle and Edward Gu, eds. *Chinese Intellectuals between State and Market* (New York: Routledge, 2004).

Gries, Peter and Stanley Rosen, eds. *Chinese Politics: State, Society and the Market* (New York: Routledge, 2010).

Harwit, Eric. *China's Telecommunications Revolution* (New York: Oxford University Press, 2008).

Mann, James. *The China Fantasy: Why Capitalism Will Not Bring Democracy to China* (New York: Penguin, 2008).

McGregor, Richard. *The Party: The Secret World of China's Communist Rulers* (New York: Harper, 2010).

Rosen, Stanley. "Contemporary Chinese Youth and the State." *Journal of Asian Studies* 68:2 (May 2009): 359–69.

Wright, Teresa. *The Perils of Protest: State Repression and Student Activism in China and Taiwan* (Honolulu: University of Hawaii Press, 2001).

—. *Accepting Authoritarianism: State-Society Relations in China's Reform Era* (Palo Alto: Stanford University Press, 2010).

Zhao, Dingxin. "An Angle on Nationalism in China Today: Attitudes among Beijing Students after Belgrade 1999." *China Quarterly* 172 (December 2002): 885–905.

—. "Nationalism and Authoritarianism: Student-Government Conflicts during the 1999 Beijing Student Protests." *Asian Perspective* 27:1 (2003): 5–34.

Zhao Ziyang, trans. and ed. Bao Pu, Renee Chiang, and Adi Ignatius. *Prisoner of the State: The Secret Journal of Zhao Ziyang* (New York: Simon and Schuster, 2009).

# 12

# A "Natural" State? Nature and Nation in North Korea

Carol Ann Medlicott

# Introduction

Most observers regard the Korean Peninsula as explicitly shared by two Korean states. The rivalry between these truculent neighbors has involved, at the best of times, each Korean government rhetorically impugning the legitimacy and authority of the other. At the worst of times, it has been punctuated by terrorism, assassinations, elaborate espionage ventures, the abrogation of human rights, cross-border fire-fights, and threats of nuclear wars. However, the expressed view of both Korean governments, and one implicitly shared by the international community, is that despite the existence of two sovereign Korean states, there is but one single Korean nation. Scholars of Korean modernity, while not reluctant to both narrate and interrogate the various ways that nationhood has been articulated and contested over the past century, rarely critique the idea of unified Korean nationhood. But when one scrutinizes the differences in how modern Korean nationhood has been constructed, expressed, and sustained by two governments, each of which refers to itself in many contexts as simply "Korea," fissures emerge in the so-called preordained Korean national unity.

A deeper critique of contemporary Korean nationhood must involve close examination of how each Korea has assembled its respective complex and distinctive national narrative. National identity involves, of course, far more than simply vague references to commonality of language, of certain cultural patterns, and of premodern history. It also entails the identification of formative myths and historical moments, whose codification as collective memory underpins contemporary nationhood. And it can also entail the recognition of certain territorial settings as material backdrops for events of crucial importance to national history, physical spaces that can assume iconic quality and lend distinctive aesthetic elements to nationalist texts and displays. Directing attention at the natural environment and the ways in which natural features become laden with political meaning is among the analytic tools often employed by human geographers who study culture and politics.

# Reflections on Korean nationhood

"Commonsense" conceptions of Korean nationhood conform to a theory of "ethnic nationalism," wherein national identity is conferred through such innate attributes as race, cultural habits, and language.[1] For the divided Korea, similar official assertions such as, "The Korean people existed as a homogeneous group . . . proud of 5,000 years of their great history" (from South Korea), and, "Our nation which for ages had lived in the same territory with one culture and one language found itself divided" (from North Korea), attest to a normative national homogeneity, based on ethnic unity.[2] These assertions also presume a collective sense of Korea's temporal and geographical coherence and collective convictions of national self-importance. As scholars of nationalism point out, ethnic nationalism is difficult to critique precisely because it appears so natural:

> (T)he self-evident status which it ascribes to itself, and which indeed attaches to it, makes those who hold it fail to see that they are holding a theory at all. They do not see that this is something contentious and to be examined . . . They think they are simply recognizing the obvious . . . What is not perceived as a contentious theory cannot be corrected.[3]

In addition to presuming that ethnic identity is the primary quality of being "Korean," many scholarly treatments of Korean nationhood since the division of Korea have been largely descriptive historical narratives that presume South Korea—not North—to be the legitimate modern inheritor of Korean nationhood.[4] Not only does this literature tend to treat "nation" as synonymous with "state" (thus, implicitly denying North Korea any political legitimacy whatsoever), it also treats "nation" as completely unproblematic in the Asian context. The appropriateness of the "nation" category in Asia has long been a concern of scholars of modern China, who have analyzed China's incorporation of Western discourses of nationalism, as part and parcel of studying China's early political modernization and its later experience of socialist revolution.[5] More recent critiques of East Asian history have taken up the question of whether "nation" is the most appropriate category when considering matters of collective self-consciousness and collective action in the history of China, among other parts of Asia, particularly when ethnicity, race, religion, class hierarchies, and territorial claims challenge the notion of homogenous national identity and present other factors around which to organize political sovereignty.[6]

Critical historians of Korea have in part interrogated the "discovery" of nationhood by the first generation of Korean intellectuals to be exposed to Western modernity, pointing to the reliance upon such cultural products as newspapers and other print media for the reinforcement of a "nation" ideal.[7] Other scholarship on Korean nationhood addresses such diverse dimensions as religion, social class, territory, the effects of geopolitics, gender, and contemporary cultural and scientific practice. A strong body of work has emerged that highlights Christianity in providing early-twentieth-century Korean nationalists an ideological framework that offered collective emotional appeal across social classes, that was both inherently provocative to the imperial authority of the Japanese (who claimed Korea as a colony from 1910 until 1945) and also attached to a practical infrastructure for modern and benevolent social services.[8] Implicit in such work is the notion that, if Christianity has been a critical component of Korean nationalism, then South Korea, where Christian practice remains extraordinarily high and church affiliation is widespread across all social classes, can claim considerably more national legitimacy than North Korea, where unregulated Christian practice has been eliminated by the state.

It is a commonplace view that South Korea has achieved a far higher degree of political legitimacy in the eyes of the international community than has North Korea. Notwithstanding South Korea's years before the

1970s of lagging behind its rival in economic growth, the South Korean government has succeeded in projecting an image of economic vigor, political sophistication, and cultural vibrancy that point to its successful balance of non-Western traditions with the prevailing imperatives of conduct for globalized economic processes and geopolitical interactions. Thus, it should be no surprise that South Korea's vision for Korean nationhood seems to be considered the more authentic. To suggest that North Korea had any claim whatsoever on credentials of Korean nationhood was tantamount to give credibility to the unthinkable—namely, the totalitarian and flagrantly anti-Western regime of Kim Il-sung and Kim Jong-il, which long adhered to an implicitly threatening mantra of armed revolution and much later came to anchor the post-Cold War "axis of evil," all the while constructing its brazenly counterfactual cult of personality. For many scholars of Korea, then, particularly those in Korea itself, to consider any sort of North Korean practice as an expression of nationalism has long been considered provocative at best, and at worst a manifestation of serious anti-South Korean political dissidence. Such work has been confined mostly to scholars with strong progressive or dissident credentials.[9]

# Landscape, memory, and nationhood

Besides being a manifestation of collective consciousness and a tool for collective resistance, nationhood also relies upon particular conceptions of the past and vivid images of the places where formative past events unfolded. Many scholars have explored the relationship between memory and nation. The power of national identity rests upon the successful articulation of a link between events in the past—both a founding moment and a "golden age"—and the past and the social, political, and cultural institutions that claim to represent the nation in the present. Sustaining such an articulation involves the "invention of tradition," so that something quite new—the nation—can legitimately claim to be something so old as to be self-justifying.[10]

And because national myths unfold in specific places, territory assumes critical importance in nationalist discourse. Schmid states, "Nationalism thrives on crisis. And crises of the nation are generally of a spatial order: where something happens determines its national significance. This explains the centrality of territorial sovereignty to nationalist discourse."[11] Altering this observation only slightly, where something is believed or is remembered to have happened determines its national significance; and inscribing these memories on the landscape is crucial to the process of transformation from natural terrain into national territory. Memory and the collective acts of commemoration enable present-day landscapes to take on potentially iconic qualities because of the power of physical and aesthetic features to conjure memories and myths of events of national significance.[12] One can readily observe this transformation in virtually any nation-state; it is ongoing in the various nationalist landscapes of daily common experience, such as capital cities, national monuments, and memorial parks. Indeed, the spatial setting of the nation's founding moment is all the more powerful as the nationalist narrative becomes central to the power of the state. Given the inherent spatiality of the state, the spatial elements of the nationalist narrative would seem to be particularly fertile for state manipulation as symbols and representative motifs.[13]

The practice of pressing history into the service of the nation is particularly striking in the Korean case. Nations are born out of conflict, and modern Korea emerged partly in response to conflict with Western ideas from the late nineteenth century, but far more decisively in response to the conflict represented by Japan's imperial domination in the period 1910–45. Moreover, key episodes of Koreans' struggles in those conflicts were enacted in particular identifiable places. The effects of each Korea's practices of manipulating the past are evident not only in the many landscapes of memory that both Korean states have constructed throughout the Peninsula to promote distinct conceptions of Korean nationhood, but also in the ways that the specific physical locales of national struggle are represented. Since Japan's 35-year occupation of Korea is widely considered the catalyst for modern Korean identity and nationhood, it follows that the foundational myths for both Korean states would draw from this experience. The two Koreas have each appealed to different interpretations and different emphases within the overall context of anti-Japanese resistance. South Korea points to the first concerted peninsula-wide resistance event, the "March First Movement" that was sparked in March 1919 when a group of Western-educated Korean nationalist intellectuals, many of whom were Christian converts and many of whom were working outside Korea from small diasporic enclaves, signaled their opposition to the Japanese colonial authorities by signing and circulating a "declaration of independence." This event is specifically named in South Korea's constitution as providing the seminal authority for a modern sovereign Korean state.[14] The North Korean regime likewise traces its authority to Koreans' early struggle against Japanese imperialism. But instead of identifying with the nationalist movement of the

Western-educated elites, North Korean nationalist texts portray a peasant struggle against the tyranny of both Japanese colonial administrators and their elitist Korean collaborators. According to this interpretation, when the March First Movement failed to oust the Japanese, it was left to Kim Il-sung later to focus anti-Japanese sentiment into an organized revolution.[15] This interpretation is clarified in Kim's 1992 multi-volume autobiography, in which he claims that the March First Movement was for him a definitive turning point (he would have been seven years old!), because he first witnessed blood being spilt in the struggle against foreign occupiers of Korea:

> The enemy used swords and guns indiscriminately against the masses, even mobilizing policemen and mounted troops. Many people were killed . . . This was the first time I saw one man killing another. This was the day when I witnessed Korean blood being spilled for the first time. My young heart burned with indignation . . . The March First Popular Uprising marked the first time that I stood in the ranks of the people and that the true image of our nation was implanted in my mind's eye.[16]

But instead of the March First Movement, the North Korean state regards the crowning achievement of colonial Korea's anti-Japanese struggle to fall somewhat later than 1919, placing it instead in the 1930s when Kim Il-sung was leading a group of partisan "guerrilla" fighters. Moreover, these events are decisively framed in a specific place: the rugged and wilderness-like China-Korea border region and surrounding the nationally symbolic Mt. Paektu (or "Paektusan," a loose phonetic rendering of the name in Korean language) a high mountain plateau straddling the border between Korea and adjacent Manchuria and steeped in the mythology of ancient Korea's primordial ethnic origins. In this locale the most significant and potent events of the Kim Il-sung-led guerrilla resistance allegedly occurred, events that the North Korean state claims are entirely responsible for the defeat of imperialist Japan and the establishment of a modern and independent Korean nation. The events in this distinctive setting form a coherent nationalist myth with the fabled young Kim at the centre.

A strong illustration of the critical importance of both history and the physical location of historic events to a particular conception of Korean nationhood can be found in North Korea's treatment of its far northern regions. In this set of practices, to which this chapter now turns, one sees the transformation of a memorial landscape into a nationalist landscape along with the prevalent manipulation of the natural motifs and aesthetic patterns associated with the physical settings of nationalist heroics.

# Physical geography of North Korean nationalism

One useful starting point for analyzing how the alleged physical setting of Kim Il-sung's exploits is mobilized aesthetically and symbolically in North Korean nationalist narratives is to consider geographers' descriptive work on that area. One comprehensive geographical treatment of Korea was produced by a German geographer, Herman Lautensach, during the late colonial period.[17] Lautensach proffers a regionalizing framework for Korea, and organizes his text largely within it. He refers to the overall border zone of Korea's far north as the "Yalu-Tumen boundary zone" (using the names of Korea's two northern rivers that mark the boundary between Korea and adjoining Manchuria) but singles out a sizeable mid-section of that border zone—the "Paektusan Area," which he delineates as "the area around Paektusan and the surrounding basalt plateau" (Figure 12.1)—as a separate and coherent region for categorical study, a region that straddles both Chinese Manchuria and northern Korea. Of the border in the Paektusan Area, Lautensach states that it is:

> . . . the only part in which the political boundary dissects a landscape of profound individuality in such a manner that only the southeastern sector belongs to Korea, whereas the other three sectors belong to Manchuria. In this area the geographical boundary cannot coincide with the political boundary. We prefer here to include the entire Paektusan area in the geographical unit of Korea.[18]

In terms of human habitation, Lautensach wrote of the dominant pattern of "fire field farmers." These he characterized as the lowest strata of landless peasants (he suggests that these are peasants who have been thrown out by landlords elsewhere), who "burn a clearing, build a log cabin nearby, raise subsistence crops for a few years, and move on."[19] Lautensach describes this cultural pattern, noted as the least sedentary of Korea's agricultural lifestyles, as being largely confined to this far northern region, with only a few pockets extant in the few thickly forested mountainous areas of the south.

In discussing the biogeography of the Paektusan area, Lautensach contends that all of Korea was probably thickly wooded in its primeval condition. He points to Korea's indigenous rural lifestyles as being particularly demanding on forest products, with relentless foraging for fuel, building materials, and other materials for medicines and foodstuffs all unfolding alongside equally relentless

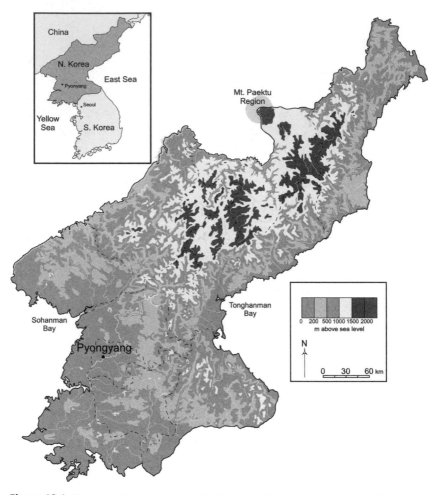

**Figure 12.1** Elevations above sea-level in North Korea. Mt. Paektu rises from a high-elevation basalt plateau, identified by geographer Herman Lautensach as the "Paektusan Area" in the northeastern part of the country.
*Source:* Map by Carol Medlicott.

clearing for agriculture. He asserts that Korean society itself recognized the need to conserve forest resources prevent their rapid squandering, and he points to restrictions that Korean kings attempted to place on forest destruction.

Plainly, the geographer Lautensach was deeply concerned with drawing an unambiguous distinction between what he regarded as the geographically anomalous area surrounding the border-straddling Paektu mountain and the remainder of Korea. Indeed, the relief patterns depicted in Figure 12.1 reinforce the uniqueness of Korea's far north. The most striking thing about

Lautensach's description of the Paektusan area is his characterization of it as not only distinctive relative to the rest of the border region and adjacent Manchuria, but also as atypical of the Korean landscape as a whole.

Lautensach clearly regarded the Paektusan area as presenting both a fieldwork conundrum and an aesthetic highlight of his work in Asia. His vivid description of the forested landscape from the volcanic pumice cone summit, where one looks downslope to see nothing but coniferous and birch forest, punctuated by lakes and marshes and huge patches of white lichen and looks inward to see the cobalt lake in the volcanic crater (Lake Chonji), is worthy of the most extravagant North Korean propaganda text: "All observers agree that the contrast that this twofold view unites makes the scene viewed from Paektusan one of the most enthralling sights on earth."

# Paektusan region and motifs of nationalism

It was to this geographically unique zone that Kim Il-sung allegedly retreated while a very young man, still using his given name of Kim Song-ju, to begin reorganizing a coherent resistance movement that, according to North Korean history, would eventually oust the Japanese colonial aggressors from Korea. Of course, Kim Song-ju's actual whereabouts have been historically established as farther north in the Manchurian interior and even in the Soviet Far East, with only occasional forays south of the Yalu-Tumen rivers to attempt the odd raid on a Japanese police outpost. But the actual setting of Kim's exploits matters, of course, far less to the construction of nationalist narrative than the alleged setting. Bruce Cumings offers a potent reminder of the power of these nationalist fables (and, by extension, of nationalist fables more generally) when he says, "At the core of almost every grandiose, prideful, hyperventilated North Korean myth . . . there is a kernel of truth . . . (O)ne underestimates the hold of these stories at one's peril."[20] In this case, the myth involves Kim's single-handed rallying of thousands of demoralized peasants throughout the Paektusan area and adjacent parts of both Manchuria and Korea, transforming them into a disciplined and uniform-clad army comprising both men and women, and conducting a full-scale revolutionary campaign against the Japanese colonial infrastructure. The North Korean Constitution proffers a summary of this myth in a strikingly biblical cadence:

> And the General said, "We must build secret bases in the form of semi-guerilla zones by creating a network of secret camps in the large forests on Mt. Paekto

for the Korean Peoples Revolutionary Army to carry on its activities and organizing the people in the surrounding wide areas. Thus we will set up bastions
of revolution invisible to the enemy."[21]

For the kernel of truth, we return to Lautensach, from whose biased narrative we can plainly infer that there was more than enough anti-Japanese
agitation, which he characterizes as "banditry," in the Paektusan area to provide grist for the North Korean propaganda mill that was to come later on:

Banditry, which has become a severe political problem in all of Manchuria,
has reached its prime in the forests of Paektusan and has encroached into the
Korean sector. The hamlets inhabited by Chinese and Koreans are raided, the
harvest robbed . . . and the inhabitants killed. The bandits' log cabins . . . are
scattered throughout the forests . . . Because of the danger from bandits the
fire-field farmers have left the plateau and retreated to the larger settlements
in the valleys. In the Korean sector, these are protected by Japanese police stations, which have been converted into small fortresses . . . It will be possible to
get rid of the bandits only when the plateau has been opened up to traffic.

Considering that Lautensach's own fieldwork in the region corresponds to
the time that Kim Il Sung may have been occasionally present, it would not
be far-fetched to speculate that his reference to "bandits" could indirectly
include the peasants with whom Kim himself was interacting. Cumings'
work reinforces the notion that the desperately poor slash-and-burn forest
peasants of the Paektusan area were being gradually transformed into Kim's
guerrilla resistance force. He quotes Japanese police records that note that
the guerrillas "had to move like monkeys through the woodmen's paths in
the dense forest," using language curiously evocative of Lautensach's mention of hunting paths as the most viable way of conveying oneself through
the region.[22]

The region's natural features, as presented in North Korean nationalist
narrative, fall into three categories: harsh winter weather, coniferous forest
vegetation, and the rugged presence of Paektu mountain itself. From each
of these three categories emerge motifs that are common in North Korean
nationalist imagery and are mobilized in ways both explicit and subtle. Of
course, in a broader sense, all nature is plainly pressed into service to reinforce the North Korean state and the cult of personality. State publications
abound with gorgeous spring blossoms, fields of waving grain, lush pastures
with grazing flocks, clear rushing streams, and fishing nets laden with their
catch. Somewhat more subtle are the images of children playing happily

in parks near plantings of two flower varieties cultivated by North Korean botanists, "Kimilsungia" and "Kimchongilia" (azalea and begonia, respectively). The ubiquitous variety-show stage backdrops depicting a red sun rising over a placid sea offer a triple-entendre of Kim Il-sung as the "Sun" of the nation, Kim's vanquishing of Japan's "rising sun" in Asia, and the red sun of socialism spreading its penetrating rays. Images of hikers amidst North Korea's more picturesque craggy peaks often include some of the many political inscriptions that have been cut into the granite rock-faces, suggesting that nature itself is a political actor in North Korea.

## Wintry weather

In considering the harsh winter weather as a motif, two things are obvious: first, that harsh winter weather is hardly confined to the Paektusan area but occurs over much of Korea; and, second, that the Paektusan area experiences four distinct seasons with extremes of heat, cold, and precipitation. However, mythologized events have conspired in at least two ways to bring the winter weather of the far northern area into focus as a virtual character in the national myths. First, the heroic actions of the young Kim Il-sung seem to be initiated, according to the nationalist narrative, when, ostensibly for the purpose of attending school, he undertook a trek from his family's transplanted home in Manchuria back to the Pyongyang area beginning in late winter. Both artistic and narrative representations of the young Kim's "1,000-ri journey for learning" depict him struggling through blizzards and "travelling snow-covered paths in deep mountains."[23] Second, Kim Jong-il's birth, which was transplanted to take place at his father's "revolutionary base in the thick forests of Mt. Paektu,"[24] was in the winter (February 16, 1942) when presumably the landscape would have been snow-covered. Consequently, the younger Kim's symbolic birth site as it appears today (a log cabin in a snowy forest with a steep mountain slope rising behind it) is rarely photographed except when the setting is fully blanketed by snow.

It seems that the winter setting of these two formative events of the North Korean nationalist narrative is meant to suggest that a winter backdrop is the most appropriate one for an overwhelming number of artistic depictions of generalized anti-Japanese struggle and guerrilla activity. Moreover, a snowy forested landscape is proffered as one of particular aesthetic value. Typical artistic renditions of Kim and his Korean People's Army fighters (KPA, as the nationalist narrative terms the resistance fighters under Kim's direction) found in public murals and museum paintings alike, depict them interacting with peasants in winter forest encampments or engaging in wintertime tactical maneuvers against the Japanese. Significantly, winter weather is treated in such art not as an obstacle but as a welcome condition. One strong indication of wintry weather being friend, not foe, to the Korean people is found in Kim Jong-il's own "directives" to North Korean filmmakers. In a set of 1989 speeches on artistic production, Kim said that special care should be taken in how filmmakers present scenes of revolutionary struggle that take place in the winter.[25] Taking into account that the elements would have affected all opponents, he pointed out, "Nevertheless, the regiment makes use of the cold and snow to make the enemy troops exhausted." Therefore, Kim said, the images of the snowy landscape should be drawn out because of the "greater sense of security it gives the audience that the headquarters of the revolution is safe, protected by the enveloping blanket of snow in which the enemy is bogged down."[26]

## Coniferous forests and trees

Nationalist myth depicts Kim Il-sung and his followers dwelling in the forest and using the thick forest vegetation to good advantage in planning their anti-Japanese tactical moves. Thus, forest landscape should logically provide a generic backdrop for myriad nationalist representations. Moreover, the idea of the forest-covered mountains as a refuge from organized authority seems to be strongly present in Korean tradition. As previously noted, Lautensach's work asserts that the vast majority of Korea's forest cover by the mid-twentieth century corresponded to its more mountainous areas. Nor can the role of forests and individual trees in particular Korean folk traditions be discounted. Coniferous trees, particularly pine, receive greater emphasis in North Korea's construction of representative landscapes of nationalism not only because of the incidental presence of pine species in the high altitude Paektusan setting but also because of the symbolic significance of pine in Korean folk tradition.

South Korean cultural geographer Je-hun Ryu has recently reviewed the various meanings of forest cover in Korean folk traditions, observing that, "From ancient times, it seems that Koreans highly esteemed the value of forests in a symbolic sense as well as in a practical sense."[27] In addition to forest groves being prized locations for a variety of shamanistic rituals, much of the significance of forest cover emerges from the broader belief framework of p'ungsu. The proximity of forest groves, together with particular patterns of landscape relief and the presence and character of water sources, were (and are) regarded as essential to the quality of auspiciousness ascribed to any site. Since forest can be both planted and eliminated, it looms large in humans' ability to affect the auspiciousness of sites and thereby also to affect the fortunes of those associated with the sites. Descriptive analysis of p'ungsu (fengshui) principles as developed in the Koryo period of Korean history tells us that pine trees growing on mountain slopes are particularly crucial in the facilitation of p'ungsu energy.[28] Of course, Paektusan is well-known to occupy the physical core of the Korean p'ungsu system of mountain relief.[29] So pine forests in the Paektusan area take on an added symbolic layer: not only did they shelter Kim Il-sung and his guerrilla army, they also accentuated the auspiciousness of the setting itself and ensured that only good fortune would accrue to those who occupied it.

Pine trees thus are indelibly associated both with the birth of North Korea as a great nation and directly with the person of Kim Il-sung. The planting of pine trees is associated with Kim's father Kim Hyong-jik, as seen in this poem ascribed to the eldest Kim:

> Comrade, do you know
> The green pine on Nam Hill?
> The rigors of snow and frost may strike it,
> But life returns when spring comes round with warm sunshine.
> If I fail, my sons will go on fighting . . .[30]

Relatedly, a North Korean cassette tape of folk songs opens with a song titled "Ggungniri" whose words read:

> I have been traveling various mountains everywhere,
> Picking up seeds, spreading them all around the mountains,
> And the pine trees are in full bloom.
> North, south, east, and west—in all directions,
> The pine trees grow to cover the mountains.
> A baby is born that will be the joy of the nation.
> Everyone is happy everywhere in this paradise called Mangyongdae.
> Pine trees, they are everywhere.

"Mangyongdae" is the birthplace of Kim Il-sung, and by implication the baby boy is Kim and the narrator of the song is Kim's father. The planting of a pine tree and the birth of Kim are equated in this song. Thus, an individual pine tree can easily represent both the North Korean nationalist cause and specifically Kim Il-sung himself. This is clearly the intent in the August 1994 issue of *DPRK Pictorial* magazine, devoted entirely to commemoration of the death of Kim Il-sung. The back cover of that issue features a full-page illustration of an aged pine tree. The caption asserts that this particular pine grows at Mangyongdae and that, "The fatherly leader will live eternally in the hearts of the people."[31]

The notion that pine trees serve in North Korean nationalist narrative as an embodiment of Kim Il-sung helps shed light on the North Korean propaganda phenomenon of "slogan trees." Slogan trees are trees purportedly discovered in recent decades by North Koreans living and working in the Paektusan area, and their trunks bear carved inscriptions praising the anti-Japanese exploits of the young Kim.[32] The intended meaning of this practice is to suggest that the guerrilla fighters serving with Kim were inspired by their loyalty to carve messages in the trunks of trees, which would go unnoticed for decades until their discovery much more recently. Once the "discovery" of slogan trees would be announced in North Korean media, the trees would be presented as part of a carefully crafted visitors' display, with their trunks encased in protective glass shells. Not only do the slogan trees serve as living reminders of Kim's ideas and influence pervading the same forest where the founding myth is set, the texts describing the discovery of these trees and the messages they convey tend to imply that their survival and readability after so many years is semi-miraculous. Although one might be tempted to regard slogan trees as among the more bizarre of North Korea's propaganda manifestations, when considered in conjunction with the symbolic meaning of Paektusan's forest cover, the practice achieves coherence.

The prevalence and explicit nature of the pine—both individually and in forests—as a motif with well-known *p'ungsu* significance, nationalist symbolism, and embodied identification with Kim Il-sung suggest that North Korean political texts addressing forest planting, conservation, and appreciation could be interpreted at a somewhat deeper level than simply superficial bureaucratic narrative. In the *Land Law of the DPRK*, a substantial section specifically addresses forestry measures.[33] Repeatedly emphasizing the need for all villages and collective farms to have "forest allotments" (preferably nearby) from which a range of building materials and other useful products could be foraged and recovered, these laws are remarkable for their implied presumption that premodern rural practices of relying upon forests for fuel and building materials are largely continuing, unaltered by modernization. The laws also enjoin people to plant more trees around their villages and on nearby hillsides, and this echoes Ryu's discussion of the importance of forest groves in various Korean folk practices. However, they also urge people to not only plant trees in groups, but also to go to forested areas in groups for hiking outings, as ways of fostering collective recreation and healthful enjoyment of the outdoors.

## Rugged mountain terrain

Finally, the distinctive contour of Paektusan itself is unmistakably prominent in North Korean nationalist imagery. In part, this derives from Paektusan's symbolic centrality to Korean p'ungsu tradition. It is commonly accepted among scholars of the inter-Korean rivalry that the North Korean state has worked hard to exploit Paektusan's complex and long-standing mytho-symbolic cultural capital and that Paektusan's image is projected incessantly across many representational genres. Paektusan is both physical metaphor for Kim Il-sung and the quintessential nationalist landscape for North Korea. Its image appears in venues ranging from the cover of Kim Il-sung's autobiography to the cover of the August 1994 pictorial magazine commemorating Kim's death to the expansive mural backdrop behind the enormous bronze statue of Kim in central Pyongyang. The profile of Pyongyang's largest and newest showpiece stadium even bears a striking resemblance to the mountain.

Moreover, rugged mountain terrain seems to be elevated in a broad generic sense in North Korean nationalist texts. Kim Il-sung's speeches and writing contain injunctions to urban-dwelling youth to acquaint themselves with Korea's mountainous areas so that they are entirely comfortable in rugged natural settings. He connected this directly to the notion that since the North Korean state had its genesis in a remote mountainous area (presuming that the KPA of the early 1940s represented the beginnings of the state, and, by deduction, that the core of any revolutionary state is its army), all citizens should be intimately familiar with all of the country's mountainous areas both as a broad nationalist gesture and in response to an implicit call to arms: "If young people are afraid of the mountains, how can they wage a revolutionary struggle and become revolutionary fighters?" Kim urged the youth to renew their emotional connections to rugged natural areas when he instructs them, "Write well about a mountain or a peak, about how you felt when you heard the hooting of an owl there at night and so on."[34] Kim reminded youth that he himself grew to maturity in the northern forest-covered mountain regions that provided both his revolutionary stronghold and a crucible for nationalist ideals. Elsewhere, Kim expressed concern that the mountain areas of the country be repopulated in numbers sufficient to undertake the same particularly laborious but noble kind of farming that had sustained their peasant guerrilla forebears.[35] Thus, all Korean people should be prepared to retreat to the rugged hills throughout the whole of Korea whenever the call to reignite the revolution is forthcoming. The explicit connection between the representative national landscape and the ideal national character strongly echoes the influential work of Lowenthal, who, in writing about the representative landscapes of British identity asserts that these are particularly "freighted with legacy." For England, Lowenthal argues, the very idea of an English landscape conveys "not simply scenery . . . but quintessential national virtues."[36] With its broad appeal to the merit of perpetual revolutionary preparedness, North Korea seems to have constructed a nationalist landscape ideology that functions in a virtually identical manner.

# Conclusion

This chapter has moved toward a deeper critique of Korean national identity by interrogating key elements of North Korea's nationalist narrative. In particular, it has sought, first, to clarify the geography of North Korean nationalism and, second, to claim that this particular geography has engendered the use of a distinctive set of nature motifs in North Korea's nationalist narratives and artistic representations. For North Korea there is an ironic disjuncture between the spatiality of Korean nation-building events and the territory claimed by the Korean nation itself. For North Korea's version of nationalist history, Kim Il-sung acted in the liminal and less-regulated wilderness zone straddling the Korea-China border. To alleviate the dilemma of Kim's nationalist heroics unfolding in a setting to which no Korean state would ever entirely lay claim, North Korea has rewritten its founding myth to set the formative activities of Kim and his guerrilla resistance movement primarily in the Paektusan area, ignoring the factual setting of much of the Manchurian-based anti-Japanese resistance. My intent has been to demonstrate that this restaging of the nationalist founding myth opens up for the North Korean state a range of motifs associated with the Paektusan region that can then easily be mobilized in the nationalist narrative. Not only does this inscribe nationalist meaning on the Paektusan region itself, it also reflexively offers nationalist meaning to other spatial settings, artistic genres, and texts alike where these motifs are manifested throughout North Korea.

I have appealed to work by colonial-era Western geographers to highlight a second ironic disjuncture—namely, that the spatial setting to which the North Korean state transplanted its founding narrative is a distinctive landscape, to be sure, but is hardly a "typical" Korean landscape. With dense forest cover dwindling to fewer and fewer pockets even in the late colonial period, coniferous forest even more scarce, and a volcanic topography completely atypical of anything else in the region, Paektusan breaks sharply from other idealized representative landscapes of nationalism in that it connotes the exception—not the rule—in terms of the character of the national territory as a whole. Still, the North Korean state has persisted in selecting potent natural motifs that can easily be related to the Paektusan region and replicating these motifs endlessly in the production of nationalist texts across a full range of genres.

With North Korea's society and economy severely crippled and quite literally in tatters, what purpose is served by analyzing its conception of nationhood? With the international community more focused upon North Korea's nuclear weapons program or its ongoing humanitarian crises, could we be beyond caring how North Korea has constructed its national narrative? Is North Korea simply a failed state whose totalitarian system needs to be dismantled—and the sooner the better? I argue that there remains an urgent need to understand how North Korea has sustained its national project for as long as it has. Realizing the patterns and continuities of North Korean cultural expression leaves us better prepared for a time when we will be interacting more frequently and directly with North Koreans in a range of social, political, and academic settings. Most are quick to criticize the North Korean state for not allowing its population any sort of exposure to the world beyond North Korea's borders. However, exposure is a two-way street. Only by seeking out encounters with the systems of knowledge that the North Korean state has produced—and seeking to understand those epistemologies for what they are—can we really be equipped for more open exchange and dialogue with North Korea.

## Five questions for discussions

1. What role does history play in North Korea's efforts to define itself as the legitimate representative of the Korean nation?
2. Given the role of nature in North Korea's construction of nationhood, what might be the role of nature in other East Asian states' processes of constructing nationhood?
3. Using North Korea as an example, what do you think is the role of adversity in helping to define a nation and in affecting its policies?
4. What role does modernity play in shaping national identity, and why does a nation arguably only exist in the context of the modern world?
5. Can history and nature help us better understand North Korea and its policies today? How can we help North Korea to connect with the outside world?

# Notes

1  Anthony Smith, *The Ethnic Origins of Nations* (New York: Blackwell, 1986); M. Ignatieff, *Blood and Belonging: Journeys into the New Nationalism* (New York: Farrar, Straus, and Giroux, 1994).

2  See, respectively, Young-soo Kim, et al., eds. *The Identity of the Korean People: A History of Legitimacy on the Korean Peninsula* (Republic of Korea: National Unification Board, 1983), p. 12; and Kim Il-sung, *On the Work of the United Front* (Pyongyang: Foreign Languages Publishing House, 1978), p. 114.

3  E. Gellner, *Nationalism* (Washington Square, NY: New York University Press, 1997), p. 7.

4  C. S. Lee, *Politics of Korean Nationalism* (Berkeley: University of California Press, 1963).

5  Within this extensive and important literature, the following are noteworthy examples: C. A. Johnson, *Peasant Nationalism and Communist Power: The Emergence of Revolutionary China, 1937–1945* (Stanford, CA: Stanford University Press, 1962); J. K. Fairbank, et al., *East Asia: The Modern Transformation* (Boston: Houghton Mifflin, 1965); J. Levenson, "The Province, the Nation, and the World: The Problem of Chinese Identity, in A. Feuerwerker, et al. eds. *Approaches to Modern Chinese History* (Berkeley: University of California Press, 1967), pp. 268–88.

6  P. Duara, *Rescuing History from the Nation: Questioning Narratives of Modern China* (Chicago and London: University of Chicago Press, 1995); K. Chow, et al., eds. *Constructing Nationhood in Modern East Asia* (Ann Arbor: University of Michigan Press, 2001).

7  The work of M. E. Robinson is crucial here. See M. E. Robinson, "Nationalism and the Korean Tradition, 1896–1920," *Korean Studies* 10 (1987): 35–53; and M. E. Robinson, *Cultural Nationalism in Colonial Korea, 1920–1925* (Seattle: University of Washington Press, 1988).

8  D. N. Clark, *Christianity in Modern Korea* (Lanham, MD: University Press of America, 1986); K. Wells, *New God, New Nation: Protestants and Self-Reconstruction Nationalism in Korea, 1896–1937* (Honolulu: University of Hawaii Press, 1990); W. J. Kang, *Christ and Caesar in Modern Korea: A History of Christianity and Politics* (Albany: State University of New York Press, 1997).

9  The work of Bruce Cumings on North Korea is particularly dominant. See B. Cumings, *North Korea: Another Country* (New York: New Press, 2004).

10  Within the substantial literature that traces the connection between nationhood and antiquity and the relationship between memory and nation, the following are particularly representative: A. Smith, "The 'Golden Age' and National Renewal," in G. Hosking and G. Schopflin, eds. *Myths and Nationhood* (New York: Routledge, 1997), pp. 36–59; A. Smith, *The Antiquity of Nations* (Malden, MA: Polity Press, 2004); E. Hobsbawm and T. Ranger, eds. *The Invention of Tradition* (Cambridge: Cambridge University Press, 1983); and J. R. Gillis, ed. *Commemorations: The Politics of National Identity* (Princeton, NJ: Princeton University Press, 1994).

11  A. Schmid, "Looking North toward Manchuria," *The South Atlantic Quarterly* 99:1 (2000): 199–240, 221. Significantly, Schmid's discussion considers the locations of the events from which North Korea derives its claims of sovereign nationhood.

12  See the classic study by S. Schama, *Landscape and Memory* (New York: Alfred A. Knopf, 1995).

13  C. Medlicott, "Symbol and Sovereignty in North Korea," *SAIS Review of International Affairs* 25:2 (Summer–Fall 2005): 69–79.

14  In its preamble, the ROK Constitution refers to the "Spirit of the March First Movement" (reprinted in Kim et al., eds. 1983:1).

15  North Korea's interpretation of modern Korea's founding events is clarified in *On the Socialist Constitution of the Democratic People's Republic of Korea* (Pyongyang: Foreign Languages Publishing House, 1975). It notes that the March First Movement "could not take a well-organised form . . . until the anti-Japanese revolutionary organisation was established between the end of the 1920s and the beginning of the 1930s . . . under the command of General Kim Il Sung" (104–5).

16  I. S. Kim, *Reminiscences with the Century, Volume I* (Pyongyang: Foreign Languages Publishing House, 1992), pp. 39 and 47.

17  Lautensach's 1945 *Korea* was published in German and in 1988 reprinted as an English translation (Berlin: Springer-Verlag, 1988). The quotations used here are all from the 1988 reprint.

18  Lautensach, p. 4.

19  Lautensach, p. 161.

20  Cumings, p. 107.

21  *On the Socialist Constitution of the Democratic People's Republic of Korea* (Pyongyang: Foreign Languages Publishing House, 1975): 105.

22  Cumings, p. 116.

23  *DPRK Pictorial*, March 1993: 4.

24  "His Childhood in Deep Forests and in War Flames," *Profile of Secretary Kim Jong Il the New Leader of the DPRK* (1988): 12–15, 13.

25  Kim Jong-il's particular obsession with filmmaking has, of course, been widely reported on in the Western and South Korean media. For analysis of nature-based national symbols in North Korean film, see C. Medlicott, "Nation and Nature in North Korean Film," in R. Fish, ed. *Cinematic Countrysides* (Manchester: Manchester University Press, 2008), pp. 35–57.

26  J. I. Kim, *Some Problems Arising in the Creation of Masterpieces* (Pyongyang: Foreign Languages Publishing House, 1989), pp. 31–2.

27  J. H. Ryu, *Reading the Korean Cultural Landscape* (Elizabeth, NJ and Seoul: Hollym, 2000), p. 214.

28  B. H. Choi, "Toson's Geomantic Theories and the Foundation of Koryo Dynasty," *Seoul Journal of Korean Studies* 2 (1989): 65–92.

29  H. K. Yoon, *The Culture of Fengshui in Korea: An Exploration of East Asian Geomancy* (New York: Lexington Books, 2008).

30  *DPRK Pictorial*, March 1993: 4.

31  *DPRK Pictorial*, August 1994.

32 *DPRK Pictorial*, February 1993: 10–11.

33 See *Land Law of the DPRK*, chapter four, "Land Conservation," Articles 30 through 39 (Pyongyang: Foreign Languages Publishing House, 1992), pp. 14–18.

34 I. S. Kim, "On Increasing the Vitality of the Work of the League of Socialist Working Youth to Suit the Character of Young People, February 3, 1971," in *On Youth Work* (Pyongyang: Foreign Languages Publishing House, 1989), pp. 94–131.

35 I. S. Kim, *On Further Accelerating the Building of the Socialist Countryside* (Pyongyang: Foreign Languages Publishing House, 1978), p. 67.

36 D. Lowenthal, "British National Identity and the English Landscape," *Rural History* 2 (1991): 205–30, 229.

# Selected bibliography

Choi, B. H. "Toson's Geomantic Theories and the Foundation of Koryo Dynasty." *Seoul Journal of Korean Studies* 2 (1989): 65–92.

Chow, K., et al., eds. *Constructing Nationhood in Modern East Asia* (Ann Arbor: University of Michigan Press, 2001).

Clark, D. N. *Christianity in Modern Korea* (Lanham, MD: University Press of America, 1986).

Cumings, B. *North Korea: Another Country* (New York: New Press, 2004).

Duara, T. *Rescuing History from the Nation: Questioning Narratives of Modern China* (Chicago and London: University of Chicago Press, 1995).

Fairbank, J. K., et al. *East Asia: The Modern Transformation* (Boston: Houghton Mifflin, 1965).

Gellner, E. *Nationalism* (Washington Square, NY: New York University Press, 1997).

Gillis, J. R. ed. *Commemorations: The Politics of National Identity* (Princeton, NJ: Princeton University Press, 1994).

Hobsbawm, E. *Nations and Nationalism since 1780: Programme, Myth, Reality* (Cambridge: Cambridge University Press, 1992).

Ignatieff, M. *Blood and Belonging: Journeys into the New Nationalism* (New York: Farrar, Straus, and Giroux, 1994).

Johnson, C. A. *Peasant Nationalism and Communist Power: The Emergence of Revolutionary China, 1937–1945* (Stanford, CA: Stanford University Press, 1962).

Kang, W. J. *Christ and Caesar in Modern Korea: A History of Christianity and Politics* (Albany: State University of New York Press, 1997).

Kim, I. S. *On Further Accelerating the Building of the Socialist Countryside* (Pyongyang: Foreign Languages Publishing House, 1978).

—. *Reminiscences with the Century, Volume I* (Pyongyang: Foreign Languages Publishing House, 1992).

Kim, J. I. *Some Problems Arising in the Creation of Masterpieces* (Pyongyang: Foreign Languages Publishing House, 1989).

Lee, C. S. *Politics of Korean Nationalism* (Berkeley: University of California Press, 1963).

Levenson, J. "The Province, the Nation, and the World: The Problem of Chinese Identity," in A. Feuerwerker, et al., eds. *Approaches to Modern Chinese History* (Berkeley: University of California Press, 1967), pp. 268–88.

Lowenthal, D. "British National Identity and the English Landscape." *Rural History* 2 (1991): 205–30.

Medlicott, C. "Symbol and Sovereignty in North Korea." *SAIS Review of International Affairs* 25:2 (Summer–Fall 2005): 69–79.

—. "Nation and Nature in North Korean Film," in R. Fish, ed. *Cinematic Countrysides* (Manchester: Manchester University Press, 2008), pp. 35–57.

*On the Socialist Constitution of the Democratic People's Republic of Korea* (Pyongyang: Foreign Languages Publishing House, 1975).

Robinson, M. E. "Nationalism and the Korean Tradition, 1896–1920." *Korean Studies* 10 (1986): 35–53.

—. *Cultural Nationalism in Colonial Korea, 1920–1925* (Seattle: University of Washington Press, 1988).

Ryu, J. H. *Reading the Korean Cultural Landscape* (Elizabeth, NJ and Seoul: Hollym, 2000), p. 214.

Schama, S. *Landscape and Memory* (New York: Alfred A. Knopf, 1995).

Schmid, A. "Looking North Toward Manchuria." *The South Atlantic Quarterly* 99:1 (2000): 199–240.

Smith, A. "The 'Golden Age' and National Renewal," in G. Hosking and G. Schopflin, eds. *Myths and Nationhood* (New York: Routledge, 1997), pp. 36–59.

Wells, K. *New God, New Nation: Protestants and Self-Reconstruction Nationalism in Korea, 1896–1937* (Honolulu: University of Hawaii Press, 1990).

Yoon, H. K. *The Culture of Fengshui in Korea: An Exploration of East Asian Geomancy* (New York: Lexington Books, 2008).

# 13

# A Global "Chinawood"? China's Cultural Policy toward Global Hollywood in the New Century

Wendy Weiqun Su

## Chapter Outline

## Introduction

By the end of 2010, the total film output of China had skyrocketed to 526 with gross box office revenue of 10.772 billion yuan, compared with the output of 91 and gross box office revenue of 960 million yuan in 2000. China had become the world's third largest film producer, trailing only

India and the United States.[1] It has also been the sole market worldwide with an annual box office growth of more than 30 percent.[2] Meanwhile, China's domestic films out-earned foreign imports in terms of box office receipts for six years consecutively from 2004 to 2009. Accordingly, some Chinese filmmakers declared that "China is the only film giant country that is not knocked down by American blockbusters."[3] On the other hand, foreign films, most of them Hollywood hits, had been flooding China at an accelerating rate and claimed one-third of China's domestic market in 2009. In 2010, *Avatar* garnered gross box office receipts of 1.32 billion yuan (roughly US$194 million) in the Chinese film market alone, making China the film's top overseas box office earner and enabling 20th Century Fox to net US$34 million in China.[4] The complex relationship between China and Hollywood raises a series of questions about the reality of China's film sector: How has a national film industry confronted omnipresent global Hollywood and managed to maintain its own growth? What's the role of the Chinese government and the government policy during this process? How has the government policy impacted the domestic film industry and how would it affect the industry's future? These are the central questions that drive this study.

Theoretically, China's evolving relationship with Hollywood-led global capital raises the question of how to conceptualize the cultural dimension of globalization, and the global dominance of popular American culture, Hollywood films in particular. To date scholars have differed and are still differing along two lines of argument: cultural imperialism versus cultural globalization, which has brought the research on "global-local dialectic" to a crucial turn in the past decade.[5] Given the uniqueness of China's integration with the global capitalist system while maintaining its political and social structures as well as its cultural traditions, its experience is considered very central to the study of global-local interplay. As such, China's cultural policy toward global Hollywood bears a profound theoretical implication. Will China's policy truly challenge the Hollywood hegemony and lead to an emergence of a "Global China"?

Situating China studies within the global context, this chapter seeks to analyze China's cultural policy and counter hegemony strategies toward global Hollywood and Hollywood-led transnational media conglomerates from 2000 to 2011. The chapter further investigates the impact of the cultural policy on China's domestic film industry as well as local and global cultural landscape.

# Policy shift: WTO challenge and redefinition of film as cultural industry

It should be noted that the cultural policy of the Chinese government during the period between mid-2000 and 2011 was, first of all, a revision of its previous policy from 1994 to early 2000. As is generally known, China's film sector was in stagnancy between the mid-1980s and the mid-1990s, due to a number of reasons: the disconnection between the government-censored film production and the market-demanded distribution and exhibition; the much tighter political control in the repressive post-1989 political environment; and the competition from commercialized television programs, rampant underground markets and theaters for pirated VCDs that had led to "audience/market fragmentation."[6] Hoping to bring the audience back to cinemas and to revitalize the film market, the Chinese government adopted the revenue-sharing system to begin importing ten foreign blockbusters annually in November 1994. By the end of the twentieth century, 10 imports, most of them Hollywood mega-productions, had conquered about 70 percent of China's film market, whereas approximately 100 domestically made films only had 30 percent of market share.[7]

In order to minimize the Hollywood influence and maintain the moral legitimacy of the ruling Communist Party, the Chinese government adopted an initial cultural policy between 1994 and early 2000. The essence of this policy was to use money earned from Hollywood imports to subsidize government-sponsored propagandistic films, so as to promote the theme of patriotism, socialism, and collectivism. However, the Chinese government's initial cultural policy was ineffective in terms of film market recouped and quality films produced. China's domestic film production kept declining: between 1990 and 1995, China's annual domestic film output was 146 on average, but the average dropped to 95 between 1996 and 2002.[8] Ten to 20 imports had beaten about 100 domestic films in terms of box office receipts. More than 70 percent of domestic films continued losing money. All these had demonstrated that the profound crisis of China's domestic film industry continued into the twenty-first century.

Facing the massive pressure of the prolonged financial crisis of the domestic film industry, and the formidable challenge after China formally rejoined the WTO in 2001, the government eventually reworked its strategy and made significant policy changes, against the larger backdrop of a newly launched reform of cultural industries. This brings us to the second and third reason for policy shift.

China's reentry to WTO and the commitment China had to make under the terms of WTO is the second reason for the shift in its cultural policy. China and the United States signed the agreement on China's accession to the WTO in November 1999, and China's accession was formally approved in November 2001. The Chinese side made considerable concessions to the United States, and Hollywood's long-standing desire for the China market seemed, finally, to be at least partially satisfied. Under the agreement, the Chinese government agreed to double the annual quotas for revenue-sharing imports to 20, to allow for a share of up to 49 percent by foreign investors in operating theaters, and to permit foreign investment in video distribution joint ventures.[9] The policy shift was a commitment that the Chinese government had to make to meet the requirements of the WTO.

The above-mentioned two reasons are external factors to the film policy shift. But the third reason is the most crucial. It is the Chinese government's redefinition of the role of films after more than 20 years of ambivalence and reluctance, and the associated launch of the reform of "cultural industries."

The status of the film sector in China had always been vague and dubious up to 2000. From the 1950s to the late 1970s, film served as the Party-state's propaganda tool, responding to the Party's political agenda. During the reform era of the 1980s, the artistic function of film was highlighted by the creative fifth generation directors. With the launch of "Main Melody" films on a large scale after the 1989 Tiananmen Incident, film's function as the conveyor of the official ideology was emphasized once more. After Deng Xiaoping's famous 1992 South China tour and the massive promotion of "socialist market economy," the reform in the film system commenced as well from 1993. Yet not till 1997, when the establishment of a "socialist market economy" became the fundamental goal for the CCP and the marketization of the cultural sector was underway, did the official definition of the film sector undergo a remarkable change.

To meet the goal set by the CCP 15th National Congress of 1998 which called for an "all-round advance of 'the socialism with the Chinese characteristics' into the 21st century," China's various sectors, including the film sector, speeded up the marketization process. In the 1998 Nan Chang film meeting, the then propaganda minister of the CCP, Ding Guangen, said "The film sector must win the market in order to prosper. Under the condition of the socialist market economy, film as a cultural product, cannot be independent of the market economy."[10] Meanwhile, the then deputy director of the State Administration of Radio Film and Television (SARFT), Zhao Shi, spoke clearly that "Film belongs to cultural industries."[11] At the same time, discussion and debate over the role and function of the film sector was going on.

By the year of 2002 when the 16th National Congress of the CCP convened and formally put forward the idea of "cultural industries," both official and unofficial voices had acknowledged the market value and the cultural industrial role of the film sector, which cleared the way for the massive transformation and for the establishment of a new film industry.

It looks like the Party-state, pushed by various external and internal forces, was finally inclined to the market and entertaining function of film, and prepared to embark on the wholesale transformation of film-included cultural industries. However, one should always bear in mind that with China's political structure and the strictest censorship, film is unlikely to be considered either a purely creative art or a purely entertaining commodity. It has to more or less carry on with a propagandistic mission. Film, like culture, can hardly enjoy a status fully independent of political restraint and government control. It is not unusual that the official utterances on the role of film vary depending on the different contexts. Like Xu Guangchun and Zhao Shi, they emphasized the market role of film as a cultural product on one occasion, while stressing the film's propagandistic role to build "socialist civilization" and reflect "Three Represents" or "socialist advanced culture" on another occasion.[12] The status of film, like the status of culture, is always ambivalent or double-functioned, and at the discursive disposal of the government. Accordingly, the film sector has to seek a balance between its different roles, negotiate its way through and "dance with shackles."

# Reworked governmental policies and new players

Within the larger background and amid theoretical preparation, several sets of reform regulations on the domestic film industry were unveiled. The SARFT promulgated Documents 18, 19, 20, 21, and other regulations in 2003.[13] In 2004 and 2005, the SARFT issued another set of supplementary regulations.[14] The key point in summary is that new players, both private and foreign, were encouraged to participate in what had formerly been a closed ideological system; this represents a significant watershed in the development of Chinese film. However, private and foreign players must stay within the parameters strictly laid down by the CCP. Therefore, it is a top-down strategy, a limited and conditional open-up with the aim of serving the CCP's agenda.

The main points of the reworked governmental regulations, among others, included:

First, direct foreign and Chinese private investment and participation were henceforth permitted in film production. Chinese state-owned institutions, studios and companies, and non-state-owned companies (collectives, share-holding companies, or privately-owned companies) were encouraged to establish joint ventures, or to establish solely owned studios. Foreign investors were permitted to establish joint ventures with state-owned studios or to hold shares of studios. Foreign investors, however, were still not permitted to establish solely owned studios or joint ventures with non-state-owned companies; nor were they permitted to hold shares of more than 49 percent of joint ventures with state-owned studios. Thus state-owned film studios still enjoyed a certain degree of state protection.

Second, in the sector of film distribution and exhibition, state-owned, non-state-owned companies, even individuals, including both citizens and foreigners, were encouraged to invest in the construction and renovation of cinemas. Although foreign investors were still banned from establishing solely owned cinemas and distribution companies, they were henceforth allowed to hold shares of up to 49 percent of joint ventures while the Chinese investors must hold shares of no less than 51 percent. Yet, in major cities including Beijing, Shanghai, Guangzhou, Xi'an, Chengdu, Wuhan, and Nanjing, foreign shares were allowed to reach as high as 75 percent and to have a cooperative term of no longer than 30 years on a trial basis.[15] The same regulation applied to Hong Kong and Macau investors as well with shares allowed to reach 75 percent.

Third, state-owned and non-state-owned institutions, studios, or companies were encouraged to hold shares of the current theater chains or establish new theater chains. Also, various provinces and regions were encouraged to build their own theater chains through vertical integration. Under the previous planned distribution system, a film, once produced, had to go through three tiers of state distribution companies at levels of province, city, and county before it finally reached exhibition theaters. The revenue earned from the distribution of that film had to be divided among these three tiers of distribution companies and exhibition theaters. As a result, the film producer could only obtain 32 percent of revenue and theaters had 28 percent. This way of distribution of revenue was considered unreasonable and unfair by film producers and exhibitors, and consequently repressed their initiative and productivity.[16] In addition, state distribution companies at various levels were not allowed to distribute films beyond their affiliated administrative areas such as a city or a county. Through the establishment of the

Hollywood-style theater chains, the distribution companies were restructured into a unified distribution complex that owns as many theaters as they can across administrative boundaries, thus breaking up administrative limitations and unleashing market force.

The supplements issued in 2004 and 2005 allowed an even higher level of market access in the order of domestic nonstate investors, Hong Kong and Macau investors, as well as foreign investors. The most noteworthy point was the greater rights and market access that Mainland Chinese government granted to Hong Kong and Macau investors, to follow the guildline of "Mainland and Hong Kong Closer Economic Partnership Arrangement" and "Mainland and Macau Closer Economic Partnership Arrangement (CEPA)."

The two CEPAs were signed respectively in Hong Kong and Macau on June 29, 2003 and October 17, 2003, which are considered the first free trade agreements aiming at the elimination of customs tariff barriers between Mainland China and its Special Administrative Regions (SARs). In terms of the cooperation in the film sector, CEPA allowed Hong Kong-produced films, upon passing the censorship, to be distributed in the Mainland without the quota limitation. Mainland-Hong Kong coproductions were treated as domestic films to be distributed. Furthermore, Hong Kong and Macau investors were allowed to invest in film theater renovations, to build solely owned new theaters, and to hold shares no more than 75 percent. Put another way, through CEPAs and related film regulations, the Chinese government granted more rights to "Greater China" investors while relatively limiting the rights of foreign investors.

The new government policies functioned as a stimulant to the domestic film industry and had drawn attention and interest of both domestic and overseas investors, bringing about an astonishing boom of film production and film market.

# The boom of domestic film production and the inflow of overseas funds

First, China's film output had been climbing up from 2003 to 2010, with the record high of 526 in 2010. In 2004, right after the implementation of new policies, the output of feature films (excluding documentaries and cartoons) jumped to 212, a 50 percent increase over 2003's number of 140, and breaking the record high of 170 that was made in 1992. In 2005, the number climbed up to 260, a 22.6 percent increase over 2004.[17] From 2006 to 2010, the output rocketed to 330, 402, 406, 456, and 526 respectively.[18]

Second, box office receipts nationwide had been soaring consecutively from 2003 to 2010, with the annual increase of more than 25 percent on average. The figures were respectively one billion yuan in 2003, 1.5 billion yuan in 2004, 2 billion yuan in 2005, 2.6 billion yuan in 2006, 3.327 billion yuan in 2007, 4.3 billion yuan in 2008, 6.21 billion in 2009, and 10.772 billion yuan in 2010.[19] See Figure 13.1 and Figure 13.2 below:

Third, Hollywood-style theater chains had been established in big cities of China. By the end of 2010, the screen number nationwide had reached 6,200, only next to the United States and India.[20]

The most drastic change that the state policy had brought to China's film industry, however, is fourth, the inflow of transnational capital into China. Transnational media conglomerates seized the opportunity occurring because of the policy shift and took advantage of reworked policies to march into China. Warner Brothers joined hands with China Film Import & Export Corporation (CFIEC) and Hengdian Company Ltd. to establish a large corporation, controlling seven theater chains that took up more than 35 percent of market share. Sony Pictures Home Entertainment also cooperated with CFIEC to set up a joint venture. Viacom collaborated with Shanghai Wenguang Group to establish the first Sino-foreign invested cartoon production company, and a second was a joint venture with Japanese Dentsu Company.[21]

Foreign investment also flowed into the renovation of theaters on a larger scale. In January 2004, Warner Brothers cooperated with Dalian Wanda Group to set up Warner Wanda International Theater, with Warner

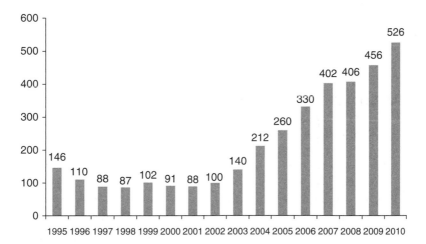

**Figure 13.1** China's film output, 1995–2010
(*Source*: *China Film Yearbook*, 1995–2010)

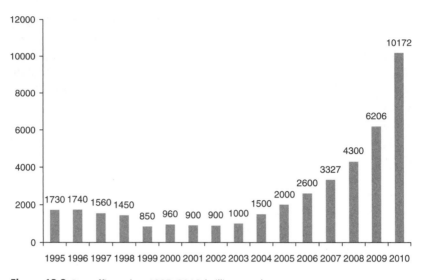

**Figure 13.2** Box office sales, 1995–2010 (million yuan)
(*Source*: *China Film Yearbook* 1995–2010)

Brothers managing and providing technological support. Warner Brothers also planned to invest in more than 30 multiple-function theaters in China in several years to come. In addition, Korea Orion and American LOEWS also invested in a number of new theaters with 75 percent of foreign share and 25 percent of Chinese share.[22] By 2005, Hollywood's seven major film studios had all set up offices in Beijing or Shanghai, awaiting further changes of state policy which would mean the arrival of opportunities.

In addition, international funds constantly flowed to China to help solve Chinese filmmakers' long-term financial difficulties. In May 2007, China Film Group and America's IDG jointly established "IDG China Media Fund," which was planning to expand the fund by 10 times and invest in the production of 60 to 80 films in the next 10 years. In addition, a film fund, titled "A3 International Film Fund" that was jointly launched by Mainland China's nonstate sector and film producers from Hong Kong, Japan, South Korea, and the United States, is expected to raise US$100 million to invest in 30 Asian coproductions among China, Japan, and South Korea in the next 5 years, and 60 percent of the fund will be invested in China. Furthermore, in October 2007, Weinstein Brothers announced it would establish an "Asian Film Fund" of US$285 million, and planned to invest more than 50 percent of the fund in 20 Chinese films in the next 5 years. It is estimated that the fund flowing into Chinese film production will reach US$60 million every year.[23]

However, while transnational corporations attempted to secure more film market share and maintained a sound footing in China, the Chinese government skillfully controlled the scale and pace of the inflow of transnational capital and the spread of foreign conglomerates into the domestic film industry. By only allowing joint adventures between state-owned companies like China Film Group and Xinhua Media Entertainment, the government aimed to guarantee state control of shareholdings in joint adventures. In late 2005, the Chinese government issued "Several Opinions in Foreign Investment in Culture Industry," which stressed once more that "Chinese mainland investors must own at least 51 percent or play a leading role in their joint ventures with foreign investors." The new rule frustrated Time Warner's strategy in China. Consequently, Warner Bros. International Cinemas (WBIC) withdrew from China in November 2006. It was stated that Warner Bros' exit from China "shows the vulnerability of foreign media and entertainment companies to the country's policy changes."[24] At the same time, state-owned companies played a more active role in seeking cooperative opportunities with foreign investors. In April, 2008, The China Film Group and Xinhua Media Entertainment, a new subsidiary of Nasdaq-listed XFMedia, announced a strategic alliance to coproduce movies from offices in Beijing and Los Angeles. Xinhua Media Entertainment will be part of XFMedia's Production Group, which produces animation drama series and special effects for Chinese television.[25]

A careful investigation of the foreign investment in China's film production, based on statistics of *China Film Yearbook 2004 to 2009*, indicates that films co funded by foreign capital merely constituted a small portion of the total film output, and the portion was relatively stable throughout a six-year period from 2003 to 2008.[26] To reiterate, the Chinese government granted "Greater China" investors more rights and market access rather than foreign conglomerates, thus to a certain degree contained the further spread of Hollywood giants into China, see Table 13.1 and Figure 13.3 below:

**Table 13.1** Ratio of total film output and films with overseas capital, 2003–8

|  | Film output | Films co-funded by Hong Kong and Taiwan companies | Films co-funded by foreign companies |
|---|---|---|---|
| 2003 | 140 (100%) | 36 (25.7%) | 16 (11.4%) |
| 2004 | 212 (100%) | 44 (20.8%) | 5 (2.4%) |
| 2005 | 260 (100%) | 34 (13.1%) | 9 (3.5%) |
| 2006 | 330 (100%) | 35 (10.6%) | 11 (3.3%) |
| 2007 | 402 (100%) | 26 (6.5%) | 15 (3.7%) |
| 2008 | 406 (100%) | 26 (6.4%) | 11 (2.7%) |

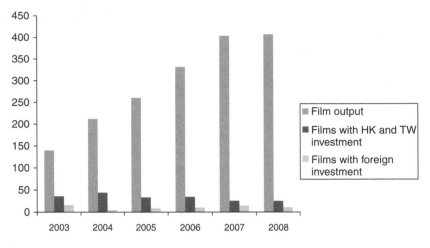

**Figure 13.3** Film output and films co-funded by overseas capital, 2003–8 (*Source*: China Film Yearbook 1995–2010)

As such, although foreign capital flowed into China in an unprecedented way, the number of films funded by foreign capital remained a very small portion in the overall Chinese film output. From 2008 to 2010, due to the policy and market changes of China, foreign capital came back again. The typical example is that EPT East Limited Company of the US and Shanghai Film Group established a joint venture "Shanghai SFG-EPT." In February 2011, IMAX Corporation announced that it was planning to operate more than 300 theaters in Greater China area in the next five years.[27] Prior to this move, IMAX had collaborated with China's Huayi Brothers to release DMR film *Aftershock* in July 2010. The trend is going on and merits further investigation.

Chinese official statistics also claimed that prior to 2003, more than 60 percent of revenue was earned from Hollywood movies, 30 percent from Hong Kong movies, and only 10 percent from Mainland China movies. After 2003, domestic films, including both Mainland and Hong Kong movies, were able to beat Hollywood imports and recover the film market. Prior to 2003, the Chinese film administration rarely made public the exact numbers of ticket sales for domestic films, and Hollywood imports in particular; after 2003, the administration felt more comfortable releasing those numbers.

It seems the government policy was showing very positive outcomes. Accordingly, the Chinese government and film researchers cheered the triumph of domestic films, and claimed that domestic films surpassed foreign imports in terms of box office receipts for consecutive seven years from 2004 to 2010. See Table 13.2 below:

**Table 13.2** Market share of domestic films (%), 2004–10

| 2004 | 55 |
| --- | --- |
| 2005 | 60 |
| 2006 | 55 |
| 2007 | 54.13 |
| 2008 | 59.04 |
| 2009 | 66 |
| 2010 | 56.3 |

(*Source: China Film Yearbook*, 2005–9; Yin, 2010; Liu, 2011, The Analysis Report of Chinese Film Enterprise in 2010. *Contemporary Cinema*, 16–22).

Director of China Film Bureau, Tong Gang, thus said: "Now the trend is that state-owned studios, non-state and overseas investors jointly create domestic films."[28]

However, are "domestic films" still domestically made films anymore? Statistics based on the official documents indicated that most "domestic films" that boasted impressive box office record were in fact either funded by overseas companies or made by overseas producers and joined by Hollywood stars. For example, the top five films of 2003 in terms of ticket sales were all coproductions either funded by Columbia Pictures Film Production Asia, or by Hong Kong companies. Among the top ten films of that year, only two were solely produced by domestic and state studios. Similarly, the top seven films of 2004 were all coproductions funded by either Columbia Pictures Corporation, Columbia Pictures Film Production Asia, or by Hong Kong companies. In 2005 and 2006, the trend continued and the scale of Sino-Foreign cooperation expanded at an unprecedented level. Joining the investment team in top ten films included Moonstone Entertainment and Ruddy Morgan Productions of the United States, Show East and Boram Entertainment Inc. of Korea, as well as Avex Inc., Gilla Company and Toho Company of Japan. Mainland China's film stars, Hong Kong stars, and internationally known stars from the United States and Japan constituted the cast and coproduced these films. In 2007, all top ten films were coproductions, co-funded, costarred, and globally distributed by overseas companies. See Table 13.3.

As such, coproductions became the major contributor to China's film revenue. Although they constituted a small number of the overall film output,

**Table 13.3** Numbers of co-productions among top ten films in receipts, 2003–9

| 2003 | HK/ TW 5, foreign 2 |
|------|---------------------|
| 2004 | HK/TW 5; foreign 3 |
| 2005 | HK/TW 3; foreign 5 |
| 2006 | HK/TW 5; foreign 2 |
| 2007 | HK/TW 5; foreign 5 |
| 2008 | HK/TW 4; foreign 5 |
| 2009 | HK/TW 5; foreign 2 |

(*Source: China Film Yearbook* 2004 to 2010)

their influence on the audience was tremendous, and their market shares had been enormous up to 2011. The impact of coproductions on Chinese film industry's growing future merits further investigation. The astonishing development of China's film industry and its relationship with Hollywood-led transnational capital provides profound implication for both China and the global cultural landscape.

# Conclusion: alliance, power, and new challenge

First of all, the Chinese government was the biggest beneficiary of its own policy and a clear winner in its tug-of-war with Hollywood-led global capital. The Chinese government's policy had provided unprecedented opportunities for transnational media conglomerates to march into China and facilitated Sino-foreign transnational partnerships. However, through its strategic and skillful operation, the Chinese government was able to prevent the domestic film market from a landslide conquest by global media capital while in the meantime making use of transnational partnerships to serve its own agenda.

The Chinese government granted "Greater China" investors more rights and market access rather than foreign conglomerates, thus the Chinese government successfully contained the further spread of Hollywood giants into China through creating a "Greater China" complex to counterbalance Hollywood's power. By doing so, the Chinese government benefited from updated film technology, industrial infrastructure, box office revenue, and financial gains while trying to minimize the Hollywood influence and the market share of transnational corporations. Therefore, through both the alliance and tug-of-war with global capital, and through the Greater China alliance, the Chinese government effectively consolidated its authoritarian power.

Second, the government's open-up policy also resulted in a striking facelift of the domestic film industry. Not only Hollywood's big-budget, high tech, spectacular model was enthusiastically emulated by Chinese film directors, but Hollywood's distribution-exhibition system was also embraced unreservedly by the state. Consequently, a strong market-oriented film industry is forming from production to distribution, and box office revenue seems to have become the sole measure to judge the success of a film up to now. Overdone Kung Fu movies that combine both spectacular Hollywood-style special effects and traditional Chinese cultural elements became the influential genre of the domestic film industry and prime market attraction, and social realism works were marginalized. Further studies are needed to investigate this phenomenon. Suffice it to say here that this trend has significantly shaped the aesthetic taste of the audience and the direction of the China film industry.

Third, accordingly, transnational, trans-regional coproductions became the major contributor to domestic film revenue and a backbone force to the domestic film industry. Their portion in the overall film output varied from approximately 37 percent in 2003 at the most to 10 percent in 2007 at the least. An intertwined partnership network is in the process of forming not only regionally in Asia but globally.

Fourth, however, a majority of films that were domestically made by state-owned or non-state-owned studios remained unwelcome and unpopular in the market, due to low quality, a lack of imagination, and/or being overly propaganda oriented. Censorship is still "The Sword of Damocles" hanging over film professionals and severely confines their agency, initiative, and enthusiasm. The Party-state needs to further loosen the grip on film production, fully liberalize minds, truly encourage diverse styles, and guarantee the freedom of expression. Moreover, the cultural policy should encourage and protect true artistic works that are not merely commercially entertaining but reflect the real living condition of the ordinary Chinese people in a transitional historical era. Their changing values, confusing identities, anxieties, struggles and aspirations, and tears and joy in a dazzling, rapidly globalizing world should become the mainstream of the film industry.

The Chinese government policy and the fundamental change in the film industry that was brought about suggests three possible consequences that may come out of China's tug-of-war with Hollywood-led global capital: First and the best, the Hollywood capital helps bring China's film industry to a higher level, and Chinese films dominate the domestic market; second, a win-win situation emerges, and Hollywood movies and Chinese movies share the domestic market; third and the worst, the Hollywood capital completely dominates China's market, and the Chinese film industry either vanishes or becomes a dependency of Hollywood.[29]

In a win-win situation, there is a possibility of "copetetion" or "cooperation in competition," which directly speaks to the nature of intertwined production between Hollywood and China. Under such a situation, Hollywood and China could both benefit from their cooperation and make money together. Hollywood could certainly benefit from the economies of scale of China and could make huge profits from China's production cost advantage, while China could benefit from Hollywood's ample capital, advanced filmmaking technique, digital technology, advanced business strategy and global distribution networks, as well as well-known directors and stars. China's rich cultural and historical heritage, as well as its untapped natural landscape is an abundant resource for both sides to draw on. Both sides would benefit from their cooperation rather than confrontation and competition. Meanwhile, China is exporting its excellent films to overseas markets and exerting indisputable influence on foreign countries. Therefore, it's not the "wolf" coming, but the "Chinese dragon" taking off by drawing on Hollywood's strength. A journalist of France's *Nice-Matin* coined the term "Chinawood." He believed "the day has come for Chinawood to challenge Hollywood!"[30]

Speaking back to the theoretical question raised earlier, the possible "Chinawood" and an emerging global China force bear profound implication for "global-local dialectic." The case study in this chapter suggests that policy is instrumental, and the role of the government is key to the elevation of China's film and cultural industries to the status as part of "soft power" and an essential element of a driving global force. However, a "Chinawood" is yet to arrive. Wise policy leads to the historical transformation and to the take-off of a nation, economically or culturally. In the global-local dialectic, it's the policy that ultimately determines a country's future and its fate in the competitive global marketplace.

## Five questions for discussions

1. What are some major policy shifts made by the Chinese government toward global Hollywood from 2000 to 2011? What is the essence of such shifts?
2. How do we understand the complex relationship between China and Hollywood from cultural and political perspectives?

3. How has the government policy impacted the domestic film industry and what are some remarkable changes in China's domestic film industry?
4. Is a "Chinawood" emerging? How will China's film industry and cultural policies challenge Hollywood?
5. Based on the China case, how do we have a deeper understanding of the cultural dimension of globalization?

# Notes

1 Xiaodong Wu, "Ershiliu bu yingpian juanzou liucheng zongpiaofang, Zhongguo dianying quexian tuxian" (Weakness of China's film industry: 26 films take away 60% box office receipts), *China Youth Daily*, January 25, 2011.

2 Tiedong Zhou, "Speech at the US-China Film Summit," Los Angeles, California, November 2, 2010.

3 Xiaoning Feng, "Zhongguo shi weiyi weibei mei dapian yakua de dianying da guo" (China is the only giant film producer that is not knocked down by American blockbusters), *Chinese Economy Network*, March 5, 2010.

4 Wei Zhang, "Avatar zhongguo piaofang jin liangyi meiyuan, weiju haiwai shichang bangshou" (*Avatar* makes China top overseas box office earner of US$ 200 million), *China News Service*, April 1, 2010.

5 John Tomlinson, "Culture Globalization and Cultural Imperialism," in *International Communication and Globalization: A Critical Introduction*, ed. Ali Mohammadi (London and New York: Sage Publications, 1997), pp. 170–90. For a literature review of these two lines of argument and their relevance to China, please see Arjun Appadurai (1996); Roland Robertson (1992a, 1992b, 1995); Frederic Jameson (1998); Nestor Garcia Canclini (1995); K. Iwabuchi (2002); Marwan Kraidy (2005); Michael Curtin (2007); and S. Lash, et al. (2010).

6 Yuezhi Zhao, *Communication in China: Political Economy, Power, and Conflict* (Rowman & Littlefield Publishers, 2008), p. 162.

7 D. Zheng, "To Be, Or Not To Be?—Jinru WTO yihou de zhongguo Dianying shengcun fenxi" (To Be, Or Not To Be—An analysis on the survival of Chinese film industry after entering into WTO), *Dianying Yishu* (2000): 4–8.

8 P. Wan, "Jinkou fenzhang yingpian shinian piaofang fenxi" (An analysis of ten years of box office of revenue-sharing imports), *Journal of Beijing Film Academy* (2005): 49–60.

9 G. Tong, 2001, "How does China's Film Industry Face the Challenge Brought by China's Join of WTO?" *China Film Yearbook 2001* (Beijing: China Film Yearbook Press), pp. 17–20.

10 Shi Zhao, "The Mission of Chinese Films to Stride into the New Century in 1999," *China Film Yearbook 2000* (Beijing: China Film Press, 2000), p. 13.

11 Ibid.

12 The quoted phrases are CCP political jargons. The Three Represents, namely, the CCP has always represented the development trend of advanced productive forces, the orientation of advanced culture and the fundamental interests of the overwhelming majority of the Chinese people, is a sociopolitical ideology credited to former CCP General Secretary and President Jiang Zemin.

13 These major regulations included: "Administration Regulations for International Film Co-production" and "Provisional Regulations for Licenses of the Film Production, Distribution and Exhibition" issued simultaneously in October 2003; "Suggestions for Further System Reform in Theater Chains" and "Provisional Regulations of the Foreign Investment in Film Theaters" issued in November 2003; as well as "Detailed Rules on Strengthening the Cooperation and Management of Film Industry between Mainland China and Hong Kong" issued in October 2003 (*China Film Yearbook 2004*, pp. 14–21).

14 These supplementary regulations included: "Provisional Regulations on Film Script Project Application and Production Approval"; "Regulations on International Film Production"; "Regulations on Administration of Radio and TV Festivals, Exhibitions and Program Exchange"; "Provisional Regulations on the Qualification of Film Corporations," etc. as well as "Supplement to Provisional Regulations on Foreign-Invested Cinemas" and "Supplement to Provisional Regulations on the Qualification of Film Corporations" that were issued in 2005 (*China Film Yearbook 2006*, pp. 47–8).

15 SARFT and MoC, "Provisional Regulations of the Foreign Investment in Film Theaters," *China Film Yearbook 2004* (Beijing: China Film Yearbook Press, 2003), pp. 18–19.

16 L. Yu, "Chinese Film: Flying in Market Economy—A Note on Cinema Chain Reform in the Past Two Years," *China Film Yearbook 2005* (Beijing: China Film Yearbook Press, 2005), pp. 203–6.

17 *China Film Yearbook 2005* (Beijing: China Film Yearbook Press, 2005), pp. 32–6; *China Film Yearbook 2006* (Beijing: China Film Yearbook Press, 2006), pp. 61–9; *China Film Yearbook 2007* (Beijing: China Film Yearbook Press, 2007), pp. 34–40.

18 See B. Chen, "Annual film revenue reaches more than 3.3 billion Yuan," *Beijing Evening Post*, January 12, 2008. Film Administration under the State Bureau of Broadcasting, Film and Television, "Film production, distribution and exhibition in 2008," Dangdai Dianying (*Contemporary Cinema*), 2009, No. 1: 27–8. H. Yin, "2009 nian zhongguo dianying chanye bei-wang (A Memo of 2009 Chinese Film Industry)," in *Annual Report on Development of China's Cultural Industries*, ed. Xiaoming Zhang, Huilin Hu, and Jiangang Zhang (Beijing: Social Sciences Academic Press, 2009), pp. 145–68. Xiaodong Wu, "Ershiliu bu yingpian juanzou liucheng zongpiaofang, Zhongguo dianying quexian tuxian" (Weakness of China's film industry: 26 films take away 60% box office receipts), *China Youth Daily*, January 25, 2011.

19 Ibid.

20 Deshu Yu, "Zhongguo yinmu shu jishen shijie disan" (China's Screen Number Ranks the Third Worldwide), January 10, 2011 at http://www.cs.com.cn/ssgs/16/201101/t20110110_2739578.html

21  G. Tong, "Fruitful Industrial Policy and New Epoch for Chinese Film—Annual Report of 2004 on Chinese Film Industry," *China Film Yearbook 2005* (Beijing: China Film Yearbook Press, 2005), pp. 32–6.

22  H. Yin and X. Wang, "The Industry Year of Chinese Film," *Dangdai Dianying* (Contemporary Cinema) (2) 2005: 18–26.

23  H. Yin and Q. Zhan, "2007 nian zhongguo dianying chanye beiwang" (A Memo of 2007 Film Industry), *Dangdai Dianying* (Contemporary Cinema) (2) 2008: 13–21.

24  Bloomberg News, "Time Warner to quit China cine business," November 8, 2006.

25  J. Landreth, "Co-prod'n unit Xinhua Media bridges China, U.S," *The Hollywood Reporter*, April 15, 2008.

26  The statistics comes from the official listings of feature films published in *China Film Yearbook 2004–2009*. They do not include underground films or art house films that were banned by the government.

27  "IMXA daju qiangzhan zhongguo shichang yuling, yingyuan fankui bugeili" (IMAX encounters unresponsive theaters of China in its attempt to conquer the Chinese market), *Huaxia Times*, February 21, 2011 at http://news.entgroup.cn/movie/219520.shtml

28  G. Tong, "Inherit the Centennial Tradition to Compose a New Chapter on Chinese Film Production," *China Film Yearbook 2006* (Beijing: China Film Yearbook Press, 2006), pp. 61–9.

29  H. Huang and Y. Wang, "2005: Zhongguo dianying shichang chixu fusu" (2005: Continuing Recovery of Chinese Film Market), *Liaowang zhoukan* (*Outlook Weekly*), 2005 (50), December 12, 54–5.

30  Y. Li, "Jingzhengxing hezuo: rushi hou zhongmei dianyingye de jiaohu taishi" (Competition: The Intertwined Situation of Sino-American Film Industry after China Reenters WTO), *Xiandai Chuanbo* (Modern Communication) (1) 2006: 14–19.

# Selected bibliography

Appadurai, A. *Modernity at Large* (Minneapolis and London: University of Minnesota Press, 1996).

Curtin, M. *Playing to the World's Biggest Audience: The Globalization of Chinese Film and TV* (Berkeley, Los Angeles and London: University of California Press, 2007).

García Canclini, N. *Hybrid Cultures: Strategies for Entering and Leaving Modernity*, trans. Christopher L. Chiappari and Silvia L. López (Minneapolis: University of Minnesota Press, 2005).

Iwabuchi, K. *Reentering Globalization: Popular Culture and Japanese Transnationalism* (Durham, NC: Duke University Press, 2002).

Jameson, F. "Notes on Globalization as a Philosophical Issue," in *The Cultures of Globalization* (Durham and London: Duke University Press, 1998), ed. Fredric Jameson and Masao Miyoshi, pp. 54–77.

Kraidy, M. *Hybridity, or the Cultural Logic of Globalization* (Philadelphia: Temple University Press, 2005).

Lash, S., Keith, M. Arnoldi, J., and Rooker, T. *Global China* (London and New York: Routledge, 2010).

Robertson, R. "Globality and Modernity." *Theory, Culture & Society* 9:2 (1992).

—. *Globalization: Social Theory and Global Culture* (London, Newbury Park, New Delhi: Sage Publication, 1992).

—. "Globalization: Time-Space and Homogeneity-Heterogeneity," in *Global Modernities* (London and New York: Sage Publications, 1995), ed. Mike Featherstone, Scott Lash, and Roland, pp. 25–44.

Tomlinson, John. "Culture Globalization and Cultural Imperialism," in *International Communication and Globalization: A Critical Introduction* (London and New York: Sage Publications, 1997), ed. Ali Mohammadi, pp. 170–90.

Zhao, Yuezhi. *Communication in China: Political Economy, Power, and Conflict* (New York: Rowman & Littlefield Publishers, 2008).

# 14

# Japan's Belated Policy Development toward a Gender-Equal Society

Atsuko Sato

## Chapter Outline

# Introduction

In the mid-late 1990s, Japan began to systematically incorporate the idea of gender equality into the government's structure and policies. In 1994, for example, the Prime Minister's Office for Women was reorganized as the Office for Gender Equality. More significantly, the government established the Basic Law for a Gender-Equal Society in 1999. Since then, the notion of a gender-equal society has been portrayed as a primary vision of the state. Yet, in spite of Japan's institutionalization of gender equality, the outcomes have not lived up to the rhetoric. In fact, according to the 2010 World Economic Forum's Global Gender Gap Index, Japan ranked 94th out of 134 countries.[1] This raises an obvious question: why is Japan's state feminism ineffective in bringing gender equality to society? This chapter argues that the answer can be found in gender equality policy discourses and the political contexts, which influence the framing of gender equality. The chapter attempts to answer this question through an in-depth analysis of the framing of gender equality in Japan's formal political institutions. Part of the analysis requires us to deconstruct the meanings of "gender equality" hidden within the Japanese government's official policy documents. Thus, we will employ "policy frame analysis" to examine how the government frames (1) gender inequality problems (i.e., diagnosis), and (2) solutions to the problem (i.e., prognosis).[2]

In addition to the framing of gender equality policy, this chapter examines another aspect of policy development: the external and internal political contexts, which, we argue, help shape the framing of gender equality policy. In this regard, the chapter first examines the political context in which existing or new policy developments have emerged. This analysis shows that state feminism does not derive solely from the idea of gender equality and women's rights. Instead, it is evident that gender policies are linked to broader political conditions and/or policy issues in the state, most evidently to its demographic trends and economic policies. More specifically, Japan's extremely low birth rate and its aging population have significantly increased demand for female labor and resulted in expansion of family-friendly policies.[3]

Furthermore, the chapter examines the concrete impact of these policies. It points out two deficiencies: the lack of effective implementation and persistent traditional gender norms. First, despite the government's policy choice about equal employment opportunity in the 1980s and a gender-equal society in the 2000s, the implementation of policies came up short in achieving gender equality in practice. Second, while the government's gender policies are important, state feminism alone is not sufficient to realize a gender-equal society. From a broader political and societal aspect, social norms are the key. Changing social norms on appropriate gender roles and social arrangements are critical in realizing a gender-equal society. The persistence of traditional gendered norms in politics and society has thus far prevented state policies from being effective.

# Three visions and strategies on gender equality

Frame analysis is a method designed to explore the underlying meaning of a certain concept.[4] It is important to emphasize that the manner in which the government understands the problem—in this case, gender inequality—already implies a solution to the problem. In other words, this approach simultaneously focuses on how "gender equality" is framed (vision) and understood, and how solutions and policies are prescribed (strategies). It is important to note that a policy-framing analysis (or critical frame analysis) of gender equality begins with the assumption that multiple interpretations of the concept of gender equality exist and the government offers different policy solutions associated with the problem of inequality.[5] These multiple interpretations of the concept of gender equality, as well as accompanying policies, are often divided into three different "visions" (see Table 14.1).[6]

The Type I vision conceptualizes the problem of gender equality as primarily the exclusion of women from the public sphere. The solution, therefore, is simple: bring women into the existing public structure. More concretely, this type of policy solution generally leads to providing "equal opportunity" and "equal treatment." Equal opportunity strategies emphasize the sameness between women and men, and assume that the problem of gender inequality is the exclusion of women in the public sphere. Thus, it focuses on legal guarantees of equal opportunity as the main solution to gender inequality. In terms of family policy, this vision does not consider work-life balance as part of gender equality issues. This perspective is apparently closely related

**Table 14.1** Three visions of gender equality

|  | Type I | Type II | Type III |
|---|---|---|---|
| Conceptualization of gender equality | Sameness | Difference | Difference |
| The solution to the problem | Inclusion of women in the existing structure | Incorporation of women's experiences in the existing structure with preferential treatment | Transformation: a deeper structural change in gender relations |
| Policy strategies | Equal opportunities Equal treatment | Positive actions | The gender mainstreaming |

*Source*: Summarized by the author.

to liberal feminism, in which existing male-dominated norms are neither problematized nor challenged.[7]

In contrast, the Type II vision assumes differences between men and women, and posits that the problem lies in hierarchically gendered norms. Because women and men are biologically and developmentally different, this vision argues that women's specific ways of knowing and thinking and their experiences have to be incorporated into the existing policy. From this perspective, the problem of gender inequality lies in the idea of patriarchal society—or the dominance of a masculinity norm in policy domains—which denigrates women's experiences and systematically disadvantages women in the workforce. The solution from this "gender differences" perspective is to be found in positive action policies. These include protective policies, such as maternity leave benefits, and affirmative action policies meant to redress past discrimination.[8] Unlike the "gender sameness perspective," the gender differences perspective questions and problematizes male-dominant policy norms. However, it focuses on providing different and special treatment for women without going further to correct gender discrimination embedded in society.

Lastly, the Type III vision further challenges the existing gendered norms and proposes a transformation of the foundations of policymaking discourses. The strategy of gender mainstreaming is particularly important in this vision.[9] The gender mainstreaming perspective asserts that: (1) there are the differences between women and between men; and (2) both women and men can be disempowered by the existing social arrangements. This perspective, therefore, not only challenges existing systems and structures, but also aims at transforming the policy process. Accordingly, while other approaches to gender equality aim to incorporate women into existing societal arrangements, the gender mainstreaming approach requires a fundamental reorganization and reconstruction of the policy process from a gender perspective (i.e., a gender-sensitive policy).

On the surface, the three "vision types" posit contesting views on gender equality; yet, the three types, in practice, can and do tend to overlap, often in a complementary fashion.[10] For example, in the gender equality policies and programs of the EU, all three strategies—equal treatment, gender-specific actions, and wider gender-based approaches—are observed.[11] This is because that "[t]he state is a contested arena, with a mixed of coherence and contradiction among a set of core institutions and complex linkages to other political and non-political domain."[12] Thus, when we analyze state policy, it is not necessarily the case that the state has a coherent vision and a single type of strategy designed to achieve gender equality. It is more likely that we will find multiple gender policy discourses (sometimes in the same official policy document), and multiple policy approaches.

Using this framework of analysis, this chapter examines how the three main visions of gender equality and their accompanying policy strategies are framed in Japan's gender equality policies during the two critical periods: the important developments in gender equality policy occurred in the 1980s (focusing on the 1985 Equal Employment Opportunity Law) and the late 1990s (focusing on the 1999 Equal Employment Opportunity Law and later development).

# Japan's gender equality policy in the 1980s

Issues of gender equality appeared in Japanese public policy relatively late compared to other industrialized democracies. It was not until 1985 that Japan passed its first domestic gender-based law, the Equal Employment Opportunity Law (EEOL, amended in 1999). The passage of EEOL, it is worth noting, was at least partly the product of nondomestic processes: in 1979, the UN General Assembly adopted a resolution on the Convention on Elimination of All Forms of Discrimination Against Women (CEDAW), which Japan signed in 1980. It was only then that the Japanese government began preparing a domestic law to comply with the Convention. In this regard, Japan's belated policy adoption is often understood as a result of growing indirect foreign pressure due to international gender-related policy development.[13] In particular, establishing an equal employment law at the national level was a prerequisite to ratify the CEDAW.

The UN Division for Advancement for Women states that "[t]he Convention provides the basis for realizing equality between women and men through ensuring women's equal access to, and equal opportunities in, political and public life—including the right to vote and to stand for election—as well as education, health, and employment."[14] As the international strategy to achieve gender equality was framed as "ensuring equal opportunity between men and women," it is not surprising to see that the Japanese government framed the new law as an equal opportunity law to act in accordance with the CEDAW. To this end, the EEOL prohibited employers from discriminating against women in education, training (Art. 6), fringe benefits (Art. 6), and retirement and dismissal (Art. 6). Article 9 prohibits employers from dismissing or giving disadvantages to women workers because of marriage, pregnancy, or childbirth. Finally, Article 8 (Special Provisions of Measures Pertaining to Women Workers) legalizes positive actions by employers to correct the past discrimination:

> The preceding three paragraphs shall not preclude employers from taking measures in connection with women workers with the purpose of improving circumstances that impede the securing of equal opportunity and treatment between men and women in employment. (Art. 8)

Despite all of these developments and changes, the law called for employers to make only voluntary efforts to prevent discrimination against women in recruiting, hiring (Art. 5), assignments, and promotion (Art. 6). Thus, the most important factors, including hiring and promotion, in gender employment equality were excluded from regulations under the law.

Indeed, while the EEOL addresses the broader issues of gender equal opportunity in employment, it is usually criticized as essentially symbolic due to a lack of critical protections, such as equal pay for equal work; even more, the law lacks an enforcement mechanism.[15] With respect to the first issue, the guidelines issued by the Women's Bureau of the Ministry of the Labor, which were supposed to clarify the ambiguity of the EEOL, allowed employers to establish the practice of a two-track system (career track for men and noncareer clerical track for women). The guidelines issued by the Women's Bureau required employers "not to exclude on the basis of their gender from those persons recruited or hired for particular recruitment and hiring classification."[16] Thus, the EEOL and the Women's Bureau's guidelines indirectly encouraged companies to establish a two-track system to legitimate differential treatment of men and women. As for a lack of enforcement mechanism, the problem is clear: the EEOL specifies no sanction or penalties, so many companies failed to make efforts to give even equal opportunities for women. In addition, because the EEOL had a weak mediation system through the Equal Opportunity Mediation Commission, few cases of gender discrimination were adequately resolved.[17]

In addition to the EEOL, it is important to discuss the 1986 Amendment to the Labor Standards Law, which was a package deal with EEOL in the 1986 Diet.[18] The original Labor Standards Law (enacted in 1947) required special protections for women, in particular "working mothers." The special treatment in the original law included restriction of overtime work (Art. 64–2), prohibition of nighttime employment (Art. 64–3) and limitations on dangerous and injurious work for expectant and nursing mothers (Arts 64–5), maternity leave (Art. 65), and menstrual period leave (Art. 68). The 1986 Amendment to the Labor Standards Law relaxed the restriction on overtime, extended maternity leave from 12 weeks to 14 weeks, and eliminated the term, "menstrual period leave." These amendments were modified in order to conform to the idea of equality in the EEOL.

Overall, the Labor Standards Law and its amendment in 1986 frame women as primary caretakers—that is, mothers. By giving working women special treatment, the reconciliation between work, on the one hand, and family, on the other hand, is framed as a problem for women. Thus, while the EEOL and the 1986 Amendment to the Labor Standards Law seemed, on the surface, to provide better opportunities and "special treatment" for women, the reality was far different. Consider, for example, a lack of provision for childcare: without adequate childcare services, women are essentially forced onto a noncareer clerical track or are forced to take part time positions; those with career-track positions are forced to leave their companies after pregnancy or giving a birth.

In addition, a new policy developed in 1986—tax breaks for working spouses—helped maintain gender inequality in Japan.[19] The tax break was included in The Law Concerning the Temporary Exception of the Spousal Deduction to Affect Income Tax for 1987. The law allowed spouses to earn no more than 1.03 million yen to receive a spousal deduction. The implication was clear: the law created a strong incentive for women to choose to work part-time as a means to limit their wages and keep the tax break. (The law was eliminated in 2004, but the 1.03 million yen cut-off technically remains.) According to the Ministry of Health, Labor and Welfare, among working women, 22 percent (3,330,000 out of 15,160, 000) were part-time workers in 1985, and the number increased to about 40 percent (8,610,000 out of 21,280,000) in 2003.[20] Although it may be argued that this indicates an increase in female economic participation, it instead reflects increasing gender gap in employment. This is not hard to see since the increase in female economic participation is based primarily on part-time jobs with low wages, little security, and low promotion and training prospects.

The series of policy developments in the 1980s suggests that the Japanese government was preoccupied with establishing the equal opportunity law in accordance with a gender-based agenda set at the international level. Specifically, the government's goal was to set the minimally acceptable policy domestically in order to comply with the CEDAW. The EEOL was framed as an "equal opportunity" measure, albeit with the acceptance of "special treatment" for women workers. It is fairly clear, however, that the government did not intend to achieve gender equality in practice or as an intended outcome. Even if the government intended to bring about significant equality the policy choices in the 1980s—which were premised on inclusion of women in the existing male-dominated employment norm/standards and the maintenance of women as mothers within traditional societal norms—this would have led to little change. The reason is clear: the policies never challenged existing male-dominated norms in the economic and societal structures.[21] What happened in the 1980s, to put it in slightly different terms, was merely the insertion of ambiguous (and toothless) gender equal opportunity clauses and protective policies for women workers into the existing male-oriented policy discourse. Ironically, but not surprisingly, this approach ended up producing even greater job and pay discrimination, since it made it more difficult for women to pursue career-track positions after marriage or childbirth. Along with other gender-related policies in the 1980s, the EEOL reinforced gender inequality by reemphasizing "motherhood."[22]

There is a clear lesson here: gender equality cannot be achieved within a male-dominant structure simply by adding women into the existing process. Structural and social constraints that cause the imbalance between women and men need to be addressed. In this sense, the policy developments of the 1980s did not alter traditional Japan's "male breadwinner / female homemaker model."

## Japan's gender equality policy in the 1990s and 2000s

The year 1990 began with a disturbing fact. For the first time, Japan's total fertility rate hit 1.57 (the "1.57 shock"); since then, the fertility rate has consistently declined, reaching 1.25 in 2006. In addition, Japan's baby-boom generation began reaching retirement age in the late 2000s. Thus, the low birth rate not only became linked to the decline of the country's working population but also to the potential collapse of the social security system in Japan. These became critical concerns, and led the Japanese government to reconsider both the roles of women in the workforce and relationship between men and women in Japanese society.

In this changing environment, an important development in gender equality policy occurred in the mid-1990s. In 1996, the Council for Gender Equality submitted Japan's Vision of Gender Equality: Creating New Values for the 21st Century, which, for the first time, introduced the concept of *danjo kyodo sankaku* (joint participation of men and women). It is important to highlight the linkage between changes in the larger social-economic context and gender equality policies. Unlike the development of the EEOL in 1986, the focus on gender equality policy in the 1990s derived primarily from domestic sources and concerns. This was clear in a statement by then-prime minister Hashimoto Ryutaro. In his speech before the *Danjo Kyodo Sankaku Shingikai* (Council for Gender Equality), Hashimoto said:

> The realization of this kind of society [a gender-equal society] is the urgent demand of these times in which we grapple with rapid changes taking place in the socioeconomic environment—the aging population, the low birthrate, and the maturation and internationalization of the economy—in our quest for a prosperous and vigorous nation. For that reason, it is my belief that building a gender-equal society can be considered a form of social reform and that gender equality will be one of the pillars of "reform and creation" in every field of society.[23]

Significantly, the primary policy goal, as articulated by Hashimoto, was to build a sustainable nation in terms of labor population, rather than to achieve gender equality per se. That is, building a gender-equal society was understood as a strategy—or a means—to solve the urgent population problem and to maintain Japan's economic power into the new millennium. Despite this qualification, the vision presented in the report established a new foundation for gender-related discourse and policy. Concretely, it led to the promulgation of the Basic Law for a Gender-Equal Society (referred to as the Basic Law), which helped to change the policy direction in a manner far more meaningful than the EEOL (and other policies of the 1980s).

So, how does the Basic Law interpret and incorporate the idea of gender equality in a way that is different from the EEOL? It would be useful to begin with the preamble of the Law, which declares: "It is vital to position the realization of a Gender-Equal Society as a top-priority task in determining the Framework of twenty-first-century Japan." Although the phrase "gender-equal society" is used in the official English language translation, it is important to note that the Japanese language version intentionally uses a new phrase: *danjo kyodo sankaku shakai,* which can be translated as "a society in which men and women jointly participate." The term "gender equality" (*danjo byodo*) is purposely not used. One reason for this is readily apparent: according to the Basic Law, gender equality is already guaranteed by the Japanese Constitution. The Preamble of the Constitution states,

"Considering respect for individuals and equality under the law expressly stipulated under the Constitution, steady progress has been made in Japan through a number of efforts toward the realization of genuine equality between women and men together with efforts taken by the international community." The idea of "joint participation of men and women" in all aspects of life, therefore, is meant to signal a shift or change in emphasis from existing notions of gender equality.

The question remains: what type of gender equality is it that the Japanese government wants to achieve? The Basic Law defines a gender equality society as a "society where both women and men shall be given *equal opportunities* to participate voluntarily in activities in all fields as equal partners in the society, and shall be able to enjoy political, economic, social and cultural benefits equally as well as to share responsibilities" (Art. 2). This definition reflects two basic frames that indicate the direction the Japanese government intended to take. First, as in the EEOL, the Basic Law ensures equal opportunity, not an equal outcome. The phrase, "securing opportunities for men and women," is repeated throughout the passages of the law. However, the Basic Law also states that building a gender-equal society requires "securing opportunities for men and women to participate jointly as equal partners in the society" (Art. 5). Second, and more significantly, the latter part of the definition suggests a move toward gender mainstreaming. This marks a major departure from the EEOL and similar legislation of the 1980s. This is clearly stated in Article 4 of the Basic Law:

> In consideration that social systems or practices can become factors impeding formation of a Gender-equal Society by reflecting the stereotyped division of roles on the basis of gender, etc., thus having a non-neutral effect on the selection of social activities by women and men, care should be taken so that social systems and practices have as neutral an impact as possible on this selection of social activities. (Art. 4)

The law recognizes, in other words, that the root cause of gender inequality rests in the social structures, institutions, values and beliefs of Japanese society; and that it is necessary to restructure the social and family roles that divide males and females. The idea of gender mainstreaming is also embedded in the Basic Plan for a Gender-Equal Society. This plan states that "to realize a gender-equal society, we have to always examine how social institutions and norms have influenced men and women."[24] Thus, the scope of the Basic Law goes beyond the public sphere. The idea of "joint participation of men and women" in all aspects of life, in sum, covers the public and private spheres, and includes the relationship between wife/mother and husband/father, the roles of family, and parenting.

In addition to securing equal opportunities for men and women, the Basic Law recognizes the state's responsibility for redressing past discrimination. This is clearly apparent in Article 2, which states, "positive provision of the opportunities stipulated in the preceding item to either women or men within the necessary limits in order to redress gender disparities in terms of such opportunities." Moreover, the Basic Plan for Gender Equality in 2000 (a plan based on the Basic Law for a Gender-Equal Society) includes the following: (1) promoting participation by women in national advisory councils and committees; (2) promoting recruitment and appointment of women national civil servants; and (3) requesting the support and cooperation of local government. The Second Basic Plan for Gender Equality in 2005 added additional numeric targets in several arenas. First, it "promotes efforts to expand women's participation in every field so that women will have at least 30 percent of the leadership positions in all fields of society by 2020." This is not an enforceable target, but the numeric target reflects the government's commitment to an "ideal" gender proportion. It is interesting to note that these measures toward the realization of a gender-equal society are framed as special institutional provisions for women (positive action). The measures, however, do not address any preestablished gendered norms and the gendered-biased structural conditions in national advisory councils and committees, and national and local public offices.

# The impact of the basic law for a Gender-Equal Society

In the ten years since the promulgation of the Basic Law, how much progress has there been toward the construction of a gender-equal society in Japan? According to the government's own assessment—as spelled out in the White Paper on Gender Equality 2009—the efforts for gender equality have not shown significant progress. With respect to equal opportunity, for example, the survey conducted by the Cabinet Office concluded that "[a]bout 60 percent of both men and women feel that women have *less* opportunity to improve their skills than men" (emphasis added). With regard to positive actions, the White Paper indicates that affirmative or positive actions have had some meaningful, albeit limited impact. Female

**Table 14.2** Percentage of women in "leadership positions"

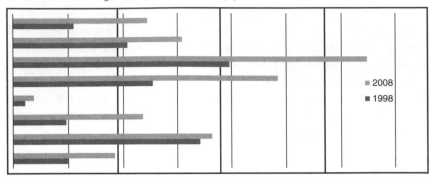

*Source*: The White Paper on Gender Equality 2009, the Cabinet Office, p. 8.

representation in national politics, for instance, showed a not-insignificant increase as the percentage of female Diet members went up from 5 percent in 1999 to 9 percent in 2009. Elsewhere, the percentage of women in "leadership positions" has increased slightly in the last ten years (Table 14.2). In particular, the percentage of members of government advisory councils has exceeded the goal of 30 percent. This increase, it is easy to surmise, is a direct result of the positive action measures taken by the government. The Council of Equality, in rather inelegant language, put it this way:

> In our country, as a typical example of measures of this kind, as stated in sec-
> tion (1), the central government and local public bodies are taking measures
> with clearly set goals and deadlines in order to promote women's participa-
> tion in advisory councils and committees, with certain results. Japan should
> further carry out "positive actions," by paying regard to the respective areas
> and measures.[25]

It is also worth noting that the percentage of national public employees recruits who passed the clerical work division of the Level I examination increased nearly two-fold from 12.7 to 24.2 percent over a ten-year period (see Table 14.2). This was due to a government-set target (established in 2004), which specified that women comprise 30 percent of recruits by 2010.[26] The government also encouraged private companies/organizations to take special efforts to review their practices in the labor, agriculture, and research fields; as with the EEOL, there are no penalties for noncompli-ance, but to encourage participation, the government offered awards to the companies. Significantly, the percentage of female managerial staff in private corporations increased from 8.2 percent to 12.7 percent in 2008. Although it is difficult to show that the proportional increase of women in managerial positions was a direct result of the government's positive action measures, there is likely a strong connection (given the timing and the long history of minimal or negligible change in this area).

While the effects of positive action measures are relatively easy to discern, this is much less the case for gender mainstreaming strategies. Indeed, it is fair to say that the implementation of gender mainstreaming policies have heretofore produced few measurable results, much less fundamental changes in Japanese society. For the most part, however, this is both understandable and expected. After all, gender mainstreaming strategies target deeply rooted, virtually naturalized societal assumptions. Changing such assumptions generally takes a great deal of time and unremitting effort. But, change invariably begins with shifts in discourse. On this point, it is worth taking a second look at key elements of the Basic Law: Work-Life Balance.

# Gender mainstreaming, work-life balance, and the Basic Law

As noted above, the Basic Law for a Gender-Equal Society clearly recognizes the importance of gender mainstreaming as a matter of principle. In practice, one of the key elements derived from the Basic Law was to promote a "work-life balance for men and women." As the Cabinet Office puts it, a work-life balance is crucial for a gender-equal society.[27]

> To achieve work-life balance, the scope of the intended recipients of support for "balancing work and family life," who once were mainly women at the childrearing and childrearing age, has been extended to those in every generation and field, regardless of gender. A major turnaround in ideas for various activities and aspects of life, including work, family life, regional activities, self-enlightenment and recreation, has been made. From the view point of gender equality that both men and women should play an equal part in the home and society demonstrating their own ability and individuality, it is important to promote the work-life balance based on such ideas, and such a balance is essential to the realization of a vigorous and sustainable society. It is thus necessary to raise society-wide awareness of and concern for the need to promote the work-life balance, and to facilitate efforts by diversified entities, including corporations.[28]

There are several elements of the government's articulation of "work-life balance" (or work-life principle) that need to be highlighted. First, in stark contrast to previous efforts, the work-life principle unequivocally locates the problem of gender inequality in the ongoing situation of work-life imbalance. Second, it understands that reconciliation of work and family, which was once defined entirely as a "women's problem," requires a different conceptualization of gender roles and gender relations in society. Third, the work-life principle assumes that solutions to gender inequality in Japanese society require "joint participation of women and men" in both the reproductive and productive spheres. Overall, it is clear that the work-life principle transcends the Type I approach, which defined the obstacles to gender equality as a problem of and for women. The work-life principle, instead, is premised on the understanding that gender equality is neither a "women's issue" nor a change that will only benefit women.

At a more concrete level, this is easy to see. Most generally, the government aims at transforming parental roles, husband and wife roles, the organization of work and time, and institutional practices (both in the private and public spheres). Some of the major initiatives and policies associated with the work-life principles include: (1) the "project for promotion of the work-life balance" with ten major socially influential companies; (2) awards to corporations, organizations, or individuals for providing child-rearing support and assisting families with their children; (3) a "No Child on a Waiting List" policy to increase childcare services; (4) promotion of an "After-School Plan for Children"; and (5) "Change! JPN" Campaign.[29] It is important to note that, while these activities are intended to facilitate changes in embedded social norms, because the immediate targets are limited to a small faction of corporations and activities, their social impact will likely be limited. In fact, the shift in the government gender policy has not produced any significant impact at people's level in society. The series of surveys conducted by the Cabinet Office show minimal changes in people's perception of gender equality at home and little change at work (see Tables 14.3 and 14.4).[30] People who feel that men are treated favorably at home decreased 4.2 percent, while people who feel that men and women are treated equally increased 3.4 percent between 2000 and 2009. However, people's perception about gender equality at home has not changed for one and half decades.

Moreover, the stereotype of gender roles in Japan is still strong among men and women. The public opinion poll in 2004 conducted by the Cabinet Office reveals that 41.2 percent of women and 49.7 percent of men still

**Table 14.3** The public perception of gender equality at home

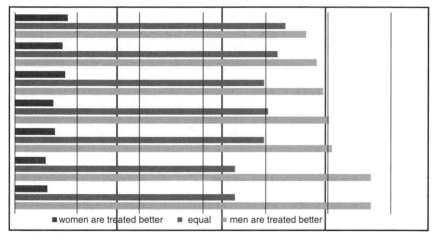

**Table 14.4** The public perception of gender equality at the workplace

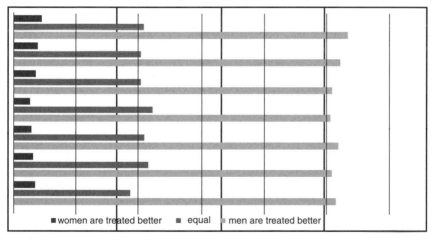

think that "the husband should be the breadwinner and the wife should stay at home" (Table 14.5). The number also shows polarization of perception of gender roles: while almost a half of people views traditional gender roles as ideal, the other half accepts the idea of gender equality roles. This indicates that the root cause of gender inequality in Japan rests on, to some degree, persistent men and women's perceptions about traditional gender roles. According to Japanese family sociologists, the persistent norm of traditional gender roles among Japanese derives from their perception

**Table 14.5** "The Husband Should Be the Breadwinner, the Wife Should Stay at Home"

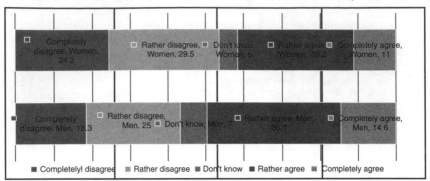

of marriage and roles of wife and husband. Based on the 2000 Japanese General Social Survey, Shima found that the perceptions of "housework by men," and "marriage and gender roles" are independent. Interestingly, this means that even people who support the relatively progressive ideas of "housework by men" and "working women" may support traditional gender roles of wife and husband after marriage.[31]

In sum, all of the above facts indicate the lack of effective implementation of gender mainstreaming and persistent traditional gender stereotypes, in particular gender roles of wife and husband in Japan. More than 10 years after Japan established the Basic Law, the rhetoric of gender mainstreaming in Japan's gender policy has not been translated into reality.

# Analysis

Analyzing Japan's gender equality policies since the 1980s, we can see that Japan has made some significant progress (in its policies, not the outcome). There are several notable driving forces in this progress. The international and domestic political contexts have influenced the development of Japan's gender policy. The progress in Japan's gender equality policy is clearly following the trends observed at the international level, including the CEDAW and the Beijing Declaration and Platform for Action. The CEDAW was the reason why Japan began to prepare for the EEOL and the 1999 Basic Law for a Gender-Equal Society was deeply influenced by the gender mainstreaming strategy, which was introduced in the Third UN World Conference of

Women (1985) and further established as the dominant norm in programs and policies in the UN in the 1990s. The influence of international norms was limited in the Japanese political context. The development of gender policies in the 1990s and 2000s, however, demonstrated the power of the domestic context to bring about more dramatic change. The policy goal of a gender-equal society derived not from the idea gender equality, but from Japan's low birthrate and declining labor force. Japan's gender-equal society policy was developed merely as a means and/or tool to achieve its sustainable population and economy in the immediate future. It is not an exaggeration to say that, if these domestic conditions were not met, the policy concept of a gender-equal society would not have been one of the main policy pillars in the 2000s.

Our examination of the framing of gender policy in the 1980s and the 1990s onward reveals multiple policy discourses in both periods. We saw that, in both periods, achieving gender equality was not the government's central concern; yet the idea of gender equality was considered a key aspect of a larger state vision. In the 1980s, gender inequality was framed as a woman's problem, so the policy prognosis was simply framed as "equal opportunity and treatment" with recognition of positive actions. Under this prognosis, giving women equal rights and the same opportunities as men and accepting the idea of positive action to redress past discrimination was ostensibly all that was needed. But, this was clearly not the case: the persistent social norms that perpetuated gender discrimination—along with poorly conceived public policies—meant that there was little real progress toward gender equality in this period.

Three visions are observed in Japan's gender policy in the latter period. The idea of equal opportunity remained the foundation of gender equality issues in Japan. However, the government has also strongly promoted "positive actions" to redress past gender discrimination in the limited areas. Further, internal demographic and economic conditions changed the landscape for gender issues, beginning in the 1990s. Women were seen as keys to resolving the country's entwined demographic and economic problems. To increase birth rates and the labor force, the ideas of a "gender-equal society" (*danjo kyodo sankaku shakai*) and "work-life balance" were introduced into the policy domain, while the older concept of "gender equality" (*danjo byodo*) was largely retired. In the Basic Law for a Gender-Equal Society and related measures, issues concerning women, family, and gender were carefully incorporated into an integrated policy framework.

# Conclusion

Despite multiple approaches the Japanese government has taken to achieve a gender-equal society, this analysis concludes that these policies and their implementation remain unsatisfactory. While the overall approach toward a gender-equal society in Japan reflects the essence of gender mainstreaming, the primary goals are economic and demographic. As a result, implementation of gender policy comes up short in terms of gender equality measures. Within the Japanese society, there are still very limited signs of a widespread acceptance of new gendered norms. As a result the top-down policy approach of building a gender-equal society has not met its goals.

Japan needs a more coherent and wider approach to implement gender mainstreaming measures in all aspects of society. As the government admits, the current policies and programs have not worked as intended. If the Japanese government wants to realize a gender-equal society in order to solve its demographic problem, it has to reconnect all of these issues in its programs: low birth rate, shortage of labor, and gender inequality. The child allowance program (*Kodomo teate*, 13,000 yen per month, per child in fiscal 2010) introduced by the DPJ government is an example of the shortfall of government family and gender policy. Although the system of child allowance rewards and/or supports parents with children and intends to improve fertility rates, the effects on gender equality, in particular women's participation in labor, are limited. Ideally, the government expects that the money distributed by the child allowance program will be used for childrearing, such as for child care. However, even people who want to use the allowance for child care face a critical barrier: a lack of government-funded child-care centers and after school-care programs.

The gap between the policy and the reality is rather wide. To realize a gender-equal society, the Japanese government needs to come up with comprehensive and coherent approaches, which deal with (1) a linkage of demographic, economic, and gender problems, and (2) the persistent perception of traditional gender roles in workplaces and at home. In particular, we argue that a gender-equal society requires promoting a family-friendly environment in the public sphere. This may include, but is not limited to, restructuring Japan's working-hour norms and workplace culture to support fathers and mothers with children to work full time for pay, and ensuring the availability of quality child-care services for working parents. The government needs to put such measures and ideas into lasting programs, which cover more people across generations, in more companies, in public services at all levels, and wider geographic areas.

## Five questions for discussions

1. What are the main differences in the framing of gender equality in the Equal Employment Opportunity Law and the Basic Law for a Gender-Equal Society?
2. Why do you think the Japanese government changed its policy on gender equality in the mid-1990s? What socioeconomic factor(s) explains Japan's gender policy change?
3. What explains the minimal impact of the Basic Law for a Gender-Equal Society? In addition to the top-down approach, what do you think is required for Japan to achieve a "gender equal society"?
4. What explains the persistence of traditional gender roles among both men and women in Japan? What can we do about it?
5. What is a gender equal society to you? Do you agree to the concept of a gender-equal society introduced by the Japanese government?

# Notes

1 The Global Gender Gap Index measures gender disparity based on political empowerment, economic participation and opportunity, educational attainment, and health and survival. For more information, see Global Gender Gap Report 2010 at http://www3.weforum.org/docs/WEF_GenderGap_Report_2010.pdf.

2 Mieke Verloo and Emanuela Lombardo, "Contested Gender Equality and Policy Variety in Europe: Introducing a Critical Frame Analysis Approach," in *Multiple Meanings of Gender Equality: A Critical Frame Analysis of Gender Policies in Europe,* ed. Mieke Verloo (Budapest, Hungary: Central European University Press, 2007), p. 33.

3 Priscilla A. Lambert, "The Political Economy of Postwar Family Policy in Japan: Economic Imperatives and Electoral Incentives," *Journal of Japanese Studies* 33:1 (2007): 1–28.

4 For details of the frame analysis, see Verloo, *Multiple Meanings of Gender Equality.*

5 Verloo and Lombardo, p. 31.

6 Rees (1998), for example, uses the following three gender equality models: (1) sameness, (2) difference, and (3) transformation. Verloo and Lombardo (2007), by contrast, refer to "inclusion," "reversal," and "displacement"; while Squires (2005) uses "equality," "difference," and "transformation." Whatever the terminology, all these scholars are describing similar conceptual differences.

7 See, for example, Squires (2005) and Verloo and Lambardo (2007).

8 Sarah l. Henderson and Alana S. Jeydel, *Participation and Protest: Women and Politics in a Global World* (Oxford: Oxford University Press, 2007), p. 115.

9    The Type III vision has been the focus of studies on gender and policy in Europe, where a strong shift to gender mainstreaming can be observed.

10    Booth and Bennett (2002).

11    Ibid.; Walby (2005).

12    Walby (2005): 338.

13    Joyce Gelb, *Gender Policies in Japan and the United States Comparing Women's Movements, Rights, and Politics* (New York: Palgrave Macmillan, 2003); Millie R. Creighton, "Marriage Motherhood, and Career Management in a Japanese Counter Culture," in *Reimaging Japanese Women,* ed. Ann Imamura (Berkeley: University California Press, 1996), pp. 192–220; Takeshi Kashima, *Otoko to Onna: Kawaru Rikigaku [Men and Women: Changing Power Relations]* (Tokyo: Iwanami, 2003).

14    http://www.un.org/womenwatch/daw/cedaw/

15    Barbara Monoly, "Japan's 1986 Equal Employment Opportunity Law and the Changing Discourse on Gender," *Signs: Journal of Women in Culture and Society* 20:2 (1995): 268–302; Gelbo (2003): 49; Yoshie Kobayashi, *A Path toward Gender Equality* (New York: Routledge, 2004), pp. 125–33; Henderson and Jeydel (2007): 118.

16    Ministry of Labor (1986), cited by Kobayashi 2004, p. 127.

17    Gelb (2003), p. 51.

18    Takashi Kashima, *Otoko to Onna: Kawaru Rikigaku [Men and Women: Changing Power Relations]* (Tokyo: Iwanami, 2003), p. 8.

19    Charles Weathers, "In Search of Strategic Partners: Japan's Campaign for Equal Opportunity," *Social Science Japan Journal* 8:1 (2005): 74–5.

20    Source: The Ministry of Health, Labour and Welfare, *Facts about Working Women in 2009.*

21    Gelb (2003), p. 51.

22    Molony (1995: 295) points out that while the 1972 Working Women's Welfare Law referred to women in the workforce as "working women," the 1986 EEOL refers them as "female workers." Although the EEOL changed the word choice, it did not treat women in the workforce in a meaningfully different way.

23    Cited by Osawa (2003): 3.

24    The Cabinet Office, the Basic Plan for a Gender-Equal Society (2000); the Second Basic Plan for Gender-Equal Society (2005).

25    http://www.gender.go.jp/english_contents/toshin-e/index.html

26    The Cabinet Office 2006, 21.

27    The Cabinet Office, *White Paper on Gender Equality 2009 Outline,* 18. On this point the Ministry of Health, Labor, and Welfare (MHLW) formulated the Charter for Work-Life Balance and Action Policy for Promoting Work-Life Balance in 2007 and "New-Zero-waiting List for Day Care Centers" in 2008.

28    The Cabinet Office, *White Paper on Gender Equality 2009 Outline,* 18–19.

29    The Cabinet Office, *White Paper on Gender Equality 2009 Outline.*

30  Gender Equality Bureau, the Cabinet Office at http://www8.cao.go.jp/survey/h21/h21-danjo/images/z03.gif. The table was produced by the author based on survey results.

31  Naoko Shima, "Yuushoku Dansei no Kazokuishiki: Seibetsuyakuwaribuntan wo Shotentoshite," *Sophia Junior College Faculty Journal* 10 (2010): 101–10.

# Selected bibliography

Booth, Christine and Cinnamon Bennett. "Gender Mainstreaming in the European Union: Towards a New Conception and Practice of Equal Opportunities?" *The European Journal of Women's Studies* 9:4 (2002): 430–46.

Bowman, John R. and Alyson M. Cole. "Do Working Mothers Oppress Women? The Swedish 'Made Debate' and the Welfare State Politics of Gender Equality." *Journal of Women in Culture and Society* 35:1 (2009): 157–84.

Chinkin, Christine. *Gender Mainstreaming in Legal and Constitutional Affairs: A Reference Manual for Governments and Other Stakeholders* (London: Commonwealth Secretariat, 2001).

Duvander, Ann-Sofie and Gunnar Andersson. "Gender Equality and Fertility in Sweden: A Study on the Impact of the Father's Uptake of Parental Leave on Continued Childbearing." *Marriage and Family Review* 39:1/2 (2006): 121–42.

Fujita, Fumiko. "The Status of Women Faculty: A View from Japan." *Journal of Women's History* 18:1 (2006): 177–80.

Fuwa, Mika. "Macro-Level Gender Inequality and the Division of Household Labor in 22 Countries." *American Sociological Review* 69:6 (2004): 751–67.

Gender Equality Bureau, Cabinet Office. *A Step towards Gender Equality in Japan* (Tokyo: Cabinet Office, 2006).

Hiroko, Takeda. "The Political Economy of Familial Relations: The Japanese State and Families in a Changing Political Economy." *Asian Journal of Political Science* 16:2 (2008): 196–214.

Kobayashi, Yoshie. *A Path toward Gender Equality* (New York: Routledge, 2004).

Lovenduski, Joni. "State Feminism and Women's Movements." *West European Politics* 31:1/2 (2008): 169–94.

Lucas, Eugenie A. "State Feminism: Norwegian Women and the Welfare State." *Feminist Issues* 10:2 (1990): 43–54.

Miyazaki, Motohiro. "1990nendai iko no hoikuseisaku no henka to sono mondaiten [Policy Changes in Child Care after 1990s and Their Problem]." *Aichikonaitankidaigaku Kiyo* 37 (2008): 107–19.

Osawa, Mari. "Government Approaches to Gender Equality in the Mid-1990s." *Social Science Japan Journal* 3:1 (2000): 3–19.

Rees, Teresa. *Mainstreaming Equality in the European Union, Education, Training and Labour Market Policies* (London: Routledge, 1998).

Rosenbluth, Frances McCall, ed. *The Political Economy of Japan's Low Fertility* (Stanford: Stanford University Press, 2006).

Squires, Judith. "Is Mainstreaming Transformative? Theorizing Mainstreaming in the Context of Diversity and Deliberation." *Social Politics* 12:3 (2005): 366–88.

Takao, Yasuo. "Japanese Women in Grassroots Politics: Building a Gender-Equal Society from the Bottom Up." *The Pacific Review* 20:2 (2006): 147–72.

Teghtsoonian, Katherine and Louise Chappell. "The Rise and Decline of Women's Policy Machinery in British Columbia and New South Wales: A Cautionary Tale." *International Political Science Review* 29:1 (1998): 29–51.

Walby, Sylvia. "Gender Mainstreaming: Productive Tensions in Theory and Practice." *Social Politics: International Studies in Gender, State and Society* 12:3 (2005): 321–43.

Yenn, Teo You. "Inequality for the Greater Good: Gender State Rule in Singapore." *Critical Asian Studies* 39:3 (2007): 423–45.

# 15

# The Local People's Congress and Grassroots Democracy in China[1]

Diqing Lou

---

## Chapter Outline

## Introduction

This chapter deals with the electoral mechanism of the local people's congress and its significance in contemporary China. We are interested in the role of the people's congress, especially the local people's congress, in grassroots politics. We are also interested in the connection between the people's congress and citizenry, such as political representation in the electoral process.

According to the PRC's Constitution, the people's congress is the fundamental political institution in China. Chinese citizens' representation and participation in local and national congresses are crucial instruments to the maintenance of China's socialist political system. Stipulated by the Constitution, the people's congress provides legitimacy to the political system and plays the role of the ultimate decision maker in the political process. The responsibilities of the people's congress include legislating at the national and local levels, overseeing activities in executive and judicial branches, approving state budget, confirmation of the candidates to government seats, etc.

Research in comparative politics has long maintained that the people's congress has been "rubber-stamps" instead of legitimate political institutions that would influence Chinese politics.[2] Conventional understanding holds that the people's congresses are not full-time political institutions, do not allow substantial and meaningful political debates, and do not provide meaningful connections between the state and citizenry. So far few studies have investigated the electoral mechanism of the local people's congress in China. We hope this chapter will contribute to the understanding of the local people's congress and how congressional elections are tied with congressional politics in China.

The materials we used in this study include published records and regulations on local elections of the people's congress, and internal records and policy documents kept in the library of the local people's congress. At the same time, the study relied on interviews we conducted with local officials from the standing committee of the people's congress in one of the largest cities in central China. These interviews were carried out in the years of 2007, 2008, 2009, and 2010. The total length of interviews exceeded 1,000 hours. The interviewees were officials of the standing committee of the local people's congress, including the heads of various agencies and departments consisting of the standing committee.

Our findings indicate, contrary to the predictions of the prevailing literature on the people's congress in China, elections to local people's congresses are actually competitive, especially for the seats that are subject to contest of private citizens. We argue that the competitiveness in local congressional elections reflects at least partially the growing status and significance of the people's congress in local Chinese politics. Even though the local people's congress may not convene frequently, the social status and prestige that the congress accords to its members, the rights and privileges that they enjoy, and the access they have to the inner-circle decision makers in local politics all helped make the electoral process competitive. We also find that congressional seats are highly sought after by private citizens, and some of the seats are obtained by a small segment of the population with considerable socioeconomic resources.

# Initiation of grassroots democracy

The PRC's Constitution stipulates:

> All power in the People's Republic of China belongs to the people. The organs through which the people exercise state power are the National People's Congress and the local people's congresses at different levels. . . . The National People's Congress and the local people's congresses at different levels are instituted through democratic election. They are responsible to the people and subject to their supervision. (Arts 2 and 3, The PRC Constitution)

Besides the preamble statement above, articles 57 to 78 of the Constitution describe the terms, responsibilities, and structure of the National People's Congress (NPC) in detail. The terms of the congressional members are five years, and the NPC's powers include amending the constitution, examining and approving state budget, deciding on war and peace, electing the President, Premier, Chief Justice of the Supreme Court, Procurator-General of the Supreme People's Procuratorate, among others.

While the NPC is accorded with a primary status in the political system of Chinese politics, previous literature suggests that legislative assemblies in authoritarian regimes generally play a more passive role in the political process.[3] Packenham observed the functionality of the congress in the third world as follows: "If the national legislatures in the third world are usually weak, some of them exert some influence with respect to some issues. It seems clear that such influence on some legislatures are able to wield takes the form of stopping things from happening more than of causing things to happen."[4]

Representatives of the people's congress are not full-time members. Except for the elections of congressional members at the grassroots level—the district or township level, China so far has only practiced indirect elections to select congressional members beyond the grassroots level. Existing literature holds that the people's congresses in China serve merely as rubber stamps, as they only occupy an auxiliary status in Chinese politics. They do not provide meaningful connections between citizens and the state. Following this argument, it could be inferred that, for the electoral process, we are likely to observe a highly orchestrated and non-contentious congressional elections, since the congressional seats may not carry substantial political significance given the peripheral status of the people's congress in Chinese politics. On the other hand, if the local people's congress occupies an increasingly important status with its members possessing political privileges and leverage, we are much likely to observe an exhilarating and competitive electoral process with meaningful political gains at stake.

In this study, we have found that the congressional elections are open to contest by citizens to a certain degree. A number of congressional seats are open for interested civilians in the electoral process, and the electoral process in congressional politics is more often than not competitive among its candidates. The segments of Chinese society that aspire political status, political access, and privileges of the congressional seats are interested in obtaining congressional seats and motivated to win candidacy.

The role of the people's congress was largely confined to that of an auxiliary political institution in China before the 1980s. Since Deng Xiaoping's economic reform in the late 1970s, the CCP has devoted increasing attention to broadening democracy and increasing civil liberties at the grassroots level. It is an effort to provide more political space to accommodate the changes brought by economic reforms. In rural areas, for example, the CCP has experimented with village elections, in which villagers are able to elect village committee leaders in free and competitive elections.[5] The village committees were drafted into Chinese Constitution in the 1980s, and the procedures of village elections were prescribed in the Organic Law in the 1990s.[6] The village election has been regarded as remarkable democratic progress in the PRC.[7]

Village elections were experimented in Guangxi Autonomous Region in the early 1980s. "When Guangxi's report on village committees reached Beijing, Peng Zhen, then vice-chairman of the NPC Standing Committee, praised villagers' committees as the perfect vehicle for practicing grassroots democracy. . . . In December 1982, thanks mainly to Peng's urging, villagers' committees were written into the Constitution as elected, mass organizations of self-government . . . In Peng's view, elections were not only compatible with the Party rule, they were also the right instruments for tightening the Party's grip in areas where its dominance was still uncertain. A measure of mass participation, in other words, would generate support for the Party's revolutionary mission while serving its state-building aspirations. 'Democracy' and government power could develop together."[8]

During our interviews, we were told that the reform of local people's congresses to broaden grassroots democracy was initiated by veteran party leaders who espoused a liberal political standing, such as Peng Zhen. Thus, through the support of the veteran leaders of the CCP who recalled favorably grassroots democracy that the CCP practiced during the Soviet period of the 1920s and 1930s, village committee elections were confirmed by Beijing and later included in China's Constitution.

When did real changes happen to the local people's congress? A congressional staff member recalled the following:

> The local people's congress did not gain momentum in its political reform until the early 1980s. It is through the vision and leadership of Comrade Peng Zhen that the local people's congress was encouraged to enhance its status and share more responsibilities with the government. The local congress was encouraged to play a more prominent role in the political process in Chinese politics.
>
> The development of the local congress started in 1979, the year when China's economic reform was carried out. Since 1986, local congresses started to have more law-making power. The increased law-making power is the most important achievement of the municipal People's Congress in recent decades.

During the interviews, we found that the municipal congress has set up formal procedures in legislative process and adhered to them closely. The municipal congress has undergone considerable transformation. Despite the trend to economize the government size at both national and local levels, the municipal congress has significantly expanded its budget and personnel since 2000. The municipal congress raised the bar to recruit better trained and more experienced staff, and new hires at the municipal congress now hold college or higher degrees in legal training. In terms of legislative work, the congress attempts to regularize the legislative procedures and strives toward the direction of systemic legislation. Also, the municipal congress plays an increasingly more independent role in supervising the government budget.[9] Overall, we have found that the municipal people's congress has been shouldering more responsibilities in shared governance, and its political status has been on the rise.

In the early 1980s, the CCP's "Resolution of Certain Questions in the History of Our Party" announced that it was the party's aim to "gradually realize direct popular participation in the democratic process at the grassroots of political power and community life."[10] The effort devoted by the CCP to broaden the grassroots democracy is well documented and researched in recent studies in comparative politics.[11] However, with the emphasis of research placed on elections at the grassroots level especially village committee elections, the democratization and institutionalization of the people's congress have received little attention in the literature so far.

# Electoral laws

Since the late 1970s, China has reformed the regulations governing electoral systems including those for the peoples' congresses. The first version of China's Election Law was adopted in 1953, and was revised for the first time in 1979, three years after the end of the Cultural Revolution. Main revisions of the 1979 Electoral Law are, first, the extension of direct elections to the grassroots level, as voters will elect congressional representatives at the district level openly; and second, the Law mandates that the number of candidates exceeds the number of the seats in grassroots congressional elections by 50 percent to 100 percent. Revisions of the 1979 Law also include articles allowing for campaigning for grassroots congressional elections and the guarantee for anonymous voting.[12] The grassroots democracy was extended to the electorate nationally for the first time.

The Electoral Law was further revised by the CCP in 1982, 1986, 1995, and 2004. These revisions focused mainly on the details in the electoral systems and regulations, aiming at refining the electoral system and including practical electoral experiences accumulated at the implementation stage.[13] More recently the NPC adopted the newest version of the Electoral Laws in March 2010. The 2010 revision of the Election Law focuses on the concept of political equality, which guarantees equal representation to the people's congress of the rural and urban population. It also emphasizes improving the representation of congressional representatives at the grassroots level.[14]

Since the late 1970s, the CCP has been focusing more on broadening the scope of democracy in both rural and urban China, especially at the grassroots level, such as instituting and refining the Electoral Law. Along with initiating economic reform and development, the democratization of the political process to broaden the scope of grassroots politics to a certain degree was on the party's agenda. Popular participation in the political process should be regarded desirable and complementary to the governance of the CCP. Mass participation and democratization at the grassroots level not only provide the CCP with popular support, but also strengthen the party's governance in the areas where its control is less certain.

# Local congressional elections

During the first week of our interviews, one of the department directors at the municipal congress asked this author: "Have you examined the Electoral Law before this interview? If not, you should take a close look. The procedure of our electoral system is stated clearly in the Electoral Law." Only after I showed him a recently obtained copy of the Electoral Law did the interviewee nod to me and the interview process became much more smooth and substantial.

According to the PRC Constitution, the electoral cycle of the people's congress is every five years. The people's congress will strictly follow the procedures of the electoral process prescribed by the Election Law. The interviewed official of the standing committee of the local people's congress said: "we are the legislature for the city, and it is very important that we carry out elections faithful to the law."

In our observation of the electoral process of the local people's congress, at least in terms of procedures, it adheres closely to what is prescribed by the Election Law. First, a list of congressional candidates would be collected from the district level along with the candidates' information. The standing committee would then tally the information and make sure that the voters would receive the information in adequate time before the date of election.

"In terms of the ratio of the candidates to the seats, we will make sure that the number of candidates exceeds the number of the seats by at least 20 percent. We will make sure that the information about candidates would be distributed to the voters before the election well in advance. The Law prescribes that the voters should have adequate time in considering candidates, and we would encourage any questions that voters may have about the candidates," said the department director.

The Election Law has been instituted in China for more than three decades and has been revised several times during its practice. It has incorporated adjustments based on electoral experiences accumulated over the years. Through practices and revisions, the Election Law has established its authority in local congressional elections.

"Besides adhering to the practice of the Election Law, within the electoral process, we pay close attention to the demographic information of our representatives, and we try to make sure that the representatives will represent different walks of the society. Every year, the congressional representatives elected would have a certain percentage of non-communist party members. It is important that the congress hears the voices of non-party members in the electoral process. Diversity is highly valued in the representation process, and in the electoral process, it is important to hear political views from those who come from different political backgrounds and from the non-party members," according to the official, "besides the requirement for admitting non-CCP members, we also aim at keeping a quota for women candidates and ethnic minority candidates, for example. It is estimated that 25 to 30 percent of the seats are reserved for women candidates."

The importance the local people's congress attached to noncommunist party members shows that the people's congress acknowledges alternative political voices in the political process, which echoes the vision of grassroots democracy initiated by the CCP as an effort to broaden the scope of public support to the communist government. It also reveals that the CCP still very much controls the political institutions and enjoys paramount political authority, as the party is confident enough to include different political voices in the political process. The nonparty members will constitute about 25 percent or so of the total congressional seats. It is unlikely that these nonparty members will challenge the political agenda or consensus adopted by the communist party. It is expected that these nonparty members will provide different perspectives, insights, and suggestions to the political process. Also, these nonparty members will help provide legitimacy of the people's congress as a representative political institution, as the CCP has a long and proud legacy of being able to work with noncommunist luminaries to broaden its support base and improve its governance.

One thing worth noting about the mandatory seating of nonparty members in the electoral process is the nature of informal politics in the political process. Once being elected as a congressional member, a nonparty member would enjoy the same political access and political privileges as party members. They would be able to raise questions and concerns about public affairs, provide suggestions to the direction of governance, and drop inquires about the decisions of executive branch and judiciaries. These rights are guaranteed by the regulations of the people's congress. In other words, once elected, these nonparty members would become full members of the people's congress disregarding their background.

Indeed, the CCP mandates the participation of nonparty members in legislative and representative political institutions, and once admitted, these nonparty members would be accorded with full membership of the congress just as the party members, enjoying the same political access, information, and privileges. It is a tacit agreement that the input of nonparty members would be welcomed during the political process dominated by the CCP, provided that these nonparty members pledge their support and loyalty to the presiding political party. While there are no formal sanctions to the responsibilities of the non-CCP congressional members, the parameters of their duties are tacitly agreed upon between them and the people's congress.

# Electoral candidacy

According to the municipal congress we interviewed, the reelection rate of the incumbent congressional representatives is about 70 percent, since the incumbent usually enjoy a fairly large advantage in elections. "Every five years, all the congressional representatives will be up for re-election, and we wish that we could keep at least 70 percent of the sitting congressional representatives. The reelection rate is actually not very high, and in some years the reelection rate could drop to 40 percent. We also hope that congress would be able to recruit and retain quality and seasoned congressional representatives," we were told.

Surprised by the relatively low percentage of the reelection rate of the incumbents as congressional representatives, we also found that some of the congressional representatives may not seek reelection. One official explained, "Some of the elected representatives may not devote a lot of time to their work of being congressional representatives. Congressional representatives are not paid positions, and it requires the representatives to be interested in and informed about civil affairs and political development of the city. Sometimes congressional members are very busy with their work and may not be able to come to the meetings and activities that are required. When a new election approaches, we may not encourage these congressional representatives to seek re-election."

Most congressional representatives have their own full-time jobs. More often than not, congressional representatives are prominent members in their own professional fields and are very busy. Even without being paid, serving as congressional members entails tasks and responsibilities. In one instance, all congressional members were invited to visit the development of a subway system in the city. The members attended a guided tour at the subway sites, got informed about the schedule of the development, followed by interviews of local TV stations. During the visit, questions and suggestions of the congressional representatives were solicited by the transportation bureau of the city. The activity was well planned, informative, and was taken seriously by the transportation bureau, and the entire tour was covered by the media. However, as it was a day-long activity set on a work day, only a small number of congressional members were able to make the trip.

The municipal people's congress organizes such activities all year around. Congressional members often postpone attending these activities or are unable to attend regularly. The local people's congress requires that each member attends at least five meetings or activities each year besides the plenary meeting. Some of the congressional members fail to meet this duty. These congressional members are not deemed as active members and may not be renominated during the electoral process.

"We wish that all our congressional representatives are informed and enthusiastic about politics and public affairs, and we wish they all possess 'participatory capability'. For congressional representatives who possess strong 'participatory capacity', such as being active in attending congressional activities and outspoken in giving advices at congressional meetings, we will encourage them to stay for the next election. For representatives who score low on participation, sometimes we will not consider them for the next election," the interviewee told us. "Some congressional candidates are government officials at the local level. Since the list of candidates for congressional seats at the municipal level is submitted by the congresses at the district level, some of the candidates submitted by the district are leaders of the government and party at the district level. Usually the head of the district and the secretary of the party bureau at the district level are likely to appear on the ballots as congressional candidates. The administrative and party leaders at the district level are likely to constitute about 20 percent of total candidacy."

The district congress sometimes would award the candidacy seats to entrepreneurs who have contributed significantly to the local economy at the district level. It is not unusual that some of the CEOs of large state-owned-enterprises at the district level would appear on the candidate list. These people lead the companies which are pillars of the local economy. It is important that these local business leaders are included in the political process so that they are informed of the public policies that the municipality adopts and their suggestions and advices are sought about the development strategy of the city.

Since the late 1970s, the economic development is regarded to be a priority on the political agenda of local governments. To maintain the fast growth of the Chinese economy, local government officials are required to ensure that the economy under their governance will grow at a certain percentage each year. The rationale is straightforward: should all sub-provincial regions be able to grow at 7 percent each year, it would help the province attain its 7 percent GDP growth rate. Local officials would be reviewed according to the performance of the local economy. If the local economy was not catching up with a designated growth rate, it would negatively affect their performance review, and it could affect their odds of career advancement.

Therefore, the performance of the local economy is crucial. Citizens who are heads of the growth-promoting businesses have a rising status in the political system. For those people who are able to contribute to the local economy, such as the CEOs of the top ten enterprises, they are likely to be awarded with such political status in the political process. When economic development becomes a task for the local government to fulfill, it may come as no surprise that the local business leaders are included in the political process more and more so.

Besides local business leaders of state-owned-enterprises, another active section of the local congress is composed of private entrepreneurs, who usually have their own successful businesses in the city and may pay substantial amount of taxes to the district government each year. The district congress tends to view their contribution to the local economy very favorably. Many of these private entrepreneurs also consider a seat at the local people's congress highly desirable as enviable political status. The district people's congress tends to honor the requests of the private entrepreneurs to become congressional candidates.

Indeed, with the significant political status associated with the people's congress in China's public life, serving as congressional representatives may help private entrepreneurs to gain public trust, as congressional memberships are likely to project the image of good, law-biding, and well-connected local community leaders. It may also indirectly promote their business, as their business partners and customers may consider them to be trust-worthy individuals, given their positions in the local people's congress. Many of the private entrepreneurs proudly reveal their positions as congressional representatives on their business cards and company brochures.

Indeed, the status as congressional representatives often brings more benefits for private entrepreneurs. The congressional membership means the access to a highly exclusive and elitist local political society. Sitting in the congress connects the representative with other members of the congress. About 20 percent of the representatives come directly from the local government, such as the mayor and secretary of municipal party bureaus. Besides the plenary congressional meeting each year, the standing committee of the municipal congress would often organize activities that request the presence of congressional members, such as the subway visit mentioned before. There are a lot of opportunities for congressional members to gain acquaintance of local political leaders, and private entrepreneurs may find it an excellent opportunity to make friends with them in a collegiate and egalitarian setting, when they serve as the same "class" in the local people's congress. Given the dominance of the CCP in local political systems, members of this elitist political club are likely to gain more political connections and receive early updates with changes in policies.

Serving as congressional members will also keep private entrepreneurs updated of development strategies of the city. Congressional members are often solicited for their opinions and suggestions about the development of their municipality. Their suggestions are pondered seriously by the local people's congress, especially as the legislative process becomes increasingly systemic and regularized. The policy of the standing committee of the local people's congress is that suggestions and policy initiatives submitted by congressional representatives should receive satisfactory responses within three months. The congressional representatives should evaluate responses given by the government, bureaucracy, or judiciary accordingly. If congressional representatives are not pleased with the responses, such process will be repeated until they are satisfied.

Congressional proposals usually receive close attention by the municipal people's congress and are handled effectively. The responses the congressional members receive come in time, and the reported satisfaction rate of the responses is high. In the city we interviewed, the satisfaction rate of responses toward congressional suggestions was around 95 percent in 2008.

Serving as congressional representatives could bring substantial and significant benefits to private entrepreneurs, such as political information, access, status, and political immunity.[15] No wonder congressional seats are highly sought after by private entrepreneurs, especially those established business leaders with considerable socioeconomic resources. At the same time, with their economic prowess and valued economy contribution, the desires of private entrepreneurs are likely to be accommodated by the local people's congress when possible. Although such pursuits may not always be successful at the individual level, private entrepreneurs as a group of the population are accorded with considerable political status.

As China's politics has become increasing pragmatism-oriented since the economic reform started, the focus of national and local politics has shifted toward development. The GDP growth and economic development are adamantly pursued by governments at all levels, and emerging capitalists who are successfully riding this new socioeconomic trend have become increasingly more powerful politically as they amass considerable personal fortune and shoulder more responsibilities in the local economy. As a group, this emerging bourgeoisie class treasures the political access to protect their private property and eagerly courts political blessings for their businesses.

According to the Electoral Law, the district people's congress provides a candidate list for congressional elections, which should constitute at least 120 percent of total seats in the municipal congress. This congressional candidacy list shall match the mandatory percentage of nonparty members, women, and minority candidates. Moreover, the leaders of the district government would constitute another 25 percent of the congressional seats. The seats that are open for civilian representatives are rather limited, approximately 35–40 percent. Given the limited number of the congressional seats that are open to be filled by civilians, the competition for congressional seats can be fierce, and such contest is often available to those candidates who possess significant amount of socioeconomic resources, such as private entrepreneurs.

In studying local congressional politics of China, we have found that the socioeconomically powerful are better represented in the political process and enjoy considerably more political access with an un-proportional magnitude. The voices and concerns of these newly emerged bourgeoisies are likely to be sent directly to decision makers and be addressed effectively. Overall, the demands of the bourgeoisies' class, including their need for protection of private property and an open business environment, receive increasing attention on the political agenda in local Chinese politics.

# Local elections, the CCP, and political reform

Given the political access and privileges associated with the memberships in local congresses, interested candidates campaign for congressional candidacy. Their campaign strategy is closely tied with their own economic status. Congressional candidacy are likely to be awarded to leaders of private entrepreneurs who contribute to the local taxation income, or leaders of emerging new industries with promising markets. While personal contacts and connections may occasionally come into play, overall the final winners of the candidacy on the ballots are likely to be determined by the applicants' economic status and their contributions to the local community.

Campaigning for congressional seats is likely to be limited in scale, and open campaigning that involves multiparties is extremely rare. More often than not, campaigning for congressional seats is conducted behind the scene.

Congressional representatives at the municipal level are directly elected by congressional representatives at the district level. However, the candidate list is composed by the standing committee of the people's congress at the district level. The actual candidate list is a balance of the demand of the standing committee of the people's congress at the upper level and requests sent from the level below. To be able to successfully get on the ballot is more than half the battle, as all nominated candidates would have a fairly good chance, above 80 percent, to be elected as congressional representative. They are intentionally chosen to provide powerful political alliances with the local congress, and these congressional representatives are expected to pledge their political support to the political system and be awarded with significant political status and privileges.[16]

As the broadened grassroots democracy is initiated by the Chinese government to generate mass support in the context of China's economic reform and development, are these measures harbinger to political reform and more opening-up of political space in China? The discussion of the reform of electoral process and political representation of the municipal people's congress in Chinese politics is tied with our inquiry of political liberalization and democratization in contemporary China.

Since the early 1980s, the Chinese government has sought to broaden the scope of grassroots democracy and increase civil liberties to accommodate changes brought by the economic reform. It permitted grassroots village committee elections in rural China, and strengthened the role of the people's congresses in the political process, especially in legislation and representation. These measures have contributed to the development of grassroots democracy in China to a certain extent, as it gives the citizenry more opportunities to share their political voices with the ruling communist party. If this trend were to continue, we are likely to witness more political space yielded to the Chinese people by the CCP.

Yet democratization efforts initiated by the CCP were aimed at improving the political support for the government by allowing more political freedom for the Chinese people. Reforms of village elections and the local people's congress were viewed by the government as instruments to generate mass support for the rule of the CCP. The political reform indeed builds more political alliance and brings more public support to the rule of the communist party. However, the scope of China's political liberalization is under the close supervision of the CCP. Today the municipal people's congress still struggles to attain an independent role in exercising oversight when it needs to check and balance the power of the municipal government, despite the progress it has made in legislation and other areas. In addition, major personnel appointments of the local people's congress are still controlled by the personnel department of the municipal party's committee. The liberalization process in China is still a cause very much dependent on the interest and willingness of the ruling party.

Moreover, not everyone benefits from this process of political liberalization equally. Observing the congressional political process and representation, the socioeconomically advantaged turned out much more likely to gain access and representation in the political process. The opened political space is disproportionately awarded to those who contribute to the economic development and those who can summon significant socioeconomic resources. China's political liberalization is not necessarily an egalitarian political process, although it seems to have provided more political access and more leverage to more citizens over time.

The revised Electoral Law governing the electoral process of the municipal people's congress, the standardized legislative process, and opened-up political representation to the citizenry suggest significant progress made by the Chinese government in political liberalization. Yet as a beginning in political reform, the political liberalization process in China still has substantial problems that need to be addressed. Critical issues such as the independent status of the legislative branch, transparency of the political process in the Chinese government, and equal political status of individual citizens have to be improved in China's political reform.

# Conclusion

This chapter has examined the local people's congress from the perspective of electoral process. With the accelerating pace of political liberalization at the grassroots level, we have tried to reconsider the role of the people's congress, especially the local people's congress, in the grassroots democracy in urban China.

Political liberalization has been ongoing in China since the late 1970s, and the local people's congress has strengthened its role and status in the political process. The change was originally envisioned by veteran CCP leaders who embraced liberal political standing and recalled favorably CCP's democratic governance during the Soviet periods. With continuous economic development in China, such political change has gained momentum in its adaptation to accommodate the changes to the Chinese society brought about by sustained economic reforms and development. The local people's congress has become more institutionalized,[17] more active and systemic in legislation, and its electoral process more established, adhering closely to the procedures prescribed by law.

We have also observed that the people's congress has been playing an increasingly important role in local politics in China, such as providing suggestions and advice for good governance at the local level. Besides representing CCP members, the people's congress has broadened congressional representation toward other segments of the society, and some of the congressional seats have been awarded to citizens who contribute to the local economy and pledge their support for the political process dominated by the CCP.

Since economic development has been deemed as the priority by the Chinese government, the congressional politics has paid more attention to local business leaders and private entrepreneurs, and solicited their voices in the political process. Meanwhile as some Chinese citizens manage to gain more personal wealth and achieve prominent socioeconomic status, they have started to seek political status that allows them to participate in the decision-making process, and to secure their socioeconomic gains through acquired political access and privilege.

Starting with China's economic reform and strengthening of grassroots democracy, the people's congress has gained its new status and expanded its responsibilities in the local politics of China. We argue that the people's congress has been playing an increasingly important role in China's local politics, accommodating societal changes brought about by economic reforms. While the people's congress has amplified its scope in political representation, the newly elected are likely to be those who possess tremendous socioeconomic resources in Chinese society today. Obviously there is still a long way to go to achieve more equal and meaningful representation in local people's congress.

## Five questions for discussions

1. What incentives do private entrepreneurs have in gaining seats at the people's congress? Does the local people's congress only represent the socioeconomically advantaged?
2. How would you evaluate the role and status of the local people's congress in China's grassroots democracy today?
3. What is the role of the CCP in the process of political liberalization?
4. Can you compare the people's congress with other legislative assemblies in East Asia?
5. How does the National People's Congress differ from the US Congress?

# Notes

1   I wish to thank the Departments of Political Science at Rider University and Texas A&M University for supporting this study. I would like to acknowledge the guidance and help provided by Professor Jon Bond. I am also grateful to Professor Zhiqun Zhu and Professor Frank Rusciano for their advice and suggestions. And I am most grateful to the members and staff of the municipal congress in the city located in central China for granting us interviews.

2   See Kevin J. O'Brien, *Reform without Liberation: China's National People's Congress and the Politics of Institutional Change* (Cambridge University Press, 1990); Minxin Pei, *China's Trapped Transition: The Limits of Developmental Democracy* (Harvard University Press, 2006).

3   See Alexander T. Edelmann, *Latin American Government and Politics* (Dorsey Press, 1969); Robert Packenham, "Functions of the Brazilian National Congress," in Weston H. Agor, ed. *Latin American Legislatures: Their Roles and Influence* (Praeger Publishers, 1971).

4   See Packenham 1971, p. 261.

5   The origin of village elections started in the rural areas of Guangxi province in southwest China. Local peasants in the villages initiated the village committees to handle village affairs and mediate conflicts while the villages were experimenting the household responsibility contract system. The village committees were initiated by local villagers, and elections conducted by local peasants. When the news of peasants establishing village committees and initiating elections on their own reached Beijing, it caused controversy and was viewed by some as a threat to local government authority. The village committee election initiated by peasants in Guangxi ultimately gained the support of Beijing.

6   The Organic Law confirms the institutional status of village elections and village committees and stipulates the specific procedures of village elections. According to the Organic Law, all village election candidates must be directly nominated by villagers; there must be more candidates than positions; and voting should be done in secret (art. 14). The Organic Law takes into account possible bureaucratic resistance and the need to strengthen the coalition pushing self-government. Toward such end, it encourages local people's congresses to enact implementing regulations and to do what it is necessary to ensure that voters can exercise their democratic rights (arts 14, 28, 29), and it also authorizes villagers to combat dishonest elections by lodging reports with local governments, people's congress, or other concerned departments (art. 15).

7   See Larry Diamond and Ramon H. Myers, "Elections and Democracy in Greater China," in Larry Diamond and Ramon H. Myers, eds. *Elections and Democracy in Greater China* (University of Oxford Press, 2001).

8   See Kevin J. O'Brien and Liangjiang Li, "Accommodating 'Democracy' in a One-Party State: Introducing Village Elections in China," in Larry Diamond and Ramon H. Myers, eds. *Elections and Democracy in Greater China* (University of Oxford Press, 2001), p. 104.

9  See Jon Bond and Diqing Lou, "The State's Rubber Stamp or Independent Agent: A Study on the Development of Municipal People's Congress in China," in Gaogang Guo and Daniel Hickey, eds. *Toward Better Governance in China: An Unconventional Pathway of Political Reform* (Rowman & Littlefield, 2009).

10  See Harold C. Hinton, *The People's Republic of China 1979–1984* (Scholarly Resources, 1986), p. 108.

11  See Kevin J. O'Brien and Lianjiang Li, "The Politics of Lodging Complaints in Rural China," *China Quarterly* 143 (1995): 757–83; O'Brien and Li, 2001; Kent Jennings, "Political Participation in the Chinese Countryside," *American Political Science Review* 91 (1997): 361–72.

12  The Electoral Law of People's Republic of China, 1979.

13  The Electoral Law of People's Republic of China, 1982, 1986, 1995, 2004.

14  "Electoral Law Revision Key to Equal Rights," *China Daily*, March 5, 2010.

15  Serving as congressional members means that they can be protected with political immunity on certain issues. Political immunity is a privilege associated with the freedom of speech provided for congressional members. This courtesy rule for congressional members can be interpreted broadly. Occasionally when private entrepreneurs run into minor legal troubles for their businesses, they may be able to walk away unscathed by contacting the local people's congress for help and invoking the political immunity article.

16  Besides private entrepreneurs, who are deemed as contributors to the local economy, a certain amount of congressional seats are awarded to professors at prestigious universities located in the city.

17  See Bond and Lou 2009.

# Selected bibliography

Bond, Jon and Diqing Lou. "The State's Rubber Stamp or Independent Agent: A Study on the Development of Municipal People's Congress in China," in Gaogang Guo and Daniel Hickey, eds. *Toward Better Governance in China: An Unconventional Pathway of Political Reform* (Lexington: Rowman & Littlefield, 2009).

Diamond, Larry and Ramon H. Myers. "Elections and Democracy in Greater China," in Larry Diamond and Ramon H. Myers, eds. *Elections and Democracy in Greater China* (Oxford: University of Oxford Press, 2001).

Hinton, Harold C. *The People's Republic of China 1979–1984* (Wilmington: Scholarly Resources, 1986).

Jennings, M. Kent. "Political Participation in the Chinese Countryside." *American Political Science Review* 91 (1997): 361–72.

O'Brien, Kevin J. *Reform without Liberation: China's National People's Congress and the Politics of Institutional Change* (New York: Cambridge University Press, 1990).

O'Brien, Kevin J. and Lianjiang Li. "The Politics of Lodging Complaints in Rural China." *China Quarterly* 143 (1995): 757–83.

—. "Accommodating 'Democracy' in a One-Party State: Introducing Village Elections in China," in Larry Diamond and Ramon H. Myers, eds. *Elections and Democracy in Greater China* (Oxford: University of Oxford Press, 2001).

Pei, Minxin. *China's Trapped Transition: The Limits of Developmental Democracy* (Cambridge: Harvard University Press, 2006).

# Index